Barron's Regents Exams and Answers

Sequential Math Course II

LESTER W. SCHLUMPF
Retired Principal
John Adams High School, Queens
Former Lecturer in Mathematics, Queens College

LAWRENCE S. LEFF
Assistant Principal
Mathematics Supervisor
Franklin D. Roosevelt High School, Brooklyn

BARRON'S

Barron's Educational Series, Inc.

All inquiries should be addressed to:
Barron's Educational Series, Inc.
250 Wireless Boulevard
Hauppauge, New York 11788
http://www.barronseduc.com

ISBN 0-8120-3126-1
ISSN 1069-2975

PRINTED IN THE UNITED STATES OF AMERICA
9 8 7 6 5 4 3 2 1

Contents

Glossary of Terms   72

Regents Examinations, Answers, and
Self-Analysis Charts   85

Contents

Preface

A HELPFUL WORD TO THE STUDENT

This book is designed to strengthen your understanding and mastery of the material in the New York State Syllabus for the Three-Year Sequence in High School Mathematics (Course II). This is the course recommended by the State for college-bound students who are now in the tenth year. The book has been specifically written to assist you in preparing for the Regents examination covering this course.

SPECIAL FEATURES INCLUDE

Complete sets of questions from 11 previous Regents examinations in this subject. Attempting to solve these will make you familiar with the topics tested on the examination and with the degree of difficulty you are expected to master in each topic. Solving the questions on many tests will provide drill, improve your understanding of the topics, and increase your confidence as the nature and language of the questions become more familiar.

Solutions to all Regents questions with step-by-step explanations of the solutions. Careful study of the solutions and explanations will improve your mastery of the subject. Each explanation is designed to show you how to apply the facts and principles you have learned in class. Since the explanation for each solution has been written with emphasis on the reasoning behind each step, its value goes far beyond the application to that particular question. You should read the explanation of the solution even if you have answered the questions correctly. It gives insight into the topic that may be valuable when answering a more difficult question on the same topic on the next test you face.

Ten Test-Taking Tips. These helpful tips and strategies will help to raise your grade on the actual Regents exam that you will take.

A unique system of self-analysis charts and classification of questions by topic. These will help you to locate weaknesses and direct your study efforts where needed. The charts classify the questions on each Regents examination into 29 topic groups. They thus enable you to locate other questions from the same topic in other Regents examinations.

A Frequency of Topic chart and a Practice Section at the front of the book consisting of questions taken from previous Regents, each with a completely explained step-by-step solution. The questions are classified into the same 29 topic groups.

This book will be valuable to you if used properly. During the term you can use the classifications in the Self-Analysis Charts to locate questions and solutions on the topics you are studying. When reviewing for end-of-term examinations, you should follow the procedure in the section titled "How to Use This Book." This will bring results in terms of greater understanding, increased self-confidence, and higher test scores.

How to Use This Book

This book has a built-in program to identify your areas of strength and weakness, and to guide you in concentrating your study on those topics where you most need assistance.

The book contains 11 of the most recent Regents examinations. There is a fully explained, step-by-step solution for each question. Following each examination there is included a specially designed Self-Analysis Chart that classifies the questions into 29 topic groups. By following the procedure below you can use the charts to identify your strengths and weak points, and to point you to particular questions on other Regents examinations whose solutions will provide help in the areas where you need additional study.

1. Do a complete Regents examination, answering *all* questions (even though you will have a choice on the actual Regents).

2. Compare your answers with those in the explained solutions.

3. On the Self-Analysis Chart, find the topic under which each question is classified, and enter the number of points you earned if you answered it correctly.

4. Obtain your percentage for each topic by dividing your earned points by the number of test points on that topic, carrying the division to two decimal places.

5. If you are not satisfied with your percentage on any topic, turn to that topic in the Practice Exercises in the front of the book and answer all questions there, comparing your results with the explained solutions.

6. If you still need additional practice on a particular topic, locate appropriate questions in other Regents examinations by using their Self-Analysis Charts to see which questions are listed for this topic. Attempting to solve them and reading their carefully explained solutions will provide you with additional practice in the topics where you need help.

Practice

HOW TO PRACTICE EFFECTIVELY AND EFFICIENTLY

1. Do not spend too much time on one question if you cannot come up with a method to be used or if you cannot complete the solution. Instead, put a slash through the number of any question you cannot complete. When you have completed as many questions as you can you will be able to return quickly to the unanswered questions and try them again.
2. After trying the unanswered questions again, check the answer key for the entire test.
3. Circle the number of each question you answered incorrectly.
4. Study the explained solutions for those questions you answered incorrectly. (If the solution uses a formula or rule you do not know, write it on a piece of paper and attach the paper to the inside of your review book.)
5. Enter the points for your correct answers on the Self-Analysis Chart following the Regents you tried, and follow the procedure given in the section on "How to Use This Book."

HOW TO PRACTICE USING A COMPLETE EXAMINATION

PART I

You should follow certain procedures when you practice on a complete Regents examination. Allow yourself between one hour and one and one-half hours of "quiet time" to do Part I. Answer *all* 35 of the Part I questions even though you will be required to choose only 30 of them on the actual Regents—those on which you believe you can get correct answers. By completing all 35 questions on the practice exams you will be in a better position to pick only 30 on the actual Regents.

On the actual Regents, if you have difficulty in finding at least 30 questions on which you are reasonably sure of your ability, it is advisable to choose some multiple-choice questions on which you can eliminate one or more of the choices as obviously incorrect. There is no penalty for guessing, but do not guess until you have first tried to solve the question. If you can validly eliminate some choices, your guess from among the remaining choices will stand a better chance of being correct. Practice this technique as you answer all the Part I questions on practice exams so that you can use it to advantage if you have to resort to it in choosing the questions you will answer on the actual exam.

PART II AND PART III

Spend one and one-half hours doing *all* seven Part II and Part III questions. Follow the same steps as you did in Part I. If the question calls for a geometric proof, prepare a "plan" before attempting to write your statements and reasons.

On the actual Regents you will have to complete only three of the five questions in Part II and only one of the two questions in Part III—those on which you believe you can score the highest (partial credit is allowed on Part II and Part III for solutions that are not completely correct if major parts are accurate.) When you do these Regents for practice, you should answer all the questions in Part II and Part III for the same reason that this was advised in Part I.

The Actual Regents

In the weeks before the Regents, you should plan to spend about one-half hour preparing each night. It is better to spread out your preparation time this way than to prepare for, say, three hours in one evening.

On the night before the Regents, read over the formulas you have attached to the review book cover. If you have prepared each night for a month or so, this is a good time to study calmly for about an hour and go to bed reasonably early.

You will have three hours to do the Course II Math Regents. If you have practiced on a number of past examinations, you will be able to complete the actual Regents in about one and one-half hours. Even so, spend the full three hours. It is better to be correct than to be fast.

ANSWERING QUESTIONS ON THE ACTUAL REGENTS

Follow steps similar to those you used for the practice exams. Before going on to Part II and Part III, go back over Part I, making sure you have answered 30 questions. Go over any of the 30 you were unsure of (those whose numbers you have marked with a slash) and try them again. If you answered more than 30 questions, cross out the ones you do not wish to have counted.

At the end of the first hour of the exam, go on to Part II and Part III. Read all the questions completely and select the three questions from Part II and the one from Part III that you have had the most success with on practice exams according to your Self-Analysis Charts. Work out each problem on scrap paper in pencil, and when you feel confident about the solution, copy it into the answer booklet *in ink*. Show all work. If you cannot completely solve three questions from Part II and one from Part III, pick those that give the potential for the most credit.

Ten Test-Taking Tips

Here are ten practical tips that can help you raise your grade on the Regents exam for Sequential Mathematics—Course II.

GENERAL STUDY TIPS

TIP 1

Know What To Expect On Test Day

SUGGESTIONS
- Become familiar with the format and directions of the Regents exam.
- Know the *types* of questions asked, particularly in Parts II and III.
- Ask your teacher to show you an actual test booklet of a previously given Course II Regents Exam.
- Find out before the day of the test where you should show scrap work and where you will write your answers to Parts I, II, and III.
- Bring to the exam room a scientific calculator that you know how to use.

TIP 2
Avoid Last-Minute Studying

SUGGESTIONS

- Start your Regents exam preparation early by: taking detailed notes in class and then reviewing your notes when you get home; completing all of your homework assignments in a neat and organized way; writing down any questions you may have about your homework so that you can ask your teacher about them; and saving your classroom tests so you can use them to help prepare for the Regents exam.
- Build your skill and confidence by completing all of the exams in this book before the day of the Regents exam. Because each exam takes up to three hours to complete, you will want to begin this process no later than several weeks before the exam is scheduled to be given.
- Get a review book early in your exam preparation so that if you need additional explanations or help, it will be at your fingertips. The recommended review book is Barron's *Let's Review: Sequential Mathematics Course II*. This book has been specially designed for fast and effective learning.
- As the day of the actual Regents exam gets closer, take the exams in this book under timed, examination conditions. Then compare your answers with the explained answers contained in this book.
- Use the Self-Analysis Chart at the end of each exam to help pinpoint any weaknesses.
- If you do not feel confident in a particular area, study the corresponding topic in your textbook or in Barron's *Let's Review: Sequential Mathematics Course II*.
- As you work your way through the exams in this book, make a list of any formulas or rules that you need to know. Learn these facts well before the day of the exam.

TIP 3

Know How to Do Questions That Are Always Asked

SUGGESTIONS

- Because Part III *always* includes a geometric proof or a logic proof, or both geometric and logic proofs, make sure you know how to analyze, plan, and write deductive proofs.
- Pick out from the Self-Analysis Charts of the last few Regents exams those topics that were stressed, and spend extra time reviewing questions involving those topics.

TIP 4

Be Rested and Come Prepared on Test Day

SUGGESTIONS

- On the night before exam day lay out all the things you must bring to the exam room.
- Prepare a checklist to make sure you bring these things:
    - ☐ Regents admission card with the room number of the exam.
    - ☐ two ink pens.
    - ☐ two sharpened pencils with erasers.
    - ☐ a ruler.
    - ☐ a compass.
    - ☐ a watch.
    - ☐ a calculator.
- If your calculator uses batteries, put fresh batteries in your scientific calculator the night before the exam.
- Eat wisely and go to bed early so you will be alert and rested when you take the exam.

- Make sure you know when your exam begins. Set your alarm clock to give you plenty of time to arrive at school before the exam starts.
- Tell your parents what time you will need to leave the house in order to get to school on time.
- Arrive to the exam room confident by being on time and by being well prepared.

CALCULATOR TIPS

TIP 5

Know How to Use Your Calculator

SUGGESTIONS
- The scientific calculator you take to the exam room should be the same calculator that you used when you completed the practice Regents exams at home.
- If you are required to use a calculator provided by your school, make sure that you practice with it before the day of the exam because not all calculators work in the same way.
- Know how to use your calculator to find the value of the sine, cosine, or tangent of an angle correct to four decimal places.
- Know how to use your calculator to find the number of degrees in an angle when the value of a trigonometric function of that angle is given. For example, if $\sin x° = 0.9511$, you should be able to use your calculator to determine that the value of angle x, correct to the nearest degree, is 72.
- Become an expert on using your calculator to find factorials ($n!$), permutations ($_nP_r$), and combinations ($_nC_r$).
- Because it is easy to press the wrong calculator key, you should first *estimate* an answer and then compare it to the answer obtained by using a calculator. If the two answers are very different, then you should start over.

TIP 6

Know When to Use Your Calculator

SUGGESTIONS

- Don't expect to have to use your calculator to answer each question. Most questions do not require a calculator.
- Expect to have to use your calculator when solving numerical problems involving the three trigonometric ratios—sine, cosine, and tangent.
- Make it a habit of using your scientific calculator to evaluate factorials, permutations, and combinations because these calculations are prone to error.

TIPS WHEN TAKING THE REAL EXAM

TIP 7

Read the Directions Carefully

SUGGESTIONS

- Before you begin to answer any questions, read the directions for each part of the Regents exam.
- Don't worry if you can't answer every question. You can omit any five short answer questions from Part I, and you only have to do four out of the seven questions contained in Parts II and III.
- Pay attention to the breakdown of points in each of the Part II questions. This can help you pick questions that will give you the maximum amount of partial credit.

TIP 8

Approach Test Questions in a Systematic Way

SUGGESTIONS

- *Read* each test question through the *first time* to get a *general idea* of the type of mathematics knowledge that the question requires. For example, one question may ask you to solve an algebraic equation, whereas another question may require that you use some geometric principle.
- *Read* the problem through a *second time* to pick out specific facts. Identify what is being *given* and what you need to *find*. Represent any unknown quantities using variables.
- *Decide on how you will get the answer*. You may need to:
  1. *Draw a sketch or diagram.* This can help you to organize the information contained in the problem so that you can arrive at a plan.
  2. *Translate the given conditions of the problem into an equation,* and then solve that equation.
- *Carry out your plan* for solving the problem.
- *Verify that your solution is correct* by making sure your answer works in the original question.
- If you have trouble answering a particular Part I question, circle the question number in the test booklet because you may want to omit this question. If you have circled more than five questions from Part I, you will know at a glance which questions you need to come back to. If you answer more than the required 30 questions in Part I, cross out the answers to the questions that you are least confident about until you are left with 30 answered questions.

TIP 9

Make Your Answers Easy to Read

SUGGESTIONS

- Make sure your answers are clear, neat, and written in ink.
- If your final answer to a Part II question is a number or an algebraic expression, draw a box around it so it stands out.
- On Part II, show all work by giving enough details so it will be clear to someone who doesn't know how you think, why and how you moved from one step of the solution to the next. If the teacher grading your paper has to try hard to figure out what you wrote, the teacher may simply decide to mark your answer wrong and give you little, if any, partial credit.
- Write a *plan* to the proof you choose to do from Part III.
- Draw graphs using a pencil so you can erase neatly, if necessary. If you receive directions that *all* work, including graphs, need to be done in ink, then when you are satisfied with the graph you have drawn, go over it with your pen.
- Don't forget to label the coordinate axes. Put "y" on top of the y-axis and "$-y$" on the bottom. Write "x" to the right of the x-axis and "$-x$" to the left. Next to the graph, write its equation.

TIP 10

Have a Plan for Budgeting Your Time

SUGGESTIONS

- In the first hour of the three-hour Course II Regents exam:
    1. Try to complete the required 30 out of 35 Part I questions.
    2. Return to the troublesome questions whose question numbers you circled.

3. In answering multiple-choice questions, first rule out any choices that are impossible. If the answer choices are numbers, you may be able to eliminate choices by plugging these numbers back into the original question to see if they work.

4. Double-check that you have answered *exactly* 30 Part I questions and that each of these answers are written neatly in ink in the appropriate space on the answer sheet that is provided.

- In the second hour of the Regents exam, complete three Part II questions and one Part III question.
  1. Make sure your solutions are neat and organized. Remember, in order to get credit, the teacher grading your paper must be able to understand what you have written.
  2. If you have difficulty choosing three questions from Part II, make sure you choose a question that allows for partial credit.
- In the next 25 minutes:
  1. Redo the 30 questions selected from Part I. Do not simply check your scrap paper because it is unlikely that you will spot a careless error by quickly scanning it.
  2. If an answer doesn't match your original answer, do the problem over until you are convinced you have the right answer. If you are undecided between two answers, choose the one that seems more reasonable to you.
- In the next 25 minutes, redo the three Part II questions and the one Part III question you chose following the same procedure used for Part I.
- In the final 10 minutes of the Regents exam:
  1. Check that you have answered 30 out of 35 Part I questions, three Part II questions, and one Part III question.
  2. Check that if a Part II or Part III question has several parts, you have clearly labeled your answer for each of the parts of that question.
  3. If you have answered more than 30 Part I questions, write **"OMIT"** next to the question number and draw a line through the answer of each question you do not want marked.
  4. If you have answered fewer than 30 Part I questions and are not sure about the remaining questions, pick out a multiple-choice question that you didn't answer that has some choices that you can eliminate. Then guess!

5. If you have answered more than three Part II questions or both Part III questions, write **"OMIT"** next to the question number and draw diagonal lines through the solutions and answers of any work you do not want marked.
6. Make sure all answers are written in ink on the answer sheets.
7. Present your proctor with a neat package of completed examination materials. Make sure it includes the Part I answer sheet, graph paper, the Part II answer sheets, all scrap work, and the test booklet. Also, make sure your name appears on each of your answer papers.

SUMMARY OF TIPS

1. Know what to expect on test day.
2. Avoid last minute studying.
3. Know how to do questions that are always asked.
4. Be rested and come prepared on test day.
5. Know *how* to use your calculator.
6. Know *when* to use your calculator.
7. Read the directions carefully.
8. Approach test questions in a systematic way.
9. Make your answers easy to read.
10. Have a plan for budgeting your time.

Frequency of Topics— Course II

Questions in the Math Course II Regents exams fall into one of 29 topic categories. The Practice Questions that follow this Frequency Chart are organized in the same manner.

The Frequency Chart shows how many questions in recent exams have been in each category, to indicate which topics have been emphasized in recent years.

The Self-Analysis Charts that follow each Regents Exam designate exactly which questions in that exam are in each category, so you can determine where your weakest areas. You may also try questions in those areas again, for more practice.

The two charts—Frequency and Self-Analysis—should give you a very good idea of the topics you need to review, and the questions that follow this chart provide more practice.

FREQUENCY OF TOPICS

	Number of Questions										
	Jan 1993	June 1993	Jan 1994	June 1994	Jan 1995	June 1995	Jan 1996	June 1996	Jan 1997	June 1997	Jan 1998
1. Properties of Number Systems; Definition of Operations	2	3	—	1	2	1	2	1	—	1	2
2. Finite Mathematical Systems	1	—	1	1	—	—	—	1	1	1	1
3. Linear Function and Graph ($y = mx + b$, slope, equations of)	2	2	2	2	3	2	—	1	2	2	1
4. Quadratic Equation (algebraic solution—factoring, formula)	1	1	2	2	1	1	2	5	2	2	1
5. Parabolas (including axis of symmetry, turning point)	3	1	2	2	2	3	2	1	3	3	3
6. System of Equations (algebraic and graphic solutions)	1	—	1	—	2	1	1	1	—	1	1
7. Supplementary, Complementary, Vertical Angles, Angle Measure	—	—	—	—	1	1	—	—	1	2	2
8. Triangle Properties (equilateral, isosceles, sum of angles)	—	3	3	2	3	2	2	3	4	3	1
9. Line Parallel to One Side of Triangle; Line Joining Midpoints of Two Sides	3	1	2	—	1	1	.	2	1	—	1
10. Inequalities in Triangles (exterior angle, unequal sides, opposite angles)	—	—	—	2	1	2	2	2	1	2	1
11. Quadrilateral Properties (parallelogram, square, rhombus, rectangle, trapezoid)	1	1	2	2	1	3	2	1	4	2	2
12. Parallel Lines	3	2	2	1	1	1	2	1	1	—	2
13. Algebraic Operations; Verbal Problems	1	2	3	4	4	2	4	3	2	3	3

FREQUENCY OF TOPICS (continued)

	Number of Questions										
	Jan 1993	June 1993	Jan 1994	June 1994	Jan 1995	June 1995	Jan 1996	June 1996	Jan 1997	June 1997	Jan 1998
14. Mean Proportional; Altitude to Hypotenuse of Right Triangle	1	2	—	1	1	2	1	1	2	1	1
15. Pythagorean Theorem; Special Right Triangles (3-4-5, 5-12-13, 30-60-90)	1	1	1	2	1	1	2	1	2	—	—
16. Similar Figures (ratios and proportions)	2	—	2	1	1	2	2	—	1	1	2
17. Areas (triangle, rectangle, parallelogram, rhombus, trapezoid)	2	2	—	1	1	—	1	2	1	2	—
18. Locus	3	3	1	2	1	1	1	2	1	1	1
19. Constructions	1	1	1	1	1	1	1	—	1	1	1
20. Deductive Proofs	2	2	3	2	1	1	2	3	1	2	2
21. Coordinate Geometry (slope, distance, midpoint, equation of circle)	2	5	3	4	4	3	4	5	3	4	5
22. Coordinate Geometry "Proofs"	1	1	1	1	—	—	1	2	1	—	1
23. Logic	4	3	3	2	3	3	4	2	2	2	2
24. Permutations; Arrangements	1	1	—	1	1	2	1	1	2	2	2
25. Combinations	1	2	1	2	2	2	1	1	2	1	1
26. Probability	—	2	1	1	4	2	—	—	1	1	—
27. Trigonometry of Right Triangle	2	3	3	2	2	3	2	2	2	2	3
28. Literal Equations	—	—	—	—	—	—	—	—	—	—	—
29. Transformations	2	4	5	2	2	3	2	5	3	2	3

Practice Exercises

This section of the book consists of 66 questions selected from former Regents examinations and classified into 29 topic groups. Step-by-step solutions are provided for each of the questions. The 29 topic groups are keyed to the Self-Analysis Charts that follow each of the 11 complete Regents examinations. This enables you to make use of the Practice Exercises to overcome any weaknesses that are revealed through the use of the Self-Analysis Charts.

1. PROPERTIES OF NUMBER SYSTEMS; DEFINITION OF OPERATIONS

1 If $*$ is an operation defined by $x * y = x^3 - y^2$, find the value of $2 * 1$.

2 If a and b are any two whole numbers, which statement is always true?
   (1) $2a + b = 2b + a$ (3) $a^b = b^a$
   (2) $a + b = b + a$ (4) $a \div b = b \div a$

3 Which set is *not* closed under addition?
   (1) natural numbers   (3) whole numbers
   (2) even integers   (4) odd integers

Solutions to Questions on Properties of Number Systems; Definitions of Operations

  1. The operation $*$ is defined by: $x * y = x^3 - y^2$
To find the value of $2 * 1$, substitute 2 for x and
1 for y in the definition of $*$: $2 * 1 = 2^3 - 1^2$
  $2^3 = 8; 1^2 = 1$: $2 * 1 = 8 - 1$
  $2 * 1 = 7$. $2 * 1 = 7$

2. Consider each choice in turn:

(1) If $2a + b = 2b + a$, then $2a - a = 2b - b$, or $a = b$. But for any two whole numbers, a and b, a may not equal b.

(2) $a + b = b + a$: This is always true by the commutative law for addition.

(3) $a^b = b^a$: Consider an example; suppose $a = 3$ and $b = 2$. $3^2 \overset{?}{=} 2^3$. $9 \neq 8$.

(4) $a \div b = b \div a$: This is not true since division is not commutative.

For example, $12 \div 3 \neq 3 \div 12$ since $4 \neq \dfrac{1}{4}$.

The correct choice is (**2**).

3. For a set to be closed under an operation, the result of performing the operation on any two members of the set must also be a member of the set.

Consider each choice in turn:

(1) natural numbers: The natural numbers comprise the set $\{1, 2, 3, 4, \ldots\}$. If any two members of this set are added, the sum will be another member of the set. The natural numbers are closed under addition.

(2) even integers: The even integers comprise the set $\{\ldots, -4, -2, 0, 2, 4, \ldots\}$. If any two members of this set are added, the sum is also an even integer. The even integers are closed under addition.

(3) whole numbers: The whole numbers comprise the set $\{0, 1, 2, 3, \ldots\}$. If any two members of this set are added, the sum is also a whole number. The whole numbers are closed under addition.

(4) odd integers: The odd integers comprise the set $\{\ldots, -5, -3, -1, 1, 3, 5, \ldots\}$. If any two members of this set are added, the sum is an even number and hence *not* a member of the set. The odd integers are not closed under addition.

The correct choice is (**4**).

2. FINITE MATHEMATICAL SYSTEMS

1   Using the accompanying table, solve for x if $x \odot H = C$.

$\odot$	C	A	T	H
C	H	C	A	T
A	C	A	T	H
T	A	T	H	C
H	T	H	C	A

2 Using the accompanying table, find the inverse of the element H.

*	M	A	T	H
M	T	H	M	A
A	H	M	A	T
T	M	A	T	H
H	A	T	H	M

3 Given the operations * and # as defined in the tables below.

*	M	O	T
M	A	N	V
O	V	A	N
T	N	V	A

#	V	A	N
V	T	M	O
A	M	O	T
N	O	T	M

a Evaluate: $T * (A \# N)$
b Evaluate: $(T * O) \# (M * T)$
c Solve for x: $(N \# A) * x = A$
d Solve for y: $(M * y) \# A = M$

Solutions to Questions on Finite Mathematical Systems
1. The given equation is: $x \odot H = C$

⊙	C	A	T	H
C	H	C	A	T
A	C	A	T	H
T	A	T	H	C
H	T	H	C	A

In the table for ⊙, $x \odot H$ is the element at the intersection of the row for some unknown element, x, with the column headed by H. In the column headed by H, look for the element C. It is on the row for T. Therefore: $T \odot H = C$
Compare to the original equation: $x = T$
$x = T$.

2.

*	M	A	T	H
M	T	H	M	A
A	H	M	A	T
T	M	A	T	H
H	A	T	H	M

First find the *identity element* for the operation *. The identity element I is an element such that $x * I = x$ and $I * x = x$ for $x = M, A, T,$ or H. Since the column for T in the table for * is identical to the left hand column, $x * T = x$ for $x = M, A, T,$ or H. Similarly, the row for T is identical to the top heading row; thus $T * x = x$ for $x = M, A , T,$ or H. Hence the identity element is T.

The *inverse* of the element H is an element y such that $H * y = T$ and $y * H = T$, where T is the identity element. In the row for H, look for the element T; it is at the intersection with the column for A. Therefore, $H * A = T$. Similarly, in the column for H, T is at the intersection with the row for A. Therefore, $A * H = T$. Thus, A is the inverse of H.

The inverse of H is **A**.

3.

*	M	O	T
M	A	N	V
O	V	A	N
T	N	V	A

#	V	A	N
V	T	M	O
A	M	O	T
N	O	T	M

a. The given expression is: $T * (A \# N)$

$A \# N$ is the element in the table for # at the inersection of the row for A with the column for N; $A \# N = T$: $T * T$

$T * T$ is the element in the table for * at the intersection of the row for T with the column for T; $T * T = A$: A

$T * (A \# N) = \mathbf{A}$.

b. The given expression is: $(T * O) \# (M * T)$

From the table for *, $(T * O) = V$ and $(M * T) = V$: $V \# V$

From the table for #, $V \# V = T$: T

$(T * O) \# (M * T) = \mathbf{T}$.

c. The given equation is: $(N \# A) * x = A$

From the table for #, $N \# A = T$: $T * x = A$

The equation says that, in the table for *, the intersection of the row for *, the intersection of the row for T with the column headed by an unknown element, x, is the element A. In the row for T, the intersection A is with the column for T: $T * T = A$

$x = \mathbf{T}$.   that is, $x = T$

d. The given equation is: $(M * y) \# A = M$

This equation states that, in the table for #, the row for some expression $(M * y)$ intersects the column for A in the element M. In the table for #, M lies in the column for A at its intersection with the row for V:

$$V \# A = M$$
$$\text{that is, } (M * y) = V$$

The equation $(M * y) = V$ states that, in the table for *, the intersection of the row for M wth the column headed by an unknown element, y, is V. In the row for M, the intersection V is with the column headed by T:

$$M * T = V$$
$$(\text{that is, } y = T)$$

$y = T$.

3. LINEAR FUNCTION AND GRAPH ($y = mx + b$, slope, equations of)

1 What is an equation of the line that is parallel to the x-axis and passes through the point $(2,3)$?

2 What is an equation of the line parallel to the line whose equation is $2x + y = 6$ and that passes through the point $(0,-1)$?
   (1) $x + 2y = -1$ (3) $2x + y = 1$
   (2) $y = -1$ (4) $y = -2x - 1$

3 What is the slope of a line that is perpendicular to the line whose equation is $y = 4x + 1$?

   (1) $-\dfrac{1}{4}$ (3) -4

   (2) $\dfrac{1}{4}$ (4) 4

Solutions to Questions on Linear Function and Graph
   1. If a line is parallel to the x-axis, its slope is 0, and its equation is in this form:

$$y = b$$

If a line passes through point $(2,3)$, its equation must be satisfied when 2 is substituted for x and 3 for y (note that the equation $y = b$ does not contain x):

$$3 = b$$

Since $b = 3$, the equation of the line is:

$$y = 3$$

The equation is $y = 3$.

2. Solve the given equation, $2x + y = 6$, for y to put it into the $y = mx + b$ form:

$$2x + y = 6$$
$$y = -2x + 6$$

The equation $y = -2x + 6$ is in the $y = mx + b$ form with $m = -2$ and $b = 6$. In this form, $m = -2$ is the slope of the line.

A line parallel to $y = -2x + 6$ must have the same slope. Therefore its equation is of this form:

$$y = -2x + b$$

If $y = -2x + b$ passes through point $(0,-1)$, the coordinates of this point must satisfy the equation of the line when substituted for x and y:

$$-1 = -2(0) + b$$
$$-1 = 0 + b$$
$$-1 = b$$

Since $b = -1$, the equation of the line in $y = mx + b$ form is:

$$y = -2x - 1$$

The correct choice is (4).

3. If an equation of a line is in the form, $y = mx + b$, then m represents the slope of the line and b represents its y-intercept. The equation, $y = 4x + 1$, is in the form, $y = mx + b$, with $m = 4$ and $b = 1$. Therefore the slope of this line is 4.

The slope of a line perpendicular to $y = 4x + 1$ must be the negative reciprocal of its slope. Consider 4 as $\frac{4}{1}$. The negative reciprocal of $\frac{4}{1}$ is $-\frac{1}{4}$. The slope of the perpendicular line must be $-\frac{1}{4}$.

The correct choice is (1).

4. QUADRATIC EQUATIONS (algebraic solution— factoring, formula)

1 Which equation has equal roots?
  (1) $2x^2 + 5x - 3^2 = 0$
  (2) $x^2 - 4x - 3^2 = 0$
  (3) $x^2 - 7x + 3 = 0$
  (4) $x^2 - 8x + 16 = 0$

2 What are the roots of the equation $x^2 + 3x - 5 = 0$?

(1) $\dfrac{-3 \pm \sqrt{29}}{2}$ (3) $\dfrac{-3 \pm \sqrt{11}}{2}$

(2) $\dfrac{3 \pm \sqrt{29}}{2}$ (4) $\dfrac{3 \pm \sqrt{11}}{2}$

3 Given the equation $x^2 - 8x + 15 = 0$. Which statement is true?
   (1) The sum of the roots is 15.
   (2) Both roots are greater than zero.
   (3) One root is less than zero and the other root is greater than zero.
   (4) One root is zero and the other root is greater than zero.

Soltuions to Questions on Quadratic Equations

1. If a quadratic equation is in the form $ax^2 + bx + c = 0$, then the nature of its roots is determined by the discriminant, $b^2 - 4ac$. For the roots to be equal, the discriminant must equal 0.

Each of the choices is in the form $ax^2 + bx + c = 0$. Calculate the discriminant for each to see which equals 0:

(1) $2x^2 + 5x - 3 = 0$ has $a = 2$, $b = 5$, and $c = -3$:

$$b^2 - 4ac = 5^2 - 4(2)(-3) = 25 + 24 = 49$$

(2) $x^2 - 4x - 32 = 0$ has $a = 1$, $b = -4$, and $c = -32$:

$$b^2 - 4ac = (-4)^2 - 4(1)(-32) = 16 + 128 = 144$$

(3) $x^2 - 7x + 3 = 0$ has $a = 1$, $b = -7$, and $c = 3$:

$$b^2 - 4ac = (-7)^2 - 4(1)(3) = 49 - 12 = 37$$

(4) $x^2 - 8x + 16 = 0$ has $a = 1$, $b = -8$, and $c = 16$:

$$b^2 - 4ac = (-8)^2 - 4(1)(16) = 64 - 64 = 0$$

The correct choice is **(4)**.

2. The given equation is a *quadratic equation:* $x^2 + 3x - 5 = 0$

The left side is a quadratic trinomial that cannot be factored, so the *quadratic formula* must be used to solve the equation: If a quadratic equation is in the form: $ax^2 + bx + c = 0$, then:

The equation $x^2 + 3x - 5 = 0$ is in the form $ax^2 + bx + c = 0$ with $a = 1$, $b = 3$, and $c = -5$:

$$x = \frac{-b \pm \sqrt{b^2 - 4ac}}{2a}$$

$$x = \frac{-3 \pm \sqrt{3^2 - 4(1)(-5)}}{2(1)}$$

$$x = \frac{-3 \pm \sqrt{9 + 20}}{2}$$

$$x = \frac{-3 \pm \sqrt{29}}{2}$$

The correct choice is **(1)**.

3. The given equation is a *quadratic equation*:

$$x^2 - 8x + 15 = 0$$

The left side is a *quadratic trinomial* that can be factored into two binomials. The factors of the first term, x^2, are x and x, and they become the first terms of the binomials:

$$(x \quad)(x \quad) = 0$$

The factors of the last term, $+15$, become the second terms of the binomials, but they must be chosen in such a way that the sum of the inner and outer cross-products of the binomials is equal to the middle term, $-8x$, of the original trinomial. Try -5 and -3 as the factors of $+15$:

$-5x = $ inner product

$$(x - 5)(x - 3) = 0$$

Since $(-5x) + (-3x) = -8x$, these are the correct factors:

$-3x = $ outer product

If the product of two factors is zero, either factor may equal zero:

$$(x - 5)(x - 3) = 0$$

The roots are 5 and 3.

$$x - 5 = 0 \lor x - 3 = 0$$
$$x = 5 \qquad x = 3$$

Consider each choice in turn:

(1) $5 + 3 = 8$, so the sum of the roots is not 15.

(2) 3 and 5 are both greater than zero so this choice is true.

(3) One root is less than zero is not true; both are positive.

(4) One root is zero is not true.

The correct choice is **(2)**.

5. PARABOLAS (including axis of symmetry, turning point)

1 The coordinates of the turning point of the graph of $y = 2x^2 - 4x + 1$ are

(1) $(1, -1)$ (3) $(-1, 5)$

(2) $(1, 1)$ (4) $(2, 1)$

2 *a* Write an equation of the axis of symmetry of the graph of $y = -x^2 + 8x - 7$.   [2]

   b Draw the graph of the equation $y = -x^2 + 8x - 7$, including all integral values of x such that $0 \le x \le 8$.   [6]

   c From the graph drawn in part *b*, find the roots of $-x^2 + 8x - 7 = 0$.   [2]

Solutions to Questions on Parabolas

1. The graph of $y = 2x^2 - 4x + 1$ is a parabola. If an equation of a parabola is in the form, $y = ax^2 + bx + c$, then an equation of its axis of symmetry is $x = -\dfrac{b}{2a}$. The equation, $y = 2x^2 - 4x + 1$, is in the form, $y = ax^2 + bx + c$, with $a = 2$, $b = -4$, and $c = 1$. An equation of its axis of symmetry is $x = -\dfrac{-4}{2(2)}$ or $x = -\dfrac{-4}{4}$ or $x = 1$.

The axis of symmetry of a parabola passes through its turning point. Therefore the x-coordinate of the turning point in this case is 1. Since the turning point is on the parabola, its coordinates must satisfy the equation of the parabola; substitute 1 for x

in the equation to determine the y-coordinate
of the turning point:

$$y = 2(1)^2 - 4(1) + 1$$
$$y = 2(1) - 4 + 1$$
$$y = 2 - 4 + 1$$
$$y = -1$$

The coordinates of the turning point are $(1,-1)$.

The correct choice is (1).

2. a. If an equation of a parabola is in the form, $y = ax^2 + bx + c$, an equation of its axis of symmetry is in the form, $x = \dfrac{-b}{2a}$.

$y = -x^2 + 8x - 7$ is in the form, $y = ax^2 + bx + c$, with $a = -1$, $b = 8$, and $c = -7$. An equation of its axis of symmetry is $x = \dfrac{-8}{2(-1)}$.

This may be simplified to $x = \dfrac{-8}{-2}$, and finally to $x = 4$.

An equation of the axis of symmetry is $x = 4$.

b. To graph $y = -x^2 + 8x - 7$ for $0 \le x \le 8$, prepare a table of values for x and y by substituting each integral value of x, from 0 to 8 inclusive, in the equation to determine the corresponding value of y.

x	$-x^2 + 8x - 7$	$= y$
0	$-0^2 + 8(0) - 7 = 0 + 0 - 7$	$= -7$
1	$-1^2 + 8(1) - 7 = -1 + 8 - 7$	$= 0$
2	$-2^2 + 8(2) - 7 = -4 + 16 - 7$	$= 5$
3	$-3^2 + 8(3) - 7 = -9 + 24 - 7$	$= 8$
4	$-4^2 + 8(4) - 7 = -16 + 32 - 7$	$= 9$
5	$-5^2 + 8(5) - 7 = -25 + 40 - 7$	$= 8$
6	$-6^2 + 8(6) - 7 = -36 + 48 - 7$	$= 5$
7	$-7^2 + 8(7) - 7 = -49 + 56 - 7$	$= 0$
8	$-8^2 + 8(8) - 7 = -64 + 64 - 7$	$= -7$

Plot the points $(0,-7)$, $(1,0)$, $(2,5)$, $(3,8)$, $(4,9)$, $(5,8)$, $(6,5)$, $(7,0)$, and $(8,-7)$ and draw a smooth curve through them. This curve is the graph of $y = -x^2 + 8x - 7$ for $0 \le x \le 8$.

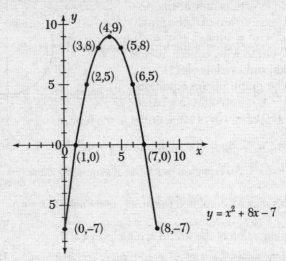

c. The roots of $-x^2 + 8x - 7 = 0$ are the values of x on the graph at the points where $y = 0$. $y = 0$ is the x-axis. There are two points where the graph crosses the x-axis; at these points, $x = 1$ and $x = 7$.

The roots are **1** and **7**.

6. SYSTEMS OF EQUATIONS (algebraic and graphic solutions)

1 If the graphs of $x^2 + y^2 = 4$ and $y = -4$ are drawn on the same axes, what is the total number of points common to both graphs?
(1) 1   (3) 3
(2) 2   (4) 0

2 Solve the following system of equations algebraically and check:

$$y = 2x^2 + 2x + 3$$
$$x = y - 3$$

[8, 2]

Solutions to Questions on Systems of Equations

1. Since the equation, $x^2 + y^2 = r^2$, represents the graph of a circle with center at the origin and a radius of r, the graph of $x^2 + y^2 = 4$ (or $x^2 + y^2 = 2^2$) is a circle with center at the origin and a radius of 2.

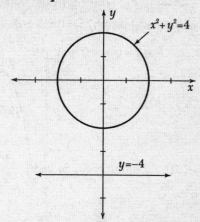

The graph of the equation, $y = -4$, is a straight line parallel to the x-axis and 4 units below it.

The two graphs do not intersect, so they have no points in common.

The correct choice is **(4)**.

2. The given system of equations is:

$$\begin{cases} y = 2x^2 + 2x + 3 \\ x = y - 3 \end{cases}$$

Rearrange the second equation so that it is solved for y:

$$x + 3 = y$$

Substitute $(x + 3)$ for y in the first equation:

$$x + 3 = 2x^2 + 2x + 3$$

This is a *quadratic equation*. Rearrange it so that all terms are on one side equal to zero:

$$0 = 2x^2 + 2x - x + 3 - 3$$

Combine like terms:

$$0 = 2x^2 + x$$

Factor out the *common monomial factor*, x, on the right side:

$$0 = x(2x + 1)$$

If the product of two factors equals zero, then either factor may equal zero:

$$x = 0 \lor 2x + 1 = 0$$
$$2x = -1$$
$$x = -\frac{1}{2}$$

Substitute 0 and $-\dfrac{1}{2}$ in the equation, $y = x + 3$, to find the corresponding values of y:

For $x = 0$: $y = 0 + 3$ For $x = -\dfrac{1}{2}$: $y = -\dfrac{1}{2} + 3$

$$y = 3 \qquad\qquad y = -\dfrac{1}{2} + \dfrac{6}{2}$$

$$y = \dfrac{5}{2}$$

The solution is $(0, 3)$ and $\left(-\dfrac{1}{2}, \dfrac{5}{2}\right)$ or $x = 0$, $y = 3$, and $x = -\dfrac{1}{2}$, $y = \dfrac{5}{2}$.

CHECK: The solutions must be checked by substituting in *both* of the *original* equations to see if they satisfy each of them:

$y = 2x^2 + 2x + 3$	$x = y - 3$
$(0, 3)$: $3 \stackrel{?}{=} 2(0)^2 + 2(0) + 3$	$0 \stackrel{?}{=} 3 - 3$
$3 \stackrel{?}{=} 2(0) + 0 + 3$	$0 = 0 \;\checkmark$
$3 \stackrel{?}{=} 0 + 0 + 3$	
$3 = 3 \;\checkmark$	
$\left(-\dfrac{1}{2}, \dfrac{5}{2}\right)$: $\dfrac{5}{2} \stackrel{?}{=} 2\left(-\dfrac{1}{2}\right)^2 + 2\left(-\dfrac{1}{2}\right) + 3$	$-\dfrac{1}{2} \stackrel{?}{=} \dfrac{5}{2} - 3$
$\dfrac{5}{2} \stackrel{?}{=} 2\left(\dfrac{1}{4}\right) - 1 + 3$	$-\dfrac{1}{2} \stackrel{?}{=} \dfrac{5}{2} - \dfrac{6}{2}$
$\dfrac{5}{2} \stackrel{?}{=} \dfrac{1}{2} + 2$	$-\dfrac{1}{2} = -\dfrac{1}{2} \;\checkmark$
$2\dfrac{1}{2} = 2\dfrac{1}{2} \;\checkmark$	

7. SUPPLEMENTARY, COMPLEMENTARY, VERTICAL ANGLES, ANGLE MEASURE

1 In the accompanying diagram, $\overleftrightarrow{AB}$ and $\overleftrightarrow{CD}$ intersect at E. If $m\angle AEC = 2x + 40$ and $m\angle CEB = x + 20$, find x.

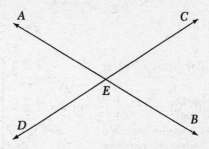

2 In the accompanying diagram, $\overline{AB} \perp \overline{BC}$, $\overline{DB} \perp \overline{BE}$, $m\angle CBE = x$, $m\angle DBC = y$, and $m\angle ABD = z$. Which statement must be true?

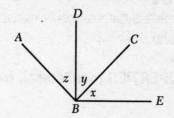

(1) $x = y$ (3) $y = z$
(2) $x = z$ (4) $2y = x + z$

Solutions to Questions on Supplementary, Complementary, Vertical Angles, Angle Measure

1. $\angle AEC$ and $\angle CEB$ are supplementary angles. The sum of the measures of two supplementary angles is $180°$:

$$m\angle AEC + m\angle CEB = 180$$
$$2x + 40 + x + 20 = 180$$
$$3x + 60 = 180$$
$$3x = 180 - 60$$
$$3x = 120$$
$$x = 40$$

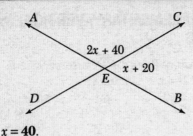

$x = 40$.

2. Perpendicular lines meet at right angles:

$\angle ABC$ is a right angle.

$\angle DBE$ is a right angle.

If the sum of two angles equals a right angle, the angles are complementary:

z is the complement of y,

x is the complement of y.

Complements of the same angle are equal in measure: $x = z$.

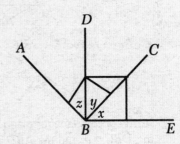

The correct choice is **(2)**.

8. TRIANGLE PROPERTIES (equilateral, isosceles, sum of angles)

1   The measures of the three angles of a triangle are in the ratio 2:3:4. Find the measure of the largest angle of the triangle.

2   In the accompanying diagram of $\triangle ABC$, $\overline{AB} \cong \overline{AC}$, $\overline{BD}$, and $\overline{DC}$ are angle bisectors, and m$\angle BAC = 20$. Find the measure of $\angle BDC$.

3 In the accompanying diagram of $\triangle ABC$, $\overline{BD}$ is drawn so that $\overline{BD} \cong \overline{DC}$. If m$\angle C = 70$, find m$\angle BDA$.

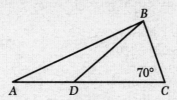

Solutions to Questions on Triangle Properties

1. Let $2x$, $3x$, and $4x$ represent, respectively, the measures of the three angles of the triangle.

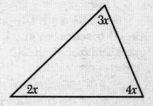

The sum of the measures of the three angles of a triangle is $180°$:

$$2x + 3x + 4x = 180$$
$$9x = 180$$

Divide both sides of the equation by 9:

$$x = 20$$

The measure of the largest angle is $4x$:

$$4x = 4(20) = 80$$

The measure of the largest angle is **80**.

2. The sum of the measures of the three angles of a triangle is $180°$:

m$\angle A = 20$:

$$\text{m}\angle A + \text{m}\angle B + \text{m}\angle C = 180$$
$$20 + \text{m}\angle B + \text{m}\angle C = 180$$
$$\text{m}\angle B + \text{m}\angle C = 180 - 20$$
$$\text{m}\angle B + \text{m}\angle C = 160$$

Since $\overline{AB} \cong \overline{AC}$, $\triangle ABC$ is isosceles; the base angles of an isosceles triangle are equal in measure:

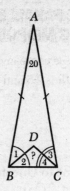

$$m\angle B = m\angle C$$
$$2(m\angle B) = 160$$
$$m\angle B = 80$$
$$m\angle C = 80$$

Since $\overline{DB}$ and $\overline{DC}$ are angle bisectors, $m\angle 1 = m\angle 2$, and $m\angle 3 = m\angle 4$:

$$2(m\angle 2) = 80 \qquad 2(m\angle 4) = 80$$
$$m\angle 2 = 40 \qquad\quad m\angle 4 = 40$$

In $\triangle BDC$, the sum of the measures of the three angles is 180°:

$$m\angle BDC + m\angle 2 + m\angle 4 = 180$$
$$m\angle BDC + 40 + 40 = 180$$
$$m\angle BDC + 80 = 180$$
$$m\angle BDC = 180 - 80$$
$$m\angle BDC = 100$$

$m\angle BDC = \mathbf{100}$.

3. Since $\overline{BD} \cong \overline{DC}$, $\triangle BDC$ is isosceles. The base angles of an isosceles triangle are equal in measure:

$$m\angle DBC = m\angle C = 70$$

$\angle ADB$ is an exterior angle of $\triangle BDC$. The measure of an exterior angle of a triangle is equal to the sum of the measures of the two remote interior angles:

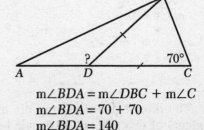

$$m\angle BDA = m\angle DBC + m\angle C$$
$$m\angle BDA = 70 + 70$$
$$m\angle BDA = 140$$

$m\angle BDA = \mathbf{140}$.

9. LINE PARALLEL TO ONE SIDE OF TRIANGLE; LINE JOINING MIDPOINTS OF TWO SIDES

1 In the accompanying diagram, $\overline{DE}$ is parallel to $\overline{AC}$. If the ratio of $AD:DB$ is 2:5 and CE measures 6, find the measure of $\overline{EB}$.

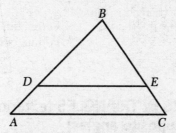

2 If the length of the line segment joining the midpoints of two sides of an equilateral triangle is 6, find the perimeter of the triangle.

Solutions to Questions on Line Parallel One Side of Triangle; Line Joining Midpoints of Two Sides

1. Let x = the measure of $\overline{EB}$.

If a line is parallel to one side of a triangle, it divides the other two sides.

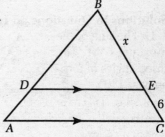

2.

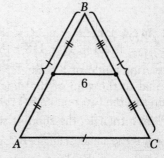

The line segment joining the midpoints of two sides of a triangle has a length equal to one-half the length of the third side:

$$6 = \frac{1}{2}AC$$
$$12 = AC$$

All sides of an equilateral triangle are of the same length:

$$AB = BC = AC = 12$$

The perimeter of a triangle is the sum of the lengths of the three sides:

Perimeter of $\triangle ABC = 3 \times 12$
Perimeter of $\triangle ABC = 36$

The perimeter is **36**.

10. INEQUALITIES IN TRIANGLES (exterior angle, unequal sides, opposite angles)

1 In $\triangle ABC$, m$\angle C = 118$ and m$\angle B = 44$. Which is the shortest side of the triangle?

2 In $\triangle ABC$, side $\overline{AC}$ is extended through C to D. If m$\angle DCB = 50$, which is the *longest* side of $\triangle ABC$?

Solutions to Questions on Inequalities in Triangles

1. The sum of the measures of the three angles of a triangle is 180°:

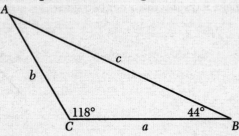

$$\text{m}\angle A + \text{m}\angle B + \text{m}\angle C = 180$$
$$\text{m}\angle A + 44 + 118 = 180$$
$$\text{m}\angle A + 162 = 180$$
$$\text{m}\angle A = 180 - 162$$
$$\text{m}\angle A = 18$$

In a triangle, the shortest side lies opposite the smallest angle. Since $\angle A$ is the smallest angle, $\overline{BC}$, or a, must be the shortest side.

$\overline{BC}$ or a is the shortest side.

2. If the exterior sides of two adjacent angles form a straight line, they are supplementary: ∠*ACB* and ∠*BCD* are supplementary.

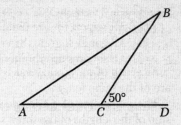

The sum of the measures of two supplementary angles is 180°:

$$m\angle ACB + m\angle BCD = 180$$
$$m\angle ACB + 50 = 180$$
$$m\angle ACB = 180 - 50$$
$$m\angle ACB = 130$$

There can be only one obtuse angle in a triangle. Since ∠*ACB* is an obtuse angle, it is the *largest* angle in △*ABC*.

In a triangle, the side opposite the *largest* angle is the *longest* side: $\overline{AB}$ is the *longest* side of △*ABC*. (It can also be designated **AB** or **c**.)

11. QUADRILATERAL PROPERTIES (parallelogram, square, rhombus, rectangle, trapezoid)

1 In parallelogram *ABCD*, diagonals $\overline{AC}$ and $\overline{BD}$ intersect at *E*. If $BE = 4x - 12$ and $DE = 2x + 8$, find x.

2 In the accompanying diagram of parallelogram *ABCD*, side $\overline{AD}$ is extended through *D* to *E* and *DB* is a diagonal. If m∠*EDC* = 65 and m∠*CBD* = 85, find m∠*CDB*.

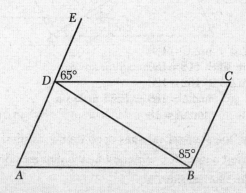

3 Which statement is *always* true?
   (1) All trapezoids are parallelograms.
   (2) All parallelograms are rectangles.
   (3) All squares are rhombuses.
   (4) All rhombuses are rectangles.

Solutions to Questions on Quadrilateral Properties

1.

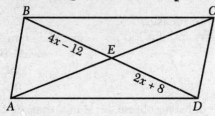

The diagonals of a parallelogram bisect each other:

$$4x - 12 = 2x + 12$$
$$4x - 2x = 8 + 12$$
$$2x = 20$$
$$x = 10$$

2.

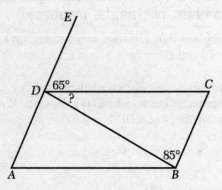

The opposite sides of a parallelogram are parallel:

$$\overline{ADE} \parallel \overline{BC}$$

If two lines are parallel, a transversal makes a pair of alternate interior angles equal in measure:

$$m\angle EDC = m\angle C$$
$$65 = m\angle C$$

The sum of the measures of the three angles of a triangle is 180:

$$m\angle CDB + m\angle C + m\angle CBD = 180$$
$$m\angle CDB + 65 + 85 = 180$$
$$m\angle CDB + 150 = 180$$
$$m\angle CDB = 180 - 150$$
$$m\angle CDB = 30$$

$m\angle CDB = 30$.

3.

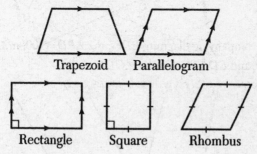

Trapezoid　Parallelogram

Rectangle　Square　Rhombus

Consider each choice in turn:

(1) All trapezoids are not parallelograms. A parallelogram has two pairs of opposite sides parallel, and a trapezoid has only one pair of parallel sides.

(2) All parallelograms are not rectangles. A rectangle is a parallelogram with one right angle; not all parallelograms have right angles.

(3) All squares are rhombuses. A rhombus is an equilateral parallelogram. So is a square. A square happens to have an additional characteristic (a right angle), but it is still a rhombus.

(4) All rhombuses are not rectangles. A rectangle is a parallelogram with one right angle. A rhombus need not have a right angle.

The correct choice is **(3)**.

12. PARALLEL LINES

1 In the accompanying diagram, $\overleftrightarrow{AB}$, $\overleftrightarrow{CD}$, $\overleftrightarrow{EF}$, and $\overleftrightarrow{GH}$ are straight lines. If m∠w = 30, m∠x = 30, and m∠z = 120, find m∠y.

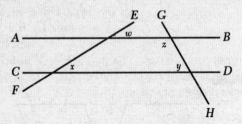

2 In the accompanying diagram, $\overline{BDG}$, m∠ABD = 100, m∠DGF = 120, $\overline{AB} \parallel \overline{CD}$, and $\overline{ED} \parallel \overline{FG}$. Find m∠CDE.

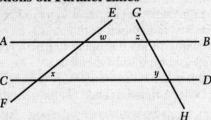

Solutions to Questions on Parallel Lines

1.

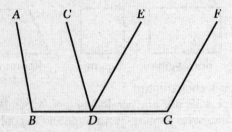

Since m∠w = 30 and m∠x = 30: m∠w = m∠x

If a transversal to two lines makes a pair of corresponding angles equal in measure, the lines are parallel: $\overline{AB} \parallel \overline{CD}$

If two lines are parallel, the interior angles on the same side of a transversal are supplementary: ∠y is the supplement of ∠z

The sum of the measures of two supplementary angles is 180:

$$m\angle y + m\angle z = 180$$

It is given that $m\angle z = 120$:

$$m\angle y + 120 = 180$$
$$m\angle y = 180 - 120$$
$$m\angle y = 60$$

$m\angle y = \mathbf{60}$.

2. If a transversal cuts two parallel lines, it makes a pair of corresponding angles congruent:

$m\angle CDG = m\angle ABD = 100$.

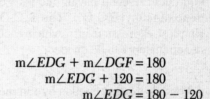

If two parallel lines are cut by a transversal, interior angles on the same side of the transversal are supplementary: $\angle EDG$ is the supplement of $\angle DGF$.

The sum of the measures of two supplementary angles is 180°:

$$m\angle EDG + m\angle DGF = 180$$
$$m\angle EDG + 120 = 180$$
$$m\angle EDG = 180 - 120$$
$$m\angle EDG = 60$$

The whole equals the sum of its parts:

$$m\angle CDG = m\angle CDE + m\angle EDG$$
$$100 = m\angle CDE + 60$$
$$100 - 60 = m\angle CDE$$
$$40 = m\angle CDE$$

$m\angle CDE = \mathbf{40}$.

13. ALGEBRAIC OPERATIONS; VERBAL PROBLEMS

1 *a* Express in simplest form:

$$\frac{5}{x-1} - \frac{3}{x}, x \neq 1,0$$

b The numerator of a certain fraction is three less than the denominator. If the numerator and the denominator are each increased by one, the value of the fraction is $\frac{2}{3}$. Find the original fraction. [*Only an algebraic solution will be accepted.*]

2 The base of a rectangle is twice the side of a square, and the height of the rectangle is 2 more than the side of the square. The area of the rectangle is 32 square units more than the area of the square. Find the dimensions of the rectangle. [*Only an algebraic solution will be accepted.*]

Solutions to Questions on Algebraic Operations; Verbal Problems

1. *a* The given expression is:

In their present form, the fractions cannot be combined because they have different denominators. Express each fraction as an equivalent fraction having the least common denominator (L.C.D.). The L.C.D. is the simplest expression into which each of the denominators can be divided:

$$\frac{5}{x-1} - \frac{3}{x}, x \neq 1,0$$

The L.C.D. for $(x-1)$ and x is $x(x-1)$

Multiply the first fraction by 1 in the form $\frac{x}{x}$, and multiply the second fraction by 1 in the form $\frac{x-1}{x-1}$:

NOTE: The above step is possible because $x \neq 1,0$ insures that we are not multiplying by 0:

$$\frac{5x}{x(x-1)} - \frac{3(x-1)}{x(x-1)}$$

$$\frac{5x}{x(x-1)} - \frac{3x-3}{x(x-1)}$$

Since the fractions now have the same denominator, they may be combined by combining their numerators:

$$\frac{5x - (3x-3)}{x(x-1)}$$

Remove the parentheses in the numerator:

$$\frac{5x - 3x + 3}{x(x-1)}$$

Combine like terms in the numerator:

$$\frac{2x+3}{x(x-1)}$$

The expression in simplest form is $\frac{2x+3}{x(x-1)}$.

b Let x = the denominator of the original fraction.

Then $x - 3$ = the numerator.

If the numerator and denominator are each increased by 1, the value of the fraction is $\dfrac{2}{3}$:

$$\frac{x - 2}{x + 1} = \frac{2}{3}$$

The equation is in the form of a proportion. In a proportion, the product of the means equals the product of the extremes (cross-multiply):

$$3(x - 2) = 2(x + 1)$$
$$3x - 6 = 2x + 2$$
$$3x - 2x = 2 + 6$$

The denominator is represented by x: $\qquad x = 8$

The numerator is represented by $x - 3$: $\qquad x - 3 = 8 - 3 = 5$

The original fraction is $\dfrac{5}{8}$.

2. Let x = the length of the side of the square.

Then $2x$ = the base of the rectangle, and $x + 2$ = the height of the rectangle.

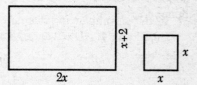

The <u>area of the rectangle</u> equals the <u>area of the square</u> plus 32.

$$\downarrow \qquad\qquad\qquad \downarrow \quad \downarrow$$

$$2x\,(x + 2) \qquad = \qquad x^2 \qquad + \quad 32$$

The equation to use is:

$$2x(x + 2) = x^2 + 32$$
$$2x^2 + 4x = x^2 + 32$$

This is a *quadratic equation.* Rearrange it so that all terms are on one side equal to 0:

$$2x^2 - x^2 + 4x - 32 = 0$$
$$x^2 + 4x - 32 = 0$$

The left side is a *quadratic trinomial* that can be factored into the product of two binomials. Be sure to check that the sum of the inner cross product and the outer cross product is equal to the middle term, $+4x$, of the original trinomial:

$+8x =$ inner product

$(x + 8)(x - 4) = 0$

$-4x =$ outer product

Since $(+8x) + (-4x) = +4x$, these are the correct factors:

$(x + 8)(x - 4) = 0$

If the product of two factors equals 0, then either factor may equal 0:

Reject the negative value as meaningless for a length:

$x + 8 = 0 \lor x - 4 = 0$

$x = -8 \qquad x = 4$

$x = 4$

The base of the rectangle $= 2x = 2(4) = 8$.
The height of the rectangle $= x + 2 = 4 + 2 = 6$.
The dimensions of the rectangle are **6** and **8** units.

14. MEAN PROPORTIONAL; ALTITUDE TO HYPOTENUSE OF RIGHT TRIANGLE

1 In the accompanying diagram of $\triangle ABC$, $m\angle ABC = 90$ and $\overline{CD}$ is an altitude. If $AD = 2$ and $DB = 6$, find AC.

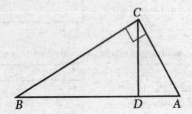

2 In right triangle ABC, $\overline{CD}$ is the altitude drawn to hypotenuse $\overline{AB}$.

The length of $\overline{AD}$ is 2 units less than the length of $\overline{DB}$, and $CD = 3$.

a Find the length of $\overline{DB}$ in radical form. [*Only an algebraic solution will be accepted.*]

b In this triangle, which statement is true?

(1) $CD < DB$

(2) $CD = DB$

(3) $CD > DB$

Solutions to Questions on Mean Proportional; Altitude to Hypotenuse of Right Triangle

1. Let $AC = x$

$AB = AD + DB = 2 + 6 = 8$

If the altitude is drawn to the hypotenuse of a right triangle, the length of either leg is the mean proportional between the length of the whole hypotenuse and the length of the adjacent segment:

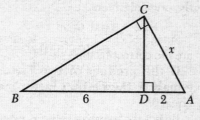

In a proportion, the product of the means equals the product of the extremes (cross-multiply):

Take the square root of both sides of the equation:

Reject the negative root as meaningless for a length:

$AC = 4.$

$$\frac{2}{x} = \frac{x}{8}$$

$$x^2 = 2(8)$$
$$x^2 = 16$$

$$x = \pm\, 4$$

$$x = 4$$

2. *a.* Let $DB = x$
Then $AD = x - 2$

If the altitude is drawn to the hypotenuse of a right triangle, the length of the altitude is the mean proportional between the lengths of the two segments of the hypotenuse:

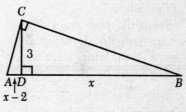

In a proportion, the product of the means equals the product of the extremes (cross-multiply):

This is a *quadratic equation*. Rearrange it so that all terms are on one side equal to zero:

$$\frac{x}{3} = \frac{3}{x - 2}$$

$$x(x - 2) = 3(3)$$
$$x^2 - 2x = 9$$

$$x^2 - 2x - 9 = 0$$

The left side is a *quadratic trinomial* that cannot be factored. Use the *quadratic formula* to solve: If a quadratic equation is in the form,

$ax^2 + bx + c = 0$, then:

$$x = \frac{-b \pm \sqrt{b^2 - 4ac}}{2a}$$

$x^2 - 2x - 9 = 0$ is in the form, $ax^2 + bx + c = 0$, with $a = 1, b = -2$, and $c = -9$:

$$x = \frac{-(-2) \pm \sqrt{(-2)^2 - 4(1)(-9)}}{2(1)}$$

$$x = \frac{2 \pm \sqrt{4 + 36}}{2}$$

$$x = \frac{2 \pm \sqrt{40}}{2}$$

To simplify the radical, factor out any perfect square factor in the radicand:

$$x = \frac{2 \pm \sqrt{4(10)}}{2}$$

Remove the perfect square factor from under the radical sign by taking its square root and writing it as a coefficient of the radical:

$$x = \frac{2 \pm 2\sqrt{10}}{2}$$

Simplify the fractional expression by dividing all terms in the numerator and denominator by 2:

$$x = 1 \pm \sqrt{10}$$

Since $\sqrt{9} = 3$, $\sqrt{10} > 3$. Therefore $(1 - \sqrt{10})$ is negative and must be rejected as a possible value for a length:

$$x = 1 + \sqrt{10}$$

The length of $\overline{DB}$ in radical form is $\mathbf{1 + \sqrt{10}}$.

b. As noted above, $\sqrt{10} > 3$. Therefore, $DB = 1 + \sqrt{10} > 1 + 3$, or $DB > 4$. Since $CD = 3$, $CD < DB$.

The correct choice is (**1**).

15. PYTHAGOREAN THEOREM; SPECIAL RIGHT TRIANGLES (3-4-5, 5-12-13, 30-60-90)

1. The diagonals of a rhombus have lengths of 12 centimeters and 16 centimeters. Find the number of centimeters in the length of one side of the rhombus.

2. The measure of the altitude of an equilateral triangle whose side has length 6 is

   (1) $\sqrt{3}$ (3) $3\sqrt{3}$

   (2) $2\sqrt{3}$ (4) $4\sqrt{3}$

Solutions to Questions on Pythagorean Theorem; Special Right Triangles

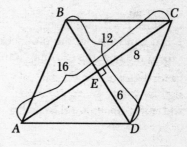

1. The diagonals of a rhombus bisect each other and are perpendicular to each other. Therefore they divide the rhombus into four right triangles, each having legs whose lengths are half that of the diagonals. Any one of the right triangles, for example $\triangle CED$, has legs whose lengths are 6 and 8 centimeters respectively.

$\triangle CED$ is a 3-4-5 right triangle with $ED = 3(2)$ and $CE = 4(2)$. Therefore hypotenuse $CD = 5(2)$ or 10. $\overline{CD}$ is also a side of the rhombus.

The length of one side of the rhombus is **10** centimeters.

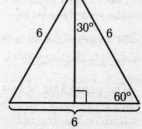

2. If a represents the length of a side of an equilateral triangle, then the length of its altitude is represented by $\frac{a}{2}\sqrt{3}$ Here, $a = 6$, so the altitude is $\frac{6}{2}\sqrt{3}$ or $3\sqrt{3}$.

The correct choice is **(3)**.

ALTERNATIVE SOLUTION: The altitude of an equilateral triangle divides it into two 30°-60°-90° triangles. In a 30°-60°-90° triangle, if the hypotenuse has length a, the length of the side opposite 60° is $\frac{a}{2}\sqrt{3}$, etc.

16. SIMILAR FIGURES (ratios and proportions)

1 The ratio of the corresponding sides of two similar polygons is 2:3. If the perimeter of the larger polygon is 27, find the perimeter of the smaller polygon.

2 Three sides of a triangle measure 4, 5, and 8. Find the length of the *longest* side of a similar triangle whose perimeter is 51.

Solutions to Questions on Similar Figures

1. Let p = the perimeter of the smaller polygon.
   Let P = the perimeter of the larger polygon.

The perimeters of two similar polygons have the same ratio as any two corresponding sides:

$$\frac{p}{P} = \frac{2}{3}$$

Since $P = 27$, we have:

$$\frac{p}{27} = \frac{2}{3}$$

In a proportion, the product of the means equals the product of the extremes (cross-multiply):

$$3p = 2(27)$$
$$3p = 54$$
$$p = 18$$

The perimeter of the smaller polygon is **18**.

2.

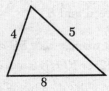 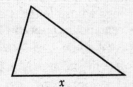

Let P = the perimeter of the first triangle.
Let x = the *longest* side of the similar triangle.
Then x will correspond to 8, the *longest* side of the first triangle.

The perimeter of a triangle is the sum of the lengths of the three sides:

$$P = 4 + 5 + 8$$
$$P = 17$$

The perimeters of two similar triangles have the same ratio as any two corresponding sides:

Reduce the fraction on the left by dividing its numerator and denominator by 17:

$$\frac{17}{51} = \frac{8}{x}$$
$$\frac{1}{3} = \frac{8}{x}$$

In a proportion, the product of the means is equal to be product of the extremes (cross-multiply):

$$x = 3(8)$$
$$x = 24$$

The longest side is **24**.

17. AREAS (triangle, rectangle, parallelogram, rhombus, trapezoid)

1 In a rectangle, the length is twice the width, and the perimeter is 48. Find the area of the rectangle.

2 Find the area of the triangle whose vertices are (0,8), (0,0), and (7,0).

Solutions to Questions on Areas

1. Let x = the width of the rectangle. Then $2x$ = the length of the rectangle.

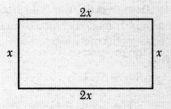

The perimeter, P, equals the sum of the lengths of all the sides:
The perimeter is 48:

$$P = x + 2x + x + 2x$$
$$48 = 6x$$
$$8 = x \text{(width is 8)}$$
$$2x = 2(8) = 16 \text{ (length is 16)}$$

The area, A, of a rectangle is equal to the product of its length and width:

$$A = 8(16)$$
$$A = 128$$

The area of the rectangle is **128**.

2.

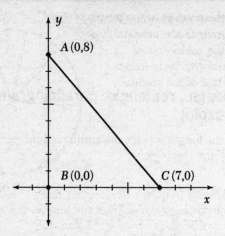

Triangle ABC is a right triangle. The area, A, of a right triangle is equal to one-half the product of the lengths of its legs:

$$A = \frac{1}{2}(AB)(BC)$$

$AB = 8$; $BC = 7$:

$$A = \frac{1}{2}(8)(7)$$
$$A = 4(7)$$
$$A = 28$$

The area of the triangle is **28**.

18. LOCUS

1 The locus of the midpoints of the radii of a circle is
   (1) a point   (3) a line
   (2) two lines   (4) a circle

2 How many points are equidistant from two intersecting lines and 3 units from their point of intersection?
   (1) 1   (3) 3
   (2) 2   (4) 4

3 An equation of the locus of points equidistant from the points $(0,6)$ and $(0,-2)$ is
   (1) $x = 2$ (3) $x = -2$
   (2) $y = 2$ (4) $y = -2$

Solutions to Questions on Locus

1. If the outer circle is the original circle, the locus of the midpoints of its radii is a smaller concentric circle whose radius is exactly half that of the original.

The correct choice is **(4)**.

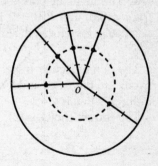

2. All points equidistant from the intersecting lines, ℓ and m, are on the angle bisectors of the angles formed at the intersection of ℓ and m. The bisectors are shown as dashed lines in the drawing.

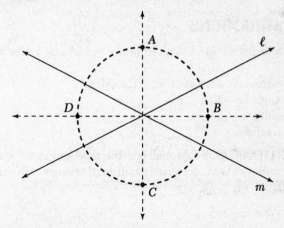

All points 3 units from the intersection of ℓ and m are on the circle whose center is the intersection and whose radius is 3 units.

Points satisfying both conditions are at the intersection of the circle with the angle bisectors. There are 4 such points, labelled A, B, C, and D in the drawing.

The correct choice is **(4)**.

3. The locus of points equidistant from $A(0,6)$ and $B(0,-2)$ is the perpendicular bisector of the line segment $\overline{AB}$.

The perpendicular bisector is a line parallel to the x-axis and 2 units above it. Its equation is $y = 2$.

The correct choice is **(2)**.

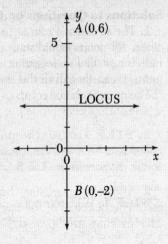

19. CONSTRUCTIONS

1 To locate a point equidistant from the vertices of a triangle, construct
   (1) the perpendicular bisectors of the sides
   (2) the angle bisectors
   (3) the altitudes
   (4) the medians

DIRECTIONS: (35): Leave all construction lines in the answer.

2 *On the answer sheet*, construct equilateral triangle ABC using the line segment $\overline{AB}$ as one side.

A ———————————————— B

Solutions to Questions on Constructions

1. The vertices of a triangle are really the two endpoints of each of its sides. All points equidistant from two points lie on the perpendicular bisector of the line segment joining those two points. Thus, locating the point equidistant from the vertices of a triangle requires construction of the perpendicular bisectors of the sides.

The correct choice is **(1)**.

2. STEP 1: With the point of the compasses on A and the compasses open to the distance from A to B, swing an arc above $\overline{AB}$.

STEP 2: With the point of the compasses on B and the compasses open the same amount as in STEP 1, swing an arc that intersects the arc of STEP 1 in a point C.

STEP 3: Draw $\overline{AC}$ and $\overline{BC}$.

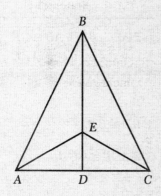

$\triangle \boldsymbol{ABC}$ is the required equilateral triangle with segment $\overline{AB}$ as one side.

20. DEDUCTIVE PROOFS

1 Given: $\triangle ABC, \overleftrightarrow{BED}, \overline{AB} \cong \overline{CB}$,
    and D is the midpoint of $\overline{AC}$.

Prove: $\overline{AE} \cong \overline{CE}$

2 Acid rain is a problem in our environment.

    Given: If industry causes acid rain, then the air is polluted.

            If the lakes are not contaminated, then the air is not polluted.

            The statement "Fish will die and industry does not cause acid rain" is not true.

            The lakes are not contaminated.

Let A represent: "Industry causes acid rain."
Let P represent: "The air is polluted."
Let C represent: "The lakes are contaminated."
Let D represent: "The fish will die."

Using laws of inference, prove: The fish will not die

Solutions to Questions on Deductive Proofs

1. Given: $\triangle ABC$, $\overline{BED}$, $\overline{AB}$, $\cong \overline{CB}$
  D is the midpoint of $\overline{AC}$

To Prove: $\overline{AE} \cong \overline{CE}$

Plan: We can prove $\overline{AE} \cong \overline{CE}$ if we can get $\triangle ADE \cong \triangle CDE$. We have two pairs of congruent sides ($\overline{AD} \cong \overline{DC}$, and the identity, $\overline{DE}$). To get included angles 1 and 2 congruent, we must first prove $\triangle ADB \cong \triangle CDB$.

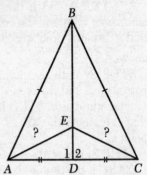

PROOF

Statements	Reasons
1. $\triangle ABC$, $\overline{BED}$, $\overline{AB} \cong \overline{CB}$	1. Given
2. D is the midpoint of $\overline{AC}$	2. Given
3. $\overline{AD} \cong \overline{DC}$	3. A midpoint divides a line segment into two congruent segments.
4. $\overline{BD} \cong \overline{BD}$	4. The reflexive property of congruence (identity).
5. $\triangle ADB \cong \triangle CDB$	5. S.S.S. $\cong$ S.S.S.
6. $\angle 1 \cong \angle 2$	6. Corresponding angles of congruent triangles are congruent.
7. $\overline{ED} \cong \overline{ED}$	7. Reason #4.
8. $\triangle ADE \cong \triangle CDE$	8. S.A.S. $\cong$ S.A.S.
9. $\overline{AE} \cong \overline{CE}$	9. Corresponding sides of congruent triangles are congruent.

2. A = "Industry causes acid rain."

P = "The air is polluted."

C = "The lakes are contaminated."

D = "The fish will die."

Using the above, convert each statement in the "Given" and "To Prove" to symbolic representation:

"If industry causes acid rain, then the air is polluted" is the *implication* or *conditional*: $\quad A \to P$

"If the lakes are not contaminated then the air is not polluted" is the *implication* that the *negation* of C implies the *negation* of P: $\quad \sim C \to \sim P$

"The statement 'Fish will die and industry does not cause acid rain' is not true" is the *negation* of the *conjunction* between D and $\sim A$: $\quad \sim(D \wedge \sim A)$

"The lakes are not contaminated" is the *negation* of C: $\quad \sim C$

Given: $A \to P$, $\sim C \to \sim P$, $\sim(D \wedge \sim A)$, and $\sim C$

To Prove: $\sim D$

PROOF

Statements	Reasons
(1) $\sim C$	(1) Given
(2) $\sim C \to \sim P$	(2) Given
(3) $\sim P$	(3) The Law of Detachment or *modus ponens* (1, 2).
(4) $A \to P$	(4) Given
(5) $\sim P \to \sim A$	(5) The Law of the Contrapositive: Inference.
(6) $\sim A$	(6) The Law of Detachment (3, 5).
(7) $\sim(D \wedge \sim A)$	(7) Given
(8) $\sim D \vee A$	(8) De Morgan's Law. Note: $\sim[\sim A]$ is the same as A.
(9) $\sim D$	(9) Law of Disjunctive Inference (6, 8).

21. COORDINATE GEOMETRY (slope, distance, midpoint, equation of circle)

1 Find the distance between the points $(-1,5)$ and $(-7,3)$.

2 What is the slope of the line that passes through the points whose coordinates are $(-1,4)$ and $(1,5)$?

3 Segment $\overline{AB}$ is the diameter of a circle whose center is $(2,0)$. If the coordinates of A are $(0,-3)$, find the coordinates of B.

4 Which is an equation of the circle whose center is $(1,3)$ and whose radius is 2?
    (1) $(x-1)^2 + (y-3)^2 = 2$
    (2) $(x-1)^2 + (y-3)^2 = 4$
    (3) $x^2 + y^2 = 4$
    (4) $(x+1)^2 + (y+3)^2 = 4$

Solutions to Questions on Coordinate Geometry

1.

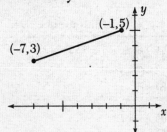

Use the formula for the distance, d, between two points (x_1, y_1) and (x_2, y_2):
Let $x_1 = -1$, $y_1 = 5$, and let $x_2 = -7$, $y_2 = 3$:

$$d = \sqrt{(x_2 - x_1)^2 + (y_2 - y_1)^2}$$

$$d = \sqrt{(-7-[-1])^2 + (3-5)^2}$$

$$d = \sqrt{(-7+1)^2 + (-2)^2}$$

$$d = \sqrt{(-6)^2 + 4}$$

$$d = \sqrt{36 + 4}$$

$$d = \sqrt{40}$$

A radical expression may be simplified by factoring out any perfect square factor in the radicand:

$$d = \sqrt{4(10)}$$

Remove the perfect square factor from under the radical sign by taking its square root and writing it as a coefficient of the radical:

$$d = 2\sqrt{10}$$

The distance is $2\sqrt{10}$.

2.

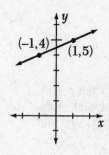

Use the formula for the slope, m, of a line joining the points (x_1, y_1) and (x_2, y_2):

$$m = \frac{y_2 - y_1}{x_2 - x_1}$$

Let $x_1 = -1$, $y_1 = 4$, and let $x_2 = 1$, $y_2 = 5$:

$$m = \frac{5 - 4}{1 - (-1)}$$

$$m = \frac{1}{1 + 1}$$

$$m = \frac{1}{2}$$

The slope $= \dfrac{1}{2}$.

3. Since $\overline{AB}$ is a diameter of the circle, the center of the circle, O, is the midpoint of $\overline{AB}$.

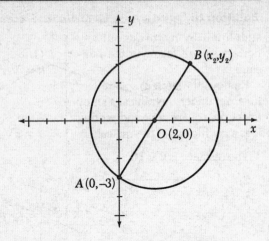

Use the formulas for the coordinates $(\overline{x}, \overline{y})$ of the midpoint of the line segment joining (x_1, y_1) and (x_2, y_2):

Here, $\overline{x} = 2$ and $\overline{y} = 0$.

Let $x_1 = 0, y_1 = -3$:

$$\overline{x} = \frac{x_1 + x_2}{2} \qquad \overline{y} = \frac{y_1 + y_2}{2}$$

$$2 = \frac{0 + x_2}{2} \qquad 0 = \frac{-3 + y_2}{2}$$

$$4 = 0 + x_2 \qquad 0 = -3 + y_2$$

$$4 = x_2 \qquad 3 = y_2$$

The coordinates of B are **(4, 3)**.

4. The equation of a circle with center at (h, k) and radius r is of this form:

For a center at $(1,3)$ and radius of $2, h = 1, k = 3$ and $r = 2$:

$$(x - h)^2 + (y - k)^2 = r^2$$

$$(x - 1)^2 + (y - 3)^2 = 2^2$$
$$\text{or } (x - 1)^2 + (y - 3)^2 = 4^2$$

The correct choice is **(2)**.

22. COORDINATE GEOMETRY "PROOFS"

1 Quadrilateral $ABCD$ has vertices $A(-3,-2)$, $B(9,2)$, $C(1,6)$, and $D(-5,4)$. Using coordinate geometry, prove that quadrilateral $ABCD$ is a trapezoid and contains a right angle.

Solution to Question on Coordinate Geometry "Proofs"

1.

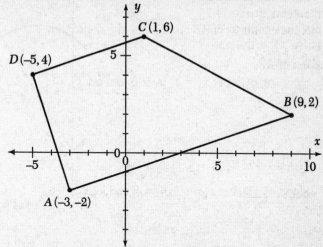

To prove that $ABCD$ is a trapezoid, we must prove that two sides are parallel and that the other two sides are not parallel. Since lines with the same slope are parallel, use the formula for the slope, m, of a line joining the points (x_1, y_1) and (x_2, y_2):

$$m = \frac{y_2 - y_1}{x_2 - x_1}$$

<u>Slope of $\overline{AB}$</u>: Let $x_1 = -3$, $y_1 = -2$, and let $x_2 = 9$, $y_2 = 2$:

$$m = \frac{2 - (-2)}{9 - (-3)}$$

$$m = \frac{2 + 2}{9 + 3}$$

$$m = \frac{4}{12} \text{ or } \frac{1}{3}$$

The slope of $\overline{AB}$ is $\frac{1}{3}$.

<u>Slope of $\overline{CD}$</u>: Let $x_1 = -5$, $y_1 = 4$, and let $x_2 = 1$, $y_2 = 6$:

$$m = \frac{6 - 4}{1 - (-5)}$$

$$m = \frac{2}{1 + 5}$$

$$m = \frac{2}{6} \text{ or } \frac{1}{3}$$

The slope of $\overline{CD}$ is $\frac{1}{3}$.

Since the slopes of $\overline{AB}$ and $\overline{CD}$ are the same, both $\frac{1}{3}$, $\overline{AB} \parallel \overline{CD}$.

<u>Slope of $\overline{BC}$</u>: Let $x_1 = 1$, $y_1 = 6$ and let $x_2 = 9$, $y_2 = 2$:

$$m = \frac{2 - 6}{9 - 1}$$

$$m = \frac{-4}{8} \text{ or } -\frac{1}{2}$$

The slope of $\overline{BC}$ is $-\frac{1}{2}$.

<u>Slope of $\overline{AD}$</u>: Let $x_1 = -5$, $y_1 = 4$, and let $x_2 = -3$, $y_2 = -2$:

$$m = \frac{-2 - 4}{-3 - (-5)}$$

$$m = \frac{-6}{-3 + 5}$$

$$m = \frac{-6}{2} \text{ or } -3$$

The slope of $\overline{AD}$ is -3.

Since the slopes of $\overline{BC}$ and $\overline{AD}$ are different, they are not parallel.

$ABCD$ is a trapezoid since it has two parallel sides ($\overline{AB}$ and $\overline{CD}$) and two opposite non-parallel sides ($\overline{BC}$ and $\overline{AD}$).

The slope of $\overline{AD}$ is -3 and the slopes of $\overline{AB}$ and $\overline{CD}$ are both $\frac{1}{3}$. The slope of $\frac{1}{3}$ is the negative reciprocal of the slope -3 (or $-\frac{3}{1}$). If two lines have slopes that are negative reciprocals of one another, the lines are perpendicular. Therefore $\overline{AD}$ is perpendicular to both $\overline{AB}$ and $\overline{CD}$, and the perpendiculars form right angles at A and D. The trapezoid $ABCD$ thus contains a right angle (in fact it contains two right angles!).

23. LOGIC

1   Given: $p \rightarrow q$
$\qquad q \rightarrow r$
What is a logically valid conclusion?
(1) $q \rightarrow \sim r$ (3) $r \rightarrow \sim q$
(2) $\sim r \rightarrow q$ (4) $\sim r \rightarrow \sim p$

2   The statement $\sim(p \wedge \sim q)$ is logically equivalent to
(1) $\sim p \wedge q$ (3) $p \wedge q$
(2) $p \vee \sim q$ (4) $\sim p \vee q$

3   Which statement is logically equivalent to the statement "If $x = 3$, then x is a prime number"?
(1) If x is a prime number, then $x = 3$.
(2) If $x \neq 3$, then x is not a prime number.
(3) If x is not a prime number, then $x \neq 3$.
(4) If x is not a prime number, then $x = 3$.

Solutions to Questions on Logic

1. Given: $p \rightarrow q$ and $q \rightarrow r$
The Law of the Syllogism (or Chain Law) states that $[(p \rightarrow q) \wedge (q \rightarrow r)] \rightarrow (p \rightarrow r)$:
$\qquad\qquad\qquad\qquad\qquad\qquad\qquad\qquad p \rightarrow r$
The Law of the Contrapositive states that $(a \rightarrow b) \leftrightarrow (\sim b \rightarrow \sim a)$, that is, if an implication is true, its contrapositive is true. The contrapositive of an implication is formed by negating both its hypothesis and conclusion and then interchanging them:
$\qquad\qquad\qquad\qquad\qquad\qquad\qquad\qquad \sim r \rightarrow \sim p$

The correct choice is **(4)**.

2. The given statement is: $\sim(p \wedge \sim q)$
From one of De Morgan's Laws,
$\sim(A \wedge B) \leftrightarrow (\sim A \vee \sim B)$.
Here let p replace A and $\sim q$ replace B: $\sim(p \wedge \sim q) \leftrightarrow (\sim p \vee \sim[\sim q])$
But the negation of $\sim q$ is q, that is, $\sim[\sim q] = q$: $\sim(p \wedge \sim q) \leftrightarrow (\sim p \vee q)$

The correct choice is **(4)**.

3. Let p represent "$x = 3$."

Let q represent "x is a prime number."

The given statement, "If $x = 3$, then x is a prime number," is represented by the *implication* or *conditional*, $p \rightarrow q$.

Consider each choice in turn:

(1) "If x is a prime number, then $x = 3$" is represented by the conditional, $q \rightarrow p$. Since the hypothesis (or antecedent), p, and conclusion (or consequent), q, of $p \rightarrow q$ have been interchanged to give $q \rightarrow p$, $q \rightarrow p$ is the *converse* of $p \rightarrow q$. The converse of a conditional is not equivalent to the conditional.

(2) "If $x \neq 3$, then x is not a prime number" is represented by $\sim p \rightarrow \sim q$. Since both the hypothesis and conclusion of $p \rightarrow q$ have been negated to form $\sim p \rightarrow \sim q$, $\sim p \rightarrow \sim q$ is the *inverse* of $p \rightarrow q$. The inverse of a conditional is not equivalent to it.

(3) "If x is not a prime number, then $x \neq 3$" is represented by $\sim q \rightarrow \sim p$. Since the hypothesis and conclusion of $p \rightarrow q$ have both been negated and then interchanged to form $\sim q \rightarrow \sim p$, $\sim q \rightarrow \sim p$ is the *contrapositive* of $p \rightarrow q$. The contrapositive of a conditional is always equivalent to it.

(4) "If x is not a prime number, then $x = 3$" is represented by $\sim q \rightarrow p$. This contradicts the contrapositive of step (3), which has already been noted as the equivalent of $p \rightarrow q$. Therefore, $\sim q \rightarrow p$ cannot be equivalent to $p \rightarrow q$.

The correct choice is **(3)**.

24. PERMUTATIONS; ARRANGEMENTS

1 How many different arrangements of seven letters can be made using the letters in the name "ULYSSES"?

2 How many different five-letter permutations can be formed from the letters of the word "DITTO"?

(1) $5!$

(2) $(5 - 2)!$

(3) $\dfrac{5!}{2!}$

(4) $_5P_2$

Solutions to Questions on Permutations; Arrangements

1. The number of different arrangements of p things where r are alike of one kind is $\dfrac{p!}{r!}$.

The name "ULYSSES" contains 7 letters but there are 3 S's.

$$\text{For } p = 7 \text{ and } r = 3, \frac{p!}{r!} = \frac{7!}{3!} = \frac{7(6)(5)(4)(3)(2)(1)}{3(2)(1)}$$

$$\frac{p!}{r!} = \frac{7(6)(5)(4)\cancel{(3)(2)(1)}^{1}}{\cancel{3(2)(1)}_{1}}$$

$$\frac{p!}{r!} = \frac{840}{1} = 840$$

840 different arrangements are possible.

2. The number of permutations, P, of n things taken n at a time when r are alike of one kind is given by the formula: $\qquad P = \dfrac{n!}{r!}$

The word "DITTO" has 5 letters but there are 2 T's. For the number of permutations of the letters in "DITTO" let $n = 5$ and $r = 2$: $\qquad P = \dfrac{5!}{2!}$

The correct choice is **(3)**.

25. COMBINATIONS

1 How many different five-person committees can be selected from nine people?

2 Which expression is *not* equivalent to $_8C_5$?
   (1) 56   (3) $_8C_3$

   (2) $_8C_5$ (4) $\dfrac{8 \cdot 7 \cdot 6}{3 \cdot 2 \cdot 1}$

Solutions to Questions on Combinations

1. The number of combinations of n things taken r at at time, $_nC_r$, is given by the formula:

$$_nC_r = \frac{n(n-1)(n-2)(n-3)\ldots \text{to } r \text{ factors}}{r!}$$

The number of different five-person committees that can be selected from nine people is the number of combinations of 9 things taken 5 at a time.

Let $n = 9$ and $r = 5$:

$$_9C_5 = \frac{9(8)(7)(6)(5)}{5(4)(3)(2)(1)}$$

$$_9C_5 = \frac{9(\overset{2}{8})(7)(\overset{\overset{1}{2}}{6})(\overset{1}{5})}{\underset{1}{5}(\underset{1}{4})(\underset{1}{3})(\underset{1}{2})(1)}$$

$$_9C_5 = \frac{126}{1} = 126$$

126 different five-person committees can be selected.

2. By definition: $\quad _nC_r = \dfrac{n(n-1)(n-2)(n-3)\ldots \text{to } r \text{ factors}}{r!}$

Evaluate $_8C_5$: $\quad _8C_5 = \dfrac{8(7)(6)}{3(2)(1)} = \dfrac{8(7)(\overset{\overset{1}{2}}{6})}{\underset{1}{3}(2)(1)} = \dfrac{56}{1} = 56$

Choice (1), 56, and choice (4), $\dfrac{8 \cdot 7 \cdot 6}{3 \cdot 2 \cdot 1}$, are both equivalent to $_8C_5$.

$_nC_r$ is always equivalent to $_nC_{n-r}$. If $n = 8$ and $r = 5$, then $n - r = 3$. Thus, $_8C_5$ is equivalent to $_8C_3$, which is choice (3).

By definition, $_nP_r = n(n-1)(n-2)(n-3)\ldots$ to r factors. Therefore, $_8P_5 = 8(7)(6)(5)(4)$. The first three factors alone are equivalent to the numerator of $_8C_5$. Therefore, $_8P_5$, which is choice (2), is *not* equivalent to $_8C_5$; in fact, it is much larger.

The correct choice is **(2)**.

26. PROBABILITY

1 If 2 cards are dealt randomly from a standard deck of 52 cards, what is the probability that they are both red queens?

(1) $\dfrac{4}{52} \cdot \dfrac{3}{51}$ (3) $\dfrac{2}{52} \cdot \dfrac{1}{51}$

(2) $\dfrac{2}{26}$ (4) $\dfrac{2}{52}$

2 A committee of 6 is to be chosen from 4 juniors and 5 seniors.
  a What is the probability that the committee will include
     the same number of juniors and seniors?
  b What is the probability that the committee will include
     all 5 seniors?
  c What is the probability that the committee will include
     no seniors?

Solutions to Questions on Probability

1. Probability of an event occurring

$$= \frac{\text{the number of successful outcomes}}{\text{the total possible number of outcomes}}.$$

There are two red queens (the queen of diamonds and the queen of hearts) in a standard deck of cards. Thus, for the first card drawn, the number of successful outcomes is 2 out of a total possible 52 outcomes.

The probability of drawing a red queen on the first draw is $\frac{2}{52}$.

One red queen remains among 51 cards after the first draw. The probability of drawing a red queen on the second draw is $\frac{1}{51}$.

The probability of drawing a red queen on both the first and second draws is the product of these probabilities: $\frac{2}{52} \times \frac{1}{51}$.

The correct choice is **(3)**.

2. Probability of an event occurring

$$= \frac{\text{the number of successful outcomes}}{\text{the total possible number of outcomes}}$$

a. If a committee of 6 is to include the same number of juniors and seniors, then it must include 3 of each.

The number of possible combinations of 3 juniors chosen from the 4 available juniors is:

$$_4C_3 = \frac{4(3)(2)}{3(2)(1)} = \frac{4\overset{1}{\cancel{(3)}\cancel{(2)}}}{\cancel{3}\cancel{(2)}(1)} = \frac{4}{1} = 4.$$

The number of possible combinations of 3 seniors chosen from the 5 available seniors is:

$$_5C_3 = \frac{5(4)(3)}{3(2)(1)} = \frac{5\overset{2}{\cancel{(4)}}\overset{1}{\cancel{(3)}}}{\underset{1}{\cancel{3}}\underset{1}{\cancel{(2)}}(1)} = \frac{10}{1} = 10.$$

Each of the 4 combinations of 3 juniors may be combined with each of the 10 combinations of 3 seniors to form 4 × 10, or 40, successful outcomes for a committee that includes the same number of juniors as seniors. The total possible number of outcomes for a committee of 6 is the number of combinations of all 9 students taken 6 at a time:

$$_9C_6 = \frac{9(8)(7)(6)(5)(4)}{6(5)(4)(3)(2)(1)} = \frac{9\overset{3}{\cancel{(8)}}\overset{4}{(7)}\overset{}{\cancel{(6)}}\overset{1}{\cancel{(5)}}\cancel{(4)}}{\underset{1}{\cancel{6}}\underset{1}{\cancel{(5)}}\cancel{(4)}\underset{1}{\cancel{(3)}}\cancel{(2)}(1)} = \frac{84}{1} = 84.$$

The probability of a committee that will include the same number of juniors and seniors $= \frac{40}{84}$ or $\frac{10}{21}$.

The probability is $\frac{\mathbf{10}}{\mathbf{21}}$.

b. There is only one combination of all 5 seniors. The committee of 6 may be formed by combining this one combination of all 5 seniors with any one of the 4 juniors. Thus, there are 4 successful outcomes for a committee of 6 that will include all 5 seniors. The total number of outcomes for the selection of such a committee is 84 (see part **a**).

The probability of a committee of 6 containing all 5 seniors $= \frac{4}{84}$ or $\frac{1}{21}$.

The probability is $\frac{\mathbf{1}}{\mathbf{21}}$.

c. To include no seniors, all 6 members of the committee would have to be juniors. But there are only 4 juniors from which to choose. Thus, there is no possible favorable outcome for a committee with no seniors.

The probability of a committee of 6 with no seniors $= \frac{0}{84}$ or 0.

The probability is **0**.

27. TRIGONOMETRY OF RIGHT TRIANGLE

1 In the accompanying diagram of rectangle $ABCD$, $AC = 22$ and
 $m\angle CAB = 24$.

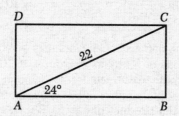

  a Find AB to the *nearest integer*
  b Find BC to the *nearest integer*
  c Using the results from parts *a* and *b*, find the number of
      square units in the area of $ABCD$

Solution to Question on Trigonometry of Right Triangle
  1.

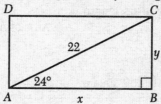

  a. Since $ABCD$ is a rectangle, $\angle B$ is a
right angle.

Let $x = AB$.

In right triangle ABC:

$$\cos \angle CAB = \frac{\text{adjacent leg}}{\text{hypotenuse}}$$

$$\cos 24° = \frac{x}{22}$$

Using a scientific calculator, $\cos 24° =$
0.9135:

In a proportion, the product of the
means equals the product of the
extremes (cross-multiply):

$$\frac{0.9135}{1} = \frac{x}{22}$$

$$x = 22(0.9135)$$
$$x = 20.0970$$

Round off to the *nearest integer*:
$AB = \mathbf{20}$ to the nearest integer.

$$x = 20$$

b. Let $y = BC$.
In right triangle ABC:

$$\sin \angle CAB = \frac{\text{opposite leg}}{\text{hypotenuse}}$$

$$\sin 24° = \frac{y}{22}$$

Using a scientific calculator, sin $24° = 0.4067$:

$$\frac{0.4067}{1} = \frac{y}{22}$$

In a proportion, the product of the means equals the product of the extremes (cross-multiply):

$$y = 22(0.4067)$$
$$y = 8.9474$$

Round off to the *nearest integer*:
$BC = \mathbf{9}$ to the *nearest integer*.

$$y = 9$$

c. The area of a rectangle is equal to the product of its length and width:

$$\text{Area of } ABCD = (AB)(BC)$$
$$= 20(9)$$
$$= 180$$

The area of $ABCD$ is **180** square units.

28. LITERAL EQUATIONS

1 If $\dfrac{a}{x} + 1 = \dfrac{c}{x}$, which is an expression for x in terms of c and a?

(1) $x = c + a$ (3) $x = a - c$
(2) $x = c - a$ (4) $x = a + c + 1$

Solution to Question on Literal Equations

1. The given equation is a literal equation:

$$\frac{a}{x} + 1 = \frac{c}{x}$$

Clear fractions by multiplying all terms on both sides of the equation by x:

$$x\left(\frac{a}{x}\right) + x(1) = x\left(\frac{c}{x}\right)$$
$$a + x = c$$
$$x = c - a$$

29. TRANSFORMATIONS

1 Find A', the image of $A(3,5)$, after a reflection in the line $y = x$.

2 A translation moves $A(-3,2)$ to $A'(0,0)$. Find B', the image of $B(5, 4)$, under the same translation.

3 Triangle ABC has coordinates $A(1,2)$, $B(4,2)$, and $C(6,4)$.
    a On graph paper, draw and label $\triangle ABC$ [1]
    b Graph and label $\triangle A'B'C'$, the image of $\triangle ABC$ after a reflection in the *x*-axis   [3]
    c Graph and label $\triangle A''B''C''$, the image of $\triangle ABC$ after a reflection in the origin   [3]
    d Graph and label $\triangle A''B''C''$, the image of $\triangle ABC$ after a dilation of constant 2.   [3]

Solutions to Questions on Transformations

1. The line $y = x$ is a line through the origin inclined at an angle of $45°$ to the positive directions of the x and y axes.

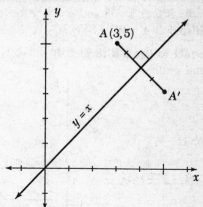

The image of a point $P(x, y)$ after a reflection in the line $y = x$ is $P'(y, x)$:

The image is **$A'(5,3)$**.

The image of $A(3,5)$ is $A'(5,3)$.

2.

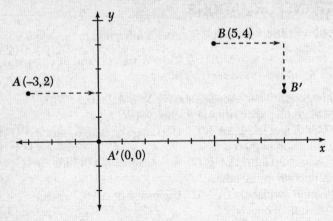

The translation that moves $A(-3,2)$ to $A'(0,0)$ is $T(x + 3, y - 2)$ since the point is moved three units to the right and 2 units down.

In $B(5,4)$, $x = 5$ and $y = 4$. After the translation, T, $B(5,4)$ becomes $B'(5 + 3, 4 - 2)$ or $B'(8,2)$.

The image is $\boldsymbol{B'(8,2)}$.

3. a.

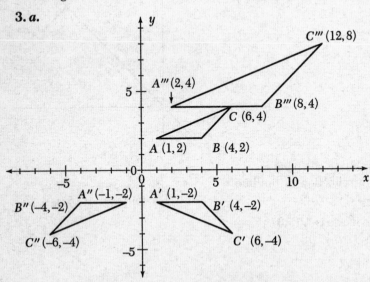

b. The image P' of a point $P(x, y)$ after a reflection in the x-axis is $P'(x, -y)$; under this reflection:

$$A(1,2) \rightarrow A'(1,-2)$$
$$B(4,2) \rightarrow B'(4,-2)$$
$$C(6,4) \rightarrow C'(6,-4)$$

c. The image of $P(x, y)$ after a reflection in the origin is $P''(-x, -y)$; after a reflection in the origin:

$$A(1,2) \rightarrow A''(-1,-2)$$
$$B(4,2) \rightarrow B''(-4,-2)$$
$$C(6,4) \rightarrow C''(-6,-4)$$

d. A dilation of constant 2 maps a point $P(x, y)$ onto its image $P'''(2x, 2y)$; under a dilation of constant 2:

$$A(1,2) \rightarrow A'''(2,4)$$
$$B(4,2) \rightarrow B'''(8,4)$$
$$C(6,4) \rightarrow C'''(12,8)$$

Glossary of Terms

abscissa The x-coordinate of a point in the coordinate plane. The abscissa of the point $(2, 3)$ is 2.

absolute value The absolute value of a number x, denoted by $|x|$, is its distance from zero on the number line. Thus, $|x|$ always represents a nonnegative number.

acute angle An angle whose degree measure is less than 90.

acute triangle A triangle that contains three acute angles.

additive inverse The opposite of a number. The additive inverse of a number x is $-x$ since $x + (-x) = 0$.

adjacent angles Two angles that have the same vertex, share a common side, but do not have any interior points in common.

alternate interior angles Two interior angles that lie on opposite sides of a transversal.

altitude A segment that is perpendicular to the side to which it is drawn.

angle The union of two rays that have the same endpoint.

angle of depression The angle formed by a horizontal line of vision and the line of sight when viewing an object beneath the horizontal line of vision.

angle of elevation The angle formed by a horizontal line of vision and the line of sight when viewing an object above the horizontal line of vision.

antecedent The part of a conditional statement that follows the word "if." Sometimes the term "hypothesis" is used in place of "antecedent."

associative property The mathematical law that states that the order in which three numbers are added or multiplied does not matter.

axis of symmetry For the parabola $y = ax^2 + bx + c$, the vertical line that contains the vertex, an equation of which is $x = -\dfrac{b}{2a}$.

base angles of an isosceles triangle The two congruent angles that include the base of an isosceles triangle.

biconditional A statement of the form p if and only if q, denoted by $p \leftrightarrow q$, which is true only when p and q have the same truth value.

binary operation An operation that is performed on two members of a set at a time.

binomial A polynomial with two unlike terms.

bisector of an angle A ray that divides the angle into two angles that have the same degree measure.

bisector of a segment A line, ray, or segment that contains the midpoint of the given segment.

circle The set of points (x, y) in a plane that are a fixed distance r from a given point (h, k) called the center. Thus, $(x - h)^2 + (y - k)^2 = r^2$.

closure property A set is closed under a binary operation if performing that operation on any two members of the set always produces a result that is a member of the same set.

coefficient The number that multiplies the literal factors of a monomial. The coefficient of $-5x^2y$ is -5.

collinear points Points that lie on the same line.

combination A subset of a group of objects in which the order of the individual objects is not considered. For example, ABC and BCA represent the *same* combination of the letters A, B, and C.

combinations formula The combination of n objects taken r at a time denoted by $_nC_r$, is given by the formula $_nC_r = \dfrac{_nP_r}{r!} = \dfrac{n!}{r!(n - r)!}$.

commutative property The mathematical law that states that the order in which two numbers are added or multiplied does not matter.

complementary angles Two angles whose degree measures add up to 90.

compound loci The locus of all points that satisfy two or more locus conditions.

compound statement A statement in logic that is formed by combining two or more simple statements using logical connectives.

conditional statement A statement that has the form "If p then q," denoted by $p \rightarrow q$, which is always true except in the case in which p is true and q is false.

congruent angles Angles that have the same degree measure.

congruent figures Figures that have the same size and the same shape. The symbol for congruence is $\cong$.

congruent polygons Two polygons having the same number of sides are congruent if their vertices can be paired so that all corresponding sides have the same length and all corresponding angles have the same degree measure.

congruent triangles Two triangles are congruent if any one of the following conditions is true: (1) the sides of one triangle are congruent to the corresponding sides of the other triangle (SSS $\cong$ SSS); (2) two sides and the included angle of one triangle are congruent to the corresponding parts of the other triangle (SAS $\cong$ SAS); (3) two angles and the included side of one triangle are congruent to the corresponding parts of the other triangle (ASA $\cong$ ASA); (4) two angles and the side opposite one of these angles of one triangle are congruent to the corresponding parts of the other triangle (AAS $\cong$ AAS).

congruent segments Line segments that have the same length.

conjugate pair The sum and difference of the same two terms, as in $a + b$ and $a - b$.

conjunct Each of the individual statements that comprise a conjunction.

conjunction A statement of the form p and q, denoted by $p \wedge q$, which is true only when p and q are true at the same time.

consequent The part of a conditional statement that follows the word "then." Sometimes the word "conclusion" is used in place of "consequent."

constant A quantity that is fixed in value. In the equation $y = x + 3$, x and y are variables and 3 is a constant.

contradiction A compound statement that is always false.

contrapositive The conditional statement formed by negating and then interchanging both parts of a conditional statement. The contrapositive of $p \rightarrow q$ is $\sim q \rightarrow \sim p$.

converse The conditional statement formed by interchanging both parts of a conditional statement. The converse of $p \rightarrow q$ is $q \rightarrow p$.

coordinate The real number that corresponds to the position of a point on a number line.

coordinate plane The region formed by a horizontal number line and vertical number line intersecting at their zero points.

corresponding angles A pair of angles that lie on the same side of the transversal, one of which is an interior angle and the other is an exterior angle.

cosine ratio In a right triangle, the ratio of the length of the leg that is adjacent to a given acute angle to the length of the hypotenuse.

degree A unit of angle measure that is defined as 1/360th of one complete rotation of a ray about its vertex.

degree of a monomial The sum of the exponents of its variable factors. For example, the degree of $3x^4$ is 4 and the degree of $-4xy^2$ is 3, since 1 (the power of x) plus 2 (the power of y) equals 3.

degree of a polynomial The greatest degree of its monomial terms. For example, the degree of $x^2 - 4x + 5$ is 2.

DeMorgan's Laws (1) $\sim (p \vee q) \leftrightarrow \sim p \wedge \sim q$ and (2) $\sim (p \wedge q) \leftrightarrow \sim p \vee \sim q$.

dilation A transformation in which a figure is enlarged or reduced in size based on a center and a scale factor.

discriminant The quantity $b^2 - 4ac$ that is underneath the radical sign in the quadratic formula. If the discriminant is positive, the two roots are real; if the discriminant is 0, the two roots are equal; and if the discriminant is negative, the two roots are not real.

disjunct Each of the statements that comprise a disjunction.

disjunction A statement of the form p *or* q, denoted by $p \vee q$, which is true when p is true, q is true, or both p and q are true.

distance formula The distance between points (x_1, y_1) and (x_2, y_2) is given by the formula $\sqrt{(x_2 - x_1)^2 + (y_2 - y_1)^2}$.

distributive property of multiplication over addition For any real numbers $a, b,$ and $c, a(b + c) = ab + ac$ and $(b + c)\, a = ba + ca$.

domain The set of all possible replacements for a variable.

equation A statement that two quantities have the same value.

equilateral triangle A triangle whose three sides have the same length.

equivalent equations Two equations that have the same solution set. Thus, $2x = 6$ and $x = 3$ are equivalent equations.

event A particular subset of outcomes from the set of all possible outcomes of a probability experiment. In flipping a coin, one event is getting a head; another event is getting a tail.

exponent In x^n, the number n is the exponent and tells the number of times the base x is used as a factor in a product. Thus, $x^3 = (x)\,(x)\,(x)$.

extremes In the proportion $\dfrac{a}{b} = \dfrac{c}{d}$, the terms a and d are the extremes.

factor A number or variable that is being multiplied in a product.

factoring The process by which a number or polynomial is written as the product of two or more terms.

factoring completely Factoring a number or polynomial into its prime factors.

factorial n Denoted by $n!$ and defined for any positive integer n as the product of consecutive integers from n to 1. Thus, $5! = 5 \cdot 4 \cdot 3 \cdot 2 \cdot 1 = 120$.

FOIL The rule for multiplying two binomials horizontally by forming the sum of the products of the first terms (F), the outer terms (O), the inner terms (I), and the last terms (L) of each binomial.

formula An equation that shows how one quantity depends on one or more other quantities.

fundamental counting principle If event A can occur in m ways and event B can occur in n ways, then both events can occur in m times n ways.

greatest common factor (GCF) The GCF of two or more monomials is the monomial with the greatest coefficient and the variable factors of the greatest degree that are common to all the given monomials. The GCF of $8a^2b$ and $20ab^2$ is $4ab$.

hypotenuse The side of a right triangle that is opposite the right angle.

image In a geometric transformation, the point or figure that corresponds to the original point or figure.

inequality A sentence that uses an inequality relation such as < (is less than), ≤ (is less than or equal to), > (is greater than), ≥ (is greater than or equal to), or ≠ (is unequal to).

integer A number from the set $\{\ldots -3, -2, -1, 0, 1, 2, 3, \ldots\}$.

inverse The statement formed by negating both the antecedent and consequent of a conditional statement. Thus, the inverse of $p \rightarrow q$ is $\sim p \rightarrow \sim q$.

irrational number A number that cannot be expressed as the quotient of two integers.

isosceles triangle A triangle in which at least two sides have the same length.

law of contrapositive inference A conditional statement and its contrapositive have the same truth value. Thus, $p \rightarrow q$ and $\sim q \rightarrow \sim p$ are logically equivalent statements.

law of disjunctive inference If a disjunction is true, then at least one of the disjuncts is true. Thus, if $p \vee q$ and $\sim p$ are true statements, then q is true.

law of conjunctive simplification If a conjunction is true, then each conjunct is true. Thus, if $p \wedge q$ is true, then p and q are both true.

law of detachment (modus ponens) If a conditional statement and its antecedent are true, then its consequent is true. Thus, if $p \rightarrow q$ and p are true, then q is true.

law of double negation The statements p and $\sim(\sim p)$ always have the same truth values.

law of modus tollens If a conditional statement is true and its consequent is false, then its antecedent is false. Thus, if $p \rightarrow q$ is true and q is false, then p is false.

law of syllogism (the chain rule) If the conditionals $p \rightarrow q$ and $q \rightarrow r$ are both true, then $p \rightarrow r$ is true.

leg of a right triangle Either of the two sides of a right triangle that is not opposite the right angle.

line Although an undefined term in geometry, it can be described as a continuous set of points that describes a straight path that extends indefinitely in two opposite directions.

linear equation An equation in which the greatest exponent of a variable is 1. A linear equation can be put into the form $Ax + By = C$, where A, B, and C are constants and A and B are not both zero.

line reflection A transformation in which each point P that is not on line ℓ is paired with a point P' on the opposite side of line ℓ so that line ℓ is the perpendicular bisector of $\overline{PP'}$. If P is on line ℓ, then P is paired with itself.

line segment Part of a line that consists of two different points on the line, called *endpoints*, and all points on the line that are between them.

line symmetry A figure has line symmetry when a line ℓ divides the figure into two parts such that each part is the reflection of the other part in line ℓ.

locus The set of all points, and only those points, that satisfy a given condition.

logical connectives The conjunction ($\wedge$), disjunction ($\vee$), conditional ($\rightarrow$), and biconditional ($\leftrightarrow$) of two statements.

logically equivalent statements Statements that always have the same truth value.

mean The mean or average of a set of n data values is the sum of the data values divided by n.

mean proportional between a and b The number x such that $\dfrac{a}{x} = \dfrac{x}{b}$.

means In the proportion $\dfrac{a}{b} = \dfrac{c}{d}$, the terms b and c are the means. If b and c have the same value, then either b or c is called the mean proportional between a and d.

median of a triangle A line segment whose endpoints are a vertex of the triangle and the midpoint of the opposite side.

midpoint The point M that lies between the endpoints of line segment AB such that $AM = BM$.

midpoint formula The midpoint of the line segment whose endpoints are (x_1, y_1) and (x_2, y_2) is $\left(\dfrac{x_1 + x_2}{2}, \dfrac{y_1 + y_2}{2} \right)$.

monomial A number, variable, or their product.

multiplicative inverse The reciprocal of a nonnegative number. For example, the multiplicative inverse of $\dfrac{3}{7}$ is $\dfrac{7}{3}$.

negation The negation of statement p is the statement, denoted by $\sim p$, that has the opposite truth value of p.

obtuse angle An angle whose degree measure is greater than 90 and less than 180.

obtuse triangle A triangle that contains an obtuse angle.

open sentence A sentence whose truth value cannot be determined until its placeholders are replaced with values from the replacement set.

opposite rays Two rays that have the same endpoint and form a line.

ordered pair Two numbers that are written in a definite order.

ordinate The y-coordinate of a point in the coordinate plane. The ordinate of the point (2, 3) is 3.

origin The zero point on a number line.

outcome A possible result in a probability experiment.

parabola The graph of a quadratic equation in which either x or y, but not both, are squared. The graph of an equation of the form $y = ax^2 + bx + c$ $(a \neq 0)$ is a parabola that has a vertical axis of symmetry, an equation of which is $x = -\dfrac{b}{2a}$.

parallel lines Lines in the same plane that do not intersect. When a third line, called a *transversal*, intersects two parallel lines, every pair of angles formed are either congruent or supplementary.

parallelogram A quadrilateral that has two pairs of parallel sides. In a parallelogram, opposite sides are congruent, opposite angles are congruent, consecutive angles are supplementary, and each diagonal divides the parallelogram into two congruent triangles.

perfect square A rational number whose square root is also rational. The perfect square integers from 1 to 100 are 1, 4, 9, 25, 36, 49, 64, 81, and 100. The number $\dfrac{4}{9}$ is an example of a fraction that is a perfect square, since $\sqrt{\dfrac{4}{9}} = \dfrac{2}{3}$ and $\dfrac{2}{3}$ is rational.

permutation An ordered arrangement of objects. For example, AB and BA represent two different permutations of the letters A and B.

perpendicular lines Lines that intersect at right angles.

plane Although undefined in geometry, it can be described as a flat surface that extends indefinitely in all directions.

point Although undefined in geometry, it can be described as indicating location with no size.

point symmetry A figure has point symmetry if after being rotated 180° the image coincides with the original figure.

polygon A simple closed curve whose sides are line segments.

polynomial A monomial or the sum or difference of two or more monomials.

power A number written with an exponent.

prime factorization The factorization of a polynomial into factors each of which are divisible only by itself and 1.

probability of an event The number of ways in which the event can occur divided by the total number of possible outcomes.

proportion An equation that states that two ratios are equal. In the proportion $\frac{a}{b} = \frac{c}{d}$, the product of the means equals the product of the extremes. Thus, $b \cdot c = a \cdot d$.

pythagorean theorem The square of the length of the hypotenuse of a right triangle is equal to the sum of the squares of the lengths of the legs of the right triangle.

quadrant One of four rectangular regions into which the coordinate plane is divided.

quadratic equation An equation that can be put into the form $ax^2 + bx + c = 0$, provided $a \neq 0$.

quadratic formula The roots of the quadratic equation $ax^2 + bx + c = 0$ are given by the formula $x = \dfrac{-b \pm \sqrt{b^2 - 4ac}}{2a}$ $(a \neq 0)$.

quadratic polynomial A polynomial like $x^2 - 3x + 4$ whose degree is 2.

quadrilateral A polygon with four sides.

radical (square root) sign The symbol $\sqrt{}$ that denotes the positive square root of a nonnegative number.

radicand The expression that appears underneath a radical sign.

ratio A comparison of two numbers by division. The ratio of a to b is the fraction $\frac{a}{b}$, provided b $\neq 0$.

rational number A number that can be written in the form $\frac{a}{b}$ where a and b are integers and $b \neq 0$. Decimals in which a set of digits endlessly repeat, like .25000 ... $\left(= \frac{1}{4}\right)$ and .33333 ... $\left(= \frac{1}{3}\right)$ represent rational numbers.

ray The part of a line that consists of a point, called an *endpoint*, and the set of points on one side of the endpoint.

real number A number that is a member of the set that consists of all rational and irrational numbers.

reciprocal The reciprocal of a nonzero number x is $\dfrac{1}{x}$. For example, the reciprocal of 3 is $\dfrac{1}{3}$ and the reciprocal of $-\dfrac{2}{5}$ is $-\dfrac{5}{2}$. The product of a nonzero number and its reciprocal is always 1.

rectangle A parallelogram with four right angles.

reflection in the origin A transformation that maps $P(x, y)$ onto $P'(-x, -y)$.

replacement set The set of values that a variable may have.

rhombus A parallelogram with four sides that have the same length.

right angle An angle whose degree measure is 90.

right triangle A triangle that contains a right angle.

root A number that makes an equation a true statement.

rotation A transformation in which a point or figure is moved about a fixed point a given number of degrees.

rotational symmetry A figure has rotational symmetry if it can be rotated so that the image coincides with the original figure.

scalene triangle A triangle in which the three sides have different lengths.

similar polygons Two polygons with the same number of sides are similar if their vertices can be paired so that corresponding angles have the same measure and the lengths or corresponding sides are in proportion.

similar triangles If two triangles have two pairs of corresponding angles that have the same degree measure, then the triangles are similar.

sine ratio In a right triangle, the ratio of the length of the leg that is opposite a given acute angle to the length of the hypotenuse.

slope A measure of the steepness of a nonvertical line. The slope of a horizontal line is 0, and the slope of a vertical line is undefined.

slope formula The slope of a nonvertical line that contains the points (x_1, y_2) and (x_2, y_2) is given by the formula $\dfrac{y_2 - y_1}{x_2 - x_1}$.

slope-intercept form An equation of a line that has the form $y = mx + b$ where m is the slope of the line and b is its y-intercept.

solution Any value from the replacement set of a variable that makes an open sentence true.

solution set The collection of all values from the replacement set of a variable that makes an open sentence true.

square A rectangle whose four sides have the same length.

square root The square root of a nonnegative number n is one of two identical numbers whose product is n. Thus, $\sqrt{9} = 3$ since $3 \times 3 = 9$.

statement Any sentence that is true or false, but not both.

success Any favorable outcome of a probability experiment.

supplementary Two angles are supplementary if the sum of their degree measures is 180.

system of equations Two or more equations whose solution is the set of values that makes each equation true at the same time. For the system of equations $x + y = 5$ and $y = x + 1$, the solution is $(2, 3)$, since $x = 2$ and $y = 3$ makes both equations true.

tangent ratio In a right triangle, the ratio of the length of the leg that is opposite a given acute angle to the length of the leg that is adjacent to the angle.

tautology A compound statement that is true regardless of the truth values of its component statements.

theorem A generalization in mathematics that can be proved.

transformation The process of "moving" each point of a figure according to some given rule.

translation A transformation in which each point of a figure is moved the same distance and in the same direction.

transversal A line that intersects two other lines in two different points.

trapezoid A quadrilateral with exactly one pair of parallel sides.

triangle A polygon with three sides.

trinomial A polynomial with three terms.

truth value Every statement has a truth value of either true *or* false, but not both.

turning point of a parabola See *vertex of a parabola*.

undefined term A term that can be described but not defined. The terms point, line, and plane are undefined in geometry.

variable The symbol, usually a letter, that represents an unspecified member of the replacement set.

vertex of a parabola The point at which the axis of symmetry intersects a parabola.

vertical angles A pair of nonadjacent angles formed by two intersecting lines.

x-axis The horizontal axis in the coordinate plane.

x-coordinate The first number in an ordered pair.

y-axis The vertical axis in the coordinate plane.

y-coordinate The second number in an ordered pair.

y-intercept The y-coordinate of the point at which the graph of an equation intersects the y-axis.

Regents Examinations, Answers, and Self-Analysis Charts

Examination January 1993

Sequential Math Course II

PART I

Answer 30 questions from this part. Each correct answer will receive 2 credits. No partial credit will be allowed. Write your answers in the spaces provided. Where applicable, answers may be left in terms of π or in radical form. [60]

1 A translation maps $A(4,1)$ onto $A'(6,6)$. Find the coordinates of the image of $B(-1,0)$ under the same translation.

1_____

2 The accompanying table defines the operation ⋈ for set $\{e,f,g,h\}$.

⋈	e	f	g	h
e	e	f	g	h
f	f	h	e	g
g	g	e	h	f
h	h	g	f	e

Using the table, solve for x: $g ⋈ x = h$

2_____

3 In right triangle ABC, m$\angle A = 2x + 2$, m$\angle B = 7x + 7$, and m$\angle C = 90$. Find the value of x.

3_____

4 In the accompanying diagram of right triangle ABC, altitude $\overline{BD}$ divides hypotenuse $\overline{AC}$ into segments with lengths of 3 and 9. Find the length of leg $\overline{AB}$.

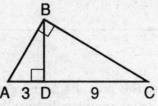

4_____

5 Solve for x: $\dfrac{x + 1}{8} = \dfrac{11}{16}$

5_____

6 In the set of rational numbers, what is the identity element for multiplication?

6_____

7 The line whose equation is $y = -3$ is reflected in the x-axis. Write an equation of the image of that line.

7_____

8 In the accompanying diagram, $\overleftrightarrow{AB} \parallel \overleftrightarrow{CD}$, $\overleftrightarrow{EF}$ intersects $\overleftrightarrow{AB}$ and $\overleftrightarrow{CD}$, and the ratio of m$\angle r$ to m$\angle s$ is 1:4. Find m$\angle r$.

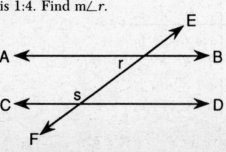

8_____

9 Vertex angle *A* of isosceles triangle *ABC* measures 70°. What is the measure, in degrees, of an *exterior* angle at *B*?

9_____

10 In the accompanying diagram of right triangle *ABC*, *AB* = 10, *BC* = 8, *CA* = 6, and ∠*C* is a right angle. Which angle of the triangle has a cosine equal to 0.8000?

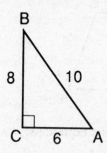

10_____

11 In the accompanying diagram, *ABCD* is an isosceles trapezoid, *AD* = *BC* = 5, *AB* = 10, and *DC* = 18. Find the length of altitude $\overline{AE}$.

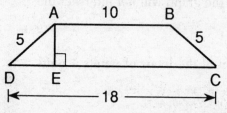

11_____

12 How many different four-letter arrangements can be formed from the letters in the word "PAPA"?

12_____

13 If $_nC_2$ = 15, find the value of *n*.

13_____

14 In a plane, what is the total number of points 5 units from the point $(4,-2)$ and 2 units from the x-axis?

14____

15 In the accompanying diagram, $ABCD$ is an isosceles trapezoid with $\overline{DE} \parallel \overline{CB}$. Find the measure of $\angle ADE$ if $m\angle C = 110$.

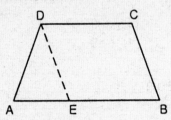

15____

16 Given the graphs of these four equations:

$$x = 4$$
$$y = 2$$
$$x = y$$
$$x + y = 1$$

If one of these graphs is picked at random, what is the probability the graph will *not* intersect the y-axis?

16____

17 Write an equation of the locus of points 4 units from the origin.

17____

Directions (18–34): For *each* question chosen, write in the space provided the *numeral* preceding the word or expression that best completes the statement or answers the question.

18 Given the true statements $\sim(p \wedge \sim q)$ and $\sim q$, which must be true?

(1) $\sim p \wedge q$ (3) p
(2) $p \vee \sim q$ (4) $\sim p$

18____

19 If the lengths of two sides of a triangle are 4 and
5, the length of the third side can *not* be
(1) 1   (3) 3
(2) 2   (4) 4   19____

20 If the hypotenuse of a right triangle measures 8
and one leg measures 5, then the other leg measures
(1) $\sqrt{3}$ (3) $\sqrt{39}$
(2) $\sqrt{13}$ (4) $\sqrt{89}$ 20____

21 In $\triangle ABC$, $m\angle A = 58$ and $m\angle B = 64$. Which
statement about the sides of the triangle is true?
(1) $AB > BC$ (3) $AB > AC$
(2) $AB = BC$ (4) $BC > AC$ 21____

22 Which statement is logically equivalent to
$\sim p \rightarrow q$?
(1) $p \rightarrow \sim q$ (3) $\sim q \rightarrow p$
(2) $q \rightarrow \sim p$ (4) $q \rightarrow p$ 22____

23 What is the midpoint of the line segment connecting the points $(-2,4)$ and $(5,-2)$?
(1) $\left(\frac{3}{2},1\right)$ (3) $\left(\frac{7}{2},1\right)$

(2) $\left(3,\frac{3}{2}\right)$ (4) $\left(\frac{3}{2},2\right)$ 23____

24 Which statement is *always* true about a parallelogram?
(1) Diagonals bisect the angles.
(2) Diagonals are perpendicular.
(3) Adjacent sides are congruent.
(4) Diagonals bisect each other.   24____

25 Which triangles must be similar?
   (1) two obtuse triangles
   (2) two scalene triangles
   (3) two right triangles
   (4) two isosceles triangles with congruent vertex
       angles   25_____

26 The graph of the equation $y = x^2$ is a
   (1) circle   (3) point
   (2) parabola   (4) straight line   26_____

27 Which is an equation of the line that passes
   through the point (0,4) and is perpendicular
   to the line whose equation is $y = -\frac{1}{2}x + 3$?

   (1) $y = -\frac{1}{2}x + 4$ (3) $y = 2x + 4$
   (2) $y = -2x + 4$ (4) $y = -2x - 4$ 27_____

28 Which statement is the converse of the statement, "If Jamie got a ticket, then Jamie was
   speeding"?
   (1) If Jamie was speeding, then Jamie got a
       ticket.
   (2) If Jamie did not get a ticket, then Jamie was
       not speeding.
   (3) If Jamie got a ticket, then Jamie was not
       speeding.
   (4) If Jamie was not speeding, then Jamie did not
       get a ticket.   28_____

29 Which must be true for x in the equation
   $\dfrac{1}{x} + \dfrac{1}{x + 3} = 2$?

   (1) $x = 0, x = -3$ (3) $x = 0, x \neq -3$
   (2) $x \neq 0, x = -3$ (4) $x \neq 0, x \neq -3$ 29_____

30 If the coordinates of a parallelogram are $Q(3,-2)$, $R(7,-2)$, $S(9,3)$, and $T(5,3)$, the area of the parallelogram is

(1) 10   (3) 30

(2) 20   (4) 40   30____

31 Which equation has -5 and 3 as its roots?

(1) $x^2 + 2x + 15 = 0$ (3) $x^2 - 2x + 15 = 0$

(2) $x^2 + 2x - 15 = 0$ (4) $x^2 - 2x - 15 = 0$ 31____

32 What is an equation of the axis of symmetry of the graph of the parabola $y = 2x^2 + 3x + 5$?

(1) $y = -\frac{3}{2}$ (3) $x = -\frac{3}{2}$

(2) $y = -\frac{3}{4}$ (4) $x = -\frac{3}{4}$ 32____

33 In the accompanying diagram, B is the midpoint of $\overline{AC}$, $\overline{DA} \perp \overline{AC}$, $\overline{EC} \perp \overline{AC}$, and $\overline{DB} \cong \overline{EB}$.

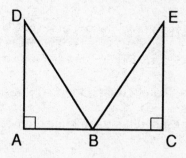

Which method of proof may be used to prove $\triangle DAB \cong \triangle ECB$?

(1) SAS $\cong$ SAS   (3) HL $\cong$ HL

(2) ASA $\cong$ ASA   (4) AAS $\cong$ AAS   33____

34 What is the slope of the line determined by the points (5,–3) and (–9,–6)?

(1) $\frac{3}{14}$ (3) $\frac{14}{3}$

(2) $-\frac{3}{14}$ (4) $\frac{9}{4}$ 34_____

DIRECTIONS (35): *Show all construction lines.*

35 *On the answer sheet*, construct the bisector of ∠*ABC*.

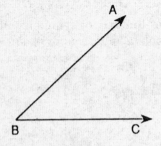

                                          35_____

PART II

Answer three questions from this part. Clearly indicate the necessary steps, including appropriate formula substitutions, diagrams, graphs, charts, etc. Calculations that may be obtained by mental arithmetic or the calculator do not need to be shown. [30]

36 *a* Solve the following system of equations algebraically:

$$y = x^2 - 6x + 6$$
$$y - x = -4 \qquad [6]$$

b For all values of *x* for which these expressions are defined, find the product in simplest form.

$$\frac{x^2 - 9}{x} \cdot \frac{x^2 + 2x}{x^2 + 5x + 6} \qquad [4]$$

37 *a* On graph paper, draw the graph of the equation $y = x^2 - 6x + 5$, including all values of *x* in the interval $0 \le x \le 6$. [5]

b On the same set of axes, sketch the image of the graph drawn in part *a* after a reflection in the *y*-axis. [3]

c Write an equation of the axis of symmetry of the graph drawn in part *b*. [2]

38 Given: points $A(8,0)$ and $B(0,4)$.

a Write an equation of $\overleftrightarrow{AB}$. [3]

b Describe fully the locus of points equidistant from *A* and *B*. [2]

c Write an equation of the locus described in part *b*. [3]

d Is the point $(1,-4)$ equidistant from *A* and *B*? Justify your answer. [2]

39 *On your answer paper*, write the letters *a*
through *e*. Next to each letter, write a valid conclusion that can be deduced from each set of true
statements. If no valid conclusion can be deduced, write "NO CONCLUSION."

a $A \lor \sim B$ [2]
　$\sim A$

b $\sim P \to Q$ [2]
　P

c $\sim X \lor \sim Y$ [2]
　$\sim X$

d $\sim A \to B$ [2]
　$C \to \sim B$

e $\sim A \to \sim B$ [2]
　B

40 In the accompanying diagram, $\overline{RT} \perp \overline{TX}$,
m$\angle TXS = 27$, m$\angle SXR = 18$, and
$SX = 21.2$ meters.

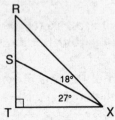

a To the *nearest tenth* of a meter, find:
　(1) TX [3]　(2) RT [2]　(3) RX [3]

b Using the answers from part *a*, find the area of
　$\triangle RTX$ to the *nearest square meter*.   [2]

PART III

Answer one question from this part. Clearly indicate the necessary steps, including appropriate formula substitutions, diagrams, graphs, charts, etc. Calculations that may be obtained by mental arithmetic or the calculator do not need to be shown. [10]

41 Points $A(-a,0)$, $B(a,0)$, $C(a,b)$, and $D(-a,b)$ form a quadrilateral.

    a Prove that quadrilateral $ABCD$ is a rectangle.
       [7]

    b If $b = 7$ and $a = 10$, prove that $ABCD$ is *not* a square. [3]

42 Given: $\overline{ADB}$, $\overline{AFC}$, $\overline{BEGC}$, $\overline{AB} \cong \overline{AC}$, $\overline{DE} \perp \overline{BC}$, $\overline{FG} \perp \overline{BC}$, and $\overline{BG} \cong \overline{CE}$.

Prove: $\overline{BD} \cong \overline{CF}$ [10]

Answers
January 1993
Sequential Math Course II

Answer Key

PART I

1. (1,5)	**13.** 6	**25.** (4)
2. g	**14.** 4	**26.** (2)
3. 9	**15.** 40°	**27.** (3)
4. 6	**16.** $\frac{1}{4}$	**28.** (1)
5. $4\frac{1}{2}$	**17.** $x^2 + y^2 = 16$	**29.** (4)
6. 1	**18.** (4)	**30.** (2)
7. $y = 3$	**19.** (1)	**31.** (2)
8. 36	**20.** (3)	**32.** (4)
9. 125	**21.** (2)	**33.** (3)
10. B	**22.** (3)	**34.** (1)
11. 3	**23.** (1)	**35.** construction
12. 6	**24.** (4)	

PARTS II AND III See answers explained section.

Answers Explained

PART I

1. A translation "slides" a point a fixed number of units in the horizontal direction and a fixed number of units in the vertical direction. If a particular translation maps $A(4,1)$ onto $A'(6,6)$, then this translation "slides" point A 2 units in the horizontal direction and 5 units in the vertical direction. In general, the image of point $P(x, y)$ under the same translation is $P'(x + 2, y + 5)$.

For point $B(-1,0)$, let $x = -1$ and $y = 0$. Under the same translation the image of $B(-1,0)$ is $B'(-1 + 2, 0 + 5) = B'(1,5)$.

The coordinates of the image $B(-1, 0)$ under the same translation are **(1,5)**.

2.

✴	e	f	g	h
e	e	f	g	h
f	f	h	e	g
g	g	e	h	f
h	h	g	f	e

The accompanying table is given.

To solve the equation g ✴ $x = h$, we need to determine the heading of the vertical column that intersects horizontal row g at element h.

Since g ✴ $g = h$, the unknown column heading, x, is g.

$x = g$.

3. The acute angles of a right triangle are complementary. Hence:

$$m\angle A + m\angle B = 90$$
$$(2x + 2) + (7x + 7) = 90$$
$$9x + 9 = 90$$
$$9x = 81$$
$$x = \frac{81}{9} = 9$$

The value of x is **9**.

4.

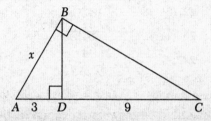

In a right triangle the altitude drawn to the hypotenuse divides the hypotenuse into two segments such that the length of either leg of the right triangle is the mean proportional between the length of the segment of the hypotenuse adjacent to it and the length of the entire hypotenuse.

In right triangle ABC, $\dfrac{AD}{AB} = \dfrac{AB}{AC}$

Since $AD = 3$, $AC = AD + DC = 3 + 9 = 12$; let $AB = x$. Then:

$$\frac{3}{x} = \frac{x}{12}$$

In a proportion, the product of the means equals the product of the extremes (cross-multiply):

$$(x)\,(x) = (3)\,(12)$$
$$x^2 = 36$$

The length of leg $\overline{AB}$ is **6**.

$$x = \sqrt{36} = 6$$

5. Given:

$$\frac{x+1}{8} = \frac{11}{16}$$

In a proportion, the product of the means equals the product of the extremes (cross-multiply):

$$16(x+1) = (8)\,(11)$$
$$16x + 16 = 88$$
$$16x = 72$$
$$x = \frac{72}{16} = 4.5$$

The value of x is **4.5**.

6. If the identity element of a set operates on any element x of the set, then the element x is always returned.

If any rational number is multiplied by 1, the product is always the original rational number. Hence, 1 is the identity element for multiplication.

In the set of rational numbers, the identity element for multiplication is **1**.

7.

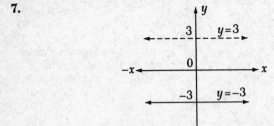

The line whose equation is given, $y = -3$, is parallel to the x-axis and 3 units below it.

The reflection of this line in the x-axis is the line that is parallel to the x-axis and is the same number of units, 3, above it. An equation of this line is $y = 3$.

The image of the reflection of $y = -3$ in the x-axis is the line whose equation is **$y = 3$**.

8.

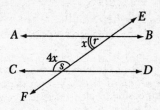

Since it is given that the ratio of the measure of $\angle r$ to the measure of $\angle s$ is 1:4, let $m\angle r = x$ and $m\angle s = 4x$.

If two lines are parallel, then interior angles on the same side of a transversal are supplementary. Hence:

$$m\angle r + m\angle s = 180$$
$$x + 4x = 180$$
$$5x = 180$$
$$x = \frac{180}{5}$$
$$x = 36$$

Thus, $m\angle r = x = 36$.
The measure of $\angle r$ is **36**.

9.

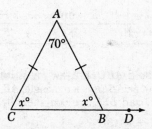

In an isosceles triangle, the base angles have the same degree measure.
Let x = the measure of each base angle of isosceles triangle ABC. If vertex angle A of isosceles triangle ABC measures 70°, then

$$x + x + 70 = 180$$
$$2x + 70 = 180$$
$$2x = 110$$
$$x = \frac{110}{2} = 55$$

At each vertex of a triangle, an exterior angle of the triangle is supplementary to the interior angle that is adjacent to it. Hence, since $m\angle B = 55$, the measure of exterior angle $DBA = 180 - 55 = 125$.
The measure, in degrees, of an *exterior* angle at B is **125**.

10.

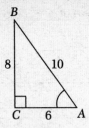

In a right triangle, the cosine of an acute angle is equal to the length of the leg adjacent to the angle divided by the length of the hypotenuse of the right triangle. Thus:

$$\cos A = \frac{AC}{AB} = \frac{6}{10} = 0.6000$$

$$\cos B = \frac{BC}{AB} = \frac{8}{10} = 0.8000$$

The cosine of angle **B** is equal to 0.8000.

11.

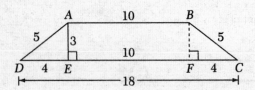

In isosceles trapezoid *ABCD*, draw an altitude from *B* to side *CD*, intersecting *CD* at *F*. Since *ABFE* is a rectangle, *AB* = *EF* = 10.

Right triangles *AED* and *BFC* are congruent by the hypotenuse-leg (H-L) method, so $DE = FC = \frac{1}{2}(8) = 4$.

The lengths of the sides of right triangle *AED* form a 3 – 4 – 5 Pythagorean triple in which *AE* = 3.

The length of altitude $\overline{AE}$ is **3**.

12. If, in a set of *n* objects, *a* objects are identical and *b* objects are also identical, then the number of different ways in which these *n* objects can be arranged is given by the formula $\dfrac{n!}{a!\,b!}$

Since the word "PAPA" consists of a total of four letters including two pairs of identical letters, let $n = 4$, $a = 2$, and $b = 2$:

$$\frac{n!}{a!\,b!} = \frac{4!}{2!\,2!}$$

$$\frac{n!}{a!\,b!} = \frac{\overset{2}{\cancel{4}} \cdot 3 \cdot \overset{1}{\cancel{2}} \cdot \overset{1}{\cancel{1}}}{\cancel{2} \cdot 1 \cdot \cancel{2} \cdot 1}$$

$$\frac{n!}{a!\,b!} = 2 \cdot 3$$

$$\frac{n}{a!\,b!} = 6$$

There are **6** different four-letter arrangements of the word "PAPA."

13. The notation $_nC_r$ means the combination of n objects taken r at a time, and is evaluated using the formula $_nC_r = \dfrac{n!}{r!\,(n-r)!}$

Since it is given that $_nC_2 = 15$, let $r = 2$. Substituting in the formula gives:

$$_nC_2 = 15 = \frac{n!}{2!\,(n-2)!}$$

$$15 = \frac{n(n-1)(n-2)!}{(2 \cdot 1)(n-2)!}$$

$$15 = \frac{n(n-1)}{2}$$

Multiply each side by 2:

$$2(15) = \overset{1}{\cancel{2}} \left[\frac{n(n-1)}{2} \right]$$

Simplify:
$$30 = n^2 - n$$

Write the quadratic equation in standard form:
$$n^2 - n - 30 = 0$$

Factor:
$$(n + ?)(n + ?) = 0$$

The missing pair of numbers must have a product of -30 and a sum of -1. The pair of numbers consists of -6 and 5:

$$(n - 6)(n + 5) = 0$$

Set each linear factor equal to 0 and solve:

$$n - 6 = 0 \text{ or } n + 5 = 0$$
$$n = 6 \text{ or } n = -5$$

Since n must be a positive integer, reject the solution $n = -5$.
The value of n is **6**.

14.

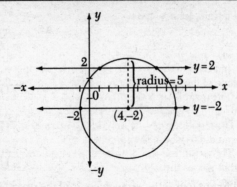

In a plane, the set of all points 5 units from (4,–2) is a circle having (4,–2) as its center and a radius of 5 units.

The set of all points 2 units from the *x*-axis is a pair of horizontal lines; one line is 2 units above the *x*-axis and the other line is 2 units below the *x*-axis.

The total number of points 5 units from (4,–2) and 2 units from the *x*-axis is the total number of points at which the pair of horizontal lines and the circle intersect. As shown in the accompanying diagram, the two parallel lines intersect the circle at a total of four points.

There are **4** points 5 units from (4,–2) and 2 units from the *x*-axis.

15.

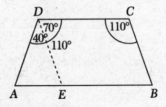

In an isosceles trapezoid, upper base angles are congruent. Thus, m∠*ADC* = m∠*C* = 110. Since $\overline{DE} \parallel \overline{CB}$, angles *C* and *EDC* are supplementary since they are interior angles on the same side of transversal $\overline{CD}$. Hence:

$$m\angle EDC = 180 - m\angle C$$

$$m\angle EDC = 180 - 110$$

$$m\angle EDC = 70$$

The measure of ∠*ADE* is found by subtracting the measure of ∠*EDC* from the measure of ∠*ADC*:

$$m\angle ADE = 110 - 70 = 40$$

The measure of ∠*ADE* is **40.**

16. Given: (1) $x = 4$
             (2) $y = 2$
             (3) $x = y$
             (4) $x + y = 1$

Where possible, put each of the given equations in the form $y = mx + b$, where m represents the slope of the line and b represents the y-intercept of the line.

Equation (1): The graph of the equation $x = 4$ is a vertical line that intersects the x-axis at $(4,0)$ and does not intersect the y-axis.

Equation (2): The equation $y = 2$ may be written as $y = 0x + 2$, which represents a horizontal line whose y-intercept is 2.

Equation (3): The equation $x = y$ may be written as $y = x + 0$, which represents a line that passes through the origin and whose y-intercept is 0.

Equation (4): The equation $x + y = 1$ may be written as $y = -x + 1$, which represents a line whose y-intercept is 1.

Only the graph of the equation $x = 4$ does not intersect the y-axis. Since exactly one out of the four graphs does not intersect the y-axis, the probability of picking this graph is $\frac{1}{4}$.

The probability a graph picked at random does *not* intersect the y-axis is $\frac{1}{4}$.

17. The locus of points 4 units from the origin is a circle whose center is the origin and whose radius is 4 units in length. In general, an equation of a circle whose center is at (h, k) and whose radius is r units is
$$(x-h)^2 + (y-k)^2 = r^2$$
Letting $h = k = 0$ and $r = 4$ gives $x^2 + y^2 = 4^2$ or $x^2 + y^2 = 16$

An equation of the locus of points 4 units from the origin is $x^2 + y^2 = 16$.

18. Using DeMorgan's laws, the given statement $\sim(p \wedge \sim q)$ is logically equivalent to $\sim p \vee \sim (\sim q)$. By the Law of Double Negation, $\sim p \vee \sim (\sim q)$ is equivalent to $\sim p \vee q$.

A statement and its negation have opposite truth values. Since $\sim q$ is given as true, q is false. In order for the conjunction $\sim p \vee q$ to be true when q is false, $\sim p$ must be true.

The correct choice is **(4)**.

19.

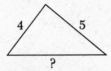

In a triangle, the sum of the lengths of any two sides must be greater than the length of the remaining side. Use this relationship to test each choice.

(1) If the third side has a length of 1, then

$$
\begin{array}{ccc}
\overset{?}{4+5>1} & \overset{?}{5+1>4} & \overset{?}{4+1>5} \\
9 > 1 \checkmark & 6 > 4 \checkmark & 5 \not> 5 \checkmark
\end{array}
$$

Since the last inequality statement is false, the length of the third side cannot be 1. You need not go further. However, if you had tested the other choices, you would have found the following:

(2) If the third side has a length of 2, then each of the required inequalities is true:

$$4 + 5 \overset{?}{>} 2 \qquad 5 + 2 \overset{?}{>} 4 \qquad 4 + 2 \overset{?}{>} 5$$
$$9 > 2 \checkmark \qquad 7 > 4 \checkmark \qquad 6 > 5 \checkmark$$

(3) If the third side has a length of 3, then each of the required inequalities is true:

$$4 + 5 \overset{?}{>} 3 \qquad 5 + 3 \overset{?}{>} 4 \qquad 4 + 3 \overset{?}{>} 5$$
$$9 > 3 \checkmark \qquad 8 > 4 \checkmark \qquad 7 > 5 \checkmark$$

(4) If the third side has a length of 4, then each of the required inequalities is true:

$$4 + 5 \overset{?}{>} 4 \qquad 4 + 4 \overset{?}{>} 5$$
$$9 > 4 \checkmark \qquad 8 > 5 \checkmark$$

The correct choice is **(1)**.

20.

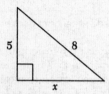

In a right triangle, the sum of the squares of the measures of the legs is equal to the square of the measure of the hypotenuse. If the hypotenuse measures 8 and one leg measures 5, lex $x =$ the measure of the remaining leg. Hence:

$$x^2 + 5^2 = 8^2$$
$$x^2 + 25 = 64$$
$$x^2 = 39$$
$$x = \sqrt{39}$$

The correct choice is **(3)**.

21.

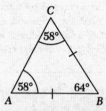

In $\triangle ABC$, if m$\angle A = 58$ and m$\angle B = 64$, then m$\angle C = 180 - (58 + 64) = 58$.

Hence, angles A and C have the same measure, and the sides opposite these angles, sides $\overline{AB}$ and $\overline{BC}$, must have the same length. Thus, $AB = BC$.

The correct choice is **(2)**.

22. Two statements are logically equivalent if they always have the same truth value. A conditional statement and its contrapositive always have the same truth value and, as a result, are logically equivalent statements.

The contrapositive of a conditional statement is formed by negating and then interchanging both parts of the conditional statement. Thus, the contrapositive of the given statement, $\sim p \to q$, is $\sim q \to \sim(\sim p)$ or, by the Law of Double Negation, $\sim q \to p$.

Hence, $\sim p \to q$ and $\sim q \to p$ are logically equivalent statements.

The correct choice is **(3)**.

23. The x- and y-coordinates of the midpoint of a line segment are the averages of the corresponding coordinates of the endpoint of the line segment.

If $M(\overline{x}, \overline{y})$ represents the midpoint of the line segment whose endpoints are (x_1, y_1) and (x_2, y_2), then $\overline{x} = \dfrac{x_1 + x_2}{2}$ and $\overline{y} = \dfrac{y_1 + y_2}{2}$

To find the coordinates of the midpoint of the line segment whose endpoints are $(-2, 4)$ and $(5, -2)$, let $x_1 = -2$, $y_1 = 4$, $x_2 = 5$, and $y_2 = -2$:

$$\overline{x} = \frac{-2 + 5}{2} \quad \text{and} \quad \overline{y} = \frac{4 + (-2)}{2}$$

$$\overline{x} = \frac{3}{2} \qquad\qquad \overline{y} = \frac{2}{2} = 1$$

The coordinates of the midpoint are $\left(\dfrac{3}{2}, 1\right)$.

The correct choice is **(1)**.

24. Consider each choice in turn:

(1) It is not *always* true that the diagonals of a parallelogram bisect the angles. The diagonals of a rhombus or a square always bisect the angles.

(2) It is not *always* true that the diagonals are perpendicular. The diagonals of a rhombus or a square are always perpendicular.

(3) It is not *always* true that the adjacent sides of a parallelogram are congruent. The adjacent sides of a rhombus or a square are always congruent.

(4) The diagonals of a parallelogram *always* bisect each other.

The correct choice is **(4)**.

25. Two triangles are similar if two pairs of corresponding angles are congruent. Consider each choice in turn:

(1) In two obtuse triangles the obtuse angles, as well as the other pairs of corresponding angles, are not necessarily congruent.

(2) Two scalene triangles do not necessarily have any pairs of congruent corresponding angles.

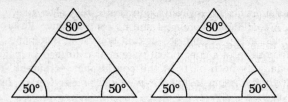

(3) Although two right triangles have one pair of corresponding congruent angles, the two pairs of corresponding acute angles are not necessarily congruent.

(4) If two isosceles triangles have congruent vertex angles, their base angles must also be congruent.

For instance, use a convenient number, say 80, to represent the measure of each of the vertex angles. Since the sum of the measures of the angles of a triangle is 180, the sum of the measures of the two base angles of each isosceles triangle is $180 - 80 = 100$.

In each isosceles triangle the base angles are congruent, so the measure of each base angle is $\frac{1}{2}$ (100) or 50. Hence, the two isosceles triangles with congruent vertex angles also have corresponding congruent base angles.

Since these two triangles have three pairs of congruent corresponding angles, they are similar.

The correct choice is **(4)**.

26. The graph of any equation of the form $y = ax^2 + bx + c$ $(a \neq 0)$ is a parabola.

The equation $y = x^2$ has this form with $a = 1$, $b = 0$, and $c = 0$. Thus, the graph of $x = x^2$ is a parabola.

The correct choice is **(2)**.

27. An equation of a line may be written in the form $y = mx + b$, where m represents its slope and b is its y-intercept.

A line that passes through point (0,4) intersects the y-axis at $y = 4$. Thus, the y-intercept of this line is 4.

If a line is perpendicular to the line whose equation is $y = -\frac{1}{2} x + 3$, then the slopes of the lines are negative reciprocals. The slope of the line $y = -\frac{1}{2} x + 3$ is $-\frac{1}{2}$.

The negative reciprocal of $-\frac{1}{2}$ is $-\left(-\frac{2}{1}\right)$ or 2, which represents the slope of the line that is perpendicular to the line $y = -\frac{1}{2} x + 3$.

Letting $m = 2$ and $b = 4$ in $y = mx + b$ gives the equation $y = 2x + 4$.
The correct choice is **(3)**.

28. The converse of a conditional statement of the form $p \rightarrow q$ is the statement $q \rightarrow p$.

Thus, to form the converse of a conditional statement that is in "If...then..." form, we interchange the statements that follow the words "If" and "then."

The converse of the statement "If Jamie got a ticket, then Jamie was speeding" is the statement "If Jamie was speeding, then Jamie got a ticket."

The correct choice is **(1)**.

29. An equation is not defined for any value of the variable that makes the denominator have a value of 0.

In the fractional equation that is given:

$$\frac{1}{x} + \frac{1}{x + 3} = 2,$$

the denominator of the first fraction is 0 when $x = 0$, and the denominator of the second fraction is 0 when $x = -3$.

Hence, the possible set of values of x must be restricted so that $x \neq 0$ and $x \neq -3$.

The correct choice is **(4)**.

30.

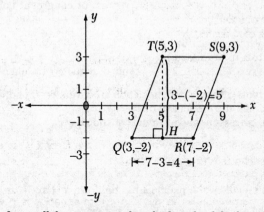

The area of a parallelogram is equal to the length of the base multiplied by the length of the altitude drawn to that base.

The coordinates of the vertices of parallelogram $QRST$ are given as $Q(3,-2)$, $R(7,-2)$, $S(9,3)$, and $T(5,3)$.

From T, draw the altitude to base $\overline{QR}$, intersecting $\overline{QR}$ at H. Since $\overline{QR}$ is a horizontal segment, its length can be determined by subtracting the x-coordinates of its endpoints. Hence, $QR = 7 - 3 = 4$.

Furthermore, point H must have the same x-coordinate as point T and the same y coordinate as points Q and R. Hence, the coordinates of H are $(5,-2)$.

Altitude $\overline{TH}$ is a vertical line segment whose length can be calculated by subtracting the y-coordinates of its endpoints. Thus, $TH = 3 - (-2) = 5$.

Area of parallelogram $QRST = AR \times TH$
Area of parallelogram $QRST = 4 \times 5$
Area of parallelogram $QRST = 20$

The correct choice is **(2)**.

31. Method 1: If -5 and 3 are the roots of a quadratic equation in variable x, then $(x + 5)$ and $(x - 3)$ must be its linear factors. Hence: $\hspace{2cm} (x + 5)(x - 3) = 0$

Use FOIL to multiply.
Multiply the <u>F</u>irst terms: $\hspace{1cm} x^2$
Multiply the <u>O</u>uter terms: $\hspace{1.5cm} -3x$
Multiply the <u>I</u>nner terms: $\hspace{2.5cm} + 5x$
Multiply the <u>L</u>ast terms: $\hspace{3.5cm} -15$
Combine these terms: $\hspace{1cm} x^2 + (-3x + 5x) - 15 = 0$
Simplify: $\hspace{2cm} x^2 + 2x - 15 = 0$

Method 2: If the roots of a quadratic equation are known, then the quadratic equation can be written in standard form as follows: $\hspace{1cm} x^2 + (- \text{sum of roots})\, x + (\text{produce of roots}) = 0$

Since the roots of a quadratic equation are given as -5 and 3, the sum of the roots is -2 and the product is -15.

Hence, the corresponding quadratic equation is

$$x^2 + [-(-2)] - 15 = 0 \quad \text{or} \quad x^2 + 2x - 15 = 0$$

The correct choice is **(2)**.

32. If the equation of a parabola has the form $y = ax^2 + bx + c$, then the equation of the axis of symmetry of the parabola is $x = -\dfrac{b}{2a}$.

For the parabola $y = 2x^2 + 3x + 5$,
let $a = 2, b = 3,$ and $c = 5$. Hence:

$$x = -\frac{b}{2a}$$

$$x = -\frac{3}{2\,(2)}$$

$$x = -\frac{3}{4}$$

The correct choice is **(4)**.

33.

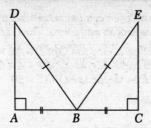

In right triangles DAB and ECB, $\overline{DB} \cong \overline{EB}$. Since these sides are opposite the right angles, they are the hypotenuses of these right triangles.

Since B is given as the midpoint of AC, leg $\overline{AB} \cong$ leg $\overline{BC}$.

The hypotenuses and a corresponding pair of legs of the two right triangles are congruent, making the two right triangles congruent by the hypotenuse-leg (H-L) method.

The correct choice is **(3)**.

34. The slope m of a line determined by points (x_1,y_1) and (x_2,y_2) is given by the formula $m = \dfrac{y_2 - y_1}{x_2 - x_1}$

For the line determined by points $(5,-3)$ and $(-9,-6)$, let $x_1 = 5$, $y_1 = -3$, and $x_2 = -9$, $y_2 = -6$. Substituting these values in the slope formula gives:

$$m = \frac{-6 - (-3)}{-9 \quad -5}$$

$$m = \frac{-6 + 3}{-14}$$

$$m = \frac{-3}{-14}$$

$$m = \frac{3}{14}$$

The correct choice is **(1)**.

35.

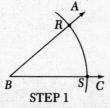

STEP 1

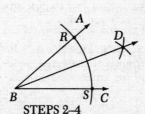

STEPS 2–4

To construct the bisector of $\angle ABC$ proceed as follows:

STEP 1: With the point of the compass on B and any convenient radius, swing an arc intersecting $\overrightarrow{BA}$ at R and $\overrightarrow{BC}$ at S.

STEP 2: With the point of the compass on R and a radius greater than half the distance from R to S, swing an arc.

STEP 3: With the point of the compass on S and the same radius as was used in Step 2, swing an arc intersecting the arc made in Step 2 in point D.

STEP 4: Using a straight-edge, draw $\overrightarrow{BD}$.

$\overrightarrow{BD}$ is the bisector of $\angle ABC$.

PART II

36. a. The given system of equations is:

$$y = x^2 - 6x + 6$$
$$y - x = -4$$

Solve the second equation for y by adding x to each side:

$$y = x - 4$$

Substitute $(x - 4)$ for y in the first equation, thereby obtaining a quadratic equation in x:

$$x - 4 = x^2 - 6x + 6$$

Put the quadratic equation in standard form so that all terms are on one side equal to 0:

$$0 = x^2 - 6x - x + 6 + 4$$
$$0 = x^2 - 7x + 10$$

Factor the right-side of the equation as the product of two binomials:

$$0 = (x + \text{?})(x + \text{?})$$

Find the missing pair of numbers such that the two numbers have a sum of -7 and a product of 10. The two numbers are -2 and -5.

$$0 = (x - 2)(x - 5)$$

If the product of two factors is 0, either factor may equal 0:

$$x - 2 = 0 \text{ or } x - 5 = 0$$
$$x = 2 \text{ or } \quad x = 5$$

Substitute each of the solutions for x in the original first-degree equation to find the corresponding value of y:

	Let $x = 2$:		Let $x = 5$:
$y - x = -4$	$y - 2 = 4$	$y - x = -4$	$y - 5 = -4$
	$y = -4 + 2$		$y = -4 + 5$
	$y = -2$		$y = 1$

The solutions are **(2,–2)** and **(5,1)**.

b. The given product is:

$$\frac{x^2 - 9}{x} \cdot \frac{x^2 + 2x}{x^2 + 5x + 6}$$

Factor each numerator and each denominator wherever possible. The first numerator is the difference of two squares. In the second numerator factor out x. The second denominator is a quadratic trinomial that can be factored as the product of two binomials:

$$\frac{(x - 3)(x + 3)}{x} \cdot \frac{x(x + 2)}{(x + 3)(x + 2)}$$

If the same factor appears in both a numerator and a denominator, divide both of them by the common factor (cancel):

$$\frac{(x - 3)\overset{1}{\cancel{(x + 3)}}}{\cancel{x}} \cdot \frac{\overset{1}{\cancel{x}}\overset{1}{\cancel{(x + 2)}}}{\cancel{(x + 3)}\cancel{(x + 2)}}$$

Multiply together the remaining factors in the numerator, and multiply together the remaining factors in the denominator:

$$\frac{(x - 3)}{1} \quad \text{or} \quad x - 3$$

The product in simplest form is $x - 3$.

37. a. Prepare a table of values for x and y by substituting each integer value of x, from 0 to 6 inclusive, in the given equation, $y = x^2 - 6x + 5$, to determine the corresponding value of y:

x	$x^2 - 6x + 5$	$= y$
0	$0^2 - 6(0) + 5 = 0 + 5$	$= 5$
1	$1^2 - 6(1) + 5 = -5 + 5$	$= 0$
2	$2^2 - 6(2) + 5 = 4 - 12 + 5$	$= -3$
3	$3^2 - 6(3) + 5 = 9 - 18 + 5$	$= -4$
4	$4^2 - 6(4) + 5 = 16 - 24 + 5$	$= -3$
5	$5^2 - 6(5) + 5 = 25 - 30 + 5$	$= 0$
6	$6^2 - 6(6) + 5 = 36 - 36 + 5$	$= 5$

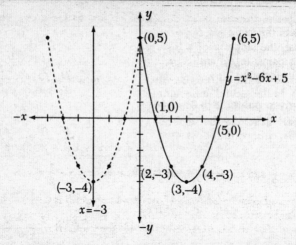

Plot points (0,5), (1,0), (2,–3), (3,–4), (4,–3), (5,0), and (6,5), and draw a smooth curve through them. This curve is a parabola and is the graph of $y = x^2 - 6x + 5$ in the interval $0 \le x \le 6$.

b. A reflection in the y-axis maps each point $P(x,y)$ of the curve onto its image, $P'(-x,y)$. Plot the image of each of the points graphed in part **a:** (0,5), (–1,0), (–2,–3), (–3,–4), (–4,–3), (–5,0), and (–6,5).

Thus, the image of the graph drawn in part **a,** after a reflection in the y-axis, is another parabola, whose turning point is (–3,–4).

c. The axis of symmetry of a parabola of the form $y = ax^2 + bx + c$ is a vertical line of symmetry whose equation has the form $x = a$, where a is the x-coordinate of the turning point. Since the turning point of the graph drawn in part **b** is (–3, 4), and equation of the axis of symmetry of this graph is **$x = -3$**.

38.

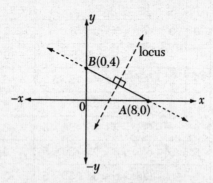

Given: points $A(8,0)$ and $B(0,4)$.

a. An equation of a line may be written in the form $y = mx + b$, where m is the slope of the line and b is its y-intercept.

Line AB passes through point $B(0,4)$, which lies on the y-axis. Since the y-coordinate of this point is 4, $b = 4$.

In general, the slope m of a line that contains points (x_1,y_1) and (x_2,y_2) is given by the formula:

$$m = \frac{y_2 - y_1}{x_2 - x_1}$$

For the given points, $A(8,0)$ and $B(0,4)$, let $x_1 = 8$, $y_1 = 0$, $x_2 = 0$, and $y_2 = 4$. Hence:

$$m = \frac{4 - 0}{0 - 8} = -\frac{4}{8} = -\frac{1}{2}$$

Since $m = -\frac{1}{2}$ and $b = 4$, an equation of line AB is $y = -\frac{1}{2}x + 4$.

b. The locus of points equidistant from points A and B is the line that is the perpendicular bisector of line segment AB.

c. The line that is the perpendicular bisector of $\overline{AB}$ must contain the midpoint of $\overline{AB}$ and also be perpendicular to $\overline{AB}$.

The x-coordinate, $\overline{x}$, of the midpoint of $\overline{AB}$ is determined by taking the average of the x-coordinates of points A and B. The y-coordinate, $\overline{y}$, of the midpoint of $\overline{AB}$ is determined by taking the average of the y-coordinates of points A and B.

For the given points, $A(8,0)$ and $B(0,4)$, let $x_1 = 8$, $y_1 = 0$, $x_2 = 4$. Hence:

$$\overline{x} = \frac{x_1 + x_2}{2} \qquad \overline{y} = \frac{y_1 + y_2}{2}$$
$$\overline{x} = \frac{8 + 0}{2} \qquad \overline{y} = \frac{0 + 4}{2}$$
$$\overline{x} = 4 \qquad \overline{y} = 2$$

Hence, the perpendicular bisector of $\overline{AB}$ contains point $(4,2)$.

If a line is perpendicular to $\overline{AB}$, then its slope must be the negative reciprocal of the slope of $\overline{AB}$. Since the slope of $\overline{AB}$ is $-\frac{1}{2}$, the slope of the line perpendicular to $\overline{AB}$ is $-\left(-\frac{2}{1}\right) = 2$.

Since the slope m of the perpendicular bisector of $\overline{AB}$ is 2, an equation of this line is $y = mx + b$, or $y = 2x + b$. This line contains point $(4, 2)$, the midpoint of $\overline{AB}$, so solve for b in $y = 2x + b$ by letting $x = 4$ and $y = 2$:

$$2 = 2(4) + b$$
$$2 = 8 + b$$
$$2 - 8 = b$$
$$-6 = b$$

Since $m = 2$ and $b = -6$, an equation of the perpendicular bisector of $\overline{AB}$ is $y = 2x - 6$.

An equation of the locus described in part **b** is $y = 2x - 6$.

d. Point $(1,-4)$ is equidistant from A and B if it is a point on the perpendicular bisector of $\overline{AB}$. Determine whether the coordinates of $(1,-4)$ satisfy the equation of the perpendicular bisector of $\overline{AB}$. Let $x = 1$ and $y = -4$

$$y = 2x - 6$$
$$-4 \overset{?}{=} 2(1) - 6$$
$$-4 \overset{?}{=} 2 - 6$$
$$-4 = -4 \checkmark$$

Yes, point $(1,-4)$ is equidistant from A and B since the point satisfies the equation of the locus of points found in part **c.**

39. a. The two given statements, (1) $A \lor {\sim}B$ and (2) ${\sim}A$, are true. The first statement is a conjunction, which is true when either, or both, of its conjuncts are true.

A statement and its negation have opposite truth values. Since ${\sim}A$ is true, A must be false. Thus, to make $A \lor {\sim}B$ a true statement, ${\sim}B$ must be true.

A valid conclusion is that **${\sim}B$ is true.**

b. The two given statements, (1) ${\sim}P \rightarrow Q$ and (2) P, are true. The first statement is a conditional, which is always true *except* in the single instance in which the hypothesis is true and the conclusion is false.

A statement and its negation have opposite truth values. Since P is true, ${\sim}P$ is false, making the statement ${\sim}P \rightarrow Q$ true regardless of the truth value of Q. Hence, it is not possible to deduce a valid conclusion about the truth value of Q.

NO CONCLUSION can be deduced.

c. The two given statements, (1) ${\sim}X \lor {\sim}Y$ and (2) ${\sim}X$, are true. The first statement is a conjunction, which is true when either, or both, of its conjunctions are true.

Since ${\sim}X$ is true, ${\sim}X \lor {\sim}Y$ is true regardless of the truth of ${\sim}Y$. Hence, it is not possible to deduce a valid conclusion about the truth value of ${\sim}Y$.

NO CONCLUSION can be deduced.

d. The two given statements, (1) ${\sim}A \rightarrow B$ and (2) $C \rightarrow {\sim}B$, are true. Consider the second statement. A conditional statement and its contrapositive are logically equivalent.

Form the contrapositive of the second statement by interchanging and then negating both parts of the original conditional statement. The contrapositive of $C \rightarrow {\sim}B$ is ${\sim}({\sim}B) \rightarrow {\sim}C$ or, using the Law of Double Negation, $B \rightarrow {\sim}C$.

Use the Chain Rule (Law of the Syllogism):

$$\sim A \rightarrow B \text{ (Given)}$$
$$\text{and } \underline{B \rightarrow \sim C} \text{ (Contrapositive of Statement (2))}$$
$$\text{Conclusion: } \sim A \rightarrow \sim C$$

A valid conclusion is that $\sim A \rightarrow \sim C$ or, equivalently, $C \rightarrow A$.

e. The two given statements, (1) $\sim A \rightarrow \sim B$ and (2) B, are true. A statement and its negation have opposite truth values.

Since B is true, its negation, $\sim B$, is false. A conditional statement is always true *except* in the single instance in which the hypothesis is true and the conclusion is false. To make $\sim A \rightarrow \sim B$ a true statement when $\sim B$ is false, $\sim A$ must be false. If $\sim A$ is false, then its negation, A, must be true.

A valid conclusion is that **A is true.**

40.

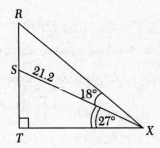

The accompanying diagram, in which $\overline{RT} \perp \overline{TX}$, $m\angle TXS = 27$, $m\angle SXR = 18$, and $SX = 21.2$ meters, is given.

a. (1) In right triangle STX, the length of hypotenuse SX is 21.2 and $\overline{TX}$ is the side adjacent to the angle whose measure is $27°$. Hence, use the cosine ratio to find TX:

$$\cos 27° = \frac{\text{side adjacent to angle}}{\text{hypotenuse}}$$
$$\cos 27° = \frac{TX}{21.2}$$

From the Tables of Natural Trigonometric Functions, $\cos 27° = 0.8910$.

$$0.8910 = \frac{TX}{21.2}$$

$$(21.2)\,0.8910 = (21.2)\,\frac{TX}{21.2}$$

$$18.89 = TX$$

TX, to the *nearest tenth* of a meter, is **18.9.**

(2) In right triangle RTX, the measure of acute angle RXT is $18° + 27° = 45°$. Angle T is a right angle so it has a measure of 90. Since the sum of the measures of the angles of a triangle is 180, the measure of acute angle R is $180 - (90 + 45) = 45$.

Since angles R and RXT are equal in measure, the lengths of the sides opposite these angles are the same. Thus, $RT = TX = 18.9$.

RT, to the *nearest tenth* of a meter, is 18.9.

(3) In right triangle RTX, RX is the hypotenuse, whose length can be found using the Pythagorean Theorem:

$$(RX)^2 = (TX)^2 + (RT)^2$$
$$(RX)^2 = (18.9)^2 + (18.9)^2$$
$$(RX)^2 = 357.21 + 357.21$$
$$(RX)^2 = 714.42$$

$$RX = \sqrt{714.42} = 26.73$$

RX, to the *nearest tenth* of a meter, is **26.7.**

b. The area of a right triangle is equal to one-half the product of the lengths of its legs.

$$\text{Area of right triangle } RTX = \frac{1}{2}(RT)(TX)$$

$$\text{Area of right triangle } RTX = \frac{1}{2}(18.9)(18.9)$$

$$\text{Area of right triangle } RTX = (9.45)(18.9)$$

$$\text{Area of right triangle } RTX = 178.605$$

The area, to the *nearest square meter*, is **179.**

PART III

41.

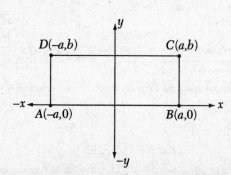

Given: The quadrilateral whose vertices are $A(-a,0)$, $B(a,0)$, $C(a,b)$, and $D(-a, b)$.

a. To prove that quadrilateral $ABCD$ is a rectangle, show that it is a parallelogram, in which the diagonals have the same length. Prove that quadrilateral ABCD is a parallelogram by showing that its opposite sides have the same length.

In general, the length of the segment whose endpoints are $P(x_1, y_1)$ and $Q(x_2, y_2)$ is given by the formula

$$PQ = \sqrt{(x_2 - x_1)^2 + (y_2 - y_1)^2}$$

To find the length of the segment whose endpoints are $A(-a,0)$ and $B(a,0)$, let $x_1 = -a$, $y_1 = 0$, $x_2 = a$, and $y_2 = 0$.

$$AB = \sqrt{(a - (-a))^2 + (0 - 0)^2}$$
$$AB = \sqrt{(a + a)^2}$$
$$AB = \sqrt{4a^2}$$
$$AB = 2a$$

To find the length of the segment whose endpoints are $B(a,0)$ and $C(a,b)$, let $x_1 = a$, $y_1 = 0$, $x_2 = a$, and $y_2 = b$.

$$BC = \sqrt{(a - a)^2 + (b - 0)^2}$$
$$BC = \sqrt{0 + b^2}$$
$$BC = b$$

To find the length of the segment whose endpoints are $C(a,b)$ and $D(-a,b)$, let $x_1 = a$, $y_1 = b$, $x_2 = -a$, and $y_2 = b$.

$$CD = \sqrt{(-a - a)^2 + (b - b)^2}$$
$$CD = \sqrt{(-2a)^2 + 0}$$
$$CD = \sqrt{4a^2}$$
$$CD = 2a$$

To find the length of the segment whose endpoints are $A(-a,0)$ and $D(-a,b)$, let $x_1 = -a$, $y_1 = 0$, $x_2 = -a$, and $y_2 = b$.

$$AD = \sqrt{(-a - (-a))^2 + (b - 0)^2}$$
$$AD = \sqrt{(-a + a)^2 + b^2}$$
$$AD = \sqrt{0 + b^2}$$
$$AD = \sqrt{b^2}$$
$$AD = b$$

Since $AB = 2a$ and $CD = 2a$, $AB = CD$. Since $BC = b$ and $AD = b$, $BC = AD$. Quadrilateral $ABCD$ is a parallelogram since its opposite sides have the same length.

To show that parallelogram $ABCD$ is a rectangle, show its diagonals, $\overline{AC}$ and $\overline{BD}$, have the same length. To find the length of the diagonal whose endpoints are $A(-a,0)$ and $C(a,b)$, let $x_1 = -a$, $y_1 = 0$, $x_2 = a$, and $y_2 = b$.

$$AC = \sqrt{(a - (-a)^2 + (b - 0)^2}$$
$$AC = \sqrt{(a + a)^2 + b^2}$$
$$AC = \sqrt{(2a)^2 + b^2}$$
$$AC = \sqrt{4a^2 + b^2}$$

To find the length of the diagonal whose endpoints are $B(a,0)$ and $D(-a,b)$, let $x_1 = a$, $y_1 = 0$, $x_2 = -a$, and $y_2 = b$.

$$BD = \sqrt{(-a - a)^2 + (b - 0)^2}$$
$$BD = \sqrt{(-2a)^2 + b^2}$$
$$BD = \sqrt{4a^2 + b^2}$$

Since $AC = \sqrt{4a^2 + b^2}$ and $BD = \sqrt{4a^2 + b^2}$, $AC = BD$. Hence, parallelogram $ABCD$ is a rectangle since its diagonals have the same length.

ALTERNATIVE STRATEGY: Use the slope formula to calculate the slope of each side of quadrilateral $ABCD$. Show that opposite sides of the quadrilateral have the same slope and are, therefore, parallel. Since the opposite sides are parallel, the quadrilateral is a parallelogram.

Compare the slopes of a pair of adjacent sides. Show that the slopes of these sides are negative reciprocals and that, as a result, the sides form a right angle. Since the parallelogram contains a right angle, it is a rectangle.

b. If a rectangle has a pair of adjacent sides that have the same length, then the rectangle is a square. In the expressions that represent the lengths of $\overline{AB}$ and $\overline{BC}$ found in part **a,** let $a = 10$ and $b = 7$:

$$AB = 2a = 2(10) = 20$$
$$BC = b = 7$$

Thus, AB and BC do not have the same length for the given values of a and b. Since a pair of adjacent sides of rectangle $ABCD$ do not have the same length, $ABCD$ is not a square.

42.

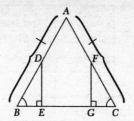

Given: $\overline{ADB}$, $\overline{AFC}$, $\overline{BEGC}$, $\overline{AB} \cong \overline{AC}$, $\overline{DE} \perp \overline{BC}$, $\overline{FG} \perp \overline{BC}$, and $\overline{BG} \cong \overline{CE}$

Prove: $\overline{BD} \cong \overline{CF}$

Plan: Since $\overline{BD}$ and $\overline{CF}$ are corresponding sides of triangles DBE and FCG, prove that these triangles are congruent by A.S.A. $\cong$ A.S.A.

PROOF

Statements	Reasons
(1) $\overline{DE} \perp \overline{BC}$ and $\overline{FG} \perp \overline{BC}$	(1) Given.
(2) Angles DEB and FGC are right angles.	(2) If two lines are perpendicular, they intersect to form right angles.
(3) $\angle DEB \cong \angle FGC$ (Angle)	(3) All right angles are congruent.
(4) $\overline{BG} \cong \overline{CE}$	(4) Given.
(5) $BG = CE$	(5) Congruent segments are equal in length.
(6) $EG = EG$	(6) Reflexive property of equality.
(7) $BE = CG$	(7) Subtraction property of equality.
(8) $\overline{BE} \cong \overline{CG}$ (Side)	(8) Segments that have the same length are congruent.
(9) $\overline{AB} \cong \overline{AC}$	(9) Given.
(10) $\angle B \cong \angle C$ (Angle)	(10) If two sides of a triangle are congruent, the angles opposite these sides are congruent.
(11) $\triangle DBE \cong \triangle FCG$	(11) A.S.A. $\cong$ A.S.A.
(12) $\overline{BD} \cong \overline{CF}$	(12) Corresponding sides of congruent triangles are congruent.

Topic	Question Numbers	Number of Points	Your Points	Your Percentage
1. Properties of Number Systems; Def. of Operations	6, 29	2 + 2 = 4		
2. Finite Mathematical Systems	2	2		
3. Linear Function & Graph ($y = mx + b$, slope, eqs. of)	16, 27	2 + 2 = 4		
4. Quadratic Equation (alg. sol.—factoring, formula)	31	2		
5. Parabola (incl. axis of symmetry, turning point)	26, 32, 37	2 + 2 + 10 = 14		
6. Systems of Equations (alg. and graphic solutions)	36a	6		
7. Quantifiers (existential and universal)				
8. Suppls., Compl., Vertical Angles, Angle Measure				
9. Triangle Properties (eq., isos., sum ∠s, 2 sides)	3, 9, 19	2 + 2 + 2 = 6		
10. Line ‖ One Side of Δ; Line Joining Midpts. of 2 Sides				
11. Inequalities in Δs (ext.∠, ≠ sides, and opp. ∠s)	21	2		
12. Quadrilateral Properties (▱, sq., rhom., rect., trap.)	11, 15, 24	2 + 2 + 2 = 6		
13. Parallel Lines	8	2		
13A. Alg. Oper.; Verbal Probs.	36b	4		
14. Mean Proportional; Alt. to Hypot. of Right Δ	4	2		
15. Pythag. Th., Special Rt. Δs (3-4-5, 5-12-13, 30-60-90)	20	2		
16. Similar Figures (ratios & proportions)	5, 25	2 + 2 = 4		
17. Areas (Δ, rect., ▱, rhom., trap.)	30, 40b	2 + 2 = 4		
18. Locus	14, 17, 38	2 + 2 + 10 = 14		
19. Constructions	35	2		
20. Deductive Proofs	33, 42	2 + 10 = 12		
21. Coordinate Geom. (slope, dist., midpt., eq. of circle)	23, 34	2 + 2 = 4		
22. Coordinate Geom. "Proofs"	41	10		
23. Logic	18, 22, 28, 39	2 + 2 + 2 + 10 = 16		
24. Permutations; Arrangements	12	2		
25. Combinations	13	2		
26. Probability				
27. Trig. of Rt. Δ	10, 40a	2 + 8 = 10		
28. Literal Eqs.				
29. Transformations	1, 7	2 + 2 = 4		

Examination
June 1993
Sequential Math Course II

PART I

Answer 30 questions from this part. Each correct answer will receive 2 credits. No partial credit will be allowed. Write your answers in the spaces provided. Where applicable, answers may be left in terms of π or in radical form.   [60]

1 In the accompanying diagram, $\overleftrightarrow{AB} \parallel \overleftrightarrow{CD}$, $\overleftrightarrow{EF} \parallel \overleftrightarrow{GH}$, and m$\angle 1$ = 105. What is m$\angle 2$?

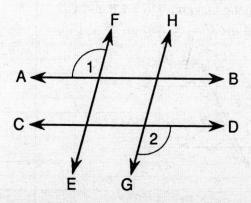

1____

2 The measures of the three sides of a triangle are 6, 8, and 10 centimeters. The midpoints of the three sides are joined to form a second triangle. How many centimeters are in the perimeter of the second triangle?

2____

3 If $\triangle JSO$ is an equilateral triangle, find the measure of an exterior angle at S.

3____

4 If $\square$ is a binary operation defined as

$a \square b = \dfrac{a + b^2}{a}$, evaluate $5 \square 3$.

4____

5 In isosceles triangle ABC, $\overline{AB} \cong \overline{CB}$. If $AB = 2x + 17$, $CB = 4x - 13$, and $AC = 2x + 16$, find the value of x.

5____

6 What is the image of point $(4,5)$ after a reflection in the y-axis?

6____

7 A square has a side of length 3, and a second square has a side of length 4. What is the ratio of the length of a diagonal of the first square to the length of a diagonal of the second square?

7____

8 In the accompanying diagram, $\overset{\leftrightarrow}{DE} \parallel \overset{\leftrightarrow}{CB}$ and $\overset{\leftrightarrow}{CD}$ is a transversal. If $m\angle 1 = 65$ and $m\angle 2 = 140$, find $m\angle CAB$.

8____

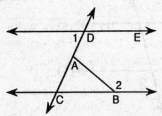

9 Solve for x: $\quad \dfrac{1}{x} + 3 = \dfrac{7}{2}$

9____

10 Express in radical form the length of the line segment joining the points whose coordinates are (2,4) and (0,–5).

10_____

11 In right triangle *ABC*, altitude $\overline{CD}$ is drawn to hypotenuse $\overline{AB}$. If *CD* = 4 and *AD* = 2, find *DB*.

11_____

12 The table below defines multiplication on the set $S = \{1, i, -1, -i\}$. Based on the table, what is the value of $(i \times i) \times i$?

×	1	i	–1	–i
1	1	i	–1	–i
i	i	–1	–i	1
–1	–1	–i	1	i
–i	–i	1	i	–1

12_____

13 Write an equation of the line that passes through the origin and is parallel to the line whose equation is $y = 3x - 7$.

13_____

14 The coordinates of the midpoint of $\overline{AB}$ are (6,8) and the coordinates of point *A* are (3,2). Find the coordinates of point *B*.

14_____

Directions (15–34): For *each* question chosen, write in the space provided the *numeral* preceding the word or expression that best completes the statement or answers the question.

15 The lengths of two sides of an isosceles triangle are 8 and 10. The length of the third side could be

(1) 6, only   (3) 10, only
(2) 8, only   (4) either 8 or 10

15_____

16 What is the image of the point (–3,–1) under the translation that shifts (x,y) to $(x - 2, y + 4)$?

(1) (–1,3)   (3) (–5,3)

(2) (–1,–5)   (4) (–5,–5)   16_____

17 What are the factors of $3x^2 + 7x - 20$?

(1) $(3x + 5)(x - 4)$

(2) $(3x - 4)(x + 5)$

(3) $(3x - 5)(x + 4)$

(4) $(3x + 4)(x - 5)$ 17_____

18 A quadrilateral has diagonals that are congruent but not perpendicular. The quadrilateral contains no right angles. The quadrilateral could be

(1) a square

(2) an isosceles trapezoid

(3) a rectangle

(4) a rhombus   18_____

19 Which set contains the number π?

(1) integers

(2) rational numbers

(3) natural numbers

(4) irrational numbers   19_____

20 Which is an equation of a line whose slope is equal to zero?

(1) $y = 1$ (3) $x + y = 5$

(2) $x = 2$ (4) $x - y = 3$ 20_____

21 The statement $\sim p \vee q$ is equivalent to

(1) $\sim(p \wedge \sim q)$ (3) $\sim(p \vee q)$

(2) $\sim(p \vee \sim q)$ (4) $\sim(p \wedge q)$ 21_____

22 The vertices of △ABC are A(0,6), B(3,0), and C(11,0). What is the area of △ABC in square units?

(1) 9   (3) 24
(2) 12   (4) 33   22____

23 In the accompanying diagram, △ABC and △RST are right triangles with right angles at B and S, respectively; $\overline{AB} \cong \overline{RS}$ and $\overline{AC} \cong \overline{RT}$.

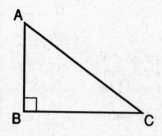 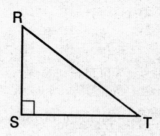

Which statement can be used to justify that △ABC ≅ △RST?

(1) SAS ≅ SAS   (3) HL ≅ HL
(2) ASA ≅ ASA   (4) SAA ≅ SAA   23____

24 Which is an equation of a line perpendicular to the line whose equation is $y = -\frac{1}{2}x + 5$?

(1) $y = 2x - 1$ (3) $y = \frac{1}{2}x - 1$

(2) $y = -2x - 1$ (4) $y = -\frac{1}{2}x - 1$ 24____

25 If $\cos x = \frac{2}{5}$, what is the measure of $\angle x$, to the *nearest degree?*

(1) 23   (3) 66
(2) 24   (4) 67   25____

26 How many different nine-letter arrangements can be formed from the letters in the word "TENNESSEE"?

(1) $\frac{9!}{3!}$

(3) $\frac{9!}{4 \cdot 2 \cdot 2}$

(2) $\frac{9!}{4!2!2!}$

(4) $\frac{9!}{4!} \cdot \frac{9!}{2!} \cdot \frac{9!}{2!}$

26____

27 An equation of the locus of points 4 units from the point (2,−1) is

(1) $(x - 2)^2 + (y + 1)^2 = 16$
(2) $(x + 2)^2 + (y - 1)^2 = 16$
(3) $(x - 2)^2 + (y - 1)^2 = 16$
(4) $(x + 2)^2 + (y + 1)^2 = 16$

27____

28 What is the y-intercept of the parabola whose equation is $y = x^2 + 5x - 6$?

(1) 1   (3) 6
(2) −1   (4) −6

28____

29 In the accompanying diagram, what is sin E?

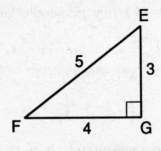

(1) $\frac{3}{4}$

(3) $\frac{3}{5}$

(2) $\frac{4}{3}$

(4) $\frac{4}{5}$

29____

30 What are the roots of the equation
$x^2 - 4x - 3 = 0$?

(1) 1,3

(3) $2 \pm \sqrt{7}$

(2) $\frac{1}{2}$,3

(4) $-2 \pm \sqrt{7}$

30____

31 Which statement is logically equivalent to the statement, "If we recycle, then the amount of trash in landfills is reduced"?

(1) If we do not recycle, then the amount of trash in landfills is not reduced.

(2) If the amount of trash in landfills is not reduced, then we did not recycle.

(3) If the amount of trash in landfills is reduced, then we recycled.

(4) If we do not recycle, then the amount of trash in landfills is reduced.

31____

32 A circle is inscribed in a square whose sides have length 2. If a dart hits the square, what is the probability that it will hit inside the circle?

(1) 1

(3) $\frac{4}{\pi}$

(2) $\frac{1}{4}$

(4) $\frac{\pi}{4}$

32____

33 How many points do the graphs of the equations $x^2 + y^2 = 16$ and $y = x$ have in common?

(1) 1

(3) 0

(2) 2

(4) 4

33____

34 The expression $_{11}C_2$ is equivalent to

(1) $_{11}P_2$

(3) $_{11}P_9$

(2) $_{11}C_9$

(4) $\frac{11!}{2!}$

34____

DIRECTIONS (35): *Show all construction lines.*

35 *On the answer sheet,* construct a line through *C*
   perpendicular to $\overleftrightarrow{ACB}$.

PART II

Answer **three** questions from this part. Clearly indicate the necessary steps, including appropriate formula substitutions, diagrams, graphs, charts, etc. Calculations that may be obtained by mental arithmetic or the calculator do not need to be shown. [30]

36 *a* On graph paper, draw the locus of points 3 units from the point (2,3). Label it *a*. [3]

    b Write the equation for the locus drawn in part *a*. [2]

    c On the same set of axes, draw the image of the graph drawn in part *a* after a reflection in the *x*-axis. Label it *c*. [2]

    d On the same set of axes, draw the image of the graph drawn in part *c* after a translation that moves (x,y) to $(x - 2, y + 3)$. Label it *d*. [3]

37 *a* On graph paper, sketch the graph of the function $y = x^2 - 6x + 7$ in the interval $0 \leq x \leq 6$. [5]

    b Between which two consecutive integers does the *smaller* root of $x^2 - 6x + 7 = 0$ lie? [2]

    c On the same set of axes, sketch the graph of the equation $y = -2$. [2]

    d Determine the number of solutions for the equations $y = x^2 - 6x + 7$ and $y = -2$. [1]

38 Given: $(K \wedge L) \rightarrow M$
$\qquad N \rightarrow \sim M$
$\qquad L \vee O$
$\qquad O \rightarrow P$
$\qquad K$
$\qquad N$

Prove: P [10]

39 In the accompanying diagram of right triangle *CAT*, altitude $\overline{AP}$ divides hypotenuse $\overline{TC}$ into segments of lengths x and $x + 7$, and $AP = 12$.

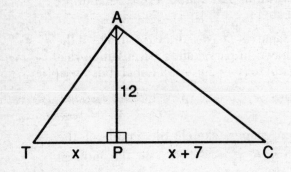

a Find the length of $\overline{TP}$. [5]

b Find the area of $\triangle CAT$. [2]

c Find the measure of $\angle T$ to the *nearest degree*. [3]

40 A change purse contains nickels, dimes, and quarters. The number of quarters is 8 more than twice the number of dimes, and the number of nickels is 4 less than the number of dimes. The probability of selecting a quarter is $\frac{3}{4}$.

a What is the total value of the coins in the purse?   [5]

b Three coins are drawn from the purse.
  (1) How many different three-coin selections can be made?   [2]
  (2) What is the probability that the three coins selected will be one of each kind? [3]

PART III

Answer one question from this part. Clearly indicate the necessary steps, including appropriate formula substitutions, diagrams, graphs, charts, etc. Calculations that may be obtained by mental arithmetic or the calculator do not need to be shown. [10]

41 Quadrilateral *ABCD* has coordinates *A*(0,0), *B*(6*a*,3*b*), *C*(3*a*,4*b*), and *D*(*a*,3*b*), $a \neq 0$ and $b \neq 0$.

   a Using coordinate geometry, show that

      (1) $\overline{AB} \parallel \overline{CD}$ [4]

      (2) $\overline{AD}$ is *not* parallel to $\overline{BC}$ [4]

   b Which kind of quadrilateral is *ABCD*? Why? [2]

42 Given: $\overline{PSRV}, \overline{PS} \cong \overline{VR}, \overline{RQ} \parallel \overline{ST}, \overline{PQ} \perp \overline{QR}$, and $\overline{VT} \perp \overline{TS}$.

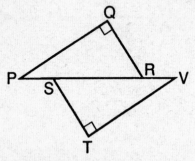

Prove: $\overline{PQ} \cong \overline{VT}$ [10]

Answers
June 1993
Sequential Math Course II

Answer Key

PART I

1. 105	**13.** $y = 3x$	**25.** 3
2. 12	**14.** (9, 14)	**26.** 2
3. 120°	**15.** 4	**27.** 1
4. $\frac{14}{5}$	**16.** 3	**28.** 4
5. 15	**17.** 3	**29.** 4
6. (–4, 5)	**18.** 2	**30.** 3
7. 3 : 4	**19.** 4	**31.** 2
8. 75	**20.** 1	**32.** 4
9. 2	**21.** 1	**33.** 2
10. $\sqrt{85}$	**22.** 3	**34.** 2
11. 8	**23.** 3	**35.** construction
12. $-i$	**24.** 1	

PARTS II AND III See answers explained section.

Answers Explained

PART I

1.

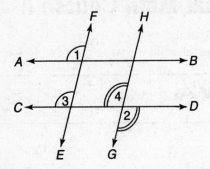

If two lines are parallel, then pairs of corresponding angles have the same measure.

Since $\overleftrightarrow{AB} \parallel \overleftrightarrow{CD}$, m∠1 = m∠3; and, since $\overleftrightarrow{EF} \parallel \overleftrightarrow{GH}$, m∠3 = m∠4. Hence, by the transitive property of equality, m∠1 = m∠4.

Since vertical angles have the same measure, m∠4 = m∠2. By the transitive property, m∠1 = m∠2. Since it is given that m∠1 = 105, and since m∠2 = m∠1, m∠2 = 105.

The measure of ∠2 is **105.**

2. The line joining the midpoints of any two sides of a triangle is parallel to the third side *and* is one-half of its length. Thus, if the midpoints of the three sides of a triangle are joined to form a second triangle, the length of each side of the second triangle is one-half the length of the side of the original triangle that is opposite it.

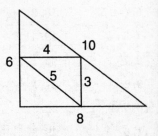

Since the lengths of the sides of the original triangle are given as 6, 8, and 10 centimeters, the lengths of the sides of the second triangle that lie opposite these sides are 3, 4, and 5 centimeters, respectively. Hence, the perimeter of the second triangle is 3 + 4 + 5 or 12 centimeters.

The perimeter of the second triangle is **12** centimeters.

3. If ∆*JSO* is equilateral, then it is also equiangular, so each angle of the triangle measures 60.

The measure of an exterior angle of a triangle is equal to the sum of the measures of the two nonadjacent interior angles of the triangle. Hence, the measure of an exterior angle at S is equal to the sum of the measures of angles J and O, which is 60 + 60 or 120.

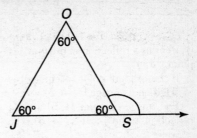

The measure of an exterior angle at S is **120**.

4. The symbol $\square$ is defined as a binary operation such that, for any two numbers a and b,

$$a \square b = \frac{a + b^2}{a}$$

To evaluate $5 \square 3$, replace a with 5 and b with 3:

Given:

$$a \square b = \frac{a + b^2}{a}$$

Let $a = 5$ and $b = 3$:

$$5 \square 3 = \frac{5 + 3^2}{5}$$

$$= \frac{5 + 9}{5}$$

$$= \frac{14}{5}$$

The value of $5 \square 3$ is $\dfrac{14}{5}$.

5. Given:

$$\overline{AB} \cong \overline{CB}$$

Since congruent segments are equal in length:

$$AB = CB$$

Substitute the given values of AB and CB:

$$2x + 17 = 4x - 13$$

Subtract $2x$ from each side of the equation:

$$
\begin{array}{rcr}
-2x & & = -2x \\
\hline
17 & = & 2x - 13
\end{array}
$$

Add 13 to each side of the resulting equation:

$$
\begin{array}{rcr}
+13 & = & +13 \\
\hline
30 & = & 2x
\end{array}
$$

Divide each side of the equation by 2:

$$\frac{30}{2} = \frac{2x}{2}$$

$$15 = x$$

The value of x is **15**.

6. In general, the image of point (x, y) after a reflection in the y-axis is point $(-x, y)$.

If the original point (preimage) is $(4, 5)$, then its image is $(-4, 5)$.

The image of point $(4, 5)$ after a reflection in the y-axis is **(–4, 5)**.

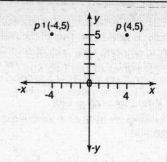

7.

 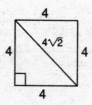

A diagonal divides a square into two isosceles right triangles. In an isosceles right triangle the length of the hypotenuse (diagonal of the square) is equal to the length of either leg (side of the square) multiplied by $\sqrt{2}$.

Hence, the length of a diagonal of the first square, whose side has a length of 3, is $3\sqrt{2}$. The length of a diagonal of the second square, whose side has a length of 4, is $4\sqrt{2}$.

The ratio of the length of the diagonal of the first square to the length of the diagonal of the second square is $\dfrac{3\sqrt{2}}{4\sqrt{2}}$ or, equivalently, $\dfrac{3}{4}$.

The ratio of the length of a diagonal of the first square to the length of a diagonal of the second square is **3:4**.

8.

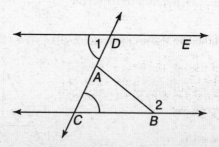

If two lines are parallel, then alternate interior angles are equal in measure. Since it is given that $\overleftrightarrow{DE} \parallel \overleftrightarrow{CB}$ and m$\angle 1$ = 65, m$\angle BCA$ = m$\angle 1$ = 65.

In a triangle, the measure of an exterior angle is equal to the sum of the measures of the two nonadjacent interior angles of the triangle:

$$m\angle CAB + m\angle BCA = m\angle 2$$

Given that m$\angle 2$ = 140:

$$m\angle CAB + 65 = 140$$

Subtract 65 from each side of the equation:

$$m\angle CAB = 140 - 65$$

$$m\angle CAB = 75$$

The measure of $\angle CAB$ is **75**.

9. Given:

$$\frac{1}{x} + 3 = \frac{7}{2}$$

Multiply each term of the equation by $2x$, the lowest common multiple of the denominators:

$$2x\left(\frac{1}{x}\right) + 2x(3) = 2x\left(\frac{7}{2}\right)$$

Subtract $6x$ from each side of the equation:

$$2 + 6x = 7x$$
$$-6x = -6x$$
$$\overline{2 = x}$$

The value of x is **2**.

10. In general, the length d of the segment whose endpoints are (x_1, y_1) and (x_2, y_2) is given by the formula

$$d = \sqrt{(x_2 - x_1)^2 + (y_2 - y_1)^2}$$

Since the given endpoints are (2,4) and (0,–5), let (x_1, y_1) = (2,4) and (x_2, y_2) = (0, –5), so that $x_1 = 2$, $y_1 = 4$, $x_2 = 0$, and $y_2 = -5$. Then,

$$d = \sqrt{(0 - 2)^2 + (-5 - 4)^2}$$
$$= \sqrt{(-2)^2 + (-9)^2}$$
$$= \sqrt{4 + 81}$$
$$= \sqrt{85}$$

The length of the line segment joining the given points is $\sqrt{85}$.

11. In a right triangle the length of the altitude drawn to the hypotenuse is the mean proportional between the lengths of the segments it forms on the hypotenuse.

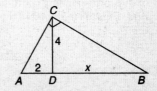

If $x = DB$, then:

$$\frac{x}{CD} = \frac{CD}{AD}$$

Substitute the given values of CD and AD:

$$\frac{x}{4} = \frac{4}{2}$$

In a proportion the product of the means equals the product of the extremes (cross-multiply):

$$2x = 4 \cdot 4$$

$$x = \frac{16}{2}$$

$$x = 8$$

The length of $\overline{DB}$ is **8**.

12. The value of $(i \times i) \times i$ is determined by first evaluating the expression within the parentheses using the accompanying table.

Since the intersection of the horizontal row labeled i and the vertical column labeled i is the element -1, $i \times i = -1$. Thus,

$\times$	1	i	-1	i
1	1	i	-1	$-i$
i	i	-1	$-i$	1
-1	-1	$-i$	1	i
$-i$	$-i$	1	i	-1

$$(i \times i) \times i = -1 \times i$$

To evaluate $-1 \times i$, find the element in the table at which the horizontal row labeled -1 intersects the vertical column labeled i. This element is $-i$. Hence, $-1 \times i = -i$.

The value of $(i \times i) \times i$ is **$-i$**.

13. A line whose equation has the form $y = mx + b$ has a slope of m and a y-intercept of b.

For the given equation, $y = 3x - 7$, $m = 3$, so the slope of the line it represents is 3. A line that is parallel to this line must have the same slope. If this line also passes through the origin, then its y-intercept is 0.

The line that passes through the origin and is parallel to the line whose equation is $y = 3x - 7$ has an equation in which $m = 3$ and $b = 0$. Hence, its equation is $y = 3x$.

An equation of the line that passes through the origin and is parallel to the given line is **$y = 3x$**.

14. The x and y coordinates of the midpoint of a segment are the averages of the corresponding coordinates of the endpoints of the segment. In general, if $(\bar{x}, \bar{y})$ is the midpoint of the segment whose endpoints are (x_1, y_1) and (x_2, y_2), then

$$\bar{x} = \frac{x_1 + x_2}{2} \quad \text{and} \quad \bar{y} = \frac{y_1 + y_2}{2}$$

Since the coordinates of the midpoint of $\overline{AB}$ are given as $(6,8)$, let $x = 6$ and $y = 8$. Since the coordinates of A are given as $(3,2)$, let $x_1 = 3$ and $y_1 = 2$.

Let (x,y) represent the coordinates of point B. Hence,

$$\bar{x} = \frac{x_1 + x_2}{2} \qquad \text{and} \qquad \bar{y} = \frac{y_1 + y_2}{2}$$

$$6 = \frac{3 + x}{2} \qquad\qquad\qquad 8 = \frac{2 + y}{2}$$

$$2 \cdot 6 = \overset{1}{\cancel{2}} \left(\frac{3 + x}{\cancel{2}} \right) \qquad 2 \cdot 8 = \overset{1}{\cancel{2}} \left(\frac{2 + y}{\cancel{2}} \right)$$

$$12 = 3 + x \qquad\qquad\qquad 16 = 2 + y$$

$$9 = x \qquad\qquad\qquad\qquad 14 = y$$

The coordinates of point B are **(9,14)**.

15. If the lengths of two sides of an *isosceles* triangle are 8 and 10, then the length of the remaining side must be equal to the length of one of the given sides of the isosceles triangle. Hence, choice (1), which gives 6 as the answer, can be eliminated.

The length of the third side of the triangle must also satisfy the condition that the length of each side of a triangle is less than the sum of the lengths of the other two sides. Test 8 and 10 as possible lengths of the third side.

Assume that the length of the third side is 8. Since $8 < 8 + 10$ and $10 < 8 + 8$ are both true statements, the length of the third side may be 8. Next, assume that the length of the third side is 10. Since $10 < 8 + 10$ and $8 < 10 + 10$, the length of the third side may also be 10. Since *both* 8 and 10 are possible answers, choices (2) and (3) are wrong.

The correct choice is **(4)**.

16. If the image of (x,y) under a certain translation is $(x - 2, y + 4)$, then the image of $(-3, -1)$ under the same translation is $(-3 - 2, -1 + 4) = (-5, 3)$.

The correct choice is **(3)**.

17. The binomial factors of the given quadratic trinominal, $3x^2 + 7x - 20$, have the form $(3x + ?)$ and $(x + ?)$ since $3x$ and x are the factors of $3x^2$.

The product of the missing terms must be -20. The choices in the question suggest that we limit the possibilities of the factors of -20 to ± 4 and ± 5. The correct pair of numbers must be chosen and placed within the parentheses so that the sum of the inner and outer cross products is $+7x$, the middle term of the quadratic trinomial that is being factored.

Try the different placements of -5 and $+4$:

$$\overset{+4x}{\overset{\wedge}{(3x+4)(x-5)}} \qquad \overset{-5x}{\overset{\wedge}{(3x-5)(x+4)}}$$
$$\underset{-15x}{} \qquad\qquad\qquad \underset{+12x}{}$$

Notice that the product $(3x + 4)(x - 5)$ is not the correct factorization since $+4x + (-15x) = -11x$. The product $(3x - 5)(x + 4)$ is the correct factorization since $(-5x) + (+12x) = +7x$.

The correct choice is **(3)**.

18. The given quadrilateral has congruent diagonals that are not perpendicular, and it contains no right angles.

Since the quadrilateral contains no right angles, it cannot be a square or a rectangle, thereby eliminating choices (1) and (3).

An isosceles trapezoid and a rhombus both have congruent diagonals. However, a rhombus has the additional property that the diagonals are perpendicular to each other, eliminating choice (4).

An isosceles trapezoid has congruent diagonals that are not perpendicular, and it contains no right angles.

The correct choice is **(2)**.

19. The number π does not have an exact decimal representation and is, therefore, irrational.

The correct choice is **(4)**.

20. An equation having the form $y = mx + b$ represents a line whose slope is m and whose y-intercept is b.

The equation in choice (1) may be written as $y = 0x + 1$, so its slope is 0.

Notice that a line whose equation has the form $y = b$ is a horizontal line whose slope is 0, and a line whose equation has the form $x = a$, as in choice (2), is a vertical line whose slope is not defined.

The equation in choice (3) may be written as $y = -x + 5$, so the line it represents has a slope of -1.

The equation in choice (4) may be written as $y = x - 3$, so the line it represents has a slope of 1.

The correct choice is **(1)**.

21. In general, DeMorgan's law states that

$$\sim(p \vee q) = \sim p \wedge \sim q \text{ and } \sim(p \wedge q) = \sim p \vee \sim q$$

Apply DeMorgan's law to each choice in turn and compare the result with the given statement, $\sim p \vee q$:

Choice (1): $\sim(p \wedge \sim q) = \sim p \vee \sim(\sim q) = \sim p \vee q.$ (This matches the given statement.)

Choice (2): $\sim(p \vee \sim q) = \sim p \wedge \sim(\sim q) = \sim p \wedge q.$

Choice (3): $\sim(p \vee q) = \sim p \wedge \sim q.$

Choice (4): $\sim(p \wedge q) = \sim p \vee \sim q.$

The correct choice is **(1)**.

22.

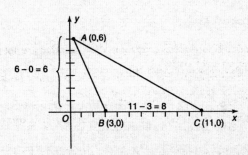

The area of a triangle is equal to one-half the product of the lengths of its base and altitude. The coordinates of the vertices of the given triangle are $A(0,6)$, $B(3,0)$, and $C(11,0)$.

Since $\overline{BC}$ is a horizontal segment, it is convenient to choose it as the base of the triangle. The length of $\overline{BC}$ is the positive difference of the x-coordinates of its endpoints, which is $11 - 3$ or 8 units.

The altitude of $\triangle ABC$ is vertical segment $\overline{OA}$. Since $\triangle ABC$ is obtuse, $\overline{OA}$ falls outside the triangle. The length of $\overline{OA}$ is the positive difference of the y-coordinates of its endpoints, which is $6 - 0$ or 6 units.

Hence,

$$\text{Area } \triangle ABC = \frac{1}{2}(8 \times 6) = \frac{1}{2}(48) = 24 \text{ square units}$$

The correct choice is **(3)**.

23.

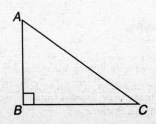 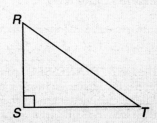

In the two given right triangles, legs $\overline{AB}$ and $\overline{RS}$ are given as congruent and hypotenuses $\overline{AC}$ and $\overline{RT}$ are given as congruent.

Two right triangles are congruent if a leg and the hypotenuse of one right triangle are congruent to the corresponding parts of the other right triangle. This theorem is sometimes abbreviated as "HL $\cong$ HL."

Hence, right triangles ABC and RST are congruent as a consequence of HL $\cong$ HL.

The correct choice is **(3)**.

24. The given equation, $y = -\frac{1}{2}x + 5$, is in the form $y = mx + b$, where m is the slope of the line and b is its y-intercept. Since $m = -\frac{1}{2}$, the slope of $y = -\frac{1}{2}x + 5$ is $-\frac{1}{2}$.

A line that is perpendicular to a line whose slope is $-\frac{1}{2}$ must have a slope that is the negative reciprocal of $-\frac{1}{2}$ of that is, a slope of 2.

The only equation among the choices in which the slope of the line is 2 is $y = 2x - 1$, choice (1).

The correct choice is **(1)**.

25. If $\cos x = \frac{2}{5}$, then $\cos x = 0.4000$. In the Table of Natural Trigonometric Functions, look in the cosine column for the two consecutive decimal numbers between which 0.4000 lies. Notice that $\cos 66° = .4067$ and $\cos 67° = .3907$.

The positive difference between .4000 and .4067 is .0067, while the positive difference between .4000 and .3907 is .0093. Since .4000 is closer to .4097 than it is to .3907, the value of x to the neareast degree is 66°.

The correct choice is **(3)**.

26. If, in a set of n objects, a are identical, b are identical, and c are identical, then the number of different ways in which the n objects can be arranged is

$$\frac{n!}{a!\,b!\,c!}$$

The word "TENNESSEE" consists of nine letters, including four identical letter E's, two identical letter N's, and two identical letter S's. To find the number of different nine-letter arrangements that can be formed from the letters in the word "TENNESSEE," let $n = 9$, $a = 4$, $b = 2$, and $c = 2$:

$$\frac{n!}{a!\,b!\,c!} = \frac{9!}{4!\,2!\,2!}$$

The correct choice is (2).

27. The locus of points 4 units from point $(2,-1)$ is a circle whose center is $(2,-1)$ and whose radius is 4. In general, the equation of a circle whose center is at (h, k) and whose radius is r is

$$(x-h)^2 + (y-k)^2 = r^2$$

Let $h = 2$, $k = -1$, $r = 4$.
Then:

$$(x-2)^2 + (y-(-1))^2 = 4^2$$
$$(x-2)^2 + (y+1)^2 = 16$$

The correct choice is (1).

28. The y-intercept of a graph is the y-coordinate of the point at which the graph crosses the y-axis.

The x-coordinate at this point is, therefore, 0. Thus, to find the y-intercept of the graph of $y = x^2 + 5x - 6$, let $x = 0$:

$$y = 0^2 + 5 \cdot 0 - 6 = -6$$

The correct choice is (4).

29. By definition,

$$\sin \angle E = \frac{\text{Length of side opposite } \angle E}{\text{Length of hypotenuse}}$$

$$= \frac{4}{5}$$

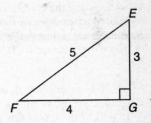

The correct choice is (4).

30. Solve the given quadratic equation, $x^2 - 4x - 3 = 0$, by substituting into the formula

$$x = \frac{-b \pm \sqrt{b^2 - 4ac}}{2a}$$

where $a = 1$, $b = -4$, and $c = -3$:

$$x = \frac{-(-4) \pm \sqrt{(-4)^2 - 4(1)(-3)}}{2(1)}$$

$$= \frac{4 \pm \sqrt{16 + 12}}{2}$$

$$= \frac{4 \pm \sqrt{28}}{2}$$

$$= \frac{4 \pm \sqrt{4 \cdot 7}}{2}$$

$$= \frac{4 \pm 2\sqrt{7}}{2}$$

$$= \frac{4}{2} \pm \frac{2\sqrt{7}}{2}$$

$$= 2 \pm \sqrt{7}$$

The correct choice is **(3)**.

31. Two statements are logically equivalent if they always have the same truth value.

A conditional, $p \rightarrow q$, and its contrapositive, $\sim q \rightarrow \sim p$, are logically equivalent statements. To form the contrapositive of the given conditional statement, "If we recycle, then the amount of trash in landfills is reduced," interchange the hypothesis and the conclusion and then negate both parts of the conditional.

The contrapositive of the given conditional is, "If the amount of trash in landfills is not reduced, then we did not recycle."

The correct choice is **(2)**.

32. The probability of an event is defined as the number of favorable outcomes divided by the total number of possible outcomes.

In finding the probability that a dart will hit inside a circle that is inscribed in a square, the area of the circle corresponds to the number of favorable outcomes.

Since it is assumed that the dart hits the square, the area of the square corresponds to the total number of possible outcomes. Thus,

$$P(\text{Dart hits inside circle}) = \frac{\text{Area of inscribed circle}}{\text{Area of square}} = \frac{\pi(\text{radius})^2}{(\text{side})^2}$$

If a circle is inscribed in a square, then the diameter of the circle will be the same length as a side of the square. Since the length of a side of the square is given as 2, the diameter of the circle is 2 and its radius is 1. Hence,

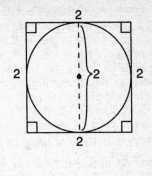

$$P(\text{Dart hits inside circle}) = \frac{\pi(\text{radius})^2}{(side)^2}$$

$$= \frac{\pi(1^2)}{(2^2)}$$

$$= \frac{\pi \cdot 1}{4} = \frac{\pi}{4}$$

The correct choice is **(4)**.

33. The graph of one given equation, $x^2 + y^2 = 16$, is a circle whose center is at the origin and whose radius is 4.

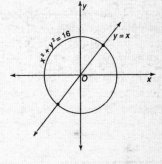

The other given equation, $y = x$, represents an oblique line that passes through the origin, so that it intersects the circle in two distinct points.

The correct choice is **(2)**.

34. The notation $_{11}C_2$ represents the number of different ways in which 2 objects can be selected from a set of 11 objects when the order of the objects selected does not matter.

This is numerically equivalent to finding the number of different ways in which 9 objects from the same set of 11 objects are *not* selected; that is, $_{11}C_2 = {_{11}C_9}$.

The correct choice is **(2)**.

35. To construct a line through C perpendicular to $\overleftrightarrow{ACB}$, follow these steps:

STEP 1: Placing the point of the compass on C and using any convenient compass setting (radius length), construct an arc that intersects $\overleftrightarrow{ACB}$ at two points. Label these points X and Y.

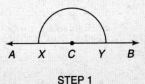

STEP 1

STEP 2: With the point of the compass on X, choose a compass setting such that the radius length is greater than the distance from X to C.

STEP 3: Using this compass setting, swing an arc. Using the same compass setting and placing the point of the compass on Y, swing another arc. Label the point at which the two arcs intersect D.

STEP 4: Using a straight-edge, draw $\overleftrightarrow{CD}$. $\overleftrightarrow{CD}$ is perpendicular to $\overleftrightarrow{ACB}$.

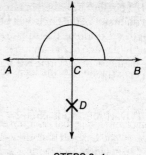

STEPS 2–4

PART II

36 a. The locus of points 3 units from point (2,3) is a circle whose center is (2,3) and whose radius is 3.

To help draw the circle, locate a few convenient points on the circle. For example, the coordinates of the endpoints of the diameter that is parallel to the y-axis are (2,6) and (2,0). The coordinates of the endpoints of the diameter that is parallel to the x-axis are (–1,3) and (5,3).

The graph is labeled a in the accompanying figure.

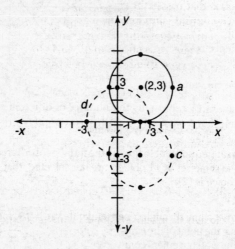

b. In general, the equation of a circle whose center is at (h,k) and whose radius is r is

$$(x-h)^2 + (y-k)^2 = r^2$$

Let $h = 2, k = 3, r = 3$.
Then:
$$(x - 2)^2 + (y - 3)^2 = 3^2$$
$$(x - 2)^2 + (y - 3)^2 = 9$$

The equation for the locus drawn in part **a** is $(x - 2)^2 + (y - 3)^2 = 9$.

c. If the circle drawn in part **a** is reflected in the x-axis, then its image is a congruent circle that is obtained by "flipping" the original circle on the opposite side of the x-axis so that the x-axis is a horizontal line of symmetry.

The image of each point (x,y) of the original circle is now the point $(x,-y)$. Since the center of the original circle is $(2,3)$ the center of the reflection of this circle is $(2,3)$.

The coordinates of a few additional image points of the circle that is being reflected may be determined by applying the rule $(x,y) \rightarrow (x,-y)$ to the four sample points used to help sketch the original circle in part **a**: $(2,6) \rightarrow (2,-6), (2,0) \rightarrow (2,0), (-1,3) \rightarrow (-1,-3)$, and $(5,3) \rightarrow (5,-3)$. Use points $(2,-6), (2,0), (-1,-3)$, and $(5, -3)$ to help sketch the reflection in the x-axis of the circle labeled a.

The reflected circle is sketched and labeled c in the accompanying figure.

d. If the circle drawn in part **c** is translated according to the given rule $(x,y) \rightarrow (x - 2, y + 3)$, then its image is a congruent circle that is obtained by "sliding" the circle labeled **c** two units horizontally to the *left* and three units vertically *up*. Since the circle that is being translated has its center at $(2,-3)$, its image has its center at $(2 - 2, -3 + 3) = (0,0)$.

The coordinates of a few additional image points may be determined by applying the translation rule $(x,y) \rightarrow (x - 2, y + 3)$ to the four sample points used to help sketch the circle in part **c**:

$(2,-6)$	$\rightarrow$	$(2 - 2, -6 + 3) = (0,-3)$
$(2,0)$	$\rightarrow$	$(2 - 2, 0 + 3) = (0,3)$
$(-1,-3)$	$\rightarrow$	$(-1 - 2, -3 + 3) = (-3,0)$
$(5,-3)$	$\rightarrow$	$(5 - 2, -3 + 3) = (3,0)$

Use points $(0,-3), (0,3), (-3,0)$, and $(3,0)$ to help sketch the translation of the graph labeled c.

The translated circle is sketched and labeled d in the accompanying figure.

37. a. Prepare a table of values for x and y by substituting each integer value of x, from 0 to 6 inclusive, in the given equation, $y = x^2 - 6x + 7$, to obtain the corresponding value of y:

x	$x^2 - 6x + 7$	$= y$
0	$0^2 - 6 \cdot 0 + 7 = 0 + 7$	$= 7$
1	$1^2 - 6 \cdot 1 + 7 = 1 - 6 + 7$	$= 2$
2	$2^2 - 6 \cdot 2 + 7 = 4 - 12 + 7$	$= -1$
3	$3^2 - 6 \cdot 3 + 7 = 9 - 18 + 7$	$= -2$
4	$4^2 - 6 \cdot 4 + 7 = 16 - 24 + 7$	$= -1$
5	$5^2 - 6 \cdot 5 + 7 = 25 - 30 + 7$	$= 2$
6	$6^2 - 6 \cdot 6 + 7 = 36 - 36 + 7$	$= 7$

Plot points $(0,7)$, $(1,2)$, $(2,-1)$, $(3,-2)$, $(4,-1)$, $(5,2)$, and $(6,7)$. Connect the points with a smooth curve that has the shape of a parabola whose turning point is at $(3,-2)$.

This curve represents the graph of $y = x^2 - 6x + 7$ in the interval $0 \le x \le 6$.

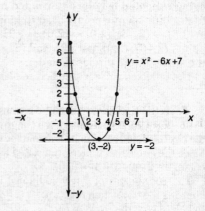

b. The x-intercepts of the graph drawn in part **a** represent the roots of $x^2 - 6x + 7 = 0$. The smaller x-intercept lies between 1 and 2.

Hence, the smaller root of $x^2 - 6x + 7 = 0$ lies between **1 and 2**.

c. As shown in the accompanying figure, the graph of $y = -2$ is a horizontal line that is 2 units below the x-axis.

d. Since the line $y = -2$ intersects the parabola at one point, its vertex, there is **1** solution for the equations $y = x^2 - 6x + 7$ and $y = -2$.

38. Given : $(K \wedge L) \rightarrow M$
             $N \rightarrow {\sim}M$
             $L \vee O$
             $O \rightarrow P$
             K
             N
   Prove : P

PROOF

Statement	Reason
1. N	1. Given.
2. $N \rightarrow \sim M$	2. Given.
3. $\sim M$	3. Law of detachment (steps 1, 2).
4. $(K \wedge L) \rightarrow M$	4. Given.
5. $\sim (K \wedge L)$	5. Law of modus tollens (steps 3, 4).
6. $\sim K \vee \sim L$	6. DeMorgan's law.
7. K	7. Given.
8. $\sim L$	8. Law of disjunctive inference (steps 6, 7).
9. $L \vee O$	9. Given.
10. O	10. Law of disjunctive inference (steps 8, 9).
11. $O \rightarrow P$	11. Given.
12. P	12. Law of detachment (steps 10, 11).

39. a. The length of the altitude drawn to the hypotenuse of a right triangle is the mean proportional between the lengths of the segments the altitude forms on the hypotenuse.

In the given right triangle, CAT: $\dfrac{TP}{AP} = \dfrac{AP}{PC}$.

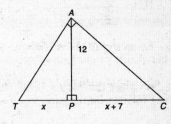

Since $TP = x$, $PC = x + 7$, and $AP = 12$: $\dfrac{x}{12} = \dfrac{12}{x + 7}$

In a proportion, the product of the means equals the product of the extremes (cross-multiply): $x(x + 7) = 12 \cdot 12$

$x^2 + 7x = 144$

Write the quadratic equation in standard form so that 0 is on the right side: $x^2 + 7x - 144 = 0$

Factor the quadratic trinomial as the product of two binomials. The first terms of each binomial factor must be x since $x \cdot x = x^2$:

$$(x + ?)(x + ?) = 0$$

The missing pair of numbers in the binomial factors must be two numbers whose product is -144 and whose sum is $+7$. The two numbers that satisfy this condition are -9 and $+16$:

$$(x - 9)(x + 16) = 0$$

If the product of two factors is 0, then either factor may equal 0:

$$x - 9 = 0 \ \lor \ x + 16 = 0$$
$$x = 9 \ \lor \ \quad x = -16$$

Reject the negative solution since x represents the length of a segment:

$$x = 9$$

The length of $\overline{TP}$ is **9**.

b. The area of a triangle is equal to one-half the product of the lengths of its base and its altitude.

In $\triangle CAT$, $\overline{AP}$ is the altitude to base $\overline{TC}$. Since $x = 9$, $TP = 9$ and $PC = 9 + 7 = 16$. Hence, $TC = 9 + 16 = 25$. Thus,

$$\text{Area } \triangle CAT = \frac{1}{2}(AP)(TC)$$
$$= \frac{1}{2}(12)(25)$$
$$= 6(25)$$
$$= 150$$

The area of $\triangle CAT$ is **150**.

c. In right triangle APT, use the tangent ratio to find the degree measure of $\angle T$.

$$\text{Tan } \angle T = \frac{\text{Length of side opposite } \angle T}{\text{Length of side adjacent to } \angle T}$$
$$= \frac{12}{9}$$
$$= 1.3333$$

In the Table of Natural Trigonometric Functions, look in the tangent column for the two consecutive decimal numbers between which 1.3333 lies. Notice that tan $53° = 1.3270$ and tan $54° = 1.3764$.

Since 1.3333 is closer to 1.3270 than it is to 1.3764, the angle is 53°.
The measure of $\angle T$ to the *nearest degree* is **53**.

40. a. The problem states that, in a purse that contains nickels, dimes, and quarters, the number of quarters is 8 more than twice the number of dimes, and the number of nickels is 4 less than the number of dimes. The number of dimes, quarters, and nickels may be represented algebraically as follows:

Let $\quad x \quad$ = the number of dimes in the change purse.
Then $2x + 8$ = the number of quarters in the change purse,
and $\quad x - 4 \quad$ = the number of nickels in the change purse.

If the probability of selecting a quarter is $\dfrac{3}{4}$, then

$$P(\text{Quarter}) = \frac{\text{Number of quarters in change purse}}{\text{Total number of coins in change purse}} = \frac{3}{4}$$

$$= \frac{2x + 8}{x + (2x + 8) + (x - 4)} \qquad = \frac{3}{4}$$

$$= \frac{2x + 8}{4x + 4} \qquad = \frac{3}{4}$$

In a proportion, the product of the means equals the product of the extremes (cross-multiply):

$$4(2x + 8) = 3(4x + 4)$$

Subtract $12x$ and 32 from each side of the equation:

$$8x + 32 = 12x + 12$$
$$\underline{-12x - 32 = -12x - 32}$$
$$-4x \quad = \quad -20$$

Divide each side of the equation by -4:

$$\frac{-4x}{-4} = \frac{-20}{-4}$$
$$x = 5$$

The number of dimes in the change purse = $\quad x = 5.$
The number of quarters in the change purse = $\quad 2x + 8 = 2(5) + 8 = 18.$
The number of nickels in the change purse = $\quad x - 4 = 5 - 4 = 1.$

To find the total value of the coins in the purse, multiply the number of each type of coin by its value in cents, and then add the resulting values:
Total Value = $5(0.10) + 18(0.25) + 1(0.05) = 0.50 + 4.50 + 0.05 = \$5.05$.
The total value of coins in the purse is **\$5.05**.

b. (1) Without regard to order, r objects may be selected from a set of n objects in ${}_nC_r$ ways, where

$$_nC_r = \frac{n!}{r!\,(n-r)!}$$

Since there are 5 dimes, 18 quarters, and 1 nickel, there is a total of 24 coins. Three coins, without considering their order, may be selected from 24 coins in $_{24}C_3$ ways, where

$$_{24}C_3 = \frac{24!}{3!\,(24-3)!} = \frac{24!}{3!\,21!} = \frac{\overset{4}{\cancel{24}} \cdot 23 \cdot 22 \cdot \overset{1}{\cancel{21}!}}{\cancel{6} \cdot \cancel{21}!}$$

$$= 4 \cdot 23 \cdot 22$$

$$= 92 \cdot 22$$

$$= 2024$$

There are **2024** different three-coin selections.

(2) The probability that the three coins selected will be one of each kind is found by writing the product of the number of ways in which 1 dime, 1 quarter, and 1 nickel can each be selected from the set of coins of the same type over the total number of different three-coin selections.

One dime can be selected from a set of 5 dimes in $_5C_1$ ways, 1 quarter can be selected from a set of 18 quarters in $_{18}C_1$ ways, and 1 nickel can be selected from a set of 1 nickel in one way. Hence, the probability that, in a three-coin selection, one of each kind of coin is selected is given by the fraction:

$$\frac{_5C_1 \cdot {}_{18}C_1 \cdot 1}{_{24}C_3}$$

From part (1), $_{24}C_3 = 2024$. Since $_nC_1 = n$, $_5C_1 = 5$, and $_{18}C_1 = 18$:

$$\frac{_5C_1 \cdot {}_{18}C_1 \cdot 1}{_{24}C_3} = \frac{5 \cdot 18 \cdot 1}{2024}$$

$$= \frac{90}{2024}$$

The probability that the three coins selected will be one of each kind is $\dfrac{90}{2024}$.

PART III

41. a. Two lines are parallel only if they have the same slope. In general, the slope, m, of the line joining points (x_1, y_1) and (x_2, y_2) is given by the formula

$$m = \frac{y_2 - y_1}{x_2 - x_1}$$

(1) Find and then compare the slopes of the line segments $\overline{AB}$ and $\overline{CD}$.

To find the slope of the segment whose endpoints are $A(0,0)$ and $B(6a,3b)$, let $(x_1,y_1) = (0,0)$ so $x_1 = 0$ and $y_1 = 0$, and let $(x_2,y_2) = (6a,3b)$ so $x_2 = 6a$ and $y_2 = 3b$. Hence,

$$\text{Slope of } \overline{AB} = \frac{y_2 - y_1}{x_2 - x_1} = \frac{3b - 0}{6a - 0} = \frac{3b}{6a} = \frac{b}{2a}$$

To find the slope of the segment whose endpoints are $C(3a,4b)$ and $D(a,3b)$, let $(x_1,y_1) = (3a,4b)$, so $x_1 = 3a$, and $y_1 = 4b$; and let $(x_2,y_2) = (a,3b)$, so $x_2 = a$, and $y_2 = 3b$. Hence,

$$\text{Slope of } \overline{CD} = \frac{y_2 - y_1}{x_2 - x_1} = \frac{3b - 4b}{a - 3a} = \frac{-b}{-2a} = \frac{b}{2a}$$

Since $\overline{AB}$ and $\overline{CD}$ have the same slope, $\frac{b}{2a}$, $\overline{AB} \parallel \overline{CD}$.

(2) Find and then compare the slopes of line segments $\overline{AD}$ and $\overline{BC}$.

To find the slope of the segment whose endpoints are $A(0,0)$ and $D(a,3b)$, let $(x_1,y_1) = (0,0)$ so $x_1 = 0$ and $y_1 = 0$, and let $(x_2,y_2) = (a,3b)$ so $x_2 = a$ and $y_2 = 3b$. Hence,

$$\text{Slope of } \overline{AD} = \frac{y_2 - y_1}{x_2 - x_1} = \frac{3b - 0}{a - 0} = \frac{3b}{a}$$

To find the slope of the segment whose endpoints are $B(6a,3b)$ and $C(3a,4b)$, let $(x_1,y_1) = (6a,3b)$ so $x_1 = 6a$ and $y_1 = 3b$, and let $(x_2,y_2) = (3a,4b)$ so $x_2 = 3a$ and $y_2 = 4b$. Hence,

$$\text{Slope of } \overline{BC} = \frac{y_2 - y_1}{x_2 - x_1} = \frac{4b - 3b}{3a - 6a} = \frac{b}{-3a} = -\frac{b}{3a}$$

Since $\overline{AB}$ and $\overline{CD}$ have different slopes, $\overline{AD}$ is *not* parallel to $\overline{BC}$.

b. Quadrilateral $ABCD$ is a trapezoid because it has exactly one pair of parallel sides.

42.

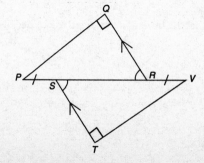

Given : $\overline{PSRV}$, $\overline{PS} \cong \overline{VR}$, $\overline{RQ} \parallel \overline{ST}$, $\overline{PQ} \perp \overline{QR}$, and $\overline{VT} \perp \overline{TS}$.

Prove : $\overline{PQ} \cong \overline{VT}$

Plan: Since $\overline{PQ}$ and $\overline{VT}$ are corresponding sides of triangles PQR and VTS. respectively, prove that these triangles are congruent by AAS $\cong$ AAS.

PROOF

Statement	Reason
1. $\overline{PQ} \perp \overline{QR}$ and $\overline{VT} \perp \overline{TS}$	1. Given.
2. Angles Q and T are right angles.	2. If two lines are perpendicular, they intersect to form right angles.
3. $\angle Q \cong \angle T$ (Angle)	3. All right angles are congruent.
4. $\overline{RQ} \parallel \overline{ST}$	4. Given.
5. $\angle PRQ \cong \angle VST$ (Angle)	5. If two lines are parallel, then alternate interior angles are congruent.
6. $\overline{PSRV}$, $\overline{PS} \cong \overline{VR}$	6. Given.
7. $PS = VR$	7. If two segments are congruent, then they are equal in length.
8. $SR = SR$	8. Reflexive property of equality.
9. $PR = VS$	9. Addition and substitution properties of equality.
10. $\overline{PR} \cong \overline{VS}$ (Side)	10. If two segments have the same length, then they are congruent.
11. $\triangle PQR \cong \triangle VTS$	11. AAS $\cong$ AAS.
12. $\overline{PQ} \cong \overline{VT}$	12. Corresponding sides of congruent triangles are congruent.

Topic	Question Numbers	Number of Points	Your Points	Your Percentage
1. Properties of Number Systems; Def. of Operations	4, 12, 19	2 + 2 + 2 = 6		
2. Finite Mathematical Systems				
3. Linear Function & Graph ($y = mx + b$, slope, eqs. of)	13, 24	2 + 2 = 4		
4. Quadratic Equation (alg. sol.—factoring, formula)	30	2		
5. Parabola (incl. axis of symmetry, turning point)	37	10		
6. Systems of Equations (alg. and graphic solutions)	—	—		
7. Suppls., Compl., Vertical Angles, Angle Measure	—	—		
8. Triangle Properties (eq., isos., sum ∠s, 2 sides)	3, 5, 15	2 + 2 + 2 = 6		
9. Line ‖ One Side of Δ; Line Joining Midpts. of 2 Sides	2	2		
10. Inequalities in Δs (ext. ∠, ≠ sides, and opp. ∠s)	—	—		
11. Quadrilateral Properties (▱, sq., rhom., rect., trap.)	18	2		
12. Parallel Lines	1, 8	2 + 2 = 4		
13. Alg. Oper.; Verbal Probs.	9, 17	2 + 2 = 4		
14. Mean Proportional; Alt. to Hypot. of Right Δ	11, 39a	2 + 5 = 7		
15. Pythag. Th., Special Rt. Δs (3-4-5, 5-12-13, 30-60-90)	7	2		
16. Similar Figures (ratios & proportions	—	—		
17. Areas (Δ, rect., ▱, rhom., trap.)	22, 39b	2 + 2 = 4		
18. Locus	27, 36a, b	2 + 3 + 2 = 7		
19. Constructions	35	2		
20. Deductive Proofs	23, 42	2 + 10 = 12		
21. Coordinate Geom. (slope, dist., midpt., eq. of circle)	10, 14, 20, 28, 33	2 + 2 + 2 + 2 +2 = 10		
22. Coordinate Geom. "Proofs"	41	10		
23. Logic	21, 31, 38	2 + 2 + 10 = 14		
24. Permutations; Arrangements	26	2		
25. Combinations	34, 40b	2 + 5 = 7		
26. Probability	32, 40a	2 + 5 = 7		
27. Trig. of Rt. Δ	25, 29, 39c	2 + 2 + 3 = 7		
28. Literal Eqs.	—	—		
29. Transformations	6, 16, 36, c, d	2 + 2 + 2 + 3 = 9		

Examination January 1994

Sequential Math Course II

PART I

Answer 30 questions from this part. Each correct answer will receive 2 credits. No partial credit will be allowed. Write your answers in the spaces provided. Where applicable, answers may be left in terms of π or in radical form. [60]

1 The lengths of the sides of a triangle are 4, 6, and 7. If the length of the longest side of a similar triangle is 21, find the perimeter of the larger triangle.

1_____

2 The measure of an exterior angle of a triangle is 120°, and the measure of one interior angle of the triangle is 50°. Find the number of degrees in the measure of the largest angle of the triangle.

2_____

3 Using the accompanying table, solve for y if $a \heartsuit y = c \heartsuit d$.

$\heartsuit$	a	b	c	d
a	b	c	d	a
b	c	d	a	b
c	d	a	b	c
d	a	b	c	d

3____

4 If $\sin A = 0.3642$, find the measure of $\angle A$ to the *nearest degree*.

4____

5 In the accompanying diagram of $\triangle ABC$, D is the midpoint of $\overline{AB}$ and E is the midpoint of $\overline{BC}$. If $DE = 5$ and $AC = 2x - 20$, find x.

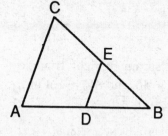

5____

6 If one root of the equation $x^2 + 5x + c = 0$ is -2, find the value of c.

6____

7 In the accompanying diagram, $\triangle IHJ \sim \triangle LKJ$. If $IH = 5$, $HJ = 2$, and $LK = 7$, find KJ.

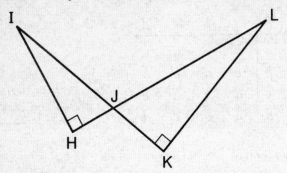

7____

8 Express, in radical form, the distance between the points whose coordinates are $(2,4)$ and $(-2,5)$.

8____

9 Solve for x: $\dfrac{2}{x} + \dfrac{1}{7} = \dfrac{4}{x}$, $x \neq 0$

9____

10 Solve for all values of x:

$$\frac{6}{x - 1} = \frac{x}{2}, \ x \neq 1$$

10____

11 In the accompanying diagram of right triangle ABC, $m\angle C = 90$, $m\angle A = 45$, and $AC = 1$. Find, in radical form, the length of $\overline{AB}$.

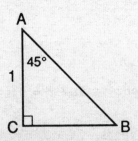

11____

12 What is the total number of ways a committee of
three can be chosen from a group of five people?   12____

13 Express in lowest terms: $\dfrac{x^2 - 9}{x^2 + 3x}$, $x \neq 0, -3$ 13____

Directions (14–34): For *each* question chosen, write in the space
provided the *numeral* preceding the word or expression that best
completes the statement or answers the question.

14 The y-intercept of the line whose equation is
$y = 3x - 2$ is

(1) -2 (3) 3

(2) 2 (4) $\frac{1}{3}$ 14____

15 In the accompanying diagram, line ℓ is parallel to
line m, and lines s and t are transversals that
intersect at a point on line m.

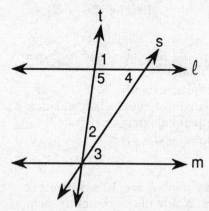

Which statement must be true?
(1) $m\angle 1 = m\angle 4$
(2) $m\angle 4 = m\angle 2$
(3) $m\angle 1 = m\angle 2 + m\angle 3$
(4) $m\angle 5 = m\angle 2 + m\angle 3$ 15____

16 Given: line ℓ and point P not on ℓ. According to the Euclidean parallel postulate, how many lines pass through P that are parallel to ℓ?

(1) 1
(2) 2
(3) an infinite number
(4) 0

16_____

17 Which is an equation of the locus of points whose ordinates are three less than twice their abscissas?

(1) $y = 2x + 3$ (3) $x = 2y + 3$
(2) $y = 2x - 3$ (4) $x = 2y - 3$

17_____

18 A translation moves point $A(4,-2)$ onto point $A'(0,2)$. What is the image of (x,y) under this translation?

(1) $(x + 2, y)$ (3) $(x - 2, y + 2)$
(2) $(x - 4, y + 4)$ (4) $(x + 4, y + 2)$

18_____

19 Which statement would *never* be used to prove that a figure is a rhombus?

(1) The figure is a quadrilateral.
(2) The figure has a pair of equal adjacent sides.
(3) The figure is a parallelogram.
(4) The figure is a rectangle.

19_____

20 The diagonals of a rhombus are 10 centimeters and 24 centimeters. A side of the rhombus measures

(1) 10 cm   (3) 24 cm
(2) 13 cm   (4) 26 cm

20_____

21 Given: points $A(1,2)$, $B(4,5)$, and $C(6,7)$. Which statement is true?
   (1) AB is equal to BC.
   (2) $\overline{AB}$ is perpendicular to $\overline{BC}$.
   (3) Points A, B, and C are collinear.
   (4) The slope of $\overline{AC}$ is -1.   21_____

22 In $\triangle QRS$, $m\angle Q = x$, $m\angle R = 8x - 40$, and $m\angle S = 2x$. Which type of triangle is $\triangle QRS$?
   (1) isosceles   (3) acute
   (2) right   (4) obtuse   22_____

23 Which statement is logically equivalent to $\sim(q \wedge \sim s)$?
   (1) $\sim q \wedge s$ (3) $\sim q \vee s$
   (2) $q \wedge \sim s$ (4) $q \vee \sim s$ 23_____

24 The coordinates of the image of $P(3,-4)$ under a reflection in the x-axis are
   (1) $(3,-4)$ (3) $(3,4)$
   (2) $(-3,4)$ (4) $(-3,-4)$ 24_____

25 Which is an equation of a line that is perpendicular to the line whose equation is $y = \frac{1}{3}x - 2$?

   (1) $y = -3x + 2$ (3) $y = -\frac{1}{3}x + 2$

   (2) $y = 3x + 2$ (4) $y = \frac{1}{3}x + 2$ 25_____

26 If the lengths of two sides of a triangle are 4 and 7, the length of the third side can *not* be

(1) 11   (3) 5

(2) 7   (4) 4   26____

27 Which is an equation of the circle whose center is (0,4) and whose radius is 3?

(1) $x^2 + (y - 4)^2 = 3$

(2) $x^2 + (y - 4)^2 = 9$

(3) $(x - 4)^2 + (y - 3)^2 = 0$

(4) $(x - 4)^2 + y^2 = 9$ 27____

28 A set contains four distinct quadrilaterals: a parallelogram, a rectangle, a rhombus, and a square. If one quadrilateral is selected from the set at random, what is the probability that the diagonals of that quadrilateral bisect each other?

(1) 1   (3) $\frac{2}{4}$

(2) $\frac{1}{4}$ (4) $\frac{3}{4}$ 28____

29 Which transformation moves (x,y) to $(5x,5y)$?

(1) reflection   (3) translation

(2) rotation   (4) dilation   29____

30 In the accompanying diagram, $\overline{MN} \perp \overline{NP}$, $\overline{QP} \perp \overline{PN}$, O is the midpoint of $\overline{NP}$, and $\overline{MN} \cong \overline{QP}$.

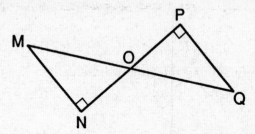

Which reason would be *least* likely to be used to prove $\triangle MNO \cong \triangle QPO$?

(1) HL $\cong$ HL

(2) AAS $\cong$ AAS

(3) SAS $\cong$ SAS

(4) ASA $\cong$ ASA   30____

31 Which is an equation of the axis of symmetry of the graph of the equation $y = 2x^2 - 5x + 3$?

(1) $x = -\frac{5}{2}$ (3) $x = -\frac{5}{4}$

(2) $x = \frac{5}{2}$ (4) $x = \frac{5}{4}$ 31____

32 In the accompanying diagram, the legs of right triangle ABC are 5 and 12 and the hypotenuse is 13.

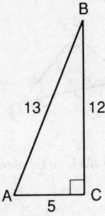

What is the value of cos A?

(1) $\frac{12}{13}$ (3) $\frac{5}{13}$

(2) $\frac{13}{5}$ (4) $\frac{12}{5}$ 32____

33 Given the true statements:

$$\sim a \lor \sim b$$
$$b$$
$$c \to a$$

Which statement is also true?

(1) c (3) $\sim c$

(2) $\sim b$ (4) a 33____

34 Which statement is logically equivalent to the statement: "If you are not part of the solution, then you are part of the problem"?

  (1) If you are part of the solution, then you are not part of the problem.

  (2) If you are not part of the problem, then you are part of the solution.

  (3) If you are part of the problem, then you are not part of the solution.

  (4) If you are not part of the problem, then you are not part of the solution.

34_____

DIRECTIONS (35): *Show all construction lines.*

35 Construct an angle congruent to angle *B* of hexagon *ABCDEF*, using point *W* as the vertex.

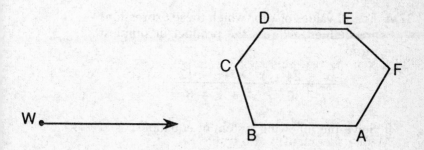

PART II

Answer three questions from this part. Clearly indicate the necessary steps, including appropriate formula substitutions, diagrams, graphs, charts, etc. Calculations that may be obtained by mental arithmetic or the calculator do not need to be shown. [30]

36 *a* On graph paper, draw the graph of the equation $y = x^2 - 4x + 3$, including all values of x in the interval $-1 \leq x \leq 5$. [4]

 b On the same set of axes, draw the graph of the image of the graph drawn in part *a* after the translation which moves (x,y) to $(x + 3, y + 2)$, and label this graph *b*. [3]

 c On the same set of axes, draw the graph of the image of the graph drawn in part *b* after a reflection in the *x*-axis, and label this graph *c*. [3]

37 *a* For all values of x for which these expressions are defined, express the product in simplest form:

$$\frac{4x - 24}{x^2 - 36} \cdot \frac{x^2 + 4x - 12}{x^2 + x - 6} \qquad [4]$$

 b Solve the following system of equations:

$$y = x + 5$$
$$x^2 + y^2 = 97 \qquad [6]$$

38 In the accompanying diagram of $\triangle ABC$, D is a point on $\overline{AB}$ and E is a point on $\overline{BC}$ such that $\overline{DE}$ is parallel to $\overline{AC}$. If DB is 2 less than AD, AC is 5 more than AD, and $DE = 4$, find the length of $\overline{AD}$ to the *nearest tenth*. [5,5]

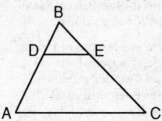

39 As shown in the accompanying diagram, a ship is headed directly toward a coastline formed by a vertical cliff $\overline{BC}$, 70 meters high. At point A, the angle of elevation from the ship to B, the top of the cliff, is 23°. A few minutes later at point D, the angle of elevation increased to 30°.

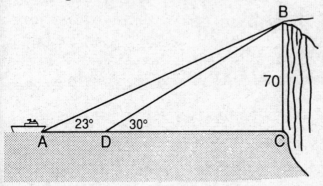

  a To the *nearest meter*, find:
  (1) DC [3]
  (2) AC [3]
  (3) AB [3]

  b To the *nearest meter*, what is the distance between the ship's position at the two sightings? [1]

40 Given: If Ronnie does not waste time in class,
then she does well in Course II.
If Ronnie is absent from class, then her
grades will go down.
Either Ronnie does not waste time in
class or Ronnie is absent from class.
Ronnie's grades do not go down.

Let T represent: "Ronnie wastes time in class."
Let A represent: "Ronnie is absent from class."
Let S represent: "Ronnie's grades go down."
Let B represent: "Ronnie does well in
Course II."

Prove: Ronnie does well in Course II.   [10]

PART III

Answer one question from this part. Clearly indicate the necessary steps, including appropriate formula substitutions, diagrams, graphs, charts, etc. Calculations that may be obtained by mental arithmetic or the calculator do not need to be shown.   [10]

41 Given: isosceles triangle ABC, $\overline{BA} \cong \overline{BC}$, $\overline{AE} \perp \overline{BC}$, and $\overline{BD} \perp \overline{AC}$.

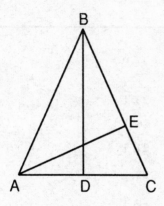

Prove: $\dfrac{AC}{BA} = \dfrac{AE}{BD}$ [10]

42 Quadrilateral $MATH$ has vertices $M(-1,4)$, $A(4,7)$, $T(7,2)$, and $H(2,-1)$. Prove that $MATH$ is a square.   [10]

Answers
January 1994
Sequential Math Course II

Answer Key

PART I

1. 51	**13.** $\dfrac{x-3}{x}$	**25.** 1
2. 70	**14.** 1	**26.** 1
3. b	**15.** 3	**27.** 2
4. 21	**16.** 1	**28.** 1
5. 15	**17.** 2	**29.** 4
6. 6	**18.** 2	**30.** 1
7. $\dfrac{14}{5}$	**19.** 4	**31.** 4
8. $\sqrt{17}$	**20.** 2	**32.** 3
9. 14	**21.** 3	**33.** 3
10. 4, –3	**22.** 4	**34.** 2
11. $\sqrt{2}$	**23.** 3	**35.** construction
12. 10	**24.** 3	

PARTS II AND III See answers explained section.

Answers Explained

PART I

1.

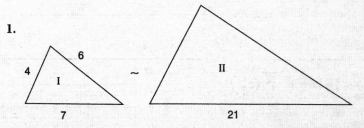

If two triangles are similar, then their perimeters have the same ratio as the lengths of any pair of corresponding sides. Hence, the longest side of the first (smaller) triangle, 7, corresponds to the longest side of the second (larger) triangle, 21.

The perimeter of the smaller triangle is $4 + 6 + 7 = 17$.

Let p = the perimeter of the larger of the two similar triangles. Then:

$$\frac{\text{Perimeter of } \Delta \text{I}}{\text{Perimeter of } \Delta \text{II}} = \frac{\text{Longest side of } \Delta \text{I}}{\text{Longest side of } \Delta \text{II}}$$

$$\frac{17}{p} = \frac{7}{21}$$

Write fractions in lowest terms:

$$\frac{17}{p} = \frac{1}{3}$$

In a proportion the product of the means equals the product of the extremes:

$$(p)\,(1) = (17)(3)$$
$$p = 51$$

The perimeter of the larger triangle is **51**.

2.   If the measure of an exterior angle of a triangle is 120°, then the angle of the triangle that is adjacent to this angle measures $180° - 120° = 60.°$ Since one of the angles of the triangle measures 50°, let x represent the measure of the remaining angle of the triangle.

The sum of the measures of the angles of the triangle is 180. Hence:

$$x + 60° + 50° = 180°$$
$$x + \quad 110° \quad = 180°$$
$$x \quad = 70°$$

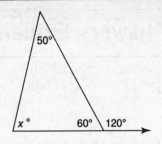

Thus, the three angles of the triangle measure 50°, 60°, and 70°.

The number of degrees in the measure of the largest angle of the triangle is **70**.

3. The accompanying table is given. To solve the given equation, $a \; \heartsuit \; y = c \; \heartsuit \; d$, use the table to determine the value of the right side of the equation.

♥	a	b	c	d
a	b	c	d	a
b	c	d	a	b
c	d	a	b	c
d	a	b	c	d

Since the intersection of the horizontal row labeled c and the vertical column labeled d is c, $c \; \heartsuit \; d = c$. Hence, $a \; \heartsuit \; y = c$.

Solve this equation by determining the heading of the vertical column that intersects horizontal row a at table element c. Since $a \; \heartsuit \; b = c$, the unknown column heading, y, is b.

The solution for y is element **b**.

4. If $\sin A = 0.3642$, then the measure of $\angle A$ can be determined by locating in the Sine column of the Table of Natural Trigonometric Functions the two consecutive decimal values between which 0.3642 lies.

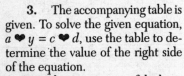

Angle	Sine	
21°	0.3584	
		Difference = 0.0058
A	0.3642	
		Difference = 0.0104
22°	0.3746	

Calculate the positive difference between 0.3642 and the two other decimal values. The measure of $\angle A$, correct to the nearest degree, is the angle that gives the smallest calculated difference.

Since 0.0058 is smaller than 0.0104, $\angle A$ is closer to 21° than it is to 22°.

Angle A, correct to the *nearest degree*, is **21°**.

5.

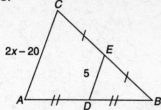

The line segment joining the midpoints of two sides of a triangle is parallel to the third side of the triangle and is one-half of its length. In the accompanying diagram, D and E are midpoints, so DE is one-half of the length of $\overline{AC}$.

Hence: $$DE = \frac{1}{2}AC$$

Substitute 5 for DE and $2x - 20$ for AC: $$5 = \frac{1}{2}(2x - 20)$$

Multiply both sides of the equation by 2: $10 = 2x - 20$
Add 20 to each side of the equation: $+20 = +20$

$$\overline{30 = 2x}$$

Divide each side of the equation by 2: $$\frac{30}{2} = \frac{2x}{2}$$

The value of x is **15**. $15 = x$

6. The given equation is: $x^2 + 5x + c = 0$
Since -2 is a root, substituting -2 for x
satisfies the equation: $(-2)^2 + 5(-2) + c = 0$

Simplify: $4 - 10 + c = 0$

$$-6 + c = 0$$

On each side of the equation add 6: $\underline{+6=+6}$

$$c = 6$$

The value of c is **6**.

7.

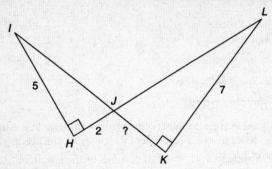

Lengths of corresponding sides of similar triangles are in proportion.   Hence:

$$\frac{KJ}{LK} = \frac{HJ}{IH}$$

Since $IH = 5$, $HJ = 2$, and $LK = 7$:
In a proportion the product of the means equals the product of the extremes:

$$\frac{KJ}{7} = \frac{2}{5}$$

$$(5)(KJ) = (7)(2)$$

Divide each side of the equation by 5:

$$KJ = \frac{14}{5}$$

The length of $\overline{KJ} = \dfrac{14}{5}$.

8.   The distance, D, between points (x_1, y_1) and (x_2, y_2) is given by this formula:

$$D = \sqrt{(x_2 - x_1)^2 + (y_2 - y_1)^2}$$

Let $(x_1, y_1) = (2,4)$ and $(x_2, y_2) = (-2,5)$.
Then $x_1 = 2$, $y_1 = 4$, $x_2 = -2$, and $y_2 = 5$:

$$= (-2 - 2)^2 + (5 - 4)^2$$
$$= (-4)^2 \quad + (1)^2$$
$$= 16 \quad + 1$$
$$= \sqrt{17}$$

The distance, in radical form, between the two given points is $\sqrt{17}$.

9. The given equation is:

$$\frac{2}{x} + \frac{1}{7} = \frac{4}{x}$$

Multiply each term of the equation by $7x$, the lowest common multiple of the denominators:

$$7x\left(\frac{2}{x}\right) + 7x\left(\frac{1}{7}\right) = 7x\left(\frac{4}{x}\right)$$

$$14 \quad + x \quad = 28$$

Subtract 14 from each side of the equation:

$$\underline{-14 \qquad\qquad = -14}$$

$$x = 14$$

The value of x is **14**.

10. The given equation is a proportion:

$$\frac{6}{x-1} = \frac{x}{2}$$

In a proportion the product of the mean is equal to the product of the extremes:

$$x(x-1) = 12$$

Remove the parentheses by multiplying each term inside the parentheses by the term in front of the parentheses:

$$x^2 - x = 12$$

Write the *quadratic* equation in standard form:

$$x^2 - x - 12 = 0$$

The left side of the equation is a quadratic trinomial that can be factored as the product of two binomials:

$$(x + ?)(x + ?) = 0$$

The factors of -12 become the last terms of the binomial factors, but they must be chosen in such a way that their sum is -1, which is the coefficient of the middle term of the quadratic trinomial. Since $(-4)(3) = -12$ and $-4 + 3 = 1$, -4 and 3 are the correct factors of -12:

$$(x - 4)(x + 3) = 0$$

If the product of two factors is 0, then either factor may be 0:

$$x - 4 = 0 \text{ or } x + 3 = 0$$

Solve each linear equation:

$$x = 4 \text{ or } \qquad x = -3$$

The values for x are **4** and **–3**.

11. Since the acute angles of a right triangle are complementary,

$$m\angle B = 90 - m\angle A$$

$$= 90 - 45$$

$$= 45$$

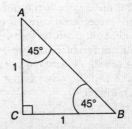

Since the acute angles of right triangle ABC are congruent, the triangle is isosceles with $BC = AC = 1$.

In a right triangle, the square of the length of the hypotenuse is equal to the sum of the squares of the lengths of the legs:

$$(AB)^2 = (BC)^2 + (AC)^2$$
$$= 1^2 + 1^2$$
$$= 2$$
$$AB = \sqrt{2}$$

The length of $\overline{AB}$ is $\sqrt{2}$.

12. The total number of ways a committee of three can be chosen from a group of five people is the number of possible combinations of five people taken three at a time. Thus:

$$_nC_r = \frac{n!}{r!(n-r)!}$$

Let $n = 5$ and $r = 3$:

$$_5C_3 = \frac{5!}{3!\,2!}$$

$$= \frac{5 \cdot \overset{2}{\cancel{4}} \cdot \cancel{3!}}{\cancel{3!} \cdot \cancel{2} \cdot 1}$$

$$= 10$$

A committee of three can be chosen from a group of five people **10** different ways.

13. To express an algebraic fraction in lowest terms, factor the numerator and the denominator and then divide out any factors that are common to both.

The given fraction is:

$$\frac{x^2 - 9}{x^2 + 3x}$$

The numerator is the difference between two perfect squares, x^2 and 9. Thus, the numerator can be factored into the product of two binomials, one of which is the sum of the square roots of the perfect squares and the other is the difference between them:

$$\frac{(x+3)(x-3)}{x^2 + 3x}$$

Factor out the common monomial factor of x from the denominator. The second factor is obtained by dividing x into each term of the original denominator:

$$\frac{(x+3)(x-3)}{x(x+3)}$$

Divide out any factor that appears in both the numerator and the denominator:

$$\frac{\cancel{(x+3)}(x-3)}{x\cancel{(x+3)}}$$

The original fraction, expressed in lowest terms, is $\dfrac{x-3}{x}$.

14.   If an equation of a line has the form $y = mx + b$, then m is the slope of the line and b is its y-intercept.

The given equation, $y = 3x - 2$, is in the form $y = mx + b$, with $m = 3$ and $b = -2$. Hence, the y-intercept of this line is -2.

The correct choice is **(1)**.

15.

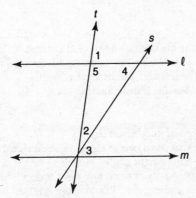

Examine each of the four choices in turn:

Choice (1): Angles 1 and 4 are alternate interior angles formed by a transversal, line ℓ, intersecting lines t and s. Since lines t and s are *not* parallel, $m\angle 1 \neq m\angle 4$. Hence, choice (1) is not correct.

Choice (2): No information is provided about the measures of the angles or the lengths of the sides of the triangle that contains angles 2, 4, and 5. Since angles 4 and 2 may or may not be equal in measure, choice (2) is not correct.

Choice (3): Angle 1 and the angle that is the sum of angles 2 and 3 are corresponding angles formed by a transversal, line t, intersecting lines ℓ and m, which are given as parallel. Since corresponding angles formed by parallel lines have the same measure, m∠1 = m∠2 + m∠3. Thus, choice (3) is correct.

Choice (4): If two lines, such as ℓ and m, are parallel, then interior angles on the same side of the transveral are supplementary. Hence, m∠5 + (m∠2 + m∠3) = 180. Choice (4) is not correct.

The correct choice is (3).

16.

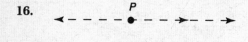

The Euclidean parallel postulate states that, through a given point *not* on a line, there is exactly one line that contains the point and is parallel to the line.

The correct choice is (1).

17. An equation of the locus of all points whose ordinates, y, are three *less than* twice their abscissas, x, is $y = 2x - 3$.

The correct choice is (2).

18. If a translation "moves" point $A(4,-2)$ onto the point $A'(0,2)$, then this translation "moves" point A 4 units horizontally to the left (from 4 to 0), and 4 units vertically up (from -2 to $+2$). Under the same translation, point (x,y) "moves" 4 units horizontally to the left and 4 units vertically up.

Hence, the image of (x, y) under this translation is $(x - 4, y + 4)$.

The correct choice is (2).

19. A rhombus is a special type of quadrilateral.

A rhombus is a parallelogram that has a pair of equal adjacent sides. A rectangle is a parallelogram that contains a right angle.

Since a rhombus does not necessarily contain any right angles, the statement in choice (4), "The figure is a rectangle," would *never* be used to prove that a figure is a rhombus.

The correct choice is (4).

20. The diagonals of a rhombus bisect each other and intersect at right angles, thus forming four congruent right triangles. Each right triangle has a side of the rhombus as its hypotenuse and, in this problem, has legs whose lengths are $\frac{1}{2}(10) = 5$ and $\frac{1}{2}(24) = 12$.

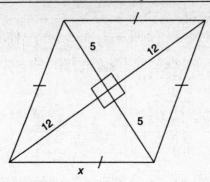

Let x = the length of a side of the rhombus. In a right triangle, the square of the length of the hypotenuse is equal to the sum of the squares of the lengths of the legs:

$$x^2 = 5^2 + 12^2$$
$$= 169$$

Take the square root of each side of the equation:

$$x = \pm \sqrt{169}$$

Reject the negative value as meaningless for length:

$$= 13$$

The correct choice is (2).

21. Given: points $A(1,2)$, $B(4,5)$, and $C(6,7)$.

Let $(x_1, y_1) = A(1,2)$, $(x_2, y_2) = B(4,5)$, and $(x_3, y_3) = C(6,7)$. Consider each of the four choices in turn.

Choice (1): $AB = BC$?

$$AB = \sqrt{(x_2 - x_1)^2 + (y_2 - y_1)^2}$$
$$= \sqrt{(4-1)^2 + (5-2)^2}$$
$$= \sqrt{9+9}$$
$$= \sqrt{18}$$

$$BC = \sqrt{(x_3 - x_2)^2 + (y_3 - y_2)^2}$$
$$= \sqrt{(6-4)^2 + (7-5)^2}$$
$$= \sqrt{4+4}$$
$$= \sqrt{8}$$

Hence, $AB \neq BC$, so choice (1) is not correct.

Choice (2): $\overline{AB} \perp \overline{BC}$?

Two lines are perpendicular if their slopes are negative reciprocals.

Slope of $\overline{AB} = \dfrac{y_2 - y_1}{x_2 - x_1}$	Slope of $\overline{BC} = \dfrac{y_3 - y_2}{x_3 - x_2}$
$= \dfrac{5-2}{4-1}$	$= \dfrac{7-5}{6-4}$
$= \dfrac{3}{3}$	$= \dfrac{2}{2}$
$= 1$	$= 1$

Since the slopes of $\overline{AB}$ and $\overline{BC}$ are equal, $\overline{AB}$ is not perpendicular to $\overline{BC}$ and choice (2) is not correct.

Choice (3): A, B, and C are collinear?

Collinear points are points that lie on the same line. Points A, B, and C are collinear if the slopes of $\overline{AB}$ and $\overline{BC}$ are equal. The work done in investigating choice (2) showed that slope $\overline{AB}$ = slope $\overline{BC}$ =1.

Hence, points A, B, and C are collinear and choice (3) is correct.

Choice (4): Slope of $\overline{AC}$ = –1? The work done in investigating choice (2) showed that slope $\overline{AC}$ = 1, so choice (4) is not correct.

The correct choice is **(3)**.

22. Given: $\qquad\qquad\qquad$ $m\angle Q = x, m\angle R = 8x - 40, m\angle S = 2x$

The sum of the measures of the
angles of a triangle is 180: $\qquad\qquad$ $x + (8x - 40) + 2x = 180$

Combine like terms: $\qquad\qquad\qquad\qquad$ $11x - 40 = 180$

On each side of the equation add 40: $\qquad\qquad$ $11x = 220$

Divide each side of the equation by 11: $\qquad\qquad\qquad$ $x = \dfrac{220}{11}$

$\qquad\qquad\qquad\qquad\qquad\qquad\qquad\qquad\qquad\qquad\qquad = 20$

Hence, $m\angle Q = x = 20$, $m\angle R = 8x - 40 = 8(20) - 40 = 120$, and $m\angle S = 2x$
$= 2(20) = 40$.

Since $\triangle QRS$ contains an angle whose measure is greater than 90, $\triangle QRS$ is obtuse.

The correct choice is **(4)**.

23. The given statement is: $\qquad\qquad\qquad\qquad\qquad$ $\sim(q \wedge \sim s)$

Apply one of DeMorgan's laws, $\sim (A \wedge B) \leftrightarrow$
$(\sim A \vee \sim B)$, by letting A be q and B be $\sim s$: $\qquad\qquad$ $\sim q \vee \sim (\sim s)$

Apply the law of double negation by replacing
$\sim(\sim s)$ with s: $\qquad\qquad\qquad\qquad\qquad\qquad\qquad$ $\sim q \vee s$

The correct choice is **(3)**.

24.

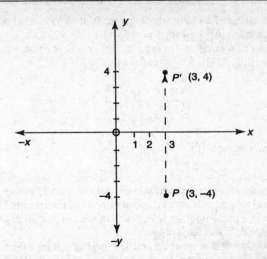

Under a reflection in the x-axis, point $P(x, y)$ is mapped onto point $P'(x,-y)$.
Thus, the coordinates of the image of $P(3,-4)$ under a reflection in the x-axis
are $(3, -(-4)) = (3,4)$.

The correct choice is **(3)**.

25. If an equation of a line has the form $y = mx + b$, then m is the slope of
the line and b is its y-intercept. The given equation, $y = \dfrac{1}{3}x - 2$, has the form
$y = mx + b$ where $m = \dfrac{1}{3}$.

If the slopes of two lines are negative reciprocals, then the lines are perpendicular. Since the negative reciprocal of $\dfrac{1}{3}$ is -3, an equation of a line that is
perpendicular to the given line must have a slope of -3.

Each of the choices is an equation in the form $y = mx + b$. The equation in
choice (1) is $y = -3x + 2$, so $m = -3$. Each of the other choices is an equation
in which $m \neq -3$.

The correct choice is **(1)**.

26. The sum of the lengths of any two sides of a triangle must be greater
than the length of the third side.

The lengths of two sides of a triangle are given as 4 and 7. Consider each of
the four choices in turn.

?	?	?	?
(1) $4 + 7 > 11$	(2) $4 + 7 > 7$	(3) $4 + 7 > 5$	(4) $4 + 7 > 4$
$11 \not> 11$	$11 > 7$	$11 > 5$	$11 > 4$

The correct choice is **(1)**.

27. An equation of a circle whose center is at (h,k) and whose radius is r units in length is $(x - h)^2 + (y - k)^2 = r^2$.

If the center of a circle is $(0,4)$ and its radius is 3, then its equation can be obtained by letting $h = 0$, $k = 4$, and $r = 3$:

$$(x - h)^2 + (y - k)^2 = r^2$$
$$(x - 0)^2 + (y - 4)^2 = 3^2$$
$$x^2 + (y - 4)^2 = 9$$

The correct choice is **(2)**.

28. The given set of four quadrilaterals contain a parallelogram, a rectangle, a rhombus, and a square. Each of these quadrilaterals is a parallelogram. Since the diagonals of a parallelogram bisect each other, the diagonals of each of the four quadrilaterals bisect each other.

The probability that a quadrilateral selected at random from this set has diagonals that bisect each other is the number of quadrilaterals in the set whose diagonals bisect each other divided by the total number of quadrilaterals in the set, or $\dfrac{4}{4} = 1$.

The correct choice is **(1)**.

29. A dilation with scale factor k ($k \neq 0$) maps each point $P(x,y)$ of a figure onto $P'(kx,ky)$.

A transformation that moves (x,y) onto $(5x,5y)$ is a *dilation* whose scale factor is 5.

The correct choice is **(4)**.

30. Given: $\overline{MN} \perp \overline{NP}$, $\overline{QP} \perp \overline{PN}$, O is the midpoint of $\overline{NP}$, $\overline{MN} \cong \overline{QP}$.

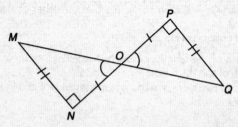

To determine which congruence method would be least likely to be used to prove $\triangle MNO \cong \triangle QPO$, consider each of the four choices in turn.

Choice (1): Triangles MNO and QPO are right triangles for which no information is provided about hypotenuse MO in $\triangle MNO$ and hypotenuse QO in $\triangle QPO$. Hence the triangles cannot be proved congruent by $HL \cong HL$.

Choice (2): $\triangle MNO \cong \triangle QPO$ by $AAS \cong AAS$ since right angle $N \cong$ right angle P, vertical angles MON and QOP are congruent, and $\overline{MN} \cong \overline{QP}$.

Choice (3) $\triangle MNO \cong \triangle QPO$ by $SAS \cong SAS$ since $\overline{NO} \cong \overline{PO}$, right angle $N \cong$ right angle P, and $\overline{MN} \cong \overline{QP}$.

Choice (4) $\triangle MNO \cong \triangle QPO$ by $ASA \cong ASA$ since right angle $N \cong$ right angle P, $\overline{NO} \cong \overline{PO}$, and vertical angles MON and QOP are congruent.

The correct choice is **(1)**.

31. The graph of an equation of the form $y = ax^2 + bx + c \ (a \neq 0)$ is a parabola whose axis of symmetry is a vertical line, an equation of which is $x = -\dfrac{b}{a}$.

In the given equation, $y = 2x^2 - 5x + 3$, $a = 2$ and $b = -5$. Thus,

$$x = -\frac{b}{2a}$$
$$= -\frac{(-5)}{2(2)}$$
$$= \frac{5}{4}$$

The correct choice is **(4)**.

32. In right triangle ABC,
$$\cos A = \frac{\text{side adjacent to } \angle A}{\text{hypotenuse}} = \frac{5}{13}$$

The correct choice is **(3)**.

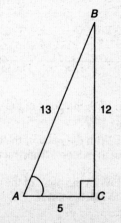

33. Given three true statements: (1) ~ a ∨ ~ b, (2) b, and (3) $c \rightarrow a$.

Since statement (2) says that b is true, ~ b, which is choice (2), is false.

Since statement (1) is true and ~ b is false, ~ a must be true by the law of disjunctive inference. Hence, a, which is choice (4), is false.

Since statement (3) is true and a is false, c, which is choice (1), is false by the law of *modus tollens*.

Since c is false, ~ c, which is choice (3), is true.

The correct choice is **(3)**.

34. A conditional statement $p \rightarrow q$ and its contrapositive, $\sim q \rightarrow \sim p$, are logically equivalent statements. Form the contrapositive of the given statement by negating and then interchanging its hypothesis and its conclusion. Thus:

Given statement: "If you are not part of the solution, then you are part of the problem."

Contrapositive: "If you are not part of the problem, then you are part of the solution."

The contrapositive, or logical equivalent, of the given statement appears as choice (2).

The correct choice is **(2)**.

35. Follow these steps to construct an angle congruent to ∠B of hexagon *ABCDEF*, using point W as the vertex.

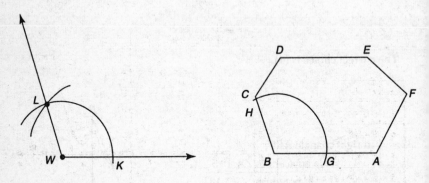

Step 1: With the point of the compass on B, construct an arc cutting $\overrightarrow{BA}$ at G and $\overrightarrow{BC}$ at H.

Step 2: With the point of the compass on point W, and with the same compass radius as in Step 1, construct an arc intersecting the ray whose endpoint is W at K.

Step 3: With the point of the compass on G, adjust the radius length of the compass to reach point H.

Step 4: With the point of the compass on W, and with the radius length GH obtained in Step 3, construct an arc intersecting at L the arc drawn in Step 2.

Step 5: Draw $\overrightarrow{WL}$.

Angle **LWK** is congruent to $\angle B$.

PART II

36. a. Prepare a table of values for x and y by substituting each integer value of x, from -1 to 5, in the given equation, $y = x^2 - 4x + 3$, to obtain the corresponding value for y:

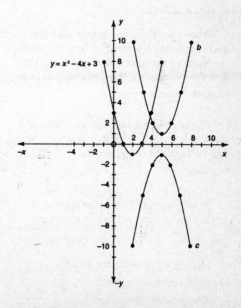

x	$x^2 - 4x + 3$	$= y$
-1	$(-1)^2 - 4(-1) + 3 = 1 + 4 + 3$	$= 8$
0	$0^2 - 4(0) + 3$	$= 3$
1	$1^2 - 4(1) + 3 = 1 - 4 + 3$	$= 0$
2	$2^2 - 4(2) + 3 = 4 - 8 + 3$	$= -1$
3	$3^2 - 4(3) + 3 = 9 - 12 + 3$	$= 0$
4	$4^2 - 4(4) + 3 = 16 - 16 + 3$	$= 3$
5	$5^2 - 4(5) + 3 = 25 - 20 + 3$	$= 8$

Plot points $(-1,8)$, $(0,3)$, $(1,0)$, $(2,-1)$, $(3,0)$, $(4,3)$, and $(5,8)$. Connect the points with a smooth curve that has the shape of a parabola whose turning point is at $(2,-1)$. This curve represents the graph of $y = x^2 - 4x + 3$ in the interval $-1 \leq x \leq 5$.

b. Under a translation that maps each point (x,y) onto $(x + 3, y + 2)$, the images of the points plotted in part **a** are as follows:

$$
\begin{aligned}
(-1,\ 8) &\rightarrow \ (-1 + 3,\ 8 + 2) = (2,10) \\
(\ 0,\ 3) &\rightarrow \ (\ 0 + 3,\ 3 + 2) = (3,\ 5) \\
(\ 1,\ 0) &\rightarrow \ (\ 1 + 3,\ 0 + 2) = (4,\ 2) \\
(\ 2,-1) &\rightarrow \ (\ 2 + 3,-1 + 2) = (5,\ 1) \\
(\ 3,\ 0) &\rightarrow \ (\ 3 + 3,\ 0 + 2) = (6,\ 2) \\
(\ 4,\ 3) &\rightarrow \ (\ 4 + 3,\ 3 + 2) = (7,\ 5) \\
(\ 5,\ 8) &\rightarrow \ (\ 5 + 3,\ 8 + 2) = (8,10)
\end{aligned}
$$

Plot the image points, connect them with a smooth curve, and label the graph b. The graph obtained after the translation that maps (x,y) onto $(x + 3, y + 2)$ is a parabola whose turning point is $(5,1)$.

c. A reflection in the x-axis maps each point (x,y) of the graph onto its image, $(x,-y)$. Plot the image of each of the points graphed in part **b**: $(2,-10)$, $(3,-5)$, $(4,-2)$, $(5,-1)$, $(6,-2)$, $(7,-5)$ and $(8,-10)$. Connect the points with a smooth curve and label this graph c. The graph obtained after a reflection in the x-axis of the graph drawn in part **b** is a parabola whose turning point is $(5,-1)$.

37. a. Given:

$$\frac{4x - 24}{x^2 - 36} \cdot \frac{x^2 + 4x - 12}{x^2 + x - 6}$$

Where possible, factor any numerator and any denominator. The first numerator contains a common factor of 4, and the first denominator is the difference of two perfect squares:

$$\frac{4(x - 6)}{(x - 6)(x + 6)} \cdot \frac{x^2 + 4x - 12}{x^2 + x - 6}$$

The second numerator and denominator are both quadratic trinomials that can be factored as the product of two binomials:

$$\frac{4(x - 6)}{(x - 6)(x + 6)} \cdot \frac{(x + 6)(x - 2)}{(x + 3)(x - 2)}$$

Divide out any factor that appears in both a numerator and a denominator:

$$\frac{\overset{1}{4\cancel{(x - 6)}}}{\cancel{(x - 6)}\cancel{(x + 6)}} \cdot \frac{\overset{1}{\cancel{(x + 6)}}\,\overset{1}{\cancel{(x - 2)}}}{(x + 3)\cancel{(x - 2)}}$$

Multiply the remaining factors:

$$\frac{4}{x + 3}$$

The product in simplest form is $\dfrac{4}{x + 3}$.

b. The given system is:

$$y = x + 5$$
$$x^2 + y^2 = 97$$

Substitute $(x + 5)$ for y in the second equation:

$$x^2 + (x + 5)^2 = 97$$

Square $(x + 5)$:

$$x^2 + x^2 + 10x + 25 = 97$$

Combine like terms:

$$2x^2 + 10x - 72 = 0$$

Divide each term of the equation by 2:

$$\frac{2x^2}{2} + \frac{10x}{2} - \frac{72}{2} = \frac{0}{2}$$

The result is a quadratic equation:

$$x^2 + 5x - 36 = 0$$

Factor the quadratic trinomial as the product of two binomials:

$$(x + 9)(x - 4) = 0$$

If the product of two factors is 0, then either factor may equal 0:

$$x + 9 = 0 \quad \text{or} \quad x - 4 = 0$$

Solve each equation:

$$x = -9 \text{ or} \qquad x = 4$$

Substitute each of the two solutions for x in the first equation to find the corresponding values of y:

Let $x = -9$: $y = (-9) + 5 \quad = -4$ | Let $x = 4$: $y = 4 + 5 \quad = 9$

The solutions are **(-9,-4)** and **(4,9)**.

38. Given:

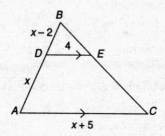

Let $x = AD$. Then:

$$DB = 2 \text{ less than } AD \quad = x - 2$$
$$AC = 5 \text{ more than } AD \quad = x + 5,$$

and $AB = AD + DB \quad = x + (x - 2) = 2x - 2$.

Since $\overline{DE}$ is parallel to $\overline{AC}$, $\angle A \cong \angle BDE$ and $\angle C \cong \angle BED$, so $\triangle DBE \sim \triangle ABC$.

The lengths of corresponding sides of similar triangles are in proportion:

$$\frac{DB}{DE} = \frac{AB}{AC}$$

Substitute $x - 2$ for DB, 4 for DE,

2$x - 2$ for AB, and $x + 5$ for AC:

$$\frac{x-2}{4} = \frac{2x-2}{x+5}$$

In a proportion the product of the means equals the product of the extremes:

$$(x - 2)(x + 5) = 4(2x - 2)$$

Collect and combine like terms:

$$x^2 + 3x - 10 = 8x - 8$$
$$x^2 - 5x - 2 = 0$$

Use the quadratic formula where $a = 1$, $b = -5$, and $c = -2$:

$$x = \frac{-b \pm \sqrt{b^2 - 4ac}}{2a}$$

$$= \frac{5 \pm \sqrt{(-5)^2 - 4(1)(-2)}}{2}$$

$$= \frac{5 \pm \sqrt{25 + 8}}{2}$$

$$= \frac{5 \pm \sqrt{33}}{2}$$

Since $\sqrt{33} \approx 5.74$

$$x_1 = \frac{5 + 5.74}{2} \text{ or } x_2 = \frac{5 - 5.74}{2}$$

Reject x_2 since a negative length is meaningless:

$$= \frac{10.74}{2} \quad \text{or} \quad = \frac{-0.74}{2} \text{ (reject)}$$

$$= 5.37$$

Round to the nearest tenth:

$$= 5.4$$

Since x represents the length of $\overline{AD}$, the length of $\overline{AD}$, correct to the *nearest tenth*, is **5.4**.

39.

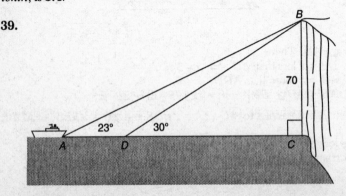

a.   (1) In right triangle BCD:

$$\tan 30° = \frac{\text{side opposite angle}}{\text{side adjacent to angle}}$$

$$= \frac{70}{DC}$$

From the Tables of Natural Trigonometric Functions, $\tan 30° = 0.5774$, so:

$$0.5774 = \frac{70}{DC}$$

$$DC(0.5774) = 70$$

$$DC = \frac{70}{0.5774}$$

$$= 121.23$$

The length of $\overline{DC}$, correct to the *nearest meter*, is **121**.

(2) In right triangle BCA:

$$\tan 23° = \frac{\text{side opposite angle}}{\text{side adjacent to angle}}$$

$$= \frac{70}{AC}$$

From the Tables of Natural Trigonometric Functions, $\tan 23° = 0.4245$, so:

$$0.4245 = \frac{70}{AC}$$

$$AC(0.4245) = 70$$

$$AC = \frac{70}{0.4245}$$

$$= 164.89$$

The length of $\overline{AC}$, correct to the *nearest meter*, is **165**.

(3) In right triangle BCA:

$$\sin 23° = \frac{\text{side opposite angle}}{\text{hypotenuse}}$$

$$= \frac{70}{AB}$$

From the Tables of Natural Trigonometric Functions, sin 23° = 0.3907, so:

$$0.3907 = \frac{70}{AB}$$

$$AB(0.3907) = 70$$

$$AB = \frac{70}{0.390}$$

$$= 179.17$$

The length of $\overline{AB}$, correct to the *nearest meter*, is **179**.

b. The distance between the ship's positions at the two sightings is AD. Using the answers obtained in part **a**, $AD = AC - DC = 165 - 121 = 44$.

The distance between the ship's positions at the two sightings is, correct to the *nearest meter*, **44** meters.

40. T represents: "Ronnie wastes time in class."

A represents: "Ronnie is absent from class."

S represents: "Ronnie's grades go down."

B represents: "Ronnie does well in Course II."

Given: "If Ronnie does not waste time in class, then she does well in Course II" is the conditional that the negation of T implies B: $\sim T \to B$

"If Ronnie is absent from class, then her grades will go down" is the conditional that A implies S: $A \to S$

"Either Ronnie does not waste time in class or Ronnie is absent from class" is the disjunction between the negation of T and A: $\sim T \vee A$

"Ronnie's grades do not go down" is the negation of S. $\sim S$

Prove: "Ronnie does well in Course II" is statement B: B

PROOF

Statement	Reason
1. $A \to S$	1. Given.
2. $\sim S$	2. Given.
3. $\sim A$	3. Law of *modus tollens* (steps 1 and 2)
4. $\sim T \vee A$	4. Given.
5. $\sim T$	5. Law of disjunctive inference (steps 3 and 4).
6. $\sim T \to B$	6. Given.
7. B	7. Law of detachment (steps 5 and 6)

PART III

___**41.** Given: Isosceles triangle ABC, $BA \cong BC$, $AE \perp BC$, and $\overline{BD} \perp \overline{AC}$.

Prove: $\dfrac{AC}{BA} = \dfrac{AE}{BD}$

PLAN: Show that triangles AEC and BDA are similar and that, as a result, the lengths of their corresponding sides are in proportion.

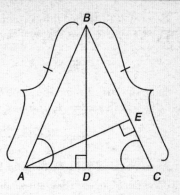

PROOF

Statements	Reason
1. $\overline{BA} \cong \overline{BC}$	1. Given.
2. $\angle BAD \cong \angle ACE$ (Angle)	2. If two sides of a triangle are congruent, then the angles opposite these sides are congruent.
3. $\overline{AE} \perp \overline{BC}$, $\overline{BD} \perp \overline{AC}$.	3. Given.
4. Angles BDA and AEC are right angles	4. Perpendicular lines meet to form right angles.
5. $\angle BDA \cong \angle AEC$ (Angle)	5. All right angles are congruent.
6. $\triangle AEC \sim \triangle BDA$	6. Two triangles are similar if two angles of one triangle are congruent to two angles of the other triangle.
7. $\dfrac{AC}{BA} = \dfrac{AE}{BD}$	7. The lengths of corresponding sides of similar triangles are in proportion.

42. A quadrilateral is a square if it is a parallelogram that contains a pair of adjacent sides that are both perpendicular and equal in length.

Prove that $MATH$ is a parallelogram by showing that its opposite sides have the same slope and, as a result, are parallel.

Slope of $\overline{MA}$: To find the slope of the side whose endpoints are $M(-1,4)$ and $A(4,7)$, let $x_1 = -1, y_1 = 4, x_2 = 4,$ and $y_2 = 7$. Thus:

$$\text{Slope of } \overline{MA} = \frac{y_2 - y_1}{x_2 - x_1} = \frac{7-4}{4-(-1)} = \frac{3}{5}$$

Slope of $\overline{TH}$: To find the slope of the side whose endpoints are $T(7,2)$ and $H(2,-1)$, let $x_1 = 7, y_1 = 2, x_2 = 2,$ and $y_2 = -1$. Thus:

$$\text{Slope of } \overline{TH} = \frac{y_2 - y_1}{x_2 - x_1} = \frac{-1-2}{2-7} = \frac{-3}{-5} = \frac{3}{5}$$

Slope of AT: To find the slope of the side whose endpoints are $A(4,7)$ and $T(7,2)$, let $x_1 = 4$, $y_1 = 7$, $x_2 = 7$, and $y_2 = 2$. Thus:

$$\text{Slope of } \overline{AT} = \frac{y_2 - y_1}{x_2 - x_1} = \frac{2-7}{7-4} = -\frac{5}{3}$$

Slope of $\overline{MH}$: To find the slope of the side whose endpoints are $M(-1,4)$ and $H(2,-1)$, let $x_1 = -1$, $y_1 = 4$, $x_2 = 2$, and $y_2 = -1$. Thus:

$$\text{Slope of } \overline{MH} = \frac{y_2 - y_1}{x_2 - x_1} = \frac{-1-4}{2-(-1)} = -\frac{5}{3}$$

Since $\overline{MA}$ and $\overline{TH}$ have the same slope they are parallel. Also, $\overline{AT}$ and $\overline{MH}$ have the same slope, so they are parallel. Hence, $MATH$ is a parallelogram.

Consider an adjacent pair of sides, say $\overline{MA}$ and $\overline{AT}$. Two lines are perpendicular if their slopes are negative reciprocals. Since the slope of $\overline{MA} = \frac{3}{5}$ and the slope of $\overline{AT} = -\frac{5}{3}$ and $\frac{3}{5}$ and $-\frac{5}{3}$ are negative reciprocals, $\overline{MA}$ is perpendicular to $\overline{AT}$. Now compare the lengths of $\overline{MA}$ and $\overline{AT}$.

Length of $\overline{MA}$: To find the length of the side whose endpoints are $M(-1,4)$ and $A(4,7)$, let $x_1 = -1$, $y_1 = 4$, $x_2 = 4$, and $y_2 = 7$. Thus:

$$MA = \sqrt{(x_2 - x_1)^2 + (y_2 - y_1)^2}$$
$$= \sqrt{(4-(-1)^2 + (7-4)^2}$$
$$= \sqrt{5^2 + 3^2}$$
$$= \sqrt{34}$$

Length of $\overline{AT}$: To find the length of the side whose endpoints are $A(4,7)$ and $T(7,2)$, let $x_1 = 4$, $y_1 = 7$, $x_2 = 7$, and $y_2 = 2$. Thus:

$$AT = \sqrt{(x_2 - x_1)^2 + (y_2 - y_1)^2}$$
$$= \sqrt{(7-4)^2 + (2-7)^2}$$
$$= \sqrt{3^2 + (-5)^2}$$
$$= \sqrt{34}$$

Hence, $\overline{MA}$ and $\overline{TH}$ have the same length, $\sqrt{34}$.

Quadrilateral $MATH$ is a square since it is a parallelogram in which a pair of adjacent sides are both perpendicular and equal in length.

	Topic	Question Numbers	Number of Points	Your Points	Your Percentage
1.	Properties of Number Systems; Def. of Operations	—	—		
2.	Finite Mathematical Systems	3	2		
3.	Linear Function & Graph ($y = mx + b$, slope, eqs. of)	14, 25	2 + 2 = 4		
4.	Quadratic Equation (alg. sol.—factoring, formula	6, 10	2 + 2 = 4		
5.	Parabola (incl. axis of symmetry, turning point)	31, 36a	2 + 4 = 6		
6.	Systems of Equations (alg. and graphic solutions)	37b	6		
7.	Suppls., Compl., Vertical Angles, Angle Measure	—	—		
8.	Triangle Properties (eq., isos., sum ∠s, 2 sides)	2, 22, 26	2 + 2 + 2 = 6		
9.	Line ‖ One Side of Δ; Line Joining Midpts. of 2 sides	5, 38	2 + 10 = 12		
10.	Inequalities of Δs (ext. ∠, ≠ sides, and opp. ∠s)	—	—		
11.	Quadrilateral Properties (▱, sq., rhom., rect., trap.)	19, 20	2 + 2 = 4		
12.	Parallel Lines	15, 16	2 + 2 = 4		
13.	Alg. Oper.; Verbal Probs.	9, 13, 37a	2 + 2 + 4 = 8		
14.	Mean Proportional; Alt. to Hypot. of Right Δ	—	—		
15.	Pythag. Th., Special Rt. Δs (3-4-5, 5-12-13, 30-60-90)	11	2		
16.	Similar Figures (ratios & proportions)	1, 7	2 + 2 = 4		
17.	Areas (Δ, rect., ▱, rhom., trap)	—	—		
18.	Locus	17	2		
19.	Constructions	35	2		
20.	Deductive Proofs	30, 40, 41	2 + 10 + 10 = 22		
21.	Coordinate Geom. (slope, dist., midpt., eq. of circle)	8, 21, 27	2 + 2 + 2 = 6		
22.	Coordinate Geom. "Proofs"	42	10		
23.	Logic	23, 33, 34	2 + 2 + 2 = 6		
24.	Permuations; Arrangements	—	—		
25.	Combinations	12	2		
26.	Probability	28	2		
27.	Trig. of Rt. Δ	4, 32, 39a, 39b	2 + 2 + 9 + 1 = 14		
28.	Literal Eqs.	—	—		
29.	Transformations	18, 24, 29, 36b, 36c	2 + 2 + 2 + 3 + 3 = 12		

Examination
June 1994

Sequential Math Course II

PART I

Answer 30 questions from this part. Each correct answer will receive 2 credits. No partial credit will be allowed. Write your answers in the spaces provided. Where applicable, answers may be left in terms of π or in radical form. [60]

1 Segment $\overline{AB}$ is parallel to segment $\overline{CD}$. If the slope of $\overline{AB} = -\dfrac{3}{7}$ and the slope of $\overline{CD} = -\dfrac{x}{14}$, find the value of x.

1_____

2 Lines $\overleftrightarrow{AB}$ and $\overleftrightarrow{CD}$ intersect at point F. What is the total number of points 4 centimeters from point F and also equidistant from $\overleftrightarrow{AB}$ and $\overleftrightarrow{CD}$?

2_____

3 In the following system, determine the value of
$(a \odot b) \odot c$.

$\odot$	a	d	b	c
a	b	a	c	d
d	a	d	b	c
b	c	b	d	a
c	d	c	a	b

3____

4 If a translation maps $(x,y) \rightarrow (x + 2, y + 3)$, what
are the coordinates of B', the image of point
$B(-3,5)$ after this translation?

4____

5 In the accompanying diagram, $\ell \parallel m$, t and s
are intersecting transversals, $m\angle 1 = 130$, and
$m\angle 2 = 60$. Find $m\angle 3$.

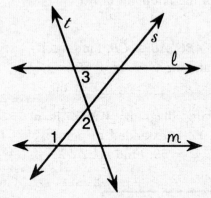

5____

6 In $\triangle ABC$, $m\angle A = 65$ and $m\angle C = 60$. Which is
the *shortest* side of the triangle?

6____

7 If $\tan A = \frac{3}{4}$, find $m\angle A$ to the *nearest degree*.

7____

8 In the accompanying diagram, the altitude to the hypotenuse of the right triangle divides the hypotenuse into two segments of lengths 3 and 12. What is the length of the altitude?

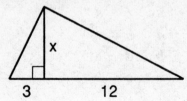

3　　　12

8___

9 What are the coordinates of P', the image of $P(1,2)$ after a reflection in the origin?

9___

10 The coordinates of A and B are $(2a,4b)$ and $(8a,6b)$, respectively. Express, in terms of a and b, the coordinates of the midpoint of $\overline{AB}$.

10___

11 In isosceles triangle ABC, $\overline{AB} \cong \overline{CB}$. Find $m\angle B$, if $m\angle A = 5x - 4$ and $m\angle C = 2x + 20$.

11___

12 In the accompanying diagram, $WXYZ$ is a parallelogram, line $\overline{YZ}$ is extended to point V, $\overline{WZ} \cong \overline{VZ}$, and $m\angle V = 50$. Find $m\angle ZWX$.

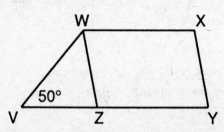

12___

13 In $\triangle ABC$, $\overline{AB} \perp \overline{BC}$ and $\overline{DE} \perp \overline{CA}$. If $DE = 8$, $CD = 10$, and $CA = 30$, find AB.

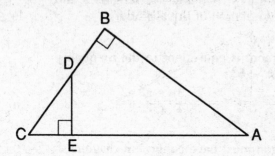

13_____

14 Write an equation of the line that passes through points (2,3) and (4,5).

14_____

15 What is the positive root of the equation $c^2 - 6c = 27$?

15_____

16 If the length of one side of a rectangle is 8 and the length of a diagonal is 10, find the area of the rectangle.

16_____

Directions (17–34): For *each* question chosen, write in the space provided the *numeral* preceding the word or expression that best completes the statement or answers the question.

17 Two consecutive angles of a parallelogram measure $2x + 10$ and $x - 10$. What is the value of x?
(1) 30   (3) 120
(2) 60   (4) −20

17_____

18 What is the length of the line segment joining points $J(1,5)$ and $K(3,9)$?
(1) $2\sqrt{5}$ (3) $13\sqrt{2}$
(2) $\sqrt{13}$ (4) $2\sqrt{13}$

18_____

19 Which statement is logically equivalent to
$\sim(a \wedge \sim b)$?

(1) $\sim a \wedge b$ (3) $\sim a \vee \sim b$
(2) $\sim a \wedge \sim b$ (4) $\sim a \vee b$ 19____

20 Which statement is equivalent to the inequality
$9 - 4x \le 3x - 5$?

(1) $x > -2$ (3) $x \le -2$
(2) $x < 2$ (4) $x \ge 2$ 20____

21 Which polygon must have congruent diagonals?

(1) parallelogram   (3) trapezoid
(2) rectangle   (4) rhombus   21____

22 What is the y-intercept of the graph of the
equation $y = 2x^2 - 5x + 7$?

(1) -5 (3) 7
(2) 2 (4) -7 22____

23 If the statements $m \rightarrow n$ and $\sim m \rightarrow s$ are true,
then which statement is a logical conclusion?

(1) $n \rightarrow s$ (3) s
(2) $s \rightarrow n$ (4) $\sim n \rightarrow s$ 23____

24 Which equation describes the locus of points
5 units from point $(3,-4)$?

(1) $(x + 3)^2 + (y - 4)^2 = 5$
(2) $(x - 3)^2 + (y + 4)^2 = 5$
(3) $(x - 3)^2 + (y + 4)^2 = 25$
(4) $(x + 3)^2 + (y - 4)^2 = 25$ 24____

25 In the solution of this problem, which property of real numbers justifies statement 5?

Statements	Reasons
1. $3x = 6$	1. Given
2. $\frac{1}{3}(3x) = \frac{1}{3}(6)$	2. Multiplication axiom
3. $\left(\frac{1}{3} \cdot 3\right)x = 2$	3. Associative property
4. $1 \cdot x = 2$	4. Multiplicative inverse
5. $x = 2$	5. _____

(1) Closure   (3) Commutative
(2) Identity   (4) Inverse   25____

26 How many 9-letter arrangements can be formed from the letters in the word "SASSAFRAS"?

(1) $\frac{4!}{3!}$ (3) $\frac{9!}{7!}$

(2) $\frac{9!}{4!3!}$ (4) $9!$ 26____

27 If the length of each leg of an isosceles triangle is 17 and the base is 16, the length of the altitude to the base is

(1) 8   (3) 15

(2) $8\frac{1}{2}$ (4) $\sqrt{32}$ 27____

28 Which equation represents the line that passes through point (0,6) and is perpendicular to the line whose equation is $y = 3x - 2$?

(1) $y = -\frac{1}{3}x + 6$ (3) $y = -3x + 6$

(2) $y = \frac{1}{3}x + 6$ (4) $y = 3x + 6$ 28____

29 Expressed as a fraction in lowest terms,

$$\frac{1}{x^2 - 4} \div \frac{x}{x - 2}, \ x \neq 2, 0, -2, \text{ is equivalent to}$$

(1) $\frac{1}{x(x + 2)}$ (3) $\frac{1}{x(x - 2)}$

(2) $\frac{-2}{x^2 - 4}$ (4) $\frac{1}{2}$

29_____

30 The lengths of two sides of a triangle are 7 and 10. The length of the third side may be

(1) 17   (3) 3
(2) 20   (4) 8

30_____

31 Which expression is *not* equivalent to $_7C_5$?

(1) $_7P_5$ (3) $\frac{7 \cdot 6 \cdot 5 \cdot 4 \cdot 3}{5 \cdot 4 \cdot 3 \cdot 2 \cdot 1}$

(2) 21   (4) $_7C_2$

31_____

32 What are the roots of the equation
$2x^2 - 6x + 3 = 0$?

(1) $\frac{-3 \pm \sqrt{3}}{2}$ (3) $\frac{3 \pm \sqrt{3}}{2}$

(2) $\frac{-3 \pm \sqrt{15}}{2}$ (4) $\frac{3 \pm \sqrt{15}}{2}$

32_____

33 The sum of $\frac{x + 4}{x}$ and $\frac{x - 4}{4}$ is

(1) $\frac{1}{2}$ (3) $\frac{x^2 + 16}{4x}$

(2) $4 + x$ (4) $\frac{2x}{x + 4}$

33_____

34 In the accompanying diagram, $\triangle ABC$ is a scalene triangle.

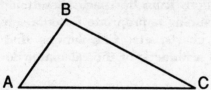

If the median is drawn from vertex B, what is the probability that its length will be greater than the length of the altitude?

(1) 1

(3) $\frac{1}{2}$

(2) 0

(4) $\frac{2}{3}$

34____

DIRECTIONS (35): *Show all construction lines.*

35 *On the answer sheet*, construct the ray that bisects $\angle B$.

PART II

Answer three questions from this part. Clearly indicate the necessary steps, including appropriate formula substitutions, diagrams, graphs, charts, etc. Calculations that may be obtained by mental arithmetic or the calculator do not need to be shown. [30]

36 Answer both *a* and *b* for all values of *x* for which these expressions are defined.

   a Express the product in simplest form:

$$\frac{x^2 - 9}{x^2 - x - 20} \cdot \frac{4x^2 - 20x}{4x^2 - 12x} \qquad [6]$$

   b Solve for *x*: $\quad \dfrac{x - 3}{2} = \dfrac{6}{x + 8} \qquad$ [4]

37 *a* On graph paper, draw the graph of the equation $y = x^2 - 4x + 4$, including all values of *x* from $x = -1$ to $x = 5$. Label the graph *a*.
    [4]

   b On the same set of axes, draw the image of the graph drawn in part *a* after a translation that maps $(x,y) \rightarrow (x - 2, y + 3)$. Label the image *b*. [2]

   c On the same set of axes, draw the image of the graph drawn in part *b* after a reflection in the *x*-axis. Label the image *c*. [2]

   d Which equation could represent the graph drawn in part *c*? [2]

    (1) $y = -x^2 + 4x - 4$ (3) $y = -x^2 - 3$

    (2) $y = x^2 - 3$ (4) $y = -x^2 + 3$

38 Alan has three detective books, two books about cars, and five comic books. He plans to lend three books to his friend David.

 a How many different selections of three books can Alan lend his friend? [2]

 b Find the probability that a three-book selection will contain
 (1) one book of each type [3]
 (2) comic books, only [3]
 (3) books about cars, only [2]

39 Trapezoid *ABCD* has coordinates *A*(−6,0), *B*(17,0), *C*(2,8), and *D*(0,8). Find the

 a area of trapezoid *ABCD* [3]

 b perimeter of trapezoid *ABCD* [4]

 c measure of ∠*B* to the *nearest degree* [3]

40 *On your answer paper*, write the numerals 1 through 8, and next to each numeral, give a reason for each statement in the proof. For statement 1, write "Given."

Given: $\triangle ABC$, $\overline{AC} \cong \overline{BC}$, $\overline{AD}$ and $\overline{BE}$ intersect at G, and $\angle 1 \cong \angle 2$.

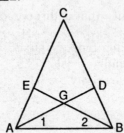

Prove: $\overline{EG} \cong \overline{DG}$

Statements	Reasons	
(1) $\triangle ABC$, $\overline{AC} \cong \overline{BC}$, $\angle 1 \cong \angle 2$	(1) Given	
(2) $\angle CAB \cong \angle CBA$	(2)	[2]
(3) $\overline{AB} \cong \overline{BA}$	(3)	[1]
(4) $\triangle EAB \cong \triangle DBA$	(4)	[2]
(5) $\angle AEB \cong \angle BDA$, $\overline{AE} \cong \overline{BD}$	(5)	[1]
(6) $\angle EGA \cong \angle DGB$	(6)	[1]
(7) $\triangle EGA \cong \triangle DGB$	(7)	[2]
(8) $\overline{EG} \cong \overline{DG}$	(8)	[1]

PART III

Answer one question from this part. Clearly indicate the necessary steps, including appropriate formula substitutions, diagrams, graphs, charts, etc. Calculations that may be obtained by mental arithmetic or the calculator do not need to be shown. [10]

41 Given: If pro basketball players compete in the Olympics, then college players do not play.

If college players do not play, then the team is not an amateur team.

If the team is not an amateur team and the team does not win the gold medal, then the people are not happy.

Pro basketball players compete in the Olympics.

The people are happy.

Let P represent: "Pro basketball players compete in the Olympics."

Let C represent: "College players play."

Let A represent: "The team is an amateur team."

Let G represent: "The team wins the gold medal."

Let H represent: "The people are happy."

Prove: The team wins the gold medal. [10]

42 The coordinates of the vertices of $\triangle TAG$ are $T(1,3)$, $A(8,2)$, and $G(5,6)$. Prove that $\triangle TAG$ is an isosceles right triangle. [10]

Answers
June 1994
Sequential Math Course II

Answer Key

PART I

1. 6	**13.** 24	**25.** (2)
2. 4	**14.** $y = x + 1$	**26.** (2)
3. b	**15.** 9	**27.** (3)
4. (−1,8)	**16.** 48	**28.** (1)
5. 70	**17.** (2)	**29.** (1)
6. $\overline{AC}$	**18.** (1)	**30.** (4)
7. 37	**19.** (4)	**31.** (1)
8. 6	**20.** (4)	**32.** (3)
9. (−1,−2)	**21.** (2)	**33.** (3)
10. (5a,5b)	**22.** (3)	**34.** (1)
11. 108	**23.** (4)	**35.** construction
12. 80	**24.** (3)	

PARTS II AND III See answers explained section.

Answers Explained

PART I

1. If two segments are parallel, their slopes are equal:

slope of $\overline{AB}$ = slope of $\overline{CD}$

$$\frac{-3}{7} = \frac{-x}{14}$$

In a proportion, the product of the means equals the product of the extremes (cross-multiply):

$$-7x = -3(14)$$

Divide each side of the equation by -7:

$$\frac{-7x}{-7} = \frac{-42}{-7}$$

$$x = 6$$

The value of x is **6**.

2. Lines $\overleftrightarrow{AB}$ and $\overleftrightarrow{CD}$ intersect at point F:

The set of all points 4 cm from point F is a circle that has F as its center and a radius of 4 cm.

The set of all points that are equidistant from $\overleftrightarrow{AB}$ and $\overleftrightarrow{CD}$ is contained on the pair of lines that bisect the pairs of vertical angles formed by lines $\overleftrightarrow{AB}$ and $\overleftrightarrow{CD}$. Since the circle intersects the pair of angle bisectors in four points, the total number of points 4 cm from point F and also equidistant from $\overleftrightarrow{AB}$ and $\overleftrightarrow{CD}$ is 4.

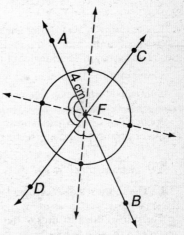

The total number of points that satisfy both conditions is **4**.

3. Evaluate $(a \circ b) \circ c$ by first evaluating the expression inside the parentheses. Since the horizontal row labeled a in the accompanying table intersects the vertical column labeled b at value c, $a \circ b = c$

$\circ$	a	d	b	c
a	b	a	c	d
d	a	d	b	c
b	c	b	d	a
c	d	c	a	b

Thus, $(a \circ b) \circ c = c \circ c$.

Since the horizontal row labeled c intersects the vertical column labeled c at value b,

$$c \circ c = b.$$

The value of $(a \circ b) \circ c$ is **b**.

4. If a translation maps $(x,y) \rightarrow (x + 2, y + 3)$, then after this translation the coordinates of the image of any point P are obtained by adding 2 to the x-coordinate of P and 3 to the y-coordinate of P. Thus, after the translation the image of $B(-3,5)$ is $B'(-3 + 2, 5 + 3) = B'(-1,8)$.

The coordinates of B' are **(−1,8)**.

5.

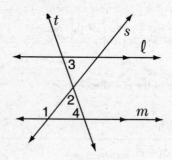

The measure of an exterior angle of a triangle is equal to the sum of the measures of the two nonadjacent interior angles of the triangle: m $\angle 1$ = m $\angle 2$ + m $\angle 4$

Given m $\angle 1$ = 130 and m $\angle 2$ = 60: 130 = 60 + m $\angle 4$

Subtract 60 from each side of the equation: $130 - 60$ = m $\angle 4$

70 = m $\angle 4$

Angles 3 and 4 have equal measures since they are alternate interior angles formed by transversal t intersecting parallel lines ℓ and m. Hence, m $\angle 3$ = m $\angle 4$ = 70.

The measure of $\angle 3$ is **70**.

6. The shortest side of a triangle lies opposite the angle of the triangle with the smallest degree measure.

The sum of the measures of the angles of a triangle is 180:

m $\angle A$ + m $\angle B$ + m $\angle C$ = 180

65 + m $\angle B$ + 60 = 180

m $\angle B$ + 125 = 180

m $\angle B$ = $180 - 125$

m $\angle B$ = 55

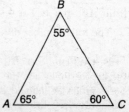

Since angle $\angle B$ has the smallest measure and lies opposite $\overline{AC}$, $\overline{AC}$ is the shortest side of the triangle.

The *shortest* side of the triangle is $\overline{AC}$.

7. Given: $\qquad\qquad\qquad\qquad\qquad\qquad\qquad\qquad\qquad$ $\tan A = \dfrac{3}{4}$

Change $\dfrac{3}{4}$ into an equivalent decimal: $\qquad\qquad\qquad\qquad$ $= 0.7500$

Consult the Table of Natural Trigonometric Functions. Under the vertical column labeled "Tangent," find the two consecutive decimal numbers between which 0.7500 lies and compare the positive differences of these numbers from 0.7500:

Angle	Tangent
36°	0.7265
?	0.7500
37°	0.7536

Difference = 0.7500 − 0.7265 = 0.0235

Difference = 0.7536 − 0.7500 = 0.0036

Since 0.0036 is smaller than 0.0235, $\angle A$, whose tangent is 0.7500, is closer to 37° than to 36°.

The measure of $\angle A$, correct to the *nearest degree,* is **37**.

8.

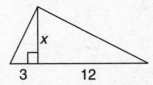

The length of the altitude drawn to the hypotenuse of a right triangle is the mean proportional between the lengths of the two segments into which the hypotenuse is divided. Thus:

$$\frac{\text{hypotenuse of segment 1}}{\text{altitude}} = \frac{\text{hypotenuse of segment 2}}{\text{altitude}}$$

$$\frac{3}{x} = \frac{x}{12}$$

In a proportion, the product of the means equals the product of the extremes (cross-multiply):

$$(x)\,(x) = (3)\,(12)$$
$$x^2 = 36$$

Take the square root of each side of the equation:

$$x = \pm\sqrt{36}$$
$$= \pm 6$$

Since a length cannot be negative, reject the negative root, so $x = 6$. The length of the altitude is **6**.

9. The reflection of point $P(x, y)$ in the origin is point $P'(-x, -y)$. Thus, the image of $P(1, 2)$ after a reflection in the origin is $P'(-1, -2)$.

The coordinates of P' are **(−1, −2)**.

10. The x- and the y-coordinates of the midpoint of $\overline{AB}$ are the averages of the corresponding coordinates of points A and B. Thus, if $M(\bar{x},\bar{y})$ is the midpoint of the segment whose endpoints are, $A(x_1,y_1)$ and $B(x_2,y_2)$, then the midpoint formula is:

$$M(\bar{x},\bar{y}) = \left(\frac{x_1+x_2}{2}, \frac{y_1+y_2}{2} \right)$$

Since the coordinates of A are $(2a,4b)$ and the coordinates of B are $(8a,6b)$, apply the midpoint formula by letting $x_1 = 2a$, $y_1 = 4b$, $x_2 = 8a$, and $y_2 = 6b$:

$$= \left(\frac{2a + 8a}{2}, \frac{4b + 6b}{2} \right)$$

$$= \left(\frac{10a}{2}, \frac{10b}{2} \right)$$

$$= (5a, 5b)$$

The coordinates of the midpoint of $\overline{AB}$ are **(5a,5b)**.

11.

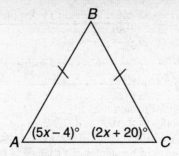

If two sides of an isosceles triangle are congruent, then the angles opposite these sides have the same measure:

$$m \angle A = m \angle C$$
$$5x - 4 = 2x + 20$$

Add 4 to each side of the equation:

$$\underline{+4 = 2x + 4}$$
$$5x = 2x + 24$$

Subtract $2x$ from each side of the equation:

$$\underline{-2x = -2x}$$
$$3x = 24$$

Divide each side of the equation by 3:

$$\frac{3x}{3} = \frac{24}{3}$$
$$x = 8$$

Since $x = 8$,

$$m \angle A = 5x - 4 = 5(8) - 4 = 40 - 4 = 36$$
$$m \angle C = 2x + 20 = 2(8) + 20 = 16 + 20 = 36$$

Since the sum of the measures of the angles of a triangle is 180,

$$36 + m \angle B + 36 = 180$$
$$m \angle B + 72 = 180$$
$$m \angle B = 180 - 72$$
$$= 108$$

The measure of $\angle B$ is **108**.

12.

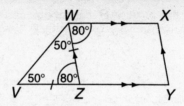

For $\triangle VZW$, it is given that $\overline{WZ} \cong \overline{VZ}$, so the angles opposite these sides, $\angle V$ and $\angle ZWV$, have equal measures. Thus, m $\angle ZWV$ = m $\angle V$ = 50.

The sum of the measures of the angles of a triangle is 180. Hence,

$$\begin{aligned}
\text{m} \angle ZWV + \text{m} \angle V + \text{m} \angle VZW &= 180 \\
50 + 50 + \text{m} \angle VZW &= 180 \\
\text{m} \angle VZW &= 180 - 100 = 80
\end{aligned}$$

Since opposite sides of a parallelogram are parallel, $\overline{VY}$ is parallel to $\overline{WX}$, which means that the alternate interior angles VZW and ZWX have equal measures. Thus, m $\angle ZWX$ = m $\angle VZW$ = 80.

The measure $\angle ZWX$ is **80**.

13.

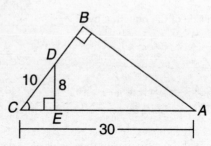

Consider right triangles DEC and ABC. Since $\angle E \cong B$ (right angles are congruent) and $\angle C \cong \angle C$ (reflexive property of congruence), these triangles are similar by the AA $\cong$ AA theorem of similarity.

The lengths of corresponding sides of similar triangles are in proportion:

$$\frac{\text{side in } \triangle ABC}{\text{corresponding side in } \triangle DEC} = \frac{AB}{DE} = \frac{CA}{CD}$$

$$\frac{AB}{8} = \frac{30}{10}$$

In a proportion, the product of the means equals the product of the extremes (cross-multiply): $10(AB) = 8(30)$

$$AB = \frac{240}{10} = 24$$

The length of $\overline{AB}$ is **24**.

14. An equation of a line for which two points are given can be determined by finding the slope of the line and then using the coordinates of either point to find the y-intercept of the line.

The slope, m, of a nonvertical line that contains points $A(x_1,y_1)$ and $B(x_2,y_2)$ is given by the formula:

$$m = \frac{\text{change in } y\text{-coordinates}}{\text{change in } x\text{-coordinates}} = \frac{y_2 - y_1}{x_2 - x_2}$$

Apply the slope formula by letting $(x_1,y_1) = (2,3)$ and $(x_2,y_2) = (4,5)$, so $x_1 = 2$, $y_1 = 3$, $x_2 = 4$, and $y_2 = 5$:

$$= \frac{5-3}{4-2}$$

$$= \frac{2}{2}$$

$$= 1$$

An equation of a nonvertical line has the form $y = mx + b$, where m is the slope of the line and b is its y-intercept. Since $m = 1$, the desired equation has the form $y = 1x + b$ or, equivalently, $y = x + b$. To find the value of b, replace x and y with the coordinates of either of the given points and then solve for b.

Using $(2,3)$, replace x by 2 and y by 3:

$$y = x + b$$
$$3 = 2 + b$$
$$3 - 2 = b$$
$$1 = b$$

Hence $b = 1$. Since $m = 1$ and $b = 1$, an equation of the line is $y = x + 1$.

An equation of the line is $\boldsymbol{y = x + 1}$.

15. The given equation is a quadratic equation: $\qquad\qquad c^2 - 6c = 27$

Rearrange the terms of the equation so that all terms are on one side equal to 0: $\qquad\qquad c^2 - 6c - 27 = 0$

The left side is a quadratic trinomial that can be factored as the product of two binomials of the form $(c + r)(c + s)$, where r and s are integers such that $r \cdot s = -27$ and $r + s = -6$. Using trial and error, we find that 3 and –9 are the correct factors of –27 since $(3)(-9) = -27$ and $3 + (-9) = -6$: $\qquad (c + 3)(c - 9) = 0$

If the product of two factors is 0, either factor may equal 0: $\qquad\qquad c + 3 = 0 \quad$ or $\quad c - 9 = 0$

$$c = -3 \text{ or } \qquad c = 9$$

Since the question asks for the positive root: $\qquad c = 9$

The positive root of the given equation is **9**.

16. Let x represent the length of the unknown side of the given rectangle:

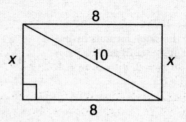

Use the Pythagorean theorem to find x: $\qquad\qquad x^2 + 8^2 = 10^2$

$$x^2 + 64 = 100$$

Subtract 64 from each side of the equation: $\qquad\qquad x^2 = 100 - 64$

$$= 36$$

Take the positive square root of each side of the equation: $\qquad\qquad x = \sqrt{36}$

$$= 6.$$

The area of a rectangle is equal to the product of a pair of adjacent sides. Thus, area = (8)(6) = 48.

The area of the rectangle is **48**.

17.

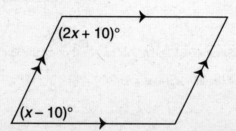

Since consecutive angles of a parallelogram are supplementary, the sum of their measures is 180:

$$(2x + 10) + (x - 10) = 180$$

Combine like terms:

$$3x = 180$$

Divide each side of the equation by 3:

$$\frac{3x}{3} = \frac{180}{3}$$

$$x = 60$$

The correct choice is **(2)**.

18. The length d of the line segment whose endpoints are (x_1, y_1) and (x_2, y_2) is given by this formula:

$$d = \sqrt{(x_2 - x_1)^2 + (y_2 - y_1)^2}$$

To find the length of the line segment joining points $J(1,5)$ and $K(3,9)$, let $(x_1, y_1) = (1,5)$ and $(x_2, y_2) = (3,9)$. Apply the distance formula by letting $x_1 = 1$, $y_1 = 5$, $x_2 = 3$, and $y_2 = 9$:

$$= \sqrt{(3 - 1)^2 + (9 - 5)^2}$$

$$= \sqrt{4 + 16}$$

$$= \sqrt{20}$$

Factor the radicand into two numbers one of which is the greatest perfect square factor of 20:

$$= \sqrt{4 \cdot 5} = \sqrt{4} \cdot \sqrt{5} = 2\sqrt{5}$$

The correct choice is **(1)**.

19. The given statement is:

$$\sim(a \wedge \sim b)$$

By one of DeMorgan's laws:

$$\sim(A \wedge \sim B) \leftrightarrow \sim A \vee \sim B$$

Let $A = a$ and $B = \sim b$:

$$\sim(a \wedge \sim b) \leftrightarrow \sim a \vee \sim(\sim b)$$

By the law of double negation, $\sim(\sim b)$ may be replaced by b:

$$\sim(a \wedge \sim b) \leftrightarrow \sim a \vee b$$

The correct choice is **(4)**.

20. The given inequality is:

$$9 - 4x \leq 3x - 5$$

Subtract 9 from each side of the inequality:

$$\frac{-9 \quad = \quad -9}{-4x \leq 3x - 14}$$

Subtract $3x$ from each side of the inequality:

$$-4x \leq \quad 3x - 14$$
$$\underline{-3x = -3x}$$
$$-7x \leq \quad \quad -14$$

Divide each side of the inequality by -7. Since the inequality is being divided by a negative quantity, change the direction of the inequality from $\leq$ to $\geq$ so an equivalent inequality results:

$$\frac{-7x}{-7} \geq \frac{-14}{-7}$$
$$x \geq 2$$

The correct choice is (**4**).

21. The diagonals of rectangle $ABCD$ form two right triangles that are congruent by SAS $\cong$ SAS since $\overline{AB} \cong \overline{DC}$, right angle 1 $\cong$ right angle 2, and $\overline{AD} \cong \overline{BC}$. Since corresponding parts of congruent triangles are congruent, diagonal $\overline{AC} \cong$ diagonal $\overline{DB}$. Thus, a rectangle always has congruent diagonals.

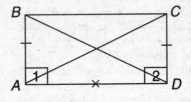

The correct choice is (**2**).

22. The y-intercept of a graph of an equation is the y-coordinate of the point at which the graph crosses the y-axis. The x-coordinate of this point is 0.

To obtain the y-intercept of the graph of $y = 2x^2 - 5x + 7$, let $x = 0$ and solve for y:

$$y = 2x^2 - 5x + 7$$
$$= 2(0)^2 - 5(0) + 7$$
$$= 7$$

The y-intercept is 7.

The correct choice is (**3**).

23. The given statements are $m \rightarrow n$ and $\sim m \rightarrow s$. A statement and its contrapositive are logically equivalent. To obtain the contrapositive of a conditional statement, interchange and then negate both parts of the conditional statement.

The contrapositive of $m \rightarrow n$ is $\sim n \rightarrow \sim m$. Thus, $\sim n \rightarrow \sim m$ and $\sim m \rightarrow s$.

The chain rule states that, if $a \rightarrow b$ and $b \rightarrow c$, then $a \rightarrow c$. Let $a = \sim n$, $b = \sim m$, and $c = s$. Therefore, by the chain rule, $\sim n \rightarrow s$.

The correct choice is **(4)**.

24. The locus of points a fixed number of units from a given point is a circle whose center is the given point and whose radius is the fixed number. If the center of the circle is at (h,k) and the radius is r, then an equation of this circle is $(x - h)^2 + (y - k)^2 = r^2$.

The locus of points 5 units from point $(3,-4)$ is a circle whose center is at $(3,-4)$ and whose radius is 5 units. Let $(h,k) = (3,-4)$ and $r = 5$. Replacing h with 3, k with -4, and r with 5 in $(x - h)^2 + (y - k)^2 = r^2$ gives $(x - 3)^2 + (y - (-4))^2 = 5^2$, which simplifies to $(x - 3)^2 + (y + 4)^2 = 25$.

The correct choice is **(3)**.

25. The number 1 is the *identity element* for multiplication for the set of real numbers since the product of 1 and *any* real number is the same real number.

Statement 4 is $1 \cdot x = 2$. Since 1 is the identity element for multiplication, the left side of the equation in statement 4 becomes x. This gives statement 5, $x = 2$. Thus, statement 5 follows from statement 4 as a result of 1 being the identity element for multiplication.

The correct choice is **(2)**.

26. If, in a set of n objects, a objects are identical and b objects are identical, then the number of different ways in which the n objects can be arranged is

$$\frac{n!}{a!\, b!}$$

The word "SASSAFRAS" consists of 9 letters, including 4 identical letter S's and 3 identical letter A's. To find the number of different 9-letter arrangements that can be formed from the letters in the word "SASSAFRAS," let $n = 9$, $a = 4$, and $b = 3$:

$$\frac{n!}{a!\, b!} = \frac{9!}{4!\, 3!}$$

The correct choices is **(2)**.

27.

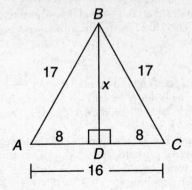

The altitude drawn to the base of an isoceles triangle intersects the base at right angles and bisects the base.

Let x represent the length of the altitude to the base. The value of x can be determined by applying the Pythagorean theorem in right triangle ADB:

$$(BD)^2 + (AD)^2 = (AB)^2$$
$$x^2 + 8^2 = 17^2$$
$$x^2 + 64 = 289$$
$$x^2 = 289 - 64$$
$$= 225$$
$$x = \sqrt{225}$$
$$= 15$$

The correct choice is **(3)**.

28.   If an equation has the form $y = mx + b$, then m is the slope of the line and b is its y-intercept.

A line that passes through point $(0,6)$ intersects the y-axis at $y = 6$, so $b = 6$.

The line whose equation is $y = 3x - 2$ has the form $y = mx + b$, where the slope $m = 3$. If two lines are perpendicular, their slopes are negative reciprocals. Since the negative reciprocal of 3 is $-\dfrac{1}{3}$, the slope m of a line perpendicular to $y = 3x - 2$ is $m = -\dfrac{1}{3}$.

Letting $m = -\dfrac{1}{3}$ and $b = 6$ in $y = mx + b$ gives

$$y = -\frac{1}{3}\,x + 6$$

as an equation of the desired line.

The correct choice is (1).

29. Given:

Change the division operation to multiplication by inverting the divisor (the second fraction):

$$\frac{1}{x^2 - 4} \div \frac{x}{x - 2} \quad (x \neq 2, 0, -2)$$

$$\frac{1}{x^2 - 4} \cdot \frac{x - 2}{x}$$

Factor the denominator of the first fraction, which is the difference of two perfect squares:

$$\frac{1}{(x + 2)(x - 2)} \cdot \frac{x - 2}{x}$$

Cancel any factor that appears in both a numerator and a denominator since the quotient of such factors is 1:

$$\frac{1}{(x + 2)\cancel{(x - 2)}} \cdot \frac{\cancel{x - 2}}{x}$$

Multiply together the remaining factors in the numerator, and multiply together the remaining factors in the denominator:

$$\frac{1}{x(x + 2)}$$

The correct choice is (1).

30. The sum of the lengths of *any* two sides of a triangle is greater than the length of the third side.

Use the lengths of the two given sides, 7 and 10, to check this relationship for each of the four choices:

Choice (1):	$7 + 10 > 17$?	False
Choice (2):	$7 + 10 > 20$?	False
Choice (3):	$7 + 10 > 3$?	True
	$3 + 10 > 7$?	True
	$7 + 3 > 10$?	False
Choice (4):	$7 + 10 > 8$?	True
	$8 + 10 > 7$?	True
	$7 + 8 > 10$?	True

The correct choice is (4).

31. The given expression, $_7C_5$, uses combination notation. In general,

$$_nC_r = \frac{n!}{r!\,(n - r)!} \quad (n \geq r)$$

Evaluate $_7C_5$ by letting $n = 7$ and $r = 5$:

$$_nC_r = \frac{n!}{r!\,(n - r)!}$$

$$= \frac{7!}{5!\,(7 - 5)!}$$

$$= \frac{7 \cdot 6 \cdot 5!}{5! \cdot 2!}$$

$$= \frac{7 \cdot \overset{3}{\cancel{6}} \cdot \overset{1}{\cancel{5!}}}{\cancel{5!} \cdot \cancel{2!} \cdot 1}$$

$$= 21$$

Compare each choice, in turn, to 21.

Choice (1): The notation $_7P_5$ means the product of the 5 greatest factors of 7! Thus, $_7P_5 = 7 \cdot 6 \cdot 5 \cdot 4 \cdot 3 \neq 21$.

Choice (2): $21 = 21$.

Choice (3): $\dfrac{7 \cdot \overset{3}{\cancel{6}} \cdot \cancel{5} \quad \cancel{4} \quad \cancel{3}}{\cancel{5} \quad \cancel{4} \quad \cancel{3} \cdot \cancel{2} \cdot 1} = 21$

Choice (4): $_7C_2 = \dfrac{7!}{2! \cdot 5!} = \dfrac{7 \cdot \overset{3}{\cancel{6}} \cdot \cancel{5!}}{\cancel{2} \cdot 1 \cdot \cancel{5!}} = 21$

Only the expression in choice (1) is *not* equivalent to $_7C_5$.

The correct choice is **(1)**.

32. The left side of the given equation, $2x^2 - 6x + 3 = 0$, is a quadratic trinomial that cannot be factored. As a result, the equation needs to be solved by using the *quadratic formula*.

If a quadratic equation is in the form $ax^2 + bx + c = 0$, then its roots are given by this formula:

$$x = \frac{-b \pm \sqrt{b^2 - 4ac}}{2a} \quad (a \neq 0)$$

The given equation is in the form $ax^2 + bx + c = 0$ with $a = 2$, $b = -6$, and $c = 3$:

$$= \frac{-(-6) \pm \sqrt{(-6)^2 - 4(2)(3)}}{2(2)}$$

$$= \frac{6 \pm \sqrt{36 - 24}}{4}$$

$$= \frac{6 \pm \sqrt{12}}{4}$$

Factor the radicand into two whole numbers, one of which is the highest perfect square factor of 12:

$$= \frac{6 \pm \sqrt{4 \cdot 3}}{4}$$

$$= \frac{6 \pm \sqrt{4}\sqrt{3}}{4}$$

$$= \frac{6 \pm 2\sqrt{3}}{4}$$

$$= \frac{2(3 \pm \sqrt{3})}{4}$$

$$= \frac{3 \pm \sqrt{3}}{2}$$

The correct choice is (**3**).

33. The given sum involves two fractions with unlike denominators:

$$\frac{x + 4}{x} + \frac{x - 4}{4}$$

Find the least common denominator (L.C.D.). The L.C.D. is $4x$, since this is the smallest expression into which each of the denominators will divide evenly.

Convert the fractions into equivalent fractions having the L.C.D. by multiplying the first fraction by 1 in the form of $\dfrac{4}{4}$, and the second fraction by 1 in the form of $\dfrac{x}{x}$:

$$\frac{4}{4}\left(\frac{x+4}{x}\right) + \frac{x}{x}\left(\frac{x-4}{4}\right)$$

$$\frac{4x+16}{4x} + \frac{x^2-4x}{4x}$$

Since the fractions now have the same denominator, they may be added by combining their numerators:

$$\frac{(4x+16)+(x^2-4x)}{4x}$$

$$\frac{x^2-4x+4x+16}{4x}$$

$$\frac{x^2+16}{4x}$$

The correct choice is (**3**).

34. A median of a triangle is a line segment drawn from a vertex of a triangle to the midpoint of the opposite side. An altitude of a triangle is a line segment drawn from a vertex of a triangle perpendicular to the opposite side.

In $\triangle ABC$, median $\overline{BM}$ and altitude $\overline{BD}$ are drawn:

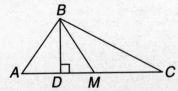

In right $\triangle BDM$, altitude $\overline{BD}$ is a leg and median $\overline{BM}$ is the hypotenuse. Hence, BM is *always* greater than BD since the hypotenuse of a right triangle is always the longest side in a right triangle.

Since the probability of a certainty is 1, the probability that the median drawn from vertex B will be greater than the altitude drawn from B is 1.

The correct choice is **(1)**.

35.

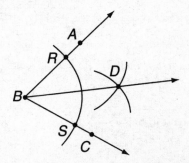

To construct the ray that bisects $\angle B$, proceed as follows:

STEP 1: Label point A on one side of $\angle B$, and label point C on the other side of $\angle B$. With the point of the compass on B and any convenient radius, swing an arc intersecting $\overrightarrow{BA}$ at R and $\overrightarrow{BC}$ at S.

STEP 2: With the point of the compass on R and a radius greater than half the distance from R to S, swing an arc.

STEP 3: With the point of the compass on S and the same radius as was used in Step 2, swing an arc intersecting the arc made in Step 2 at point D.

STEP 4: Using a straight-edge, draw $\overrightarrow{BD}$.

$\overrightarrow{BD}$ is the ray that bisects $\angle B$.

PART II

36. a. The given product is:

$$\frac{x^2 - 9}{x^2 - x - 20} \cdot \frac{4x^2 - 20x}{4x^2 - 12x}$$

Where possible, factor any numerator and any denominator. The first numerator is the difference of two squares, and the first denominator is a quadratic trinomial that can be factored as the product of two binomials:

$$\frac{(x - 3)(x + 3)}{(x + 4)(x - 5)} \cdot \frac{4x^2 - 20x}{4x^2 - 12x}$$

In the second fraction, $4x$ is the greatest common factor of both the numerator and the denominator:

$$\frac{(x-3)(x+3)}{(x+4)(x-5)} \cdot \frac{4x(x-5)}{4x(x-3)}$$

Divide out any factor that appears in both a numerator and a denominator:

$$\frac{\overset{1}{\cancel{(x-3)}}(x+3)}{(x+4)\underset{1}{\cancel{(x-5)}}} \cdot \frac{\overset{1}{\cancel{4x}}\cancel{(x-5)}}{\cancel{4x}\cancel{(x-3)}}$$

Multiply the remaining factors together in the numerator, and multiply the remaining factors together in the denominator:

$$\frac{x+3}{x+4}$$

The product in simplest form is $\dfrac{x+3}{x+4}$.

b. The given equation is:

$$\frac{x-3}{2} = \frac{6}{x+8}$$

In a proportion, the product of the means is equal to the product of the extremes (cross-multiply):
Simplify:
Combine and collect like terms:

$$(x-3)(x+8) = (2)(6)$$
$$x^2 - 3x + 8x - 24 = 12$$
$$x^2 + 5x - 36 = 0$$

Factor the quadratic trinomial as the product of two binomials:

$$(x+9)(x-4) = 0$$

If the product of two factors is 0, then either or both factors are 0:

$$x + 9 = 0 \quad \text{or } x - 4 = 0$$
$$x = -9 \text{ or} \qquad x = 4$$

The solutions for x are **–9** and **4**.

37. a. Prepare a table of values for x and y by substituting each integer value of x, from $x = -1$ to $x = 5$, in the given equation, $y = x^2 - 4x + 4$, to obtain the corresponding value for y.

x	$x^2 - 4x \quad + 4$	$= y$
-1	$(-1)^2 - 4(-1) + 4 = \quad 1 + 4 + 4$	$= 9$
0	$0^2 - 4(0) \quad + 4 = \quad 0 + 0 + 4$	$= 4$
1	$1^2 - 4(1) \quad + 4 = \quad 1 - 4 + 4$	$= 1$
2	$2^2 - 4(2) \quad + 4 = \quad 4 - 8 + 4$	$= 0$
3	$3^2 - 4(3) \quad + 4 = \quad 9 - 12 + 4$	$= 1$
4	$4^2 - 4(4) \quad + 4 = 16 - 16 + 4$	$= 4$
5	$5^2 - 4(5) \quad + 4 = 25 - 20 + 4$	$= 9$

Plot points $(-1,9)$, $(0,4)$, $(1,1)$, $(2,0)$, $(3,1)$, $(4,4)$, and $(5,9)$. Connect these points with a smooth curve that has the shape of a parabola whose turning point is at $(3,1)$. This curve labeled a, represents the graph of $y = x^2 - 4x + 4$ over the interval from $x = -1$ to $x = 5$.

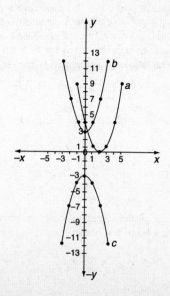

b. Under a translation that maps (x,y) onto $(x - 2, y + 3)$, the images of the points plotted in part **a** are as follows:

(x,y)	$\rightarrow$	$(x - 2, y + 3)$	=	Image Points
$(-1, 9)$	$\rightarrow$	$(-1 - 2, 9 + 3)$	=	$(-3, 12)$
$(0, 4)$	$\rightarrow$	$(0 - 2, 4 + 3)$	=	$(-2, 7)$
$(1, 1)$	$\rightarrow$	$(1 - 2, 1 + 3)$	=	$(-1, 4)$
$(2, 0)$	$\rightarrow$	$(2 - 2, 0 + 3)$	=	$(0, 3)$
$(3, 1)$	$\rightarrow$	$(3 - 2, 1 + 3)$	=	$(1, 4)$
$(4, 4)$	$\rightarrow$	$(4 - 2, 4 + 3)$	=	$(2, 7)$
$(5, 9)$	$\rightarrow$	$(5 - 2, 9 + 3)$	=	$(3, 12)$

Plot the image points, connect them with a smooth curve, and label the graph b. The graph obtained after a translation that maps $(x,y) \rightarrow (x - 2, y + 3)$ is a parabola whose turning point is $(2,0)$.

c. A reflection in the x–axis maps each point (x,y) of the graph onto its image, $(x, -y)$. Plot the image of each of the points graphed in part **b** to obtain $(-3,-12)$, $(-2,-7)$, $(-1,-4)$, $(0,-3)$, $(1,-4)$, $(2,-7)$, and $(3,-12)$. Connect these points with a smooth curve and label this graph c. The graph obtained after a reflection in the x–axis of the graph drawn in part **b** is a parabola whose turning point is $(0,-3)$ and that opens downward.

d. Since the parabola drawn in part **c** has the y-axis as its axis of symmetry, its equation has the form $y = ax^2 + b$, where b represents the y-intercept of the graph. The graph labeled c has a y-intercept of -3, so $b = -3$. Since the graph labeled c opens downward, the coefficient of the x^2-term of its equation is *negative*. Hence, a possible equation for this graph is $y = -x^2 - 3$.

The correct choice is **(3)**.

38. a. Without regard to order, r objects may be selected from a set of n objects in $_nC_r$ ways, where

$$_nC_r = \frac{n!}{r! \, (n - r)!}$$

Since it is given that Allan has three detective books, two books about cars, and five comic books, he has a total of ten books.

To find the number of different selections of three books that Allan can lend his friend, evaluate $_nC_r$ for $r = 3$ and $n = 10$:

$$_nC_r = \frac{n!}{r!\,(n-r)!}$$

$$_{10}C_3 = \frac{10!}{3!\,(10-3)!}$$

$$= \frac{10 \cdot 9 \cdot 8 \cdot \overset{1}{\cancel{7!}}}{3! \cdot \cancel{7!}}$$

$$= \frac{10 \cdot \overset{3}{\cancel{9}} \cdot \overset{4}{\cancel{8}}}{\cancel{3} \cdot \cancel{2} \cdot 1}$$

$$= 10 \cdot 3 \cdot 4$$

$$= 120$$

There are **120** different selections of three books.

b. (1) The probability that a three-book selection will contain one book of each type is obtained by writing the product of the number of ways in which one detective book, one book about cars, and one comic book can be selected from the total number of three-book selections determined in part **a**.

One detective book can be selected from three detective books in $_3C_1$ ways, one book about cars can be selected from two books about cars in $_2C_1$ ways, and one comic book can be selected from five comic books in $_5C_1$ ways. Hence, the probability that in a three-book selection one of each type of book will be selected is given by the fraction

$$\frac{_3C_1 \cdot {_2C_1} \cdot {_5C_1}}{_{10}C_3}$$

From part **a**, $_{10}C_3 = 120$. Since $_nC_1 = n$, we have $_3C_1 = 3$, $_2C_1 = 2$, and $_5C_1 = 5$. Thus:

$$\frac{_3C_1 \cdot {_2C_1} \cdot {_5C_1}}{_{10}C_3} = \frac{3 \cdot 2 \cdot 5}{120}$$

$$= \frac{30}{120}$$

The probability that a three-book selection will contain one book of each type is $\dfrac{30}{120}$.

(2) The probability that a three-book selection will contain only comic books is obtained by writing the product of the number of ways in which no (zero) detective book, no book about cars, and three comic books can be selected from the total number of three-book selections determined in part **a**. Hence, the probability that a three-book selection will contain only comic books is given by the fraction

$$\frac{_3C_0 \cdot {}_2C_0 \cdot {}_5C_3}{_{10}C_3}$$

Since $_nC_0 = 1$, we have $_3C_0 = {}_2C_0 = 1$. From part **a**, $_{10}C_3 = 120$. Thus:

$$\frac{_3C_0 \cdot {}_2C_0 \cdot {}_5C_3}{_{10}C_3} = \frac{1 \cdot 1 \cdot {}_5C_3}{120}$$

$$= \frac{1}{120} \cdot \frac{5!}{3!\,(5-3)!}$$

$$= \frac{1}{120}\; \frac{5 \cdot \overset{2}{\cancel{4}} \cdot \overset{1}{\cancel{3!}}}{\cancel{3!} \cdot \cancel{2} \cdot 1}$$

$$= \frac{1}{120}(10)$$

$$= \frac{10}{120}$$

The probability that a three-book selection will contain only comic books is $\dfrac{10}{120}$.

(3) There are *two* books about cars. Hence, it is not possible that a *three*-book selection will contain *only* books about cars. Since the probability of an impossibility is 0, the probability that a three-book selection will contain only books about cars is **0**.

39. The coordinates of trapezoid $ABCD$ are given as $A(-6, 0)$, $B(17, 0)$, $C(2,8)$, and $D(0,8)$. Trapezoid $ABCD$ is sketched in the accompanying figure.

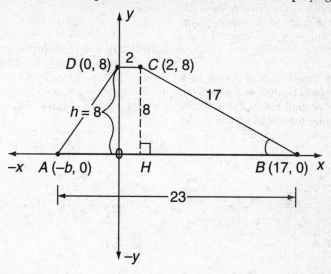

Since AB and CD are horizontal segments, their lengths can be determined by subtracting the x-coordinate of the left endpoint of the segment from the x-coordinate of the right endpoint. Thus:

$$AB = 17 - (-6) = 17 + 6 = 23$$
$$CD = 2 - 0 = 2$$

An altitude of the trapezoid coincides with the y-axis. The endpoints of this altitude are the origin $(0,0)$ and $D(0,8)$, so its length is $8 - 0 = 8$.

a. The area of a trapezoid is equal to one-half the product of the length of an altitude of the trapezoid and the sum of the lengths of its bases. Thus:

$$\text{area of trapezoid } ABCD = \frac{1}{2} h(AB + CD)$$

Since $h = 8$, $AB = 23$, and $CD = 2$: $= \frac{1}{2}(8)(23 + 2)$

$$= 4(25)$$

$$= 100$$

The area of trapezoid $ABCD$ is **100 square units**.

b. The perimeter of the trapezoid is the sum of the lengths of its four sides. From part **a**, $AB = 23$ and $CD = 2$. The lengths of $\overline{AD}$ and $\overline{BC}$ can be determined by using the distance formula.

The distance d between points (x_1, y_1) and (x_2, y_2) is given by the formula:

$$d = \sqrt{(x_2 - x_1)^2 + (y_2 - y_1)^2}$$

To find the length of the segment joining points $A(-6, 0)$ and $D(0, 8)$, let $(x_1, y_1) = A(-6, 0)$ and $(x_2, y_2) = D(0, 8)$. In applying the distance formula, let $x_1 = -6$ and $y_1 = 0$, and let $x_2 = 0$ and $y_2 = 8$:

$$AD = \sqrt{(0 - (-6))^2 + (8 - 0)^2}$$

$$= \sqrt{6^2 + 8^2}$$

$$= \sqrt{36 + 64}$$

$$= \sqrt{100}$$

$$= 10$$

To find the length of the segment joining points $B(17, 0)$ and $C(2, 8)$, let $(x_1, y_1) = B(17, 0)$ and $(x_2, y_2) = C(2, 8)$. In applying the distance formula, let $x_1 = 17$ and $y_1 = 0$, and let $x_2 = 2$ and $y_2 = 8$:

$$BC = \sqrt{(2 - 17)^2 + (8 - 0)^2}$$

$$= \sqrt{(-15)^2 + 8^2}$$

$$= \sqrt{225 + 64}$$

$$= \sqrt{289}$$

$$= 17$$

$$\begin{aligned}
\text{perimeter of trapezoid } ABCD &= AB + CD + AD + BC \\
&= 23 + 2 + 10 + 17 \\
&= 52
\end{aligned}$$

The perimeter of trapezoid $ABCD$ is **52**.

c. To find the measure of $\angle B$, a right triangle that contains $\angle B$ must be formed. As shown on the accompanying illustration, drop an altitude from C to $\overline{AB}$, intersecting $\overline{AB}$ at H. Since the height of the trapezoid is 8, the length of altitude $\overline{CH}$ is 8 and, from part **b**, $BC = 17$. Hence, in right triangle CHB the sine ratio can be used to find the measure of $\angle B$:

$$\sin B = \frac{\text{side opposite } \angle B}{\text{hypotenuse}}$$

$$= \frac{8}{17}$$

Use a calculator: $= 8 \div 17 \approx 0.4706$

Consult the Table of Natural Trigonometric Functions. Under the vertical column labeled "Sine," find the two consecutive decimal numbers between which 0.4706 lies. Observe that $\sin 28° = 0.4695$ and $\sin 29° = 0.4848$. Since 0.4706 is closer to 0.4695 than to 0.4848, $\angle B$, correct to the nearest degree, is 28°.

The measure of $\angle B$, to the *nearest degree*, is **28**.

40. Given: $\triangle ABC$, $\overline{AC} \cong \overline{BC}$, $\overline{AD}$ and $\overline{BE}$ intersect at G, and $\angle 1 \cong \angle 2$.
Prove: $\overline{EG} \cong \overline{DG}$
PLAN: Show $\triangle EAB \cong \triangle DBA$ by $ASA \cong ASA$. Then use corresponding parts of these triangles to show $\triangle EGA \cong \triangle DGB$ by $AAS \cong AAS$.

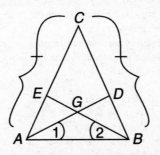

Statements	Reasons
1. $\triangle ABC$, $\overline{AC} \cong \overline{BC}$, $\angle 1 \cong \angle 2$	1. Given.
2. $\angle CAB \cong \angle CBA$	2. If two sides of a triangle are congruent, the angles opposite these sides are also congruent.
3. $\overline{AB} \cong \overline{BA}$	3. Reflexive property of congruence.
4. $\triangle EAB \cong \triangle DBA$	4. ASA $\cong$ ASA.
5. $\angle AEB \cong \angle BDA$, $\overline{AE} \cong \overline{BD}$	5. Corresponding parts of congruent triangles are congruent.
6. $\angle EGA \cong \angle DGB$	6. The angles in a vertical pair of angles are congruent.
7. $\triangle EGA \cong \triangle DGB$	7. AAS $\cong$ AAS
8. $\overline{EG} \cong \overline{DG}$	8. Corresponding parts of congruent triangles are congruent.

PART III

41. Given:

P represents: "Pro basketball players compete in the Olympics."
C represents: "College players play."
A represents: "The team is an amateur team."
G represents: "The team wins the gold medal."
H represents: "The people are happy."

"If pro basketball players compete in the Olympics, then college players do not play" is the conditional that P implies the negation of C: $P \rightarrow \sim C$

"If college players do not play, then the team is not an amateur team" is the conditional that the negation of C implies the negation of A: $\sim C \rightarrow \sim A$

"If the team is not an amateur team and the team does not win the gold medal, then the people are not happy" is the conditional that the conjunction of the negation of A and the negation of G implies the negation of H:

$$(\sim A \wedge \sim G) \rightarrow \sim H$$

"Pro basketball players compete in the Olympics" is the statement P:

$$P$$

"The people are happy" is the statement H:

$$H$$

Prove: "The team wins the gold medal" is the statement G.

Statements	Reasons
1. $P \rightarrow \sim C$	1. Given.
2. $\sim C \rightarrow \sim A$	2. Given.
3. $P \rightarrow \sim A$	3. Chain rule (steps 1 and 2).
4. P	4. Given.
5. $\sim A$	5. Law of detachment (steps 3 and 4).
6. $(\sim A \wedge \sim G) \rightarrow \sim H$	6. Given.
7. H	7. Given
8. $\sim (\sim A \wedge \sim G)$	8. Law of *modus tollens* (steps 6 and 7).
9. $\sim (\sim A) \vee \sim (\sim G)$	9. De Morgan's law.
10. $A \vee G$	10. Law of double negation.
11. G	11. Law of disjunctive inference (steps 5 and 10).

42. The coordinates of the vertices of $\triangle TAG$ are given as $T(1,3)$, $A(8,2)$, and $G(5,6)$. Use the converse of the Pythagorean theorem to prove that $\triangle TAG$ is a right triangle. A right triangle is an isosceles right triangle if its two legs have the same length.

Find the length of each side of the triangle by applying the distance formula, where d represents the length of a segment whose endpoints are (x_1, y_1) and (x_2, y_2):

$$d = \sqrt{(x_2 - x_1)^2 + (y_2 - y_1)^2}$$

Length of $\overline{TA}$: Let $(x_1, y_1) = T(1,3)$ and $(x_2, y_2) = A(8,2)$. Hence, $x_1 = 1$, $y_1 = 3$, $x_2 = 8$, and $y_2 = 2$:

$$TA = \sqrt{(8-1)^2 \neq (2-3)^2}$$

$$= \sqrt{7^2 + (-1)^2}$$

$$= \sqrt{49+1}$$

$$= \sqrt{50}$$

Length of $\overline{GT}$: Let $(x_1, y_1) = G(5,6)$ and $(x_2, y_2) = T(1,3)$. Hence, $x_1 = 5$, $y_1 = 6$, $x_2 = 1$, and $y_2 = 3$:

$$GT = \sqrt{(1-5)^2 + (3-6)^2}$$

$$= \sqrt{(-4)^2 + (-3)^2}$$

$$= \sqrt{16+9}$$

$$= \sqrt{25}$$

Length of $\overline{GA}$: Let $(x_1, y_1) = G(5,6)$ and $(x_2, y_2) = A(8,2)$. Hence, $x_1 = 5$, $y_1 = 6$, $x_2 = 8$ and $y_2 = 2$:

$$GA = \sqrt{(8-5)^2 + (2-6)^2}$$

$$= \sqrt{(3)^2 + (-4)^2}$$

$$= \sqrt{9+16}$$

$$= \sqrt{25}$$

If the square of the length of the longest side of the triangle, side $\overline{TA}$, is equal to the sum of the squares of the lengths of the other two sides, then the triangle is a right triangle.

$$(TA)^2 \stackrel{?}{=} (GT)^2 + (GA)^2$$

$$\left(\sqrt{50}\right)^2 \stackrel{?}{=} \left(\sqrt{25}\right)^2 + \left(\sqrt{25}\right)^2$$

$$50 \stackrel{?}{=} 25 + 25$$

$$50 \stackrel{\checkmark}{=} 50$$

Thus, $\triangle TAG$ is a right triangle. Since right triangle TAG has two sides, $\overline{GA}$ and $\overline{GT}$, that have the same length, the triangle is an isosceles right triangle.

Topic	Question Numbers	Number of Points	Your Points	Your Percentage
1. Properties of Number Systems; Def. of Operations	25	2		
2. Finite Mathematical Systems	3	2		
3. Linear Function & Graph ($y = mx + b$, slope, eqs. of)	14, 28	2 + 2 = 4		
4. Quadratic Equation (alg. sol.—factoring, formula)	15, 32	2 + 2 = 4		
5. Parabola (incl. axis of symmetry, turning point)	22, 37	2 + 10 = 12		
6. Systems of Equations (alg. and graphic solutions)				
7. Suppls., Compl., Vertical Angles, Angle Measure				
8. Triangle Properties (eq., isos., sum ∠s, 2 sides)	11, 12	2 + 2 = 4		
9. Line ‖ One Side of Δ; Line Joining Midpts. of 2 Sides				
10. Inequalities in Δs (ext. ∠, ≠ sides, and opp. ∠s)	6, 30	2 + 2 = 4		
11. Quadrilateral Properties (▱, sq., rhom., rect., trap.)	17, 21	2 + 2 = 4		
12. Parallel Lines	5	2		
13. Alg. Oper.; Verbal Probs.	20, 29, 33, 36	2 + 2 + 2 + 10 = 16		
14. Mean Proportional; Alt. to Hypot. of Right Δ	8	2		
15. Pythag. Th., Special Rt. Δs (3-4-5, 5-12-13, 30-60-90)	16, 27	2 + 2 = 4		
16. Similar Figures (ratios & proportions	13	2		
17. Areas (Δ, rect., ▱, rhom., trap.)	39a	3		
18. Locus	2, 24	2 + 2 = 4		
19. Constructions	35	2		
20. Deductive Proofs	40, 41	10 + 10 = 20		
21. Coordinate Geom. (slope, dist., midpt., eq. of circle)	1, 10, 18, 39b	2 + 2 + 2 + 4 = 10		
22. Coordinate Geom. "Proofs"	42	10		
23. Logic	19, 23	2 + 2 = 4		
24. Permutations; Arrangements	26	2		
25. Combinations	31, 38	2 + 10 = 12		
26. Probability	34	2		
27. Trig. of Rt. Δ	7, 39c	2 + 3 = 5		
28. Literal Eqs.				
29. Transformations	4, 9	2 + 2 = 4		

Examination January 1995

Sequential Math Course II

PART I

Answer 30 questions from this part. Each correct answer will receive 2 credits. No partial credit will be allowed. Write your answers in the spaces provided. Where applicable, answers may be left in terms of π or in radical form.   [60]

1 In the accompanying diagram, $\overleftrightarrow{RS} \parallel \overleftrightarrow{TU}$ and $\overleftrightarrow{GH} \parallel \overleftrightarrow{MN}$. If m$\angle x = 115$, find m$\angle y$.

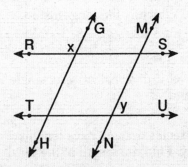

1_____

2 In the accompanying diagram, $ABCD$ is a parallelogram with altitude $\overline{DE}$ drawn to side $\overline{AB}$. If $DE = AE$, find the measure of $\angle A$.

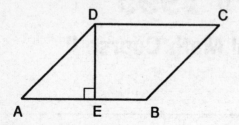

2 _____

3 The sides of $\triangle ABC$ are 6.8, 6.8, and 8.4 meters. Find the perimeter of the triangle that is formed by joining the midpoints of the sides of $\triangle ABC$.

3 _____

4 Point $A(6,3)$ is reflected in the x-axis. Find the coordinates of A', its image.

4 _____

5 If $a \spadesuit b$ is defined as $\dfrac{a - b}{a + b}$, find the value of $-3 \spadesuit 1$.

5 _____

6 In $\triangle ABC$, side $\overline{AC}$ is extended through C to D and $m\angle DCB = 60$. Which is the longest side of $\triangle ABC$?

6 _____

7 What is the length of a diagonal of a rectangle whose sides are 3 and 7?

7 _____

8 Two sides of an isosceles triangle have lengths 2 and 12, respectively. Find the length of the third side.

8 _____

9 The sides of a triangle have lengths 3, 5, and 7. In a similar triangle, the shortest side has length $x - 3$, and the longest side has length $x + 5$. Find the value of x.   9_____

10 Find the number of square units in the area of a triangle whose vertices are $A(2,0)$, $B(6,0)$, and $C(4,5)$.   10_____

11 Find, in radical form, the distance between points $(-1,-2)$ and $(5,0)$.   11_____

12 What are the coordinates of the center of a circle if the endpoints of a diameter are $(-6,2)$ and $(4,6)$?   12_____

13 In equilateral triangle ABC, $AB = 3x$ and $BC = 2x + 12$. Find the numerical value of the perimeter of $\triangle ABC$.   13_____

Directions (14–35): For *each* question chosen, write in the space provided the *numeral* preceding the word or expression that best completes the statement or answers the question.

14 Which coordinate pair is a solution for the following system of equations?

$$x^2 + y^2 = 8$$
$$x = 2$$

(1) $(2,4)$ (3) $(2,\sqrt{8})$

(2) $(2,2)$ (4) $(4,2)$ 14_____

15 In parallelogram *ABCD*, diagonal $\overline{BD}$ is drawn. Which statement must be true?

  (1) △*ABD* must be an obtuse triangle.
  (2) △*CDB* must be an acute triangle.
  (3) △*ABD* must be an isosceles triangle.
  (4) △*ABD* must be congruent to △*CDB*.   15____

16 In the accompanying diagram, *AB* intersects $\overleftrightarrow{CE}$ and $\overrightarrow{CD} \perp \overleftrightarrow{AB}$.

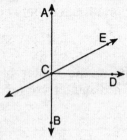

Which statement is true?

  (1) ∠*ACE* ≅ ∠*BCD*.
  (2) *B*, *C*, and *D* are collinear.
  (3) ∠*ACE* and ∠*ECD* are complementary.
  (4) ∠*ACE* and ∠*ECD* are supplementary.   16____

17 Which property is illustrated by
□(△ + O) = □△ + □O?

  (1) distributive   (3) commutative
  (2) associative   (4) transitive   17____

18 From a deck of 52 cards, two cards are randomly drawn without replacement. What is the probability of drawing two hearts?

  (1) $\frac{2}{52}$ (3) $\frac{13}{52} \cdot \frac{12}{51}$

  (2) $\frac{13}{52} \cdot \frac{13}{51}$ (4) $\frac{13}{52} \cdot \frac{13}{52}$ 18____

19 Which is logically equivalent to $\sim(\sim p \vee q)$?

  (1) $p \wedge \sim q$ (3) $\sim p \vee \sim q$

  (2) $\sim p \wedge \sim q$ (4) $p \vee \sim q$ 19_____

20 Which is an equation of the circle whose center is the origin and whose radius is 4?

  (1) $y = x^2 + 8$ (3) $x^2 + y^2 = 16$

  (2) $x^2 + y^2 = 4$ (4) $x + y = 8$ 20_____

21 Expressed in simplest form, $\dfrac{x}{2} - \dfrac{x}{3} + \dfrac{x}{4}$ is equivalent to

  (1) $\dfrac{x}{3}$ (3) $\dfrac{3x}{24}$

  (2) $\dfrac{x}{24}$ (4) $\dfrac{5x}{12}$ 21_____

22 If a translation maps point $A(-3,1)$ to point $A'(5,5)$, the translation can be represented by

  (1) $(x + 8, y + 4)$ (3) $(x + 2, y + 6)$

  (2) $(x + 8, y + 6)$ (4) $(x + 2, y + 4)$ 22_____

23 When the statement "If A, then B" is true, which statement must also be true?

  (1) If B, then A.

  (2) If not A, then B.

  (3) If not B, then A.

  (4) If not B, then not A.   23_____

24 In right triangle ABC, altitude $\overline{CD}$ is drawn to hypotenuse $\overline{AB}$. If $AD = 5$ and $DB = 24$, what is the length of $\overline{CD}$?

(1) 120

(3) $2\sqrt{30}$

(2) $\sqrt{30}$

(4) $4\sqrt{30}$

24____

25 The graph of which equation has a *negative* slope?

(1) $y = 5x - 3$

(3) $y - 2 = 4x$

(2) $x + y = 5$

(4) $y = 0$

25____

26 What is the equation of the locus of points passing through point $(3,-2)$ and 3 units from the y-axis?

(1) $x = -2$

(3) $x = 3$

(2) $y = -2$

(4) $y = 3$

26____

27 Which expression is a perfect square?

(1) $x^2 - 4x + 4$

(3) $x^2 - 9x + 9$

(2) $x^2 - 4x - 4$

(4) $x^2 - 9x - 9$

27____

28 The roots of the equation $2x^2 + 5x - 2 = 0$ are

(1) $\dfrac{5 \pm \sqrt{41}}{2}$

(3) $2, \dfrac{1}{2}$

(2) $-\dfrac{1}{2}, -2$

(4) $\dfrac{-5 \pm \sqrt{41}}{4}$

28____

29 How many different 13-letter permutations can be formed from the letters of the word "QUADRILATERAL"?

(1) $13!$

(3) $\frac{13!}{3!2!2!}$

(2) $\frac{13!}{7!}$

(4) $\frac{13!}{6!}$

29_____

30 The hypotenuse of right triangle ABC is 10 and $m\angle A = 60$. What is the measure, to the *nearest tenth*, of the leg opposite $\angle A$?

(1) 5.0

(3) 7.1

(2) 5.8

(4) 8.7

30_____

31 Which equation represents a line parallel to the line whose equation is $y = 2x - 7$?

(1) $y = 2x$

(3) $y = -7$

(2) $y = \frac{1}{2}x - 7$

(4) $y = -\frac{1}{2}x + 7$

31_____

32 Expressed in simplest form, $\frac{2x^2}{x^2 - 1} \cdot \frac{x - 1}{x}$, $x \neq 1, 0, -1$, is equivalent to

(1) $\frac{2x}{x - 1}$

(3) $\frac{2}{x}$

(2) 2

(4) $\frac{2x}{x + 1}$

32_____

33 A set contains five isosceles trapezoids, three squares, and a rhombus that is not a square. A figure is chosen at random. What is the probability that its diagonals will be congruent?

(1) 1

(3) $\frac{5}{9}$

(2) $\frac{8}{9}$

(4) $\frac{3}{9}$

33_____

34 Which graph could represent the equation $y = x^2 - 4$?

(1)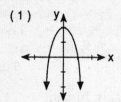

(3)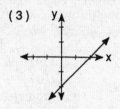

(2)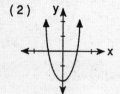

(4)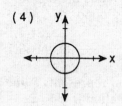

34_____

35 In the accompanying diagram, $\triangle ABC$ is scalene.

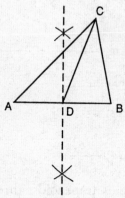

The construction on this triangle shows that $\overline{CD}$ is the

(1) median to side $\overline{AB}$
(2) bisector of angle C
(3) altitude to side $\overline{AB}$
(4) perpendicular bisector of side $\overline{AB}$

35_____

PART II

Answer three questions from this part. Clearly indicate the necessary steps, including appropriate formula substitutions, diagrams, graphs, charts, etc. Calculations that may be obtained by mental arithmetic or the calculator do not need to be shown. [30]

36 Answer both *a* and *b* for all values of *x* for which these expressions are defined.

   a Solve for *x*: $\dfrac{x + 3}{3x} = \dfrac{x}{12}$ [5]

   b Express the product as a single fraction in lowest terms:

$$\frac{x}{3x + 15} \cdot \frac{2x^2 + 11x + 5}{2x^2 + x}$$ [5]

37 *a* On graph paper, draw the graph of the equation $y = -x^2 + 4x - 1$, including all values of *x* in the interval $-1 \le x \le 5$.   [5]

   b On the same set of axes, draw the graph of the equation $x - y = 5$.   [3]

   c From the graphs drawn in parts *a* and *b*, determine the solution(s) of this system of equations:

$$\begin{aligned} y &= -x^2 + 4x - 1 \\ x - y &= 5 \end{aligned}$$ [2]

38 There are seven boys and three girls on a school tennis team. The coach must select four people from this group to participate in a county championship.

   a How many four-person teams can be formed from the group of ten students?   [3]

   b In how many ways can two boys and two girls be chosen to participate in the county championship?   [3]

   c What is the probability that two boys and two girls are chosen for the team?   [2]

   d What is the probability that a four-member team will contain at least one boy?   [2]

39 In the accompanying diagram of rhombus *ABCD*, m∠*BAD* = 36 and the length of diagonal $\overline{AEC}$ = 16.

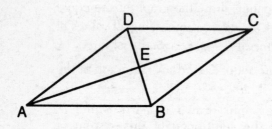

   a Find the length of diagonal $\overline{BD}$ to the *nearest tenth.*   [4]

   b Find the perimeter of rhombus *ABCD* to the *nearest integer.*   [6]

40 The endpoints of $\overline{AB}$ are $A(1,4)$ and $B(5,1)$.

   a On graph paper, draw and label $\overline{AB}$.   [1]

   b Graph and state the coordinates of $\overline{A'B'}$, the image of $\overline{AB}$ under a reflection in the y-axis. [2]

   c Graph and state the coordinates of $\overline{A''B''}$, the image of $\overline{AB}$ under a dilation of 2 with respect to the origin.   [2]

   d Using coordinate geometry, show that a line segment and its image are congruent under a line reflection and are *not* congruent under a dilation.   [5]

PART III

Answer one question from this part. Clearly indicate the necessary steps, including appropriate formula substitutions, diagrams, graphs, charts, etc. Calculations that may be obtained by mental arithmetic or the calculator do not need to be shown. [10]

41 Given: $B \rightarrow D$
$\qquad D \rightarrow \sim E$
$\qquad (\sim A \wedge \sim B) \rightarrow C$
$\qquad \sim F \rightarrow E$
$\qquad \sim A$
$\qquad \sim C$

Prove: F [10]

42 Prove: In an isosceles triangle, the line segment that bisects the vertex angle bisects the base.
[10]

Answers
January 1995
Sequential Math Course II

Answer Key

PART I

1. 65	**13.** 108	**25.** (2)
2. 45	**14.** (2)	**26.** (3)
3. 11	**15.** (4)	**27.** (1)
4. (6,–3)	**16.** (3)	**28.** (4)
5. 2	**17.** (1)	**29.** (3)
6. $\overline{AB}$	**18.** (3)	**30.** (4)
7. $\sqrt{58}$	**19.** (1)	**31.** (1)
8. 12	**20.** (3)	**32.** (4)
9. 9	**21.** (4)	**33.** (2)
10. 10	**22.** (1)	**34.** (2)
11. $\sqrt{40}$ or $2\sqrt{10}$	**23.** (4)	**35.** (1)
12. (–1,4)	**24.** (3)	

PARTS II AND III See answers explained section.

Answers Explained

PART I

1.

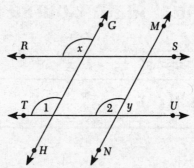

If two lines are parallel, then corresponding angles have the same measure.

Since $\overleftrightarrow{RS} \parallel \overleftrightarrow{TU}$, m$\angle x$ = m$\angle 1$; and, since $\overleftrightarrow{GH} \parallel \overleftrightarrow{MN}$, m$\angle 1$ = m$\angle 2$. Hence, by the transitive property of equality, m $\angle x$ = m $\angle 2$.

Since it is given that m$\angle x$ = 115, m$\angle 2$ = 115. Angles y and 2 are supplementary. Hence:

$$m\angle y = 180 - m\angle 2$$
$$= 180 - 115$$
$$= 65$$

The measure of $\angle y$ is **65**.

2.

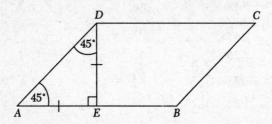

It is given that $\overline{DE} \perp \overline{AB}$ and $DE = AE$. Thus, $\triangle DEA$ is an isosceles right triangle.

In an isosceles right triangle, the acute angles are both complementary and equal in measure. The sum of the measures of two complementary angles is 90. Hence, the measure of each acute angle of right triangle DEA is one-half of 90, or 45.

The measure of $\angle A$ is **45**.

3.

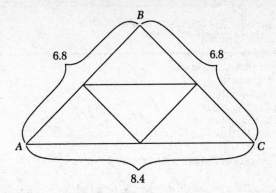

The line joining the midpoints of two sides of a triangle is parallel to the third side and is one-half of its length. Thus, if the midpoints of the three sides of △ABC are joined to form a new triangle, each side of the new triangle is one-half the length of the side of △ABC that is opposite it.

Since the lengths of the sides of △ABC are 6.8, 6.8, and 8.4 meters, the lengths of the sides of the new triangle that lie opposite these sides are 3.4, 3.4, and 4.2 meters, respectively. Hence, the perimeter of the new triangle is $3.4 + 3.4 + 4.2 = 11$ meters.

The perimeter is **11** meters.

4. The image point $P(x,y)$ after a reflection in the x-axis is point $P'(x,-y)$. If point $A(6,3)$ is reflected in the x-axis, the coordinates of A', the image of point A, are $(6,-3)$.

The coordinates of A' are $(6,-3)$.

5. If $a \spadesuit b$ is defined as $\dfrac{a-b}{a+b}$,

then the value of $-3 \spadesuit 1$ is obtained by substituting -3 for a and 1 for b:

$$a \spadesuit b = \frac{a-b}{a+b}$$

Let $a = -3$ and $b = 1$:

$$-3 \spadesuit 1 = \frac{-3-1}{-3+1}$$

$$= \frac{-4}{-2}$$

Simplify:

$$= 2$$

The value of $-3 \spadesuit 1$ is **2**.

6. In the accompanying diagram, side $\overline{AC}$ is extended through C to D. It is given that m$\angle DCB = 60$. Then, since angles DCB and ACB are supplementary, m$\angle ACB = 180 - 60 = 120$.

The longest side of
a triangle is the side that is
opposite the angle that has
the greatest measure. Since
an obtuse angle of a triangle
must be the angle with
the greatest measure, the
longest side of triangle ABC
is the side that is opposite
obtuse angle ACB, that is,
side $\overline{AB}$.

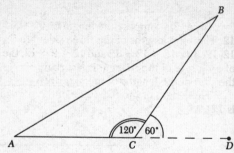

The longest side of $\triangle ABC$ is $\overline{AB}$.

7. A diagonal of a rectangle divides the rectangle into two right triangles.
The adjacent sides of the rectangle form the legs of each right triangle, and
the diagonal is the hypotenuse of both right triangles.

In a right triangle, the square of
the length of the hypotenuse is equal
to the sum of the squares of
the lengths of the legs. If x
represents the length of a
diagonal of a rectangle whose
adjacent sides measure 3 and 7,
then

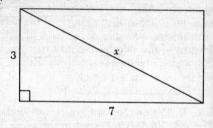

$$x^2 = 3^2 + 7^2$$
$$= 9 + 49$$
$$= 58$$
$$x = \pm \sqrt{58}$$

The length of the diagonal is $\sqrt{58}$.

8. An isosceles triangle has two sides that have the same length. If the
lengths of two sides of an isosceles triangle are 2 and 12, the length of the third
side must be either 2 or 12.

To determine whether the length of the third side is 2 or 12, check
whether, in each case, the length of each side of the triangle is less than the
sum of the lengths of the other two sides.

Case (1): Suppose
the length of the third side
is 2. Then the lengths of
the three sides are 2, 2, and
12. Since it is *not* true that
$12 < 2 + 2$, the length of
the third side is not 2.

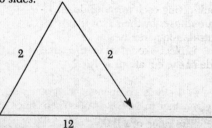

Case (2): Suppose the length of the third side is 12. Then the lengths of the three sides are 2, 12, 12. Since $2 < 12 + 12$ and $12 < 2 + 12$, the length of each side of the triangle is less than the sum of the lengths of the other two sides.

The length of the third side of the triangle is **12**.

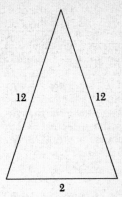

9.

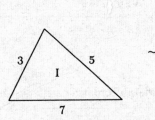

The lengths of corresponding sides of similar triangles are in proportion:

$$\frac{\text{shortest side of } \triangle \text{I}}{\text{shortest side of } \triangle \text{II}} = \frac{\text{longest side of } \triangle \text{I}}{\text{longest side of } \triangle \text{II}}$$

Substitute the given values for the lengths of the sides:

$$\frac{3}{x-3} = \frac{7}{x+5}$$

In a proportion the product of the means equals the product of the extremes (cross-multiply):

$$7(x-3) = 3(x+5)$$

Remove the parentheses by multiplying each term inside the parentheses by the factor that is outside the parentheses:

$$7x - 21 = 3x + 15$$

Collect like terms on the same side of the equation:

$$7x - 3x = 15 + 21$$

$$4x = 36$$

The value of x is **9**.

$$x = \frac{36}{4} = 9$$

10. The area of a triangle is equal to one-half the product of the lengths of its base and the altitude drawn to that base.

In the accompanying figure, the length of base $\overline{AB}$ is $6 - 2 = 4$, and the length of altitude $\overline{CH}$ is 5.

Thus:

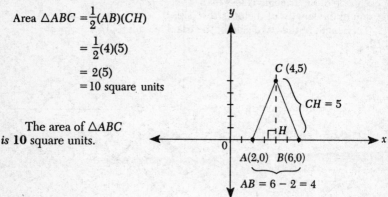

Area $\triangle ABC = \frac{1}{2}(AB)(CH)$

$\quad\quad\quad\quad = \frac{1}{2}(4)(5)$

$\quad\quad\quad\quad = 2(5)$

$\quad\quad\quad\quad = 10$ square units

The area of $\triangle ABC$
is **10** square units.

11. The distance d between the points whose coordinates are (x_1, y_1) and (x_2, y_2) is given by the formula

$$d = \sqrt{(x_2 - x_1)^2 + (y_2 - y_1)^2}$$

To find the distance between points $(-1, -2)$ and $(5, 0)$, let $x_1 = -1$, $y_1 = -2$, $x_2 = 5$, and $y_2 = 0$. Thus:

$$\begin{aligned}
d &= \sqrt{(5 - (-1))^2 + (0 - (-2))^2} \\
&= \sqrt{(5 + 1)^2 + (0 + 2)^2} \\
&= \sqrt{6^2 + 2^2} \\
&= \sqrt{36 + 4} \\
&= \sqrt{40}
\end{aligned}$$

The distance between the given points is $\sqrt{40}$ or $2\sqrt{10}$.

12. The coordinates of the midpoint of a line segment are the averages of the corresponding coordinates of the endpoints of the line segment. In general, if the endpoints of a line segment are (x_1, y_1) and (x_2, y_2), then the coordinates of the midpoint $M(\overline{x}, \overline{y})$ are given by the formulas

$$\overline{x} = \frac{x_1 + x_2}{2} \quad \text{and} \quad \overline{y} = \frac{y_1 + y_2}{2}$$

The center of a circle is the midpoint of any diameter of that circle. To find the coordinates of the center of a circle in which the endpoints of a diameter are $(-6, 2)$ and $(4, 6)$, let $x_1 = -6$, $y_1 = 2$, $x_2 = 4$, $y_2 = 6$. Thus:

$$\bar{x} = \frac{x_1 + x_2}{2} \quad \text{and} \quad \bar{y} = \frac{y_1 + y_2}{2}$$

$$= \frac{-6 + 4}{2} \qquad\qquad = \frac{2 + 6}{2}$$

$$= \frac{-2}{2} \qquad\qquad\quad = \frac{8}{2}$$

$$= -1 \qquad\qquad\quad\; = 4$$

The coordinates of the center of the circle are $(-1, 4)$.

13. An equilateral triangle is a triangle in which all three sides have the same length.

It is given that, in equilateral triangle ABC, $AB = 3x$ and $BC = 2x + 12$. Thus:

$$AB = BC$$
$$3x = 2x + 12$$
$$x = 12$$

Hence, $AB = 3x = 3(12) = 36$. Since each of the three sides has the same length, the perimeter of the triangle is $36 + 36 + 36 = 108$.

The numerical value of the perimeter of $\triangle ABC$ is **108**.

14. The system of equations given is:

$$x^2 + y^2 = 8$$
$$x = 2$$

Substitute 2 for x in the first equation:

$$2^2 + y^2 = 8$$
$$4 + y^2 = 8$$

Isolate y^2:

$$y^2 = 4$$

Take the square root of each side of the equation:

$$y = \pm\sqrt{4} = \pm 2$$

Write the two solutions: $(2, 2)$ and $(2, -2)$

Choice (2) contains the solution $(2, 2)$.

The correct choice is **(2)**.

15. A diagonal of a parallelogram always divides the parallelogram into two congruent triangles.

The correct choice is **(4)**.

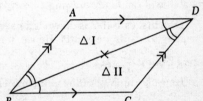

$$\triangle \text{ I} \cong \triangle \text{ II by ASA} \cong \text{ASA}$$

16.

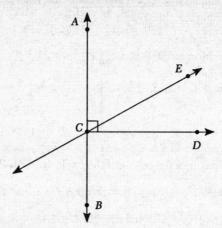

It is given that $\overline{CD} \perp \overline{AB}$. Since the exterior sides of adjacent angles ACE and ECD form a right angle, m$\angle ACE$ + m$\angle ECD$ = 90. Thus, angles ACE and ECD are complementary.

The correct choice is **(3)**.

17. If a, b, and c, are real numbers, the distributive property states that

$$a(b + c) = ab + bc$$

The given equation

$$\square(\triangle + O) = \square\triangle + \square O$$

has the form $a(b + c) = ab + bc$, where $a = \square$, $b = \triangle$, and $c = O$.

The correct choice is **(1)**.

18. Since a standard deck of 52 playing cards contains 13 hearts, the probability of randomly drawing a heart is $\frac{13}{52}$.

If the first card that is drawn is a heart and is not replaced, then 12 of the remaining 51 cards are hearts. Hence, the probability of randomly drawing a second heart is $\frac{12}{51}$.

Using the multiplication principle of counting, we find that the probability of randomly drawing two hearts without replacement is $\frac{13}{52} \cdot \frac{12}{51}$.

The correct choice is **(3)**.

19. A statement that is logically equivalent to the negation of a disjunction or conjunction may be obtained by using one of De Morgan's laws.

The given statement is:	$\sim(\sim p \vee q)$
One of De Morgan's laws states:	$\sim(A \vee B) \leftrightarrow \sim A \wedge \sim B$
Let $A = \sim p$ and $B = q$:	$\sim(\sim p \vee q) \leftrightarrow \sim(\sim p) \wedge \sim q$
By the law of double negation $\sim(\sim p)$ may be replaced by p:	$\sim(\sim p \vee q) \leftrightarrow \quad p \wedge \sim q$

The correct choice is (**1**).

20. An equation of a circle whose center is the origin and whose radius is r is $x^2 + y^2 = r^2$.

To obtain an equation of a circle whose center is the origin and whose radius is 4, replace r with 4:

$$x^2 + y^2 = 4^2 \quad \text{or} \quad x^2 + y^2 = 16$$

The correct choice is (**3**).

21. The given expression $\dfrac{x}{2} - \dfrac{x}{3} + \dfrac{x}{4}$. The Lowest Common Denominator (LCD) is 12 since 12 is the smallest positive integer into which 2, 3, and 4 divide evenly.

To change the first fraction into an equivalent fraction that has the LCD as its denominator, multiply it by 1 in the form of $\dfrac{6}{6}$. Similarly, multiply the second fraction by $\dfrac{4}{4}$ and

the last fraction by $\dfrac{3}{3}$:

$$\frac{x}{2} - \frac{x}{3} + \frac{x}{4} = \frac{x}{2}\left(\frac{6}{6}\right) - \frac{x}{3}\left(\frac{4}{4}\right) + \frac{x}{4}\left(\frac{3}{3}\right)$$

$$= \frac{6x}{12} - \frac{4x}{12} + \frac{3x}{12}$$

Write the sum of the numerators over the common denominator:

$$= \frac{6x - 4x + 3x}{12}$$

Simplify the numerator:

$$= \frac{2x + 3x}{12}$$

$$= \frac{5x}{12}$$

The correct choice is (**4**).

22. If a translation "moves" a point $P(x,y)$ h units in the horizontal direction and k units in the vertical direction, then the coordinates of the image point can be represented by $(x + h, y + k)$.

The given translation maps points $A(-3,1)$ to point $A'(5,5)$. The constant h is the value that, when added to -3, gives 5. Since $-3 + h = 5$, $h = 8$. Similarly, since $1 + k = 5$, $k = 4$.

Hence, the given translation maps (x,y) to $(x + 8, y + 4)$.

The correct choice is **(1)**.

23. A conditional statement and its contrapositive always have the same truth values.

To form the contrapositive of a conditional statement, interchange the two parts of the conditional statement and then negate both parts. If the original statement is "If A, then B," then the contrapositive is "If not B, then not A."

Thus, when the given statement, "If A, then B" is true, the statement "If not B, then not A" must also be true.

The correct choice is **(4)**.

24.

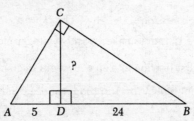

In a right triangle, the length of the altitude drawn to the hypotenuse is the mean proportional between the lengths of the two segments of the hypotenuse that are formed by the altitude:

$$\frac{AD}{CD} = \frac{CD}{DB}$$

Substitute the given values $AD = 5$ and $DB = 24$, and let $CD = x$:

$$\frac{5}{x} = \frac{x}{24}$$

In a proportion the product of the means equals the product of the extremes (cross-multiply):

$$x \cdot x = 5 \cdot 24$$
$$x^2 = 120$$

Take the square root of each side of the equation:

$$x = \pm\sqrt{120}$$

Reject the negative value of x since x represents the length of a side of the triangle:

$$= \sqrt{120}$$

Factor the radicand so that one of its factors is the highest perfect square factor of 120:

$$= \sqrt{4 \cdot 30}$$

Distribute the radical sign over each
factor of the radicand: $= \sqrt{4} \cdot \sqrt{30}$

Evaluate $\sqrt{4}$: $= 2\sqrt{30}$

The correct choice is **(3)**.

25. The graph of an equation that has the form $y = mx + b$ is a line
whose slope is m and whose y-intercept is b.

Examine each choice in turn. If necessary, put the equation given in the
form $y = mx + b$ so that you can tell the slope of its graph.

Choice (1): The given equation is $y = 5x - 3$. Since $m = 5$, the slope of
the graph of this equation is 5.

Choice (2): The given equation is $x + y = 5$. Solve for y by subtracting
x on each side of the equation: $y = -x + 5$. Since $m = -1$, the slope of the
graph of this equation is -1.

Choice (3): The given equation is $y - 2 = 4x$. Solve for y by adding 2 on
each side of the equation: $y = 4x + 2$. Since $m = 4$, the slope of the graph of
this equation is 4.

Choice (4): The given equation is $y = 0$, which may also be written as
$y = 0 \cdot x$. Since $m = 0$, the slope of the graph of this equation is 0.

The correct choice is **(2)**.

26. The locus of points
3 units from the y-axis is the pair
of vertical lines on either sides of
the y-axis, whose equations are
$x = -3$ and $x = 3$.

It is given that the desired
locus passes through point $(3, -2)$.
Since the line whose equation
is $x = 3$ passes through
$(3, -2)$, $x = 3$ describes the
locus of points that pass through
point $(3, -2)$ and are 3 units
from the y-axis.

The correct choice is **(3)**.

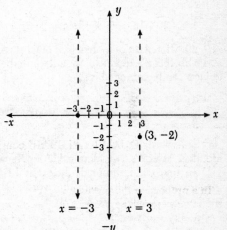

27. A perfect square trinomial is a trinomial that can be factored as the
square of a binomial. Try to factor the quadratic trinomial in each choice. In
choice (1),

$$x^2 - 4x + 4 = (x - 2)(x - 2) = (x - 2)^2$$

The correct choice is **(1)**.

28. The given equation is $2x^2 + 5x - 2 = 0$. Since the quadratic trinomial on the left side of the equation cannot be factored over the set of integers, use the quadratic formula to find the roots of the given equation.

If a quadratic equation is in the form $ax^2 + bx + c = 0$, then its roots are given by the formula:

$$x = \frac{-b \pm \sqrt{b^2 - 4ac}}{2a} \quad (a \neq 0)$$

Since the given equation is in the form $ax^2 + bx + c = 0$, substitute the values $a = 2, b = 5$, and $c = -2$ in the formula:

$$= \frac{-5 \pm \sqrt{5^2 - 4(2)(-2)}}{2(2)}$$

$$= \frac{-5 \pm \sqrt{25 + 16}}{4}$$

$$= \frac{-5 \pm \sqrt{41}}{4}$$

The correct choice is **(4)**.

29. If in a set of n objects, a objects are identical, b objects are identical, and c objects are identical, then the number of different ways in which the n objects can be arranged is

$$\frac{n!}{a!\,b!\,c!}$$

The word "QUADRILATERAL" consists of 13 letters, including three identical letter A's, two identical letter R's, and two identical letter L's.

To find the number of different 13-letter arrangements that can be formed from the letters of the word "QUADRILATERAL," let $n = 13$, $a = 3, b = 2$, and $c = 2$:

$$\frac{n!}{a!\,b!\,c!} = \frac{13!}{3!\,2!\,2!}$$

The correct choice is **(3)**.

30. To find the length of a leg of a right triangle, given the measure of an acute angle of the triangle that is opposite it and the length of the hypotenuse, use the sine ratio:

$$\sin \angle A = \frac{\text{leg opposite } \angle A}{\text{hypotenuse}}$$

$$= \frac{BC}{\text{hypotenuse}}$$

$$\sin 60° = \frac{BC}{10}$$

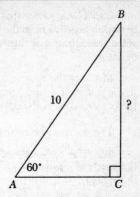

Look under the column labeled "Angle" in the Table of Natural Trigonometric Functions. Locate 60°, and read across on the same line until you locate the value under the column labeled "Sine."

Record 0.8660 as the value of sin 60°.
Thus:

$$0.8660 = \frac{BC}{10}$$

Multiply each side of the
equation by 10:

$$10(0.8660) = BC$$
$$8.660 = BC$$

The length of side $\overline{BC}$, correct to the *nearest tenth*, is 8.7.
The correct choice is **(4)**.

31. If two lines have the same slope but different y-intercepts, they are parallel.

A line whose equation has the form $y = mx + b$ has a slope of m and a y-intercept of b. The equation of the given line is $y = 2x - 7$. Since $m = 2$ and $b = -7$, the slope of the line is 2 and its y-intercept is -7.

Each of the equations in the four choices has the form $y = mx + b$. Look for an equation in which $m = 2$ and $b \neq -7$.

The equation in choice (1) is $y = 2x$, so $m = 2$ and $b = 0$. This line has the same slope as $y = 2x - 7$ and a different y-intercept. Thus, the lines represented by the equations $y = 2x - 7$ and $y = 2x$ are parallel.

The correct choice is **(1)**.

32. The given product is:

$$\frac{2x^2}{x^2 - 1} \cdot \frac{x - 1}{x} \quad (x \neq 1, 0, -1)$$

Where possible, factor any numerator
and denominator. The first denominator
is the difference of two squares:

$$\frac{2x^2}{(x + 1)(x - 1)} \cdot \frac{x - 1}{x}$$

Cancel any factor that appears
in both a numerator and a denominator
since the quotient of these factors is 1:

$$\frac{\overset{x}{\cancel{2x^2}}}{(x+1)\underset{1}{(\cancel{x-1})}} \cdot \frac{\overset{1}{\cancel{x-1}}}{\underset{1}{\cancel{x}}}$$

Multiply the remaining factors together
in the numerator, and multiply the remaining
factors together in the denominator:

$$\frac{2x}{x+1}$$

The correct choice is **(4)**.

33. The diagonals of an isosceles trapezoid are congruent, as are the diagonals of a square. The diagonals of a rhombus that is not a square are not congruent.

If a set contains five isosceles trapezoids, three squares, and a rhombus that is not a square, then eight of the nine figures have diagonals that are congruent. Hence, the probability of randomly choosing a figure from this set whose diagonals will be congruent is $\frac{8}{9}$.

The correct choice is **(2)**.

34. The given equation, $y = x^2 - 4$, represents a parabola.

The graph in choice (3) can be eliminated since it is a line, and the graph in choice (4) can be eliminated since it is a circle.

Since the coefficient of the x^2-term is positive, the turning point (vertex) of its graph will be the lowest point on the graph. The parabola in choice (2) has this feature.

The correct choice is **(2)**.

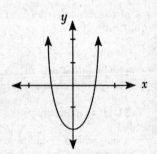

35. A *median* of a triangle is a segment drawn from a vertex of the triangle to the midpoint of the side opposite that vertex.

An *altitude* of a triangle is a segment that is drawn from a vertex of the triangle and is perpendicular to the side that is opposite that vertex.

A *bisector* of an angle (or side) divides that angle (or side) into two congruent parts.

In the diagram, the broken line that is determined by the intersection of the two pairs of compass arcs on either side of $\overline{AB}$ represents the perpendicular bisector of $\overline{AB}$. Hence, point D is the midpoint of $\overline{AB}$. Since $\overline{CD}$ is drawn from vertex C to the midpoint of $\overline{AB}$, it is the *median* to side $\overline{AB}$.

The correct choice is **(1)**.

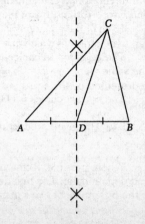

PART II

36. a. The given equation is:

$$\frac{x+3}{3x} = \frac{x}{12}$$

In a proportion, the product of the means equals the product of the extremes (cross-multiply):

$$x(3x) = 12(x+3)$$
$$3x^2 = 12x + 36$$

Collect all terms on the left side of the equation:

$$3x^2 - 12x - 36 = 0$$

Divide each term of the equation by 3:

$$\frac{3x^2}{3} - \frac{12x}{3} - \frac{36}{3} = \frac{0}{3}$$

$$x^2 - 4x - 12 = 0$$

Factor the left side of the equation as the product of two binomials:

$$(x - 6)(x + 2) = 0$$

If the product of two factors is 0, then either or both factors are 0:

$$x - 6 = 0 \quad or \quad x + 2 = 0$$
$$x = 6 \quad or \quad x = -2$$

The solutions for x are **6** and **−2**.

b. The given product is:

$$\frac{x}{3x + 15} \cdot \frac{2x^2 + 11x + 5}{2x^2 + x}$$

Where possible, factor any numerator and denominator. The first denominator has a common factor of 3, and the second denominator has a common factor of x. The second numerator can be factored as the product of two binomials:

$$\frac{x}{3(x + 5)} \cdot \frac{(2x + 1)(x + 5)}{x(2x + 1)}$$

Cancel any factor that appears in both a numerator and a denominator since the quotient of these factors is 1:

$$\frac{\overset{1}{\cancel{x}}}{3\cancel{(x + 5)}} \cdot \frac{\overset{1}{\cancel{(2x + 1)}}\overset{1}{\cancel{(x + 5)}}}{\cancel{x}\underset{1}{\cancel{(2x + 1)}}}$$

Multiply the remaining factors together in the numerator, and multiply the remaining factors together in the denominator:

$$\frac{1}{3}$$

The product in lowest terms is $\frac{1}{3}$.

37. a. Before drawing the graph of $y = -x^2 + 4x - 1$ over the interval $-1 \leq x \leq 5$, prepare a table of values for x and y by substituting each integer value of x, from -1 to 5, into the given equation to obtain the corresponding value of y:

x	$-x^2 + 4x - 1$	$= y$
-1	$-(-1)^2 + 4(-1) - 1 = -1 - 4 - 1$	$= -6$
0	$-(0)^2 + 4(0) - 1 = 0 - 1$	$= -1$
1	$-(1)^2 + 4(1) - 1 = -1 + 4 - 1$	$= 2$
2	$-(2)^2 + 4(2) - 1 = -4 + 8 - 1$	$= 3$
3	$-(3)^2 + 4(3) - 1 = -9 + 12 - 1$	$= 2$
4	$-(4)^2 + 4(4) - 1 = -16 + 16 - 1$	$= -1$
5	$-(5)^2 + 4(5) - 1 = -25 + 20 - 1$	$= -6$

Now plot points $(-1, -6)$, $(0, -1)$, $(1, 2)$, $(2, 3)$, $(3, 2)$, $(4, -1)$, and $(5, -6)$. Connect these points with a smooth curve that has the shape of a parabola whose turning point (vertex) is at $(2, 3)$. Label this graph with its equation, $y = -x^2 + 4x - 1$, as shown in the accompanying figure.

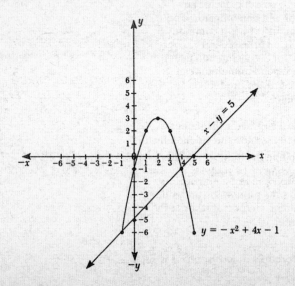

b. To draw the graph of $x - y = 5$, first prepare a table of values of x and y. Before preparing this table, solve the equation for y : $y = x - 5$. Choose three convenient values for x, and substitute them into the equation $y = x - 5$ to find the corresponding values of y:

x	$x - 5$	$= y$
0	$0 - 5$	$= -5$
3	$3 - 5$	$= -2$
5	$5 - 5$	$= 0$

On the same set of axes used for part **a**, plot points $(0,-5)$, $(3,-2)$, and $(5,0)$, and then draw a straight line through them. Label this line with its equation, $x - y = 5$, as shown in the accompanying figure.

c. The real solution(s) of a system comprised of a linear equation and a quadratic equation can be expressed as the coordinates of those points, if any, at which the graphs of the two equations intersect. Since the graphs drawn in parts **a** and **b** intersect at $(-1,-6)$ and $(4,-1)$, the coordinates of these points are the solutions to the system of equations

$$y = -x^2 + 4x - 1$$
$$x - y = 5$$

The solutions are $(-1,-6)$ and $(4,-1)$.

38. The problem states that, from a group of seven boys and three girls on a school tennis team, the coach must select four people to participate in a county championship.

Without regard to order, r objects may be selected from a group of n objects in $_nC_r$ ways, where

$$_nC_r = \frac{n!}{r!(n - r)!}$$

a. To find the number of different four-person teams that can be formed from the group of 10 students, evaluate $_nC_r$ for $r = 4$ and $n = 10$:

$$_nC_r = \frac{n!}{r!(n - r)!}$$

$$_{10}C_4 = \frac{10!}{4!(10 - 4)!}$$

$$= \frac{10!}{4! \cdot 6!}$$

$$= \frac{10 \cdot \overset{3}{\cancel{9}} \cdot \overset{1}{\cancel{8}} \cdot 7 \cdot \overset{1}{\cancel{6!}}}{\cancel{4} \cdot \cancel{3} \cdot \cancel{2} \cdot 1 \cdot \cancel{6!}}$$

$$= 10 \cdot 3 \cdot 7$$

$$= 210$$

From the group of 10 students, **210** four-person teams can be formed.

b. Two boys can be chosen from a group of seven boys in $_7C_2$ different ways. Two girls can be chosen from a group of three girls in $_3C_2$ different ways.

The product of $_7C_2$ and $_3C_2$ gives the number of different ways in which two boys *and* two girls can be chosen from a group of seven boys and three girls. Since

$$_7C_2 = \frac{7!}{2!(7-2)!} = \frac{7!}{2! \cdot 5!} \quad \text{and} \quad _3C_2 = \frac{3!}{2!(3-2)!} = \frac{3!}{2!},$$

$$_7C_2 \cdot {}_3C_2 = \frac{7!}{2! \cdot 5!} \cdot \frac{3!}{2!}$$

$$= \frac{7 \cdot \overset{3}{\cancel{6}} \cdot \overset{1}{\cancel{5!}}}{\cancel{2} \cancel{1} \cdot \cancel{5!}} \cdot \frac{3 \cdot \overset{1}{\cancel{2!}}}{\cancel{2!}}$$

$$= 7 \cdot 3 \cdot 3$$

$$= 63$$

There are **63** ways in which two boys and two girls can be chosen to participate in the county championship.

c. To find the probability that two boys and two girls will be chosen for the team, divide the number of ways in which the two boys and two girls can be chosen, obtained in part **b**, by the number of four-person teams that can be formed, obtained in part **a**: $\frac{63}{210}$.

The probability that two boys and two girls will be chosen for the team is $\frac{63}{210}$.

d. Since there are only three girls in the group of 10 students, every four-member team must include at least one boy. Since the probability of a certainty is 1, the probability that a four-member team will include at least one boy is 1.

The probability that a four-member team will include at least one boy is **1**.

39.

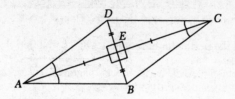

a. The diagonals of a rhombus:

• bisect the angles of the rhombus. Hence, if m∠BAD = 36, m∠BAE
= $\frac{1}{2}$(36) = 18.

• bisect each other. Hence, if the length of $\overline{AEC}$ is 16, then AE = $\frac{1}{2}$(16)
= 8.

• intersect at right angles. Hence ∠AEB is a right angle, and m∠AEB
= 90.

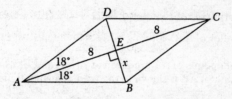

To find the length of diagonal $\overline{BD}$, first find the length of $\overline{BE}$ in right
triangle AEB. If x = BE, then

$$\tan \angle BAE = \frac{\text{leg opposite } \angle BAE}{\text{leg adjacent to } \angle BAE}$$

$$= \frac{BE}{AE}$$

$$\tan 18° = \frac{x}{8}$$

Look under the column labeled "Angle" in the Table of Natural Trigonometric Functions. Locate 18°, and read across on the same line until you
locate the value under the column labeled "Tangent."

Record 0.3249 as the value of tan 18°. Thus:

$$0.3249 = \frac{x}{8}$$

$$8(0.3249) = x$$

$$2.5992 = x$$

Since $x = BE = 2.5992$, $BD = 2(2.5992) = 5.1984$.
The length of $\overline{BD}$, correct to the *nearest tenth*, is **5.2**.

b. To find the perimeter of rhombus $ABCD$, first find the length of a side of the rhombus.

In right triangle AEB, apply the Pythagorean relationship, where side $\overline{AB}$ is the hypotenuse of the right triangle:

$$(AB)^2 = (AE)^2 + (BE)^2$$

From part **a**, let $AE = 8$ and, to the nearest tenth, let $BE = 2.6$:

$$= (8)^2 + (2.6)^2$$
$$= 64 + 6.76$$
$$= 70.76$$

Take the square root of each side of the equation:

$$AB = \sqrt{70.76} = 8.412$$

Since each side of a rhombus has the same length, the perimeter of rhombus $ABCD$ is four times the length of side $\overline{AB}$:

Perimeter of rhombus $ABCD = 4(8.412) = 33.648$

The perimeter of the rhombus, correct to the *nearest integer*, is **34**.

40. The endpoints of $\overline{AB}$ are given as $A(1,4)$ and $B(5,1)$.
a. The graph of $\overline{AB}$ is shown in the accompanying figure.

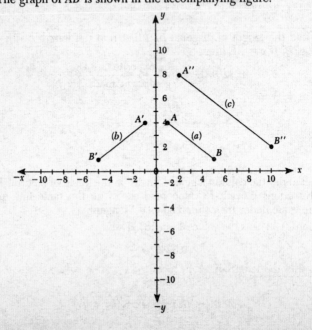

b. If the point whose coordinates are (x,y) is reflected in the y-axis, then $(-x, y)$ are the coordinates of the image of that point. Thus, if $\overline{AB}$ is reflected in the y-axis, then the coordinates of the endpoints of $\overline{A'B'}$, the image of $\overline{AB}$, are $A'(-1,4)$ and $B'(-5,1)$. The graph of $\overline{A'B'}$ is shown in the accompanying figure.

The coordinates of the endpoints of $\overline{A'B'}$ are **$A'(-1,4)$ and $B'(-5,1)$.**

c. If a segment is dilated with respect to the origin, using a scale factor of k, then each point $P(x, y)$ on the segment is mapped onto the image point $P'(kx, ky)$. Thus, the image of $\overline{AB}$ under a dilation whose scale factor is 2 is the segment $\overline{A''B''}$ whose endpoints have coordinates that are twice the x- and y-coordinates of the corresponding endpoints of $\overline{AB}$. Hence, the coordinates of A'' are $(2(1), 2(4)) = (2,8)$ and the coordinates of B'' are $(2(5), 2(1)) = (10,2)$. The graph of $\overline{A''B''}$ is shown in the accompanying figure.

The coordinates of the endpoints of $\overline{A''B''}$ are **$A''(2,8)$ and $B''(10,2)$.**

d. In general, the distance d between the points whose coordinates are (x_1, y_1) and (x_2, y_2) is given by the formula

$$d = \sqrt{(x_2 - x_1)^2 + (y_2 - y_1)^2}$$

To show that a line segment and its image are congruent under a line reflection and *not* congruent under a dilation with a scale factor different than ± 1, use the distance formula to find the lengths of $\overline{AB}$, $\overline{A'B'}$, and $\overline{A''B''}$.

To find the length of $\overline{AB}$: Find the distance between points $A(1,4)$ and $B(5,1)$:

$$AB = \sqrt{(x_2 - x_1)^2 + (y_2 - y_1)^2}$$

Let $x_1 = 1$, $y_1 = 4$, $x_2 = 5$, and $y_2 = 1$; then

$$AB = \sqrt{(5 - 1)^2 + (1 - 4)^2}$$

$$= \sqrt{4^2 + (-3)^2}$$

$$= \sqrt{16 + 9}$$

$$= \sqrt{25}$$

$$= 5$$

To find the length of $\overline{A'B'}$: Find the distance between points $A'(-1,4)$ and $B'(-5,1)$:

$$A'B' = \sqrt{(x_2 - x_1)^2 + (y_2 - y_1)^2}$$

Let $x_1 = -1$, $y_1 = 4$, $x_2 = -5$,
and $y_2 = 1$; then

$$A'B' = \sqrt{(-5 - (-1))^2 + (1 - 4)^2}$$

$$= \sqrt{(-5 + 1)^2 + (-3)^2}$$

$$= \sqrt{(-4)^2 + (-3)^2}$$

$$= \sqrt{16 + 9}$$

$$= \sqrt{25}$$

$$= 5$$

Since $\overline{AB}$ and $\overline{A'B'}$ have the same length, a line segment and its image are congruent under a line reflection.

To find the length of $\overline{A''B''}$: Find the distance between points A'' (2,8) and B''(10, 2):

$$A''B'' = \sqrt{(x_2 - x_1)^2 + (y_2 - y_1)^2}$$

Let $x_1 = 2$, $y_1 = 8$, $x_2 = 10$, and $y_2 = 2$; then

$$A''B'' = \sqrt{(10 - 2)^2 + (2 - 8)^2}$$

$$= \sqrt{(-8)^2 + (-6)^2}$$

$$= \sqrt{64 + 36}$$

$$= \sqrt{100}$$

$$= 10$$

Since $\overline{AB}$ and $\overline{A''B''}$ have different lengths, a line segment and its image are *not* congruent under a dilation whose scale factor is 2.

PART III

41. Given: $B \rightarrow D$
$D \rightarrow \sim E$
$(\sim A \wedge \sim B) \rightarrow C$
$\sim F \rightarrow E$
$\sim A$
$\sim C$

Prove: F

PROOF

Statement	Reason
1. ~C	1. Given.
2. (~A ∧ ~B) → C	2. Given.
3. ~(~A ∧ ~B)	3. Law of *modus tollens* (1, 2).
4. ~(~A) ∨ ~(~B)	4. De Morgan's law.
5. A ∨ B	5. Law of double negation.
6. ~A	6. Given.
7. B	7. Law of disjunctive inference (5, 6).
8. B → D	8. Given.
9. D	9. Law of detachment (7, 8).
10. D → ~E	10. Given.
11. ~E	11. Law of detachment (9, 10).
12. ~F → E	12. Given.
13. ~(~F)	13. Law of *modus tollens* (11, 12).
14. F	14. Law of double negation.

42. Given:

△ABC is isosceles with
$\overline{AB} \cong \overline{CB}$.
$\overline{BD}$ bisects ∠ABC.

Prove: $\overline{AD} \cong \overline{CD}$

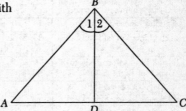

PLAN: Prove △ABD ≅ △CBD by SAS ≅ SAS.

PROOF

Statement	Reason
1. △ABC is isosceles with $\overline{AB} \cong \overline{CB}$ (Side ≅ Side).	1. Given.
2. $\overline{BD}$ bisects ∠ABC.	2. Given.
3. ∠1 ≅ ∠2 (Angle ≅ Angle)	3. The bisector of an angle divides the angle into two congruent angles.
4. $\overline{BD} \cong \overline{BD}$ (Side ≅ Side)	4. Reflexive property of congruence.
5. △ABD ≅ △CBD	5. SAS ≅ SAS
6. $\overline{AD} \cong \overline{CD}$	6. Corresponding sides of congruent triangles are congruent.

Topic	Question Numbers	Number of Points	Your Points	Your Percentage
1. Properties of Number Systems; Def. of Operations	5, 17	$2 + 2 = 4$		
2. Finite Mathematical Systems				
3. Linear Function & Graph ($y = mx + b$, slope, eqs. of)	25, 31, 37(b)	$2 + 2 + 3 = 7$		
4. Quadratic Equation (alg. sol.—factoring, formula)	28	2		
5. Parabola (incl. axis of symmetry, turning point)	34, 37(a)	$2 + 5 = 7$		
6. Systems of Equations (alg. and graphic solutions)	14, 37(c)	$2 + 2 = 4$		
7. Suppls., Compl., Vertical Angles, Angle Measure	16	2		
8. Triangle Properties (eq., isos., sum ∠s, 2 sides)	2, 8, 13	$2 + 2 + 2 = 6$		
9. Line ∥ One Side of △; Line Joining Midpts. of 2 Sides	3	2		
10. Inequalities in △s (ext. ∠, ≠ sides, and opp. ∠s)	6	2		
11. Quadrilateral Properties (▱, sq., rhom., rect., trap.)	15	2		
12. Parallel Lines	1	2		
13. Alg. Oper.; Verbal Probs.	21, 27, 32, 36	$2 + 2 + 2 + 10 = 16$		
14. Mean Proportional; Alt. to Hypot. of Right △	24	2		
15. Pythag. Th., Special Rt. △s (3-4-5, 5-12-13, 30-60-90)	7	2		
16. Similar Figures (ratios & proportions	9	2		
17. Areas (△, rect., ▱, rhom., trap.)	10	2		
18. Locus	26	2		
19. Constructions	35	2		
20. Deductive Proofs	42	10		
21. Coordinate Geom. (slope, dist., midpt., eq. of circle)	11, 12, 20, 40	$2 + 2 + 2 + 10 = 16$		
22. Coordinate Geom. "Proofs"	—	—		
23. Logic	19, 23, 41	$2 + 2 + 10 = 14$		
24. Permutations; Arrangements	29	2		
25. Combinations	38(a), (b)	$3 + 3 = 6$		
26. Probability	18, 33, 38(c), (d)	$2 + 2 + 2 + 2 = 8$		
27. Trig. of Rt. △	30, 39	$2 + 10 = 12$		
28. Literal Eqs.	—	—		
29. Transformations	4, 22	$2 + 2 = 4$		

Examination
June 1995
Sequential Math Course II

PART I

Answer 30 questions from this part. Each correct answer will receive 2 credits. No partial credit will be allowed. Write your answers in the spaces provided. Where applicable, answers may be left in terms of π or in radical form. [60]

1 In the accompanying diagram, $\overleftrightarrow{AB}$ is parallel to $\overleftrightarrow{CD}$, and transversal $\overleftrightarrow{EH}$ intersects $\overleftrightarrow{AB}$ and $\overleftrightarrow{CD}$ at F and G, respectively. If $m\angle AFG = 2x + 10$ and $m\angle FGD = x + 20$, find the value of x.

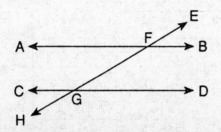

1____

2 In the accompanying diagram, *ABCD* is a parallelogram, $\overline{DA} \cong \overline{DE}$, and m∠*B* = 70. Find m∠*E*.

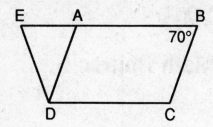

2____

3 In △*ABC*, m∠*A* = 35 and m∠*C* = 77. Which is the longest side of the triangle?

3____

4 The sides of a triangle measure 6, 8, and 10. The shortest side of a similar triangle is 15. Find the perimeter of the larger triangle.

4____

5 Rectangle *PROM* has coordinates *P*(2,1), *R*(8,1), *O*(8,5), and *M*(2,5). What are the coordinates of the point of intersection of the diagonals?

5____

6 Find, to the *nearest tenth*, the distance between points (1,3) and (–2,0).

6____

7 Solve for *x*: $\dfrac{2x - 4}{3} = \dfrac{3x + 4}{2}$

7____

8 In the accompanying diagram of right triangle MNQ, $\overline{NP}$ is the altitude to hypotenuse $\overline{MQ}$. If $QP = 16$ and $PM = 9$, find the length of $\overline{NP}$.

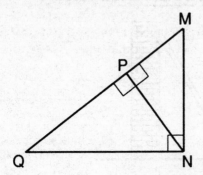

8____

9 How many distinct five-letter permutations can be formed using the letters of the word "GAUSS"?

9____

10 Under a translation, the image of point $(3,2)$ is $(-1,3)$. What are the coordinates of the image of point $(-2,6)$ under the same translation?

10____

11 In $\triangle BAT$, M is the midpoint of $\overline{BA}$ and N is the midpoint of $\overline{BT}$. If $AT = 3x + 12$ and $MN = 15$, find x.

11____

12 How many different bowling teams of five persons can be formed from a group of ten persons?

12____

13 A 20-foot ladder is leaning against a wall. The foot of the ladder makes an angle of 58° with the ground. Find, to the *nearest foot*, the vertical distance from the top of the ladder to the ground.

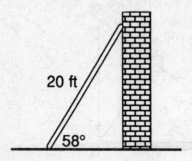

13_____

14 In quadrilateral *ABCD*, m∠*A* = 57, m∠*B* = 65, and m∠*C* = 118. What is the measure of an exterior angle at *D*?

14_____

15 Under a dilation with constant of dilation *k*, the image of the point (2,3) is (8,12). What is the value of *k*?

15_____

Directions (16–34): For *each* question chosen, write in the space provided the *numeral* preceding the word or expression that best completes the statement or answers the question.

16 An equation of the line that passes through point (0,3) and whose slope is –2 is

(1) $y = -2x + 3$ (3) $y = 2x + 3$
(2) $y = -2x - 3$ (4) $y = 2x - 3$ 16_____

17 Given: $p \rightarrow q$

$$\frac{p}{\therefore q}$$

What is this argument called?

(1) DeMorgan's Law
(2) Law of Detachment
(3) Law of Disjunctive Inference
(4) Law of Contrapositive   17_____

18 If $x \clubsuit y = \dfrac{x^2 - 2xy + y^2}{x - y}$ defines the binary operation $\clubsuit$, what is the value of $5 \clubsuit 3$?

(1) 1   (3) 9
(2) 2   (4) 32   18_____

19 If $(x - 3)$ and $(x + 7)$ are the factors of the trinomial $x^2 + ax - 21$, what is the value of a?

(1) –3   (3) 7
(2) –4   (4) 4   19_____

20 Which statement is *not* always true about a parallelogram?

(1) Opposite sides are parallel.
(2) Opposite sides are congruent.
(3) Opposite angles are congruent.
(4) Diagonals are congruent.   20_____

21 The parabola shown in the diagram is reflected
in the *x*-axis.

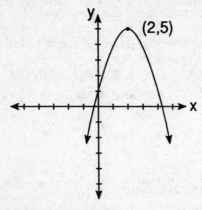

What is the image of the turning point after the
reflection?

(1) (2,−5)   (3) (−2,−5)

(2) (−2,5)   (4) (5,2)   21____

22 If $\angle C$ is the complement of $\angle A$, and $\angle S$ is the
supplement of $\angle A$, which statement is *always*
true?

(1) $m\angle C + m\angle S = 180$

(2) $m\angle C + m\angle S = 90$

(3) $m\angle C > m\angle S$

(4) $m\angle C < m\angle S$ 22____

23 Which equation describes the locus of points
equidistant from points (2,2) and (2,6)?

(1) $y = 8$ (3) $x = 8$

(2) $y = 4$ (4) $x = 4$ 23____

24 In equilateral triangle *ABC*, the bisectors of
angles *A* and *B* intersect at point *F*. What is
$m\angle AFB$?

(1) 60   (3) 120

(2) 90   (4) 150   24____

25 Two sides of a triangle have lengths 5 and 8. Which length can *not* be the length of the third side?

(1) 5   (3) 3

(2) 6   (4) 4   25_____

26 In the accompanying diagram of right triangle *ABC*, what is tan *C*?

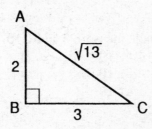

(1) $\frac{2}{3}$ (3) $\frac{\sqrt{13}}{3}$

(2) $\frac{3}{2}$ (4) $\frac{2}{\sqrt{13}}$ 26_____

27 In the accompanying diagram, $\overleftrightarrow{ACE}$ is parallel to $\overleftrightarrow{DB}$, m∠*DBA* = 40, and m∠*BCE* = 105.

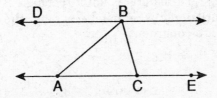

Which statement is true?

(1) $\overline{AB}$ is the longest side of △*ABC*.

(2) $\overline{AC}$ is the longest side of △*ABC*.

(3) △*ABC* is an isosceles triangle.

(4) △*ABC* is an obtuse triangle.   27_____

28 Which equation represents the circle whose center is (−4,2) and whose radius is 3?

(1) $(x + 4)^2 + (y - 2)^2 = 9$
(2) $(x + 4)^2 + (y - 2)^2 = 3$
(3) $(x - 4)^2 + (y + 2)^2 = 9$
(4) $(x - 4)^2 + (y + 2)^2 = 3$

28_____

29 If two legs of a right triangle measure 3 and $\sqrt{10}$, then the hypotenuse must measure
(1) 1
(3) 10
(2) $\sqrt{19}$
(4) 19

29_____

30 Which statement is equivalent to "If a quadrilateral is a rectangle, the diagonals are congruent"?
(1) If the diagonals of a quadrilateral are congruent, the quadrilateral is a rectangle.
(2) If a quadrilateral is not a rectangle, the diagonals of the quadrilateral are not congruent.
(3) If the diagonals of a quadrilateral are not congruent, the quadrilateral is not a rectangle.
(4) If a quadrilateral is a parallelogram, the diagonals are congruent.

30_____

31 In how many points do the graphs of the equations $x^2 + y^2 = 9$ and $y = 2x - 1$ intersect?
(1) 1
(3) 3
(2) 2
(4) 4

31_____

32 Which quadratic equation has irrational roots?

(1) $x^2 + 2x - 8 = 0$ (3) $x^2 - 3x + 2 = 0$

(2) $x^2 - x - 30 = 0$ (4) $x^2 - 4x - 7 = 0$ 32_____

33 Which equation represents the axis of symmetry of the graph of the equation $y = x^2 - 6x + 5$?

(1) $x = -3$ (3) $x = 3$

(2) $y = -3$ (4) $y = 3$ 33_____

34 Which equation represents a line that is parallel to the line whose equation is $y = \frac{1}{2}x - 2$?

(1) $y = 2x - 3$ (3) $2y = x - 3$

(2) $y = -2x - 3$ (4) $2y = -x - 3$ 34_____

DIRECTIONS (35): *Show all construction lines.*

35   Construct the angle bisector of $\angle C$ of $\triangle ABC$.

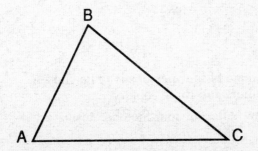

PART II

Answer three questions from this part. Clearly indicate the necessary steps, including appropriate formula substitutions, diagrams, graphs, charts, etc. Calculations that may be obtained by mental arithmetic or the calculator do not need to be shown. [30]

36 *a* On graph paper, draw the graph of the equation $y = x^2 - 2x - 3$ for all values of x in the interval $-2 \leq x \leq 4$. [6]

    b What are the roots of the equation $x^2 - 2x - 3 = 0$? [2]

    c On the same set of axes, draw the image of the graph drawn in part *a* after a reflection in the y-axis. [2]

37 Answer both *a* and *b* for all values of x for which these expressions are defined.

    a Simplify: $\dfrac{x^2 + 9x + 20}{x^2 - 16} \div \dfrac{x^2 + 5x}{4x - 16}$ [6]

    b Solve for x: $\dfrac{2}{x} = \dfrac{x - 3}{5}$ [4]

38 A debating team of four persons is to be chosen from five juniors and three seniors.

    a How many different four-member teams are possible? [2]

    b How many of these teams will consist of exactly two juniors and two seniors? [3]

c What is the probability that one of the four-member teams will consist of exactly one junior and three seniors? [3]

d What is the probability that one four-member team will consist of juniors only? [2]

39 In the accompanying diagram of right triangle *ABD*, *AB* = 6 and altitude $\overline{BC}$ divides hypotenuse $\overline{AD}$ into segments of lengths *x* and 8.

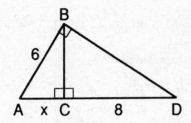

a Find *AC* to the *nearest tenth*. [7]

b Using the answer from part *a*, find the measure of ∠*A* to the *nearest degree*. [3]

40 An 8- by 10-inch photo has a frame of uniform width placed around it.

a If the uniform width of the frame is *x* inches, express the outside dimensions of the picture frame in terms of *x*. [4]

b If the area of the picture and frame is 143 in^2, what is the uniform width of the frame? [6]

PART III

Answer one question from this part. Clearly indicate the necessary steps, including appropriate formula substitutions, diagrams, graphs, charts, etc. Calculations that may be obtained by mental arithmetic or the calculator do not need to be shown. [10]

41 *a* Given:

> Either I go to camp or I get a summer job.
> If I get a summer job, then I will earn money.
> If I earn money, then I will buy new sneakers.
> I do not buy new sneakers.

Let *C* represent: "I go to camp."
Let *J* represent: "I get a summer job."
Let *M* represent: "I earn money."
Let *S* represent: "I buy new sneakers."

Prove: I go to camp. [8]

b Given the true statements:

> If Michael is an athlete and he is salaried, then Michael is a professional.
> Michael is not a professional.
> Michael is an athlete.

Which statement must be true? [2]

(1) Michael is an athlete and he is salaried.
(2) Michael is a professional or he is salaried.
(3) Michael is not salaried.
(4) Michael is not an athlete. 41____

42 Given: quadrilateral $PQRT$, $\overline{QSV}$, $\overline{RST}$, $\overline{PTV}$, $\overline{QV}$
bisects $\overline{RT}$, and $\overline{QR} \parallel \overline{PV}$.

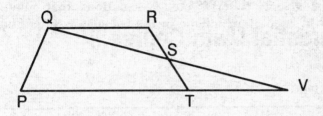

Prove: $\overline{QS} \cong \overline{VS}$ [10]

Answers
June 1995
Sequential Math Course II

Answer Key

PART I

1. 10	**13.** 17	**25.** (3)
2. 70	**14.** 60°	**26.** (1)
3. $\overline{AB}$	**15.** 4	**27.** (1)
4. 60	**16.** (1)	**28.** (1)
5. (5, 3)	**17.** (2)	**29.** (2)
6. 4.2	**18.** (2)	**30.** (3)
7. –4	**19.** (4)	**31.** (2)
8. 12	**20.** (4)	**32.** (4)
9. 60	**21.** (1)	**33.** (3)
10. (–6, 7)	**22.** (4)	**34.** (3)
11. 6	**23.** (2)	**35.** construction
12. 252	**24.** (3)	

PARTS II AND III See answers explained section.

Answers Explained

PART I

1. If two lines are parallel, alternate interior angles have the same degree measure. Since $\overleftrightarrow{AB}$ is parallel to $\overleftrightarrow{CD}$, alternate interior angles AFG and FGD are equal in measure. Thus:

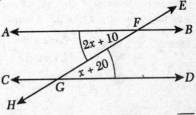

$$\begin{aligned} \text{m}\angle AFG &= \text{m}\angle FGD \\ 2x + 10 &= x + 20 \\ 2x &= x + 20 - 10 \\ 2x - x &= 10 \\ x &= 10 \end{aligned}$$

The value of x is **10**.

2. In the accompanying diagram, $ABCD$ is a parallelogram, so $\overline{DA} \parallel \overline{CB}$. If two lines are parallel, corresponding angles have the same degree measure. Hence:

$$\text{m}\angle DAE = \text{m}\angle B = 70.$$

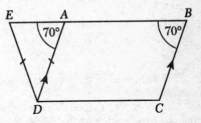

It is also given that $\overline{DA} \cong \overline{DE}$; as a result, the angles in $\triangle EDA$ that are opposite these sides have the same degree measure. Thus:

$$\text{m}\angle E = \text{m}\angle DAE = 70.$$

$\text{m}\angle E = \textbf{70}$.

3. The longest side of a triangle is the side that is opposite the angle of the triangle with the greatest degree measure.

The sum of the degree measures of the angles of a triangle is 180. In $\triangle ABC$, $\text{m}\angle A = 35$ and $\text{m}\angle C = 77$. Hence:

$$\begin{aligned} \text{m}\angle B &= 180 - (35 + 77) \\ &= 180 - 112 \\ &= 68 \end{aligned}$$

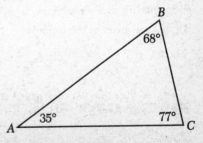

In $\triangle ABC$ the angle with the greatest measure is $\angle C$. Since $\overline{AB}$ is the side opposite $\angle C$, $\overline{AB}$ is the longest side of the triangle.

The longest side of $\triangle ABC$ is $\overline{AB}$.

4.

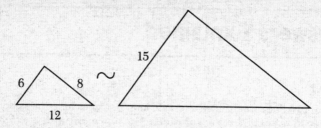

If two triangles are similar, the perimeters of the two triangles have the same ratio as the lengths of any pair of corresponding sides. Let x represent the perimeter of the larger triangle. Then:

$$\frac{\text{shortest side of smaller } \triangle}{\text{shortest side of larger } \triangle} = \frac{\text{perimeter of smaller } \triangle}{\text{perimeter of larger } \triangle}$$

$$\frac{6}{15} = \frac{6+8+10}{x}$$

$$= \frac{24}{x}$$

$$6x = 15(24)$$

$$x = \frac{15\overset{4}{\cancel{(24)}}}{\cancel{6}}$$

$$= 15(4)$$

$$= 60$$

The perimeter of the larger triangle is **60**.

5. Since the diagonals of a rectangle bisect each other, the diagonals intersect each other at their midpoints. Thus, to find the coordinates of the point at which the diagonals of rectangle *PROM* intersect, find the coordinates of the midpoint of either diagonal.

The coordinates of the midpoint of a line segment are the averages of the corresponding coordinates of the endpoints of the segment. In general, if the endpoints of a line segment are (x_1, y_1) and (x_2, y_2), the coordinates of midpoint $M(\bar{x}, \bar{y})$ are given by the formulas

$$\bar{x} = \frac{x_1 + x_2}{2} \quad \text{and} \quad \bar{y} = \frac{y_1 + y_2}{2}$$

To find the midpoint of diagonal $\overline{PO}$, which has endpoints $(2,1)$ and $(8,5)$, let $x_1 = 2$, $y_1 = 1$, $x_2 = 8$, and $y_2 = 5$. Thus:

$$\bar{x} = \frac{x_1 + x_2}{2} \quad \text{and} \quad \bar{y} = \frac{y_1 + y_2}{2}$$

$$= \frac{2+8}{2} \qquad\qquad = \frac{1+5}{2}$$

$$= \frac{10}{2} \qquad\qquad = \frac{6}{2}$$

$$= 5 \qquad\qquad\qquad = 3$$

The coordinates of the point of intersection of the diagonals are **(5,3)**.

6. The distance d between the points whose coordinates are (x_1, y_1) and (x_2, y_2) is given by the formula

$$d = \sqrt{\left(x_2 - x_1\right)^2 + \left(y_2 - y_1\right)^2}$$

To find the distance between points (1,3) and (–2,0), let $x_1 = 1$, $y_1 = 3$, $x_2 = -2$, and $y_2 = 0$. Thus:

$$d = \sqrt{\left(-2-1\right)^2 + \left(0-3\right)^2}$$

$$= \sqrt{\left(-3\right)^2 + \left(-3\right)^2}$$

$$= \sqrt{9+9}$$

$$= \sqrt{18}$$

Use a calculator: $= 4.242...$

The distance between points (1,3) and (–2,0), to the *nearest tenth*, is **4.2**.

7. The given equation is:

$$\frac{2x-4}{3} = \frac{3x+4}{2}$$

In a proportion, the product of the means is equal to the product of the extremes (cross-multiply):

$$3(3x+4) = 2(2x-4)$$

Remove the parentheses by multiplying each term inside the parentheses by the number in front of the parentheses:

$$9x + 12 = 4x - 8$$

On each side of the equation subtract 12:

$$9x = 4x - 8 - 12$$
$$= 4x - 20$$

On each side of the equation subtract 4x:

$$9x - 4x = -20$$
$$5x = -20$$

Divide each side of the equation by 5:

$$x = \frac{-20}{5} = -4$$

The value of x is **–4**.

8.

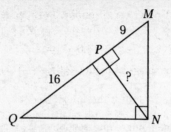

If the altitude is drawn to the hypotenuse of a right triangle, the length of the altitude is the mean proportional between the lengths of the segments into which the hypotenuse is divided. Thus:

$$\frac{QP}{NP} = \frac{NP}{PM}$$

$$\frac{16}{NP} = \frac{NP}{9}$$

Cross-multiply:

$$(NP)^2 = 16 \times 9 = 144$$

$$NP = \sqrt{144} = 12$$

The length of $\overline{NP}$ is **12**.

9. If, in a set of n objects, a are identical, the number of distinct ways in which the n objects can be arranged is $\frac{n!}{a!}$.

The word "GAUSS" contains two identical letters, S and S. To find the number of distinct five-letter permutations that can be formed using the letters of the word "GAUSS," let $n = 5$ and $a = 2$. Thus:

$$\frac{n!}{a!} = \frac{5!}{2!} = \frac{5 \cdot 4 \cdot 3 \cdot \cancel{2} \cdot \cancel{1}}{\cancel{2} \cdot \cancel{1}}$$

$$= 5 \cdot 4 \cdot 3$$

$$= 60$$

The number of distinct five-letter permutations that can be formed from the letters of the word "GAUSS" is **60**.

10. A translation "slides" each point of a figure a fixed number of units in the horizontal direction and a fixed number of units in the vertical direction.

If under a certain translation the image of point $(3,2)$ is $(-1,3)$, this translation slides $(3,2)$ 4 units horizontally to the *left* and 1 unit vertically *up*. Thus, the image of any point (x,y) under the same translation is point $(x - 4, y + 1)$.

To find the image of point (–2,6) under the same translation, apply the translation rule $(x,y) \rightarrow (x-4, y+1)$, where $x = -2$ and $y = 6$:

$$(-2, 6) \rightarrow (-2-4, 6+1) = (-6, 7)$$

The coordinates of the image of point (–2,6) are **(–6,7)**.

11. In a triangle, the length of the line segment that connects the midpoints of two sides of a triangle is one-half the length of the third side of the triangle. Hence:

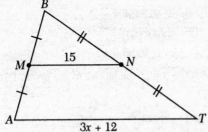

$$MN = \frac{1}{2}(AT)$$

$$15 = \frac{1}{2}(3x + 12)$$

Multiply each side of the equation by 2:

$$30 = 3x + 12$$
$$18 = 3x$$
$$\frac{18}{3} = x$$
$$6 = x$$

The value of x is **6**.

12. The total number of ways in which a team of r persons can be selected from a group of n persons is the number of possible combinations of n persons taken r at a time. Thus:

$$_nC_r = \frac{n!}{r!(n-r)!}$$

Let $n = 10$ and $r = 5$:

$$_{10}C_5 = \frac{10!}{5!(10-5)!}$$

$$= \frac{\overset{2}{\cancel{10}} \cdot 9 \cdot \overset{2}{\cancel{8}} \cdot 7 \cdot \overset{1}{\cancel{6}} \cdot \overset{1}{\cancel{5!}}}{\cancel{5} \cdot \cancel{4} \cdot \cancel{3} \cdot 2 \cdot 1(\cancel{5!})}$$

$$= 2 \cdot 9 \cdot 2 \cdot 7$$
$$= 252$$

The number of different five-person bowling teams that can be formed from a group of ten people is **252**.

13. Let x represent the vertical distance from the top of the ladder to the ground. Then:

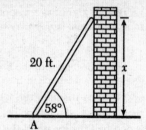

$$\sin A = \frac{\text{length of leg opposite} \angle A}{\text{length of hypotenuse}}$$

$$\sin 58° = \frac{x}{20}$$

From the Tables of Natural Trigonometric Functions, $\sin 58° = 0.8480$. Hence:

$$0.8480 = \frac{x}{20}$$
$$20(0.8480) = x$$
$$16.96 = x$$

The vertical distance from the top of the ladder to the ground, to the *nearest foot*, is **17 feet**.

14. The sum of the degree measures of the angles of a quadrilateral is 360. In quadrilateral $ABCD$, $m\angle A = 57$, $m\angle B = 65$, and $m\angle C = 118$. Thus:

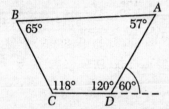

$$m\angle D = 360 - (57 + 65 + 118)$$
$$= 360 - 240$$
$$= 120$$

At each vertex of a polygon, an interior angle is supplementary to an exterior angle drawn at that vertex. Since $m\angle D = 120$, the measure of an exterior angle at vertex D is $180 - 120$ or 60.

The measure of an exterior angle at D is **60**.

15. A dilation is a size transformation of a figure. Under a dilation, the x and the y coordinates of each point of a figure are multiplied by the same nonzero number k, called the *scale factor* or *constant of dilation*.

If the image of point $(2,3)$ is $(8,12)$, the x and the y coordinates of the original point are each multiplied by 4.

The value of k is **4**.

16. The equation $y = mx + b$ represents an equation of a line that has a slope of m and a y-intercept of b.

If a line has a slope of -2, then $m = -2$. The y-intercept of a line is the y-coordinate of the point at which the line crosses the y-axis. At this point, $x = 0$. Since it is given that the line passes through point $(0,3)$, $b = 3$.

Since $m = -2$ and $b = 3$, an equation of this line is $y = -2x + 3$.

The correct choice is **(1)**.

17. Given:

$$p \rightarrow q$$
$$\underline{p}$$
$$\therefore q$$

Examine each choice in turn.

- (1) DeMorgan's Law states that

$$\sim(p \wedge q) \leftrightarrow \sim p \vee \sim q \quad \text{and} \quad \sim(p \vee q) \leftrightarrow \sim p \wedge \sim q$$

- (2) The Law of Detachment states that, if a conditional $(p \rightarrow q)$ and its antecedent (p) are true, its consequent (q) must also be true. In argument form,

$$p \rightarrow q$$
$$\underline{p}$$
$$\therefore q$$

Thus, choice (2) denotes the given argument.

- (3) The Law of Disjunctive Inference states that, if a disjunction is true, at least one of the disjuncts must also be true.
- (4) The Law of Contrapositive Inference states that a conditional statement and its contrapositive always have the same truth value.

The correct choice is **(2)**.

18. The given binary operation is:

$$x * y = \frac{x^2 - 2xy + y^2}{x - y}$$

To evaluate $5 * 3$, let $x = 5$ and $y = 3$:

$$= \frac{5^2 - 2(5)(3) + 3^2}{5 - 3}$$
$$= \frac{25 - 30 + 9}{2}$$
$$= \frac{4}{2}$$
$$= 2$$

The correct choice is **(2)**.

19. It is given that $(x - 3)$ and $(x + 7)$ are the factors of $x^2 + ax - 21$. To find the value of a, multiply the binomial factors together and then compare the coefficients of the resulting trinomial with the coefficients of $x^2 + ax - 21$. Thus:

$$x^2 + ax - 21 = (x - 3)(x + 7)$$
$$= x^2 + 7x - 3x - 21$$
$$= x^2 + 4x - 21$$

Hence, the value of a, the coefficient of x, is 4.
The correct choice is **(4)**.

20. Although the diagonals of a rectangle and of a square are congruent, the diagonals of a parallelogram may or may not be congruent. For example, the diagonals of a rhombus that is not a square are not congruent.

The correct choice is **(4)**.

21. A reflection of a figure in the x-axis maps each point (x,y) of the figure onto $(x,-y)$, its image point. Thus, a reflection in the x-axis of a parabola whose turning point is $(2,5)$ maps $(2,5)$ onto $(2,-5)$. The correct choice is **(1)**.

22. Two angles are complementary if the sum of their degree measures is 90, and are supplementary if the sum of their measures is 180. If $\angle C$ is the complement of $\angle A$, angles A and C are both acute angles. If $\angle S$ is the supplement of $\angle A$, an acute angle, $\angle S$ is an obtuse angle.

Thus, $m\angle C < m\angle S$.

The correct choice is **(4)**.

23. The locus of points equidistant from two fixed points is the line that is the perpendicular bisector of the segment whose endpoints are the two fixed points.

On graph paper, draw the segment whose endpoints are $(2,2)$ and $(2,6)$. The midpoint of this vertical segment is $(2,4)$.

A horizontal line that contains $(2,4)$ represents the locus of points equidistant from $(2,2)$ and $(2,6)$. An equation of this horizontal line is $y = 4$.

The correct choice is **(2)**.

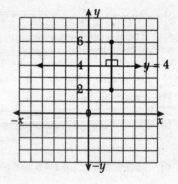

24.

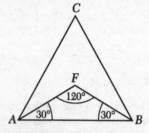

An equilateral triangle is also equiangular. Hence, each angle of an equilateral triangle measures 60. Since the bisector of an angle divides the angle into two angles that have the same measure:

$$m\angle FAB = \frac{1}{2}(60) = 30 \quad \text{and} \quad m\angle FBA = \frac{1}{2}(60) = 30$$

Since the sum of the measures of the angles of a triangle is 180,

$$m\angle AFB = 180 - (30 + 30)$$
$$= 180 - 60$$
$$= 120$$

The correct choice is **(3)**.

25. The sum of the lengths of *any* two sides of a triangle is greater than the length of the third side. Use the lengths of the two given sides, 5 and 8, to check this relationship for each of the four choices:

- (1): $5 + 5 > 8$? True.
  $5 + 8 > 5$? True.

- (2): $6 + 5 > 8$? True.
  $5 + 8 > 6$? True.
  $6 + 8 > 5$? True.

- (3): $3 + 5 > 8$? False.   Thus, 5, 8, and 3 cannot represent the lengths of the sides of a triangle.

- (4): $4 + 5 > 8$? True.
  $4 + 8 > 5$? True.
  $5 + 8 > 4$? True.

The correct choice is **(3)**.

26. $\tan C = \dfrac{\text{length of leg opposite } \angle C}{\text{length of leg adjacent to } \angle C}$

$$= \frac{AB}{BC}$$
$$= \frac{2}{3}$$

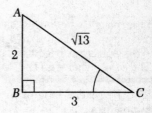

The correct choice is **(1)**.

27.

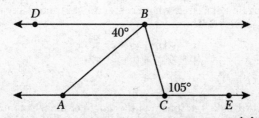

The question states that in the accompanying diagram $\overset{\leftrightarrow}{ACE}$ is parallel to $\overset{\leftrightarrow}{DB}$, $m\angle DBA = 40$, and $m\angle BCE = 105$.

Find the measure of each of the three angles of $\triangle ABC$:

- Since parallel lines form congruent alternate interior angles,

$$\text{m}\angle CAB = \text{m}\angle DBA = 40$$

- Since angles ACB and BCE are supplementary,

$$\begin{aligned}
\text{m}\angle ACB &= 180 - \text{m}\angle BCE \\
&= 180 - 105 \\
&= 75
\end{aligned}$$

- Since the sum of the degree measures of the angles of a triangle is 180,

$$\begin{aligned}
\text{m}\angle ACB &= 180 - (\text{m}\angle CAB + \text{m}\angle ACB) \\
&= 180 - (40 + 75) \\
&= 180 - 115 \\
&= 65
\end{aligned}$$

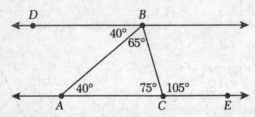

In a triangle, the longest side lies opposite the angle with the greatest degree measure. Since $\angle ACB$ has the greatest measure, the side opposite $\angle ACB$, $\overline{AB}$, is the longest side of $\triangle ABC$.

The correct choice is **(1)**.

28. The general form of an equation of a circle whose center is at (h,k) and whose radius is r is

$$(x - h)^2 + (y - k)^2 = r^2$$

To find an equation of a circle whose center is $(-4,2)$ and whose radius is 3, let $h = -4$, $k = 2$, and $r = 3$. Thus:

$$\begin{aligned}
(x - (-4))^2 + (y - 2)^2 &= 3^2 \\
(x + 4)^2 \quad + (y - 2)^2 &= 9
\end{aligned}$$

The correct choice is **(1)**.

29. In a right triangle, the square of the length of the hypotenuse is equal to the sum of the squares of the lengths of the two legs. If the lengths of the two legs of a right triangle are 3 and $\sqrt{10}$, and x represents the length of the hypotenuse, then:

$$x^2 = 3^2 + \left(\sqrt{10}\right)^2$$
$$= 9 + 10$$
$$= 19$$
$$x = \sqrt{19}$$

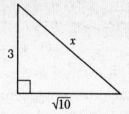

The correct choice is **(2)**.

30. A conditional statement and its contrapositive always have the same truth value and, as a result, are logically equivalent statements.

The given statement, "If a quadrilateral is a rectangle, the diagonals are congruent," is a conditional statement. To form the contrapositive, interchange and then negate both parts of the original conditional, obtaining the equivalent statement

"If the diagonals of a quadrilateral are not congruent, the quadrilateral is not a rectangle."

The correct choice is **(3)**.

31. To find the number of points at which the graphs of the equations $x^2 + y^2 = 9$ and $y = 2x - 1$ intersect, sketch the two graphs on the same set of axes, as shown in the accompanying figure.

The graph of $x^2 + y^2 = 9$ is a circle whose center is at $(0,0)$ and whose radius is 3.

The graph of $y = 2x - 1$ is a line that contains points $(0,-1)$ and $\left(\dfrac{1}{2}, 0\right)$.

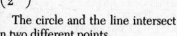

The circle and the line intersect in two different points.

The correct choice is **(2)**.

32. In general, the quadratic equation $ax^2 + bx + c = 0$ has irrational roots if its discriminant, $b^2 - 4ac$, is *not* a perfect square. Calculate the discriminant for the quadratic equation given in each choice.

- **(1):** If $x^2 + 2x - 8 = 0$, then $a = 1$, $b = 2$, and $c = -8$.

$$b^2 - 4ac = (2)^2 - 4(1)(-8)$$
$$= 4 + 32$$
$$= 36$$

Since 36 is a perfect square, the roots of $x^2 + 2x - 8 = 0$ are rational.

- (2): If $x^2 - x - 30 = 0$, then $a = 1$, $b = -1$, and $c = -30$.

$$b^2 - 4ac = (-1)^2 - 4(1)(-30)$$
$$= 1 + 120$$
$$= 121$$

Since 121 is a perfect square, the roots of $x^2 - x - 30 = 0$ are rational.

- (3): If $x^2 - 3x + 2 = 0$, then $a = 1$, $b = -3$, and $c = 2$.

$$b^2 - 4ac = (-3)^2 - 4(1)(2)$$
$$= 9 - 8$$
$$= 1$$

Since 1 is a perfect square, the roots of $x^2 - 3x + 2 = 0$ are rational.

- (4): If $x^2 - 4x - 7 = 0$, then $a = 1$, $b = -4$, and $c = -7$.

$$b^2 - 4ac = (-4)^2 - 4(1)(-7)$$
$$= 16 + 28$$
$$= 44$$

Since 44 is not a perfect square, the roots of $x^2 - 4x - 7 = 0$ are irrational. The correct choice is **(4)**.

33. If the equation of a parabola is in the form $y = ax^2 + bx + c$ ($a \neq 0$), an equation of the axis of symmetry is $x = -\dfrac{b}{2a}$. Since the given equation is $y = x^2 - 6x + 5$, let $a = 1$ and $b = -6$. Thus:

$$x = -\frac{b}{2a}$$
$$= -\frac{-6}{2(1)}$$
$$= \frac{6}{2}$$
$$= 3$$

The correct choice is **(3)**.

34. If an equation of a line has the form $y = mx + b$, then m is the slope of the line and b is the y-intercept.

Two lines are parallel if they have the same slope. Since the equation of the given line is $y = \dfrac{1}{2}x - 2$, $m = \dfrac{1}{2}$, the slope of the line is $\dfrac{1}{2}$. Examine each choice in turn for an equation that represents a line whose slope is $\dfrac{1}{2}$.

- (1): The equation is $y = 2x - 3$, so $m = 2$. The slope of the line is 2 so it is not parallel to the given line.

- (2): The equation is $y = -2x - 3$, so $m = -2$. The slope of the line is -2, so it is not parallel to the given line.

- (3): The equation is $2y = x - 3$. Dividing each member of the equation by 2 gives $y = \frac{1}{2}x - \frac{3}{2}$. Since $m = \frac{1}{2}$, the slope of the line is $\frac{1}{2}$. Hence, the line is parallel to the given line.

- (4): The equation is $2y = -x - 3$. Dividing each member of the equation by 2 gives $y = -\frac{1}{2}x - \frac{3}{2}$. The slope of the line is $-\frac{1}{2}$, so it is not parallel to the given line.

The correct choice is **(3)**.

35.

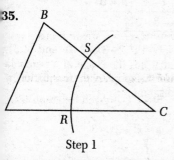

Step 1

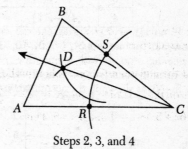

Steps 2, 3, and 4

construct the bisector of ∠C of △ABC proceed as follows:

STEP 1: With the pivot point of the compass on C and any convenient ius, swing an arc intersecting $\overline{AC}$ at R and $\overline{BC}$ at S.

STEP 2: With the pivot point of the compass on R and a radius greater ι half the distance from R to S, swing an arc.

STEP 3: With the pivot point of the compass on S and the same radius as used in step 2, swing an arc intersecting in point D the arc made in step 2.

STEP 4: Using a straight-edge, draw $\overrightarrow{CD}$.

$\overrightarrow{CD}$ is the bisector of ∠C of △ABC.

PART II

36. a. Before drawing the graph of the equation $y = x^2 - 2x - 3$ for all values of x in the interval $-2 \le x \le 4$, prepare a table of values for x and y by substituting each integer value of x, from -2 to 4, into the given equation to obtain the corresponding value of y:

x	$x^2 - 2x - 3$	$= y$
-2	$(-2)^2 - 2(-2) - 3 = 4 + 4 - 3$	$= 5$
-1	$(-1)^2 - 2(-1) - 3 = 1 + 2 - 3$	$= 0$
0	$(0)^2 - 2(0) - 3$	$= -3$
1	$(1)^2 - 2(1) - 3 = 1 - 2 - 3$	$= -4$
2	$(2)^2 - 2(2) - 3 = 4 - 4 - 3$	$= -3$
3	$(3)^2 - 2(3) - 3 = 9 - 6 - 3$	$= 0$
4	$(4)^2 - 2(4) - 3 = 16 - 8 - 3$	$= 5$

Now plot points $(-2,5)$, $(-1,0)$, $(0,-3)$, $(1,-4)$, $(2,-3)$, $(3,0)$, and $(4,5)$. Connect these points with a smooth curve that has the shape of a parabola whose turning point (vertex) is at $(1,-4)$. Label this graph with its equation, $y = x^2 - 2x - 3$, as shown in the accompanying diagram.

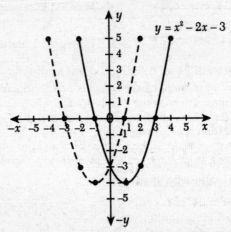

b. The x-coordinates of the points at which the graph drawn in part **a** crosses the x-axis must satisfy the equation $x^2 - 2x - 3 = 0$ since the y-coordinates of these points are 0.

The roots of the equation $x^2 - 2x - 3 = 0$ are $x = -1$ and $x = 3$.

c. A reflection in the y-axis maps each point (x,y) of the graph onto the point $(-x,y)$. The images of the points plotted in part **a** are as follows:

(x,y)	$\rightarrow$	$(-x,y)$
$(-2,5)$	$\rightarrow$	$(2,5)$
$(-1,0)$	$\rightarrow$	$(1,0)$
$(0,-3)$	$\rightarrow$	$(0,-3)$
$(1,-4)$	$\rightarrow$	$(-1,-4)$
$(2,-3)$	$\rightarrow$	$(-2,-3)$
$(3,0)$	$\rightarrow$	$(-3,0)$
$(4,5)$	$\rightarrow$	$(-4,5)$

Plot the image points and connect them with a smooth curve that has the shape of a parabola whose vertex is at $(-1,-4)$, as shown as a broken curve in the diagram in part **a**.

37. a. The given expression is:

Change the division by a fractional expression to multiplication by inverting the second fraction:

Factor each numerator and each denominator wherever possible. The first numerator is a quadratic trinomial that can be factored as the product of two binomials using the reverse of FOIL:

The first denominator is the difference of two perfect squares, so it can be factored as the sum and difference of the same two terms:

A common factor can be removed from the numerator and from the denominator of the second fraction:

If the same factor appears in both a numerator and a denominator, divide both of them by that factor so their quotient is 1 (cancel):

Multiply together the remaining factors in the numerators and multiply together the remaining factors in the denominators:

The quotient in simplest form is $\dfrac{4}{x}$.

$$\frac{x^2+9x+20}{x^2-16} \div \frac{x^2+5x}{4x-16}$$

$$\frac{x^2+9x+20}{x^2-16} \cdot \frac{4x-16}{x^2+5x}$$

$$\frac{(x+4)(x+5)}{x^2-16} \cdot \frac{4x-16}{x^2+5x}$$

$$\frac{(x+4)(x+5)}{(x+4)(x-4)} \cdot \frac{4x-16}{x^2+5x}$$

$$\frac{(x+4)(x+5)}{(x+4)(x-4)} \cdot \frac{4(x-4)}{x(x+5)}$$

$$\frac{\cancel{(x+4)}\cancel{(x+5)}}{\cancel{(x+4)}\cancel{(x-4)}} \cdot \frac{4\cancel{(x-4)}}{x\cancel{(x+5)}}$$

$$\frac{4}{x}$$

b. The given equation is:

In a proportion, the product of the means equals the product of the extremes (cross-multiply):

$$\frac{2}{x} = \frac{x-3}{5}$$

$$x(x-3) = 5(2)$$
$$x^2 - 3x = 10$$

On each side of the quadratic equation subtract 10 so that all of the nonzero terms appear on the left side of the equation:

$$x^2 - 3x - 10 = 0$$

Factor the left side of the equation as the product of two binomials that have the form $(x + ?)(x + ?)$. The missing numbers are the two factors of -10 that add up to -3. The correct factors of -10 are -5 and 2:

$$(x - 5)(x + 2) = 0$$

Set each binomial factor equal to 0 and then solve the resulting equations:

$$x - 5 = 0 \text{ or } x + 2 = 0$$
$$x = 5 \qquad x = -2$$

The values of x are **5** and **−2**.

38. a. In general, r people can be selected from a group of n people, without regard to their order, in $_nC_r$ different ways, where

$$_nC_r = \frac{n!}{r!(n-r)!}$$

The total number of students from which the four members of the debating team will be selected is eight (five juniors + three seniors). Hence, to find the number of different four-member teams that can be chosen from five juniors and three seniors, evaluate $_nC_r$ by letting $n = 8$ and $r = 4$:

$$_8C_4 = \frac{8!}{4!(8-4)!}$$

$$= \frac{8!}{4! \cdot 4!}$$

$$= \frac{\overset{2}{\cancel{8}} \cdot 7 \cdot \overset{1}{\cancel{6}} \cdot 5 \cdot \overset{1}{\cancel{4!}}}{\cancel{4} \cdot \cancel{3} \cdot \cancel{2} \cdot 1 \cdot \cancel{4!}}$$

$$= 70$$

The number of different four-member teams that can be chosen is **70**.

b. Two juniors can be selected from a group of five juniors in $_5C_2$ different ways. Two seniors can be selected from a group of three seniors in $_3C_2$ different ways. Thus, the product $_5C_2 \cdot {}_3C_2$ represents the total number of teams each of which will consist of exactly two juniors and two seniors:

$$_5C_2 = \frac{5!}{2! \cdot (5-2)!} \quad \text{and} \quad {}_3C_2 = \frac{3!}{2! \cdot (3-2)!}$$

$$= \frac{5 \cdot \overset{2}{\cancel{4}} \cdot \overset{1}{\cancel{3!}}}{\cancel{2} \cdot 1 \cdot \cancel{3!}} \qquad = \frac{3 \cdot \overset{1}{\cancel{2!}}}{\cancel{2!} \cdot 1}$$

$$= 10 \qquad\qquad = 3$$

Since $_5C_2 = 10$ and $_3C_2 = 3$;

$$_5C_2 \cdot {}_3C_2 = 10 \cdot 3 = 30$$

Thus, **30** teams will consist of exactly two juniors and two seniors.

c. One junior can be selected from a group of five juniors in $_5C_1$ different ways. Three seniors can be selected from a group of three seniors in $_3C_3$ different ways.

Thus, the product $_5C_1 \cdot {}_3C_3$ represents the total number of teams each of which will consist of exactly one junior and three seniors. Since

$$_5C_1 = \frac{5!}{1! \cdot 4!} = \frac{5 \cdot \overset{1}{\cancel{4!}}}{\cancel{4!}} = 5, \quad {}_3C_3 = \frac{\overset{1}{\cancel{3!}}}{\cancel{3!} \cdot 0!} = 1, \quad \text{and} \quad 5 \cdot 1 = 5,$$

five teams can be formed with exactly one junior and three seniors. From part **a**, a total of 70 four-member teams can be formed. Hence,

$$P(1 \text{ junior, 3 seniors}) = \frac{\text{number of teams with one junior and three seniors}}{\text{total number of four-member teams}}$$

$$= \frac{5}{70}$$

The probability that one of the four-member teams will consist of exactly one junior and three seniors is $\dfrac{5}{70}$.

d. Four juniors can be selected from a group of five juniors in $_5C_4$ different ways. Since

$$_5C_4 = \frac{5!}{4! \cdot (5-4)!} = \frac{5 \cdot \overset{1}{\cancel{4!}}}{\cancel{4!} \cdot 1!} = 5,$$

five teams can be formed with exactly four juniors. From part **a**, a total of 70 four-member teams can be formed. Hence;

$$P(4 \text{ juniors}) = \frac{\text{number of teams with four juniors}}{\text{total number of four-member teams}}$$

$$= \frac{5}{70}$$

The probability that one of the four-member teams will consist of juniors only is $\frac{5}{70}$.

39. a.

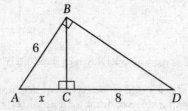

In a right triangle, the length of either leg is the mean proportional between the length of the segment of the hypotenuse adjacent to that leg and the length of the whole hypotenuse. Thus:

$$\frac{AC}{AB} = \frac{AB}{AD}$$

$$\frac{x}{6} = \frac{6}{x+8}$$

Cross-multiply:

$$x(x+8) = 36$$
$$x^2 + 8x = 36$$

On each side of the equation subtract 36 so that all the nonzero terms are on the left side of the equation:

$$x^2 + 8x - 36 = 0$$

Use the quadratic formula with $a = 1$, $b = 8$, and $c = -36$:

$$x = \frac{-b \pm \sqrt{b^2 - 4ac}}{2a}$$

$$= \frac{-8 \pm \sqrt{8^2 - 4(1)(-36)}}{2(1)}$$

$$= \frac{-8 \pm \sqrt{64 + 144}}{2}$$

$$= \frac{-8 \pm \sqrt{208}}{2}$$

Use a calculator to find that $\sqrt{208}$ is
approximately 14.42:

$$= \frac{-8 \pm 14.42}{2}$$

$$x_1 = \frac{-8 + 14.42}{2} \text{ or } x_2 = \frac{-8 - 14.42}{2}$$

$$= \frac{6.42}{2} \qquad\qquad = \frac{-22.42}{2}$$

$$= 3.21 \qquad\qquad = -11.21$$

Reject since
x must be
positive.

Thus, AC, correct to the *nearest tenth*, is **3.2**.

b. To find the measure of $\angle A$, use the answer from part **a** and the cosine
ratio in right triangle ACB:

$$\cos A = \frac{\text{length of leg adjacent to } \angle A}{\text{length of hypotenuse}}$$

$$= \frac{AC}{AB}$$

$$= \frac{3.2}{6}$$

$$= 0.5333$$

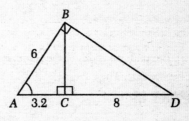

Since $\cos 58° = 0.5299$ and $\cos 57° = 0.5446$, the measure of $\angle A$ is
closer to 58°.

The measure of $\angle A$ correct to the *nearest degree* is **58°**.

40.

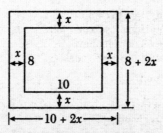

a. If the uniform width of a frame around an 8- by 10-inch photo is x
inches, the width of the photo with the frame is $x + 8 + x = 8 + 2x$ inches and
the length of the photo with the frame is $x + 10 + x = 10 + 2x$ inches.

The outside dimensions of the picture frame are as follows: width = **8 + 2x inches** and length = **10 + 2x inches**.

b. Since the area of the picture and the frame is 143 in.²:

$$(10 + 2x)(8 + 2x) = 143$$

Multiply the two binomials together using FOIL:

$$80 + 20x + 16x + 4x^2 = 143$$

On each side of the equation subtract 143. Then collect and rearrange the terms in descending order of powers of x:

$$4x^2 + 36x - 63 = 0$$

Factor as the product of two binomials (or use the quadratic formula):

$$(2x - 3)(2x + 21) = 0$$

Set each factor equal to 0 and then solve the resulting equations:

$$2x - 3 = 0 \quad \text{or} \quad 2x + 21 = 0$$

$$x = \frac{3}{2} \qquad\qquad x = -\frac{21}{2}$$

Reject since x must be positive.

The uniform width of the frame is $\frac{3}{2}$ or **1.5 inches**.

PART III

41. a. Given:

    Either I go to camp or I get a summer job.
    If I get a summer job, then I will earn money.
    If I earn money, then I will buy new sneakers.
    I do not buy new sneakers.

Let C represent: "I go to camp."
Let J represent: "I get a summer job."
Let M represent: "I earn money."
Let S represent: "I buy new sneakers."

Prove: I go to camp.

"Either I go to camp or I get a summer job" is the disjunction of statements C and J: $C \vee J$

"If I get a summer job, then I will earn money" is the conditional that J implies M: $J \to M$

"If I earn money, then I will buy new sneakers" is the conditional that M implies S: $M \to S$

"I do not buy new sneakers" is the negation of statement S: ~S

Prove: "I go to camp" is statement C.

PROOF

Statement	Reason
1. $M \to S$ ~S	1. Given.
2. ~M	2. Law of *Modus Tollens*.
3. $J \to M$	3. Given.
4. ~M	4. Law of *Modus Tollens* (2, 3).
5. $C \vee J$	5. Given.
6. C	6. Law of Disjunctive Inference (4, 5).

b. Write each of the given statements in symbolic form:

Statement A   Statement S

If Michael is an athlete and he is salaried,

then Michael is a professional. $(A \wedge S) \to P$

Statement P

"Michael is not a professional":   ~P

"Michael is an athlete": A

• By the Law of *Modus Tollens*,

$$(A \wedge S) \to P$$
$$\frac{\sim P}{\therefore \sim(A \wedge S)}$$

• By DeMorgan's laws,

$$\sim(A \wedge S) \leftrightarrow \sim A \vee \sim S$$

• Since it is given that A is true, ~A is false. By the Law of Disjunctive Inference, ~S is true. Hence, "Michael is not salaried" is a true statement.

The correct choice is **(3)**.

42.

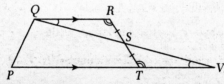

Given: Quadrilateral $PQRT$,
$\overline{QV}$ bisects $\overline{RT}$, and $\overline{QR} \parallel \overline{PV}$.

Prove: $\overline{QS} \cong \overline{VS}$

PLAN: Prove $\triangle QRS \cong \triangle VTS$ by $AAS \cong AAS$.

PROOF

Statement	Reason
1. $\overline{QR} \parallel \overline{PV}$	1. Given.
2. $\angle TVS \cong \angle RQS$ (*Angle*) $\angle VTS \cong \angle QRS$ (*Angle*)	2. If two lines are parallel, alternate interior angles are congruent.
3. $\overline{QV}$ bisects $\overline{RT}$.	3. Given.
4. $\overline{TS} \cong \overline{RS}$ (*Side*)	4. If a segment is bisected, it is divided into two congruent segments.
5. $\triangle QRS \cong \triangle VTS$	5. $AAS \cong AAS$
6. $\overline{QS} \cong \overline{VS}$	6. Corresponding sides of congruent triangles are congruent.

Topic	Question Numbers	Number of Points	Your Points	Your Percentage
1. Properties of Number Systems; Def. of Operations	18	2		
2. Finite Mathematical Systems	—	—		
3. Linear Function & Graph ($y = mx + b$, slope, eqs. of)	16, 34	2 + 2 = 4		
4. Quadratic Equation (alg. sol.—factoring, formula)	32	2		
5. Parabola (incl. axis of symmetry, turning point	19, 33, 36	2 + 2 + 10 = 14		
6. Systems of Equations (alg. and graphic solutions)	31	10		
7. Suppls., Compl., Vertical Angles, Angle Measure	22	2		
8. Triangle Properties (eq., isos., sum ∠s, 2 sides)	24, 27	2 + 2 = 4		
9. Line ∥ One Side of △; Line Joining Midpts. of 2 Sides	11	2		
10. Inequalities in △s (ext. ∠, ≠ sides, and opp. ∠s)	3, 25	2 + 2 = 4		
11. Quadrilateral Properties (□, sq., rhom., rect., trap.)	2, 14, 20	2 + 2 + 2 = 6		
12. Parallel Lines	1	2		
13. Alg. Oper.; Verbal Probs.	37, 40	10 + 10 = 20		
14. Mean Proportional; Alt. to Hypot. of Right △	8, 39a	2 + 7 = 9		
15. Pythag. Th., Special Rt. △s (3-4-5, 5-12-13, 30-60-90)	29	2		
16. Similar Figures (ratios & proportions)	4, 7	2 + 2 = 4		
17. Areas (△, rect., □, rhom., trap.)	—	—		
18. Locus	23	2		
19. Constructions	35	2		
20. Deductive Proofs	42	10		
21. Coordinate Geom. (slope, dist., midpt., eq. of circle)	5, 6, 28	2 + 2 + 2 = 6		
22. Coordinate Geom. "Proofs"	—	—		
23. Logic	17, 30, 41	2 + 2 + 10 = 14		
24. Permutations; Arrangements	9, 12	2 + 2 = 4		
25. Combinations	38a, b	2 + 3 = 5		
26. Probability	38c, d	3 + 2 = 5		
27. Trig. of Rt. △	13, 26, 39b	2 + 2 + 3 = 7		
28. Literal Eqs.	—	—		
29. Transforamtions	10, 15, 21	2 + 2 + 2 = 6		

Examination January 1996

Sequential Math Course II

PART I

Answer 30 questions from this part. Each correct answer will receive 2 credits. No partial credit will be allowed. Write your answers in the spaces provided. Where applicable, answers may be left in terms of π or in radical form. [60]

1 If $a \Delta b$ is a binary operation defined as $\dfrac{2a + b}{a}$ evaluate $2 \Delta 4$.

1 _____

2 In the accompanying diagram, $\triangle ABC$ is isosceles, $\overline{BC}$ is extended to D, $\overline{AB} \cong \overline{AC}$, and $m\angle A = 80$. Find $m\angle ACD$.

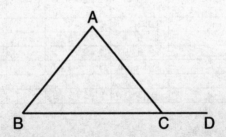

2 _____

3 In $\triangle PEN$, m$\angle P$ = 40 and m$\angle N$ = 80. Which side
   of the triangle is the longest?   3 _____

4 Solve for x: $\dfrac{x-2}{x+4} = \dfrac{x+2}{x+12}$ 4 _____

5 The lengths of the sides of a triangle are 4, 5, and
   6. If the length of the longest side of a similar
   triangle is 15, what is the length of the *shortest*
   side of this triangle?   5 _____

6 The coordinates of the vertices of $\triangle ABC$ are
   $A(0,0)$, $B(3,0)$, and $C(0,4)$. What is the length of
   $\overline{BC}$?   6 _____

7 What is the slope of the line determined by points
   $(-1,3)$ and $(3,-1)$?   7 _____

8 What are the coordinates of N', the image of
   $N(5,-3)$ under a reflection in the y-axis?   8 _____

9 In the accompanying diagram, line ℓ is parallel to
   line m and line t is a transversal. If m$\angle 1$ = $2x + 20$
   and m$\angle 2$ = $4x + 10$, what is the number of degrees
   in $\angle 3$?

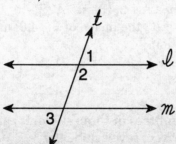

                                                        9 _____

10 Find the number of square units in the area of the triangle whose vertices are points $A(2,0)$, $B(6,0)$, and $C(8,5)$.

10 _____

11 The measure of one angle of a triangle equals the sum of the measures of the other two angles. Find the number of degrees in the measure of the largest angle of the triangle.

11 _____

12 In the accompanying diagram, $\overleftrightarrow{AB} \parallel \overleftrightarrow{CD}$, $m\angle x = 50$, and $m\angle y = 60$. What is $m\angle z$?

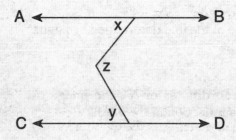

12 _____

13 A translation maps $A(-3,4)$ onto $A'(2,-6)$. Find the coordinates of B', the image of $B(-4,0)$ under the same translation.

13 _____

14 How many committees of three students can be chosen from a class of seven students?

14 _____

15 In the accompanying diagram of right triangle ABC, $b = 40$ centimeters, $m\angle A = 60$, and $m\angle C = 90$. Find the number of centimeters in the length of side c.

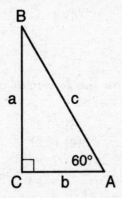

15 _____

16 Factor completely: $3x^2 - 15x - 42$ 16 _____

Directions (17–35): For *each* question chosen, write in the space provided the *numeral* preceding the word or expression that best completes the statement or answers the question.

17 Which statement is the negation of $p \wedge \sim q$?

(1) $\sim p \vee q$ (3) $p \wedge q$

(2) $p \vee \sim q$ (4) $\sim p \wedge \sim q$ 17 _____

18 Which equation illustrates the additive inverse property?

(1) $a + (-a) = 0$ (3) $a \div (-a) = -1$

(2) $a + 0 = a$ (4) $a \cdot \dfrac{1}{a} = 1$ 18 _____

19 In right triangle ABC, altitude $\overline{CD}$ is drawn to hypotenuse $\overline{AB}$. If $AD = 2$ and $DB = 6$, then AC is

   (1) $4\sqrt{3}$ (3) 3

   (2) $2\sqrt{3}$ (4) 4 19 _____

20 What is a solution for the system of equations $x - y = 2$ and $y = 2x - 4$?

   (1) $(0,2)$ (3) $(3,2)$

   (2) $(2,0)$ (4) $(4,2)$ 20 _____

21 If $a \rightarrow b$ and $\sim c \rightarrow \sim b$ are given, which statement must be true?

   (1) $a \rightarrow c$ (3) $c \rightarrow a$

   (2) $b \rightarrow a$ (4) $c \rightarrow b$ 21 _____

22 Which equation represents the graph of a circle?

   (1) $y = x$

   (2) $y = x^2$

   (3) $x^2 + y^2 = 9$

   (4) $x = 4$ 22 _____

23 What is the length of the altitude of an equilateral triangle whose side has length 4?

   (1) $2\sqrt{3}$ (3) $4\sqrt{3}$

   (2) 2 (4) 4 23 _____

24 Which statement about two equilateral triangles is *always* true?

(1) They are similar.
(2) They are congruent.
(3) They are equal in area.
(4) They have congruent altitudes.   24 _____

25 In the accompanying diagram of right triangle *ABC*, the hypotenuse is $\overline{AB}$, $AC = 3$, $BC = 4$, and $AB = 5$.

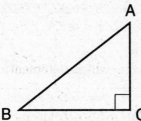

Sin *B* is equal to

(1) sin *A*   (3) tan *A*
(2) cos *A*   (4) cos *B*   25 _____

26 If *C* is the midpoint of line segment $\overline{AB}$ and *D* is the midpoint of line segment $\overline{AC}$, which statement is true?

(1) $AC > BC$ (3) $DB = AC$
(2) $AD < CD$ (4) $DB = 3CD$ 26 _____

27 Which statement is logically equivalent to $\sim a \rightarrow b$?

(1) $a \rightarrow \sim b$ (3) $\sim b \rightarrow a$
(2) $b \rightarrow \sim a$ (4) $\sim b \rightarrow \sim a$ 27 _____

28 In the accompanying diagram of △ABC, if AB < BC < AC, then which statement is *false*?

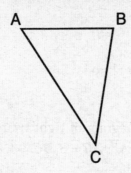

(1) m∠A > m∠C   (3) m∠B > m∠C
(2) m∠A < m∠B   (4) m∠B < m∠A   28 ____

29 In the accompanying diagram of quadrilateral ABCD, diagonal $\overline{AC}$ bisects ∠BAD and ∠BCD.

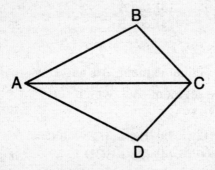

Which statement can be used to prove that △ABC ≅ △ADC?

(1) HL ≅ HL   (3) ASA ≅ ASA
(2) SSS ≅ SSS   (4) SAS ≅ SAS   29 ____

30 How many different six-letter arrangements can be formed using the letters in the word "DIVIDE"?

(1) 6!

(3) $\frac{6!}{2!2!}$

(2) $_6P_6$

(4) $\frac{6!}{4!}$

30 _____

31 The roots of the equation $x^2 + 3x - 1 = 0$ are

(1) $\frac{-3 \pm \sqrt{5}}{2}$

(3) $\frac{3 \pm \sqrt{5}}{2}$

(2) $\frac{-3 \pm \sqrt{13}}{2}$

(4) $\frac{3 \pm \sqrt{13}}{2}$

31 _____

32 Which is an equation of the axis of symmetry of the graph of the equation $y = x^2 - 6x + 2$?

(1) $x = -3$ (3) $x = 3$

(2) $y = -3$ (4) $y = 3$

32 _____

33 In the coordinate plane, what is the total number of points that are 8 units from the origin and equidistant from the axes?

(1) 1   (3) 0

(2) 2   (4) 4

33 _____

34 In rhombus $PQRS$, diagonals $\overline{PR}$ and $\overline{QS}$ intersect at T. Which statement is *always* true?

(1) Quadrilateral $PQRS$ is a square.

(2) Triangle RTQ is a right triangle.

(3) Triangle PQS is equilateral.

(4) Diagonals $\overline{PR}$ and $\overline{QS}$ are congruent.

34 _____

35 In the accompanying diagram, the bisector of an angle has been constructed.

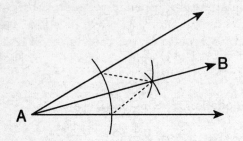

In proving this construction, which reason is used for the congruence involved?

(1) ASA   (3) AAS

(2) SSS   (4) SAS   35 _____

PART II

Answer three questions from this part. Clearly indicate the necessary steps, including appropriate formula substitutions, diagrams, graphs, charts, etc. Calculations that may be obtained by mental arithmetic or the calculator do not need to be shown. [30]

36 For all values of x for which these expressions are defined, perform the indicated operation and express in simplest form.

a $\dfrac{3x - 9}{x^2 - 9} - \dfrac{1}{x + 3}$ [5]

b $\dfrac{x^2 + 3x - 4}{5x - 5} \cdot \dfrac{10x^2 - 40x}{x^2 - 16}$ [5]

37 *a* On graph paper, draw the graph of the equation $y = -x^2 - 2x + 8$, including all values of x in the interval $-5 \leq x \leq 3$.   [6]

   b On the same set of axes, draw the graph of the equation $y = x + 4$.   [2]

   c What is the solution for the following system of equations?

$$y = -x^2 - 2x + 8$$
$$y = x + 4$$
   [1,1]

38 The vertices of $\triangle ABC$ are $A(-3,-2)$, $B(2,3)$, and $C(5,-4)$.

   a On graph paper, draw and label $\triangle ABC$.   [1]

   b Graph and state the coordinates of $\triangle A'B'C'$, the image of $\triangle ABC$ after a dilation of 2.   [3]

   c Find the area of $\triangle A'B'C'$.   [6]

39 In the accompanying diagram of isosceles trapezoid $ABCD$, $m\angle A = 53$, $DE = 6$, and $DC = 10$.

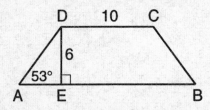

   a Find AE to the *nearest tenth*.   [4]

   b Find, to the *nearest integer*, the perimeter of isosceles trapezoid $ABCD$.   [6]

40   *a*   Find the positive solution of $3x^2 + 2x = 7$ to the *nearest tenth.*   [4]

    b   Given: If I receive a check for $500, then we will go on a trip.

               If the car breaks down, then we will not go on a trip.

               Either I receive a check for $500 or we will not buy souvenirs.

               The car breaks down.

Let *C* represent: "I receive a $500 check."
Let *T* represent: "We will go on a trip."
Let *B* represent: "The car breaks down."
Let *S* represent: "We will buy souvenirs."

Using the laws of logic, prove that we will not buy souvenirs.   [6]

PART III

Answer one question from this part. Clearly indicate the necessary steps, including appropriate formula substitutions, diagrams, graphs, charts, etc. Calculations that may be obtained by mental arithmetic or the calculator do not need to be shown.　[10]

41　Given: rectangle $ABCD$, $\overline{BNPC}$, $\overline{AEP}$, $\overline{DEN}$, and $\overline{AP} \cong \overline{DN}$.

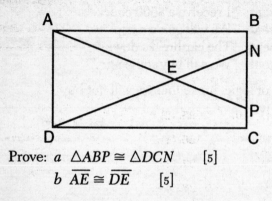

Prove: a　$\triangle ABP \cong \triangle DCN$　　[5]
　　　　b　$\overline{AE} \cong \overline{DE}$　　[5]

42　The vertices of quadrilateral $GAME$ are $G(r, s)$, $A(0,0)$, $M(t,0)$, and $E(t + r, s)$. Using coordinate geometry, prove that quadrilateral $GAME$ is a parallelogram.　[10]

Answers
January 1996
Sequential Math Course II

Answer Key

PART I

1. 4	**13.** $(1, -10)$	**25.** (2)
2. 130	**14.** 35	**26.** (4)
3. $\overline{PE}$	**15.** 80	**27.** (3)
4. 8	**16.** $3(x+2)(x-7)$	**28.** (4)
5. 10	**17.** (1)	**29.** (3)
6. 5	**18.** (1)	**30.** (3)
7. -1	**19.** (4)	**31.** (2)
8. $(-5, -3)$	**20.** (2)	**32.** (3)
9. 70	**21.** (1)	**33.** (4)
10. 10	**22.** (3)	**34.** (2)
11. 90	**23.** (1)	**35.** (2)
12. 110	**24.** (1)	

PARTS II AND III See answers explained section.

Answers Explained

PART I

1. If $a\Delta b$ is defined as $\dfrac{2a+b}{a}$, the value of $2\Delta 4$ is obtained by substituting 2 for a and 4 for b.

The given formula is:
$$a\Delta b = \frac{2a+b}{a}$$

Let $a = 2$ and $b = 4$:
$$2\Delta 4 = \frac{2(2)+4}{2}$$

Simplify the right side of the equation:
$$= \frac{4+4}{2}$$
$$= \frac{8}{2}$$
$$= 4$$

The value of $2\Delta 4$ is **4**.

2. If two sides of a triangle are congruent, the angles opposite these sides are also congruent. Since $\overline{AB} \cong \overline{AC}$, $\angle B$ and $\angle ACB$ have equal measures.

Let $x = \mathrm{m}\angle B = \mathrm{m}\angle ACB$. Since the sum of the measures of the three angles of a triangle add up to 180:

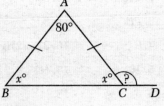

$$\mathrm{m}\angle A + \mathrm{m}\angle B + \mathrm{m}\angle ACB = 180$$
$$80 \;+\; x \;+\; x \;= 180$$
$$80 \;+\; 2x \;= 180$$
$$2x = 180 - 80$$
$$x = \frac{100}{2} = 50$$

Hence, $\mathrm{m}\angle B = \mathrm{m}\angle ACB = 50$.

Angle ACD is an exterior angle of $\triangle ABC$ at vertex C. The measure of an exterior angle of a triangle is equal to the sum of the measures of the two non-adjacent interior angles of the triangle. Thus:

$$\mathrm{m}\angle ACD = \mathrm{m}\angle A + \mathrm{m}\angle B$$
$$= 80 \;+\; 50$$
$$= 130$$

The measure of $\angle ACD$ is **130**.

3. In a triangle, the longest side is opposite the angle with the greatest degree measure.

It is given that, in ΔPEN, m$\angle P = 40$ and m$\angle N = 80$. Since the sum of the measures of the angles of a triangle is 180,

$$m\angle E = 180 - (40 + 80) = 60.$$

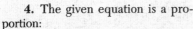

In ΔPEN, $\angle N$ has the greatest measure, so the side opposite $\angle N$, $\overline{PE}$, is the side of the triangle with the greatest length.

The longest side of the triangle is $\overline{PE}$.

4. The given equation is a proportion:

In a proportion, the product of the means is equal to the product of the extremes (cross-multiply):

On each side of the equation, multiply the two binomials:

Since both sides of the equation contain x^2, subtracting x^2 from each side of the equation eliminates this term:

Combine like terms:

Add 24 to each side of the equation:

Subtract $6x$ from each side of the equation:

Divide each side of the equation by 4:

$x = 8$.

$$\frac{x-2}{x+4} = \frac{x+2}{x+12}$$

$$(x + 12)(x - 2) = (x + 4)(x + 2)$$

$$x^2 + 12x - 2x - 24 = x^2 + 4x + 2x + 8$$

$$12x - 2x - 24 = 4x + 2x + 8$$
$$10x - 24 = 6x + 8$$
$$10x = 6x + 32$$

$$4x = 32$$

$$x = \frac{32}{4} = 8$$

5.

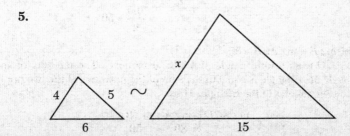

The lengths of corresponding sides of similar triangles are in proportion:

$$\frac{\text{longest side of larger } \Delta}{\text{longest side of smaller } \Delta} = \frac{\text{shortest side of larger } \Delta}{\text{shortest side of smaller } \Delta}$$

$$\frac{15}{6} = \frac{x}{4}$$

$$6x = 4(15)$$

Cross-multiply: $6x = 60$

$$x = \frac{60}{6} = 10$$

The length of the *shortest* side of the similar triangle is **10**.

6.

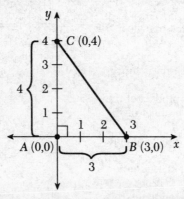

If the vertices of $\triangle ABC$ are $A(0,0)$, $B(3,0)$, and $C(0,4)$, then $\triangle ABC$ is a right triangle in which the length of leg $\overline{AB}$ is 3 and the length of leg $\overline{AC}$ is 4. Since the lengths of the sides of right triangle ABC form a 3-4-5 Pythagorean triple, the length of hypotenuse $\overline{BC}$ is 5.

The length of hypotenuse $\overline{BC}$ is **5**.

7. To find the slope m of the line determined by points $(-1,3)$ and $(3,-1)$, let $(x_1, y_1) = (-1,3)$ and $(x_2, y_2) = (3,-1)$. Then use the slope formula:

$$m = \frac{y_2 - y_1}{x_2 - x_1}$$

$$= \frac{-1 - 3}{3 - (-1)}$$

$$= \frac{-4}{3 + 1}$$

$$= \frac{-4}{4}.$$

$$= -1$$

The slope of the line determined by the given points is **−1**.

8. In general, if point (x,y) is reflected in the y-axis, its image is point $(-x,y)$. Therefore, if N' is the image of $N(5,-3)$ under a reflection in the y-axis, the coordinates of N' are $(-5,-3)$.

The coordinates of N' are **(-5,-3)**.

9.

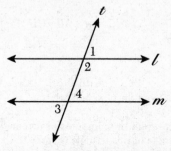

It is given that, in the accompanying diagram, line ℓ is parallel to line m, $m\angle 1 = 2x + 20$, and $m\angle 2 = 4x + 10$. Since adjacent angles 1 and 2 form a straight line, their measures add up to 180. Thus:

$$
\begin{aligned}
m\angle 1 \ + \ m\angle 2 &= 180 \\
(2x+20)+(4x+10) &= 180 \\
6x+30 &= 180 \\
6x &= 150 \\
x &= \frac{150}{6} = 25
\end{aligned}
$$

Hence, $m\angle 1 = 2x + 20 = 2(25) + 20 = 70$.

Since parallel lines form corresponding angles with equal measures, $m\angle 4 = m\angle 1 = 70$. Also, vertical angles have equal measures, so $m\angle 3 = m\angle 4 = 70$.

The number of degrees in $\angle 3$ is **70**.

10.

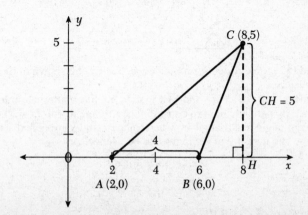

The area of a triangle is one-half the product of the length of its base and height. In the accompanying diagram, the length of base $\overline{AB}$ is $6 - 2$ or 4.

From C drop a perpendicular that intersects the x–axis at point H. The height CH of the triangle is 5. Thus:

$$\Delta ABC = \frac{1}{2} \times AB \times CH$$

$$= \frac{1}{2} \times 4 \times 5$$

$$= 10$$

There are **10** square units in the area of ΔABC.

11. Let x and y represent the measures of two angles of a triangle. If the measure of the third angle of this triangle is equal to the sum of the measures of the other two angles, then $x + y$ represents the measure of the largest angle of the triangle.

Since the sum of the measures of the three angles of a triangle is 180:

$$x + y + (x + y) = 180$$
$$2x + 2y = 180$$
$$x + y = 90$$

Hence, the number of degrees in the measure of the largest angle of the triangle is **90**.

12.

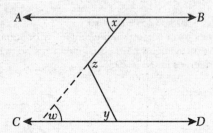

Extend the segment that forms angle x to line CD, as shown in the accompanying diagram.

It is given that $\overleftrightarrow{AB} \parallel \overleftrightarrow{CD}$ and that $m\angle x = 50$. Since alternate interior angles formed by parallel lines are equal in measure, $m\angle w = m\angle x = 50$. Angle z is an exterior angle of a triangle in which angles w and y are nonadjacent interior angles. The measure of $\angle y$ is given as 60. Hence:

$$m\angle z = m\angle w + m\angle y$$
$$= 50 \quad + \quad 60$$
$$= 110$$

The measure of $\angle z$ is **110**.

13. If a translation maps $A(-3,4)$ onto $A'(2,-6)$, then the translation "moves" point A horizontally 5 units since $-3 + 5 = 2$. The translation also "moves" point A vertically -10 units since $4 + (-10) = -6$. Hence, the general rule for this translation is

$$(x,y) \to (x+5, y-10).$$

If B' is the image of $B(-4,0)$ under the same translation, then the coordinates of B' are $(-4+5, 0-10) = (1,-10)$.

The coordinates of B' are **(1,–10)**.

14. The number of committees with three students that can be chosen from a class of seven students is the number of combinations of seven things taken three at a time.

The number of n things taken r at a time is given by this formula:

$$_nC_r = \frac{_nP_r}{r!}$$

Let $n = 7$ and $r = 3$:

$$_7C_3 = \frac{_7P_3}{3!}$$

$$= \frac{\overset{1}{7 \times \cancel{6} \times 5}}{\cancel{3 \times 2} \times 1}$$

$$= 35$$

35 three-student committees can be formed.

15.

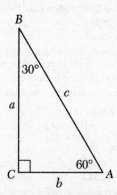

Since $m\angle C = 90$, and $m\angle A = 60$, then $m\angle B = 90 - 60 = 30$.

In a 30-60 right triangle, the length of the side opposite the 30° angle is one-half the length of the hypotenuse. In $\triangle ABC$, b is the side that is opposite the 30° angle, so its length is one-half the length of the hypotenuse. Since $b = 40$ centimeters and side c is the hypotenuse, $c = 80$ centimeters.

The number of centimeters in the length of side c is **80**.

16. The given expression to be factored completely is:

$$3x^2 - 15x - 42$$

First factor out the greatest common factor, if any. Since each term is divisible by 3, factor out 3:

$$3(x^2 - 5x - 14)$$

The expression inside the parentheses is a quadratic trinomial. Try to factor it into the product of two binomials that have the form $(x + ?)(x + ?)$. The missing numbers in the two binomials are the two factors of -14 whose sum is -5. These numbers are 2 and -7:

$$3(x + 2)(x - 7)$$

The completely factored form of the given equation is $3(x + 2)(x - 7)$.

17. To negate the conjunction $p \wedge \sim q$, use one of De Morgan's laws.

Apply De Morgan's Law that states

$$\sim(A \wedge B) \leftrightarrow \sim A \vee \sim B$$

by letting $A = p$ and $B = \sim q$: $\sim(p \wedge \sim q) \leftrightarrow \sim p \vee \sim(\sim q)$

Use the Law of Double Negation: $\sim(p \wedge \sim q) \leftrightarrow \sim p \vee q$

Thus, the negation of $p \wedge \sim q$ is $\sim p \vee q$.

The correct choice is **(1)**.

18. The equation $a + (-a) = 0$ states that the sum of any number a and its additive inverse (opposite) is 0.

The correct choice is **(1)**.

19. If an altitude is drawn to the hypotenuse of a right triangle, the length of either leg is the mean proportional between the hypotenuse and the segment of the hypotenuse that is adjacent to that leg. Thus, since $AD = 2$ and $DB = 6$:

$$\frac{AB}{AC} = \frac{AC}{AD}$$

$$\frac{2+6}{AC} = \frac{AC}{2}$$

$$\frac{8}{AC} = \frac{AC}{2}$$

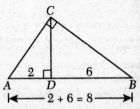

Cross-multiply: $(AC)^2 = 16$

$$AC = \sqrt{16} = 4$$

The correct choice is **(4)**.

20. The given system of equations is:

$$x - y = 2$$
$$y = 2x - 4$$

Eliminate y in the first equation by substituting its equal, $2x - 4$:

$$x - (2x - 4) = 2$$

Remove the parentheses by taking the opposite of each term that is inside the parentheses:

$$x - 2x + 4 = 2$$

Solve for x:

$$-x + 4 = 2$$
$$x = 2$$

Find the corresponding value of y by substituting 2 for x in the second equation:

$$y = 2(2) - 4 = 0$$

The solution is (2,0).
The correct choice is (**2**).

21. The given statements are:

$$a \rightarrow b \quad [1]$$
$$\sim c \rightarrow \sim b \quad [2]$$

Apply the Law of Contrapositive Inference to statement [2]: $b \rightarrow c \quad [3]$
Apply the Chain Rule to statements [1] and [3]: $a \rightarrow c$
The correct choice is (**1**).

22. The graph of an equation that has the form $x^2 + y^2 = c$ is a circle provided that $c > 0$. The equation $x^2 + y^2 = 9$ has this form.
The correct choice is (**3**).

23. An equilateral triangle is also equiangular, so each angle measures 60°.

An altitude drawn to a side of an equilateral triangle forms two 30-60 right triangles in which the altitude is the side that is opposite the 60° angle. Hence, the altitude is one-half the length of the hypotenuse times $\sqrt{3}$.

Since it is given that the length of a side of the equilateral triangle is 4, the length of the altitude is $\frac{1}{2} \times 4 \times \sqrt{3}$ or $2\sqrt{3}$.

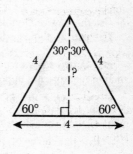

The correct choice is (**1**).

24. Since an equilateral triangle is also equiangular, each angle of an equiangular triangle measures 60°. As a result, two equilateral triangles will *always* be similar since they have three pairs of congruent angles.
The correct choice is (**1**).

25. In a right triangle, the sine of an acute angle is equal to the cosine of the other acute angle of the triangle. In given right triangle ABC, angles A and B are the acute angles,

so $\sin A = \cos B$ and $\sin B = \cos A$.

Since the question asks for an equivalent expression for sin *B*, look for the choice that is cos *A*.

The correct choice is (**2**).

26.

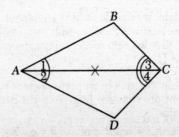

In the accompanying diagram, *C* is the midpoint of $\overline{AB}$ and *D* is the midpoint of $\overline{AC}$.

Pick any convenient number for the length of $\overline{AB}$, say *AB* = 12. Then figure out the length of each segment that appears in the four choices:

$$AC = BC = 6, \quad AD = CD = 3, \quad DB = DC + BC = 3 + 6 = 9.$$

Check the truth of each choice.
Since $3CD = 3(3) = 9$, $DB = 3CD$ is a true statement.
The correct choice is (**4**).

27. A conditional statement and its contrapositive are logically equivalent.

The given statement is: $\qquad\qquad\qquad \sim a \to b$

Form the contrapositive of the given conditional by negating each of its parts and then switching their positions: $\qquad\qquad \sim b \to \sim(\sim a)$

Use the Law of Double Negation: $\qquad\qquad \sim b \to a$

The correct choice is (**3**).

28. If two sides of a triangle have different lengths, the angle with the smaller measure lies opposite the shorter side.

- Since *AB* < *BC*, m∠*C* < m∠*A* (or, equivalently, m∠*A* > m∠*C*). Hence, choice (1) is true.
- Since *BC* < *AC*, m∠*A* < m∠*B*. Hence, choice (2) is true and choice (3) is true but choice (4) is *false*.

The correct choice is (**4**).

29.

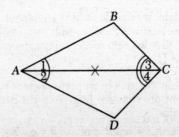

Since it is given that $\overline{AC}$ bisects $\angle BAD$ and $\angle BCD$:

- $\angle 1 \cong \angle 2$ (A)
- $\overline{AC} \cong \overline{AC}$ (S)
- $\angle 3 \cong \angle 4$ (A)

Hence, $\triangle ABC \cong \triangle ADC$ by ASA $\cong$ ASA.
The correct choice is **(3)**.

30. If, in a set of n objects, p objects are identical and q objects of another kind are identical, then the number of different ways in which the n objects can be arranged is $\dfrac{n!}{p!\,q!}$.

The word "DIVIDE" has six letters, including two identical letter D's and two identical letter I's. To find the number of different six-letter arrangements that can be formed using the letters in "DIVIDE," let $n = 6$, $p = 2$ and $q = 2$:

$$\frac{n!}{p!\,q!} = \frac{6!}{2!\,2!}$$

The correct choice is **(3)**.

31. The given equation, $x^2 + 3x - 1 = 0$, is a quadratic equation. Each of the four choices give irrational numbers as possible roots. Since the roots of the quadratic equation are irrational, use the quadratic formula to solve the equation.

If a quadratic equation is in the form $ax^2 + bx + c = 0$, its roots are given by this formula:

$$x = \frac{-b \pm \sqrt{b^2 - 4ac}}{2a} \quad (a \neq 0)$$

The given equation is in the form $ax^2 + bx + c = 0$ with $a = 1$, $b = 3$, and $c = -1$:

$$= \frac{-3 \pm \sqrt{3^2 - 4(1)(-1)}}{2(1)}$$

$$= \frac{-3 \pm \sqrt{9 + 4}}{2}$$

$$= \frac{-3 \pm \sqrt{13}}{2}$$

The correct choice is **(2)**.

32. The graph of an equation that has the form $y = ax^2 + bx + c$ $(a \neq 0)$ is a parabola. An equation of the axis of symmetry for this parabola is $x = -\dfrac{b}{2a}$.

The given equation, $y = x^2 - 6x + 2$, is in the form $y = ax^2 + bx + c$, where $a = 1$, $b = -6$, and $c = 2$. Hence, an equation of the axis of symmetry for this parabola is

$$x = -\frac{b}{2a} = -\frac{(-6)}{2(1)} = \frac{6}{2} = 3$$

The correct choice is **(3)**.

33. The set of all points that are 8 units from the origin is a circle with a radius of 8 units whose center is at the origin.

The set of all points that are equidistant from the axes is a pair of lines that pass through the origin and make a 45° angle with either axis, as shown in the accompanying diagram.

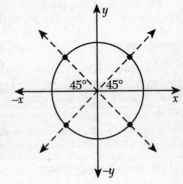

The pair of lines intersect the circle in four different points. Hence, the total number of points that are 8 units from the origin and equidistant from the axes is 4.

The correct choice is **(4)**.

34. A rhombus is an equilateral parallelogram. As shown in the accompanying diagram, the diagonals of a rhombus:

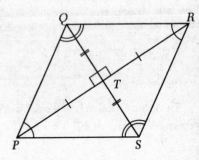

- bisect each other;
- bisect opposite angles of the parallelogram; and
- intersect at right angles.

In rhombus $PQRS$, diagonals $\overline{PR}$ and $\overline{QS}$ form right angles at T, so the statement $\triangle RTQ$ is a right triangle is *always* true

The correct choice is **(2)**.

35.

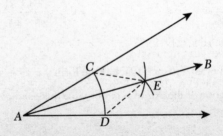

In the accompanying construction, ray AB bisects $\angle A$ if $\triangle ACE \cong \triangle ADE$.

- The arc drawn using A as its center makes $\overline{AC} \cong \overline{AD}$ (S).
- The arcs with C and E as their centers are drawn with the same compass setting, making $\overline{CE} \cong \overline{DE}$ (S).
- Since $\overline{AE} \cong \overline{AE}$ (S), $\triangle ACE \cong \triangle ADE$ by SSS $\cong$ SSS. Since corresponding parts of congruent triangles are congruent, $\angle CAE \cong \angle DAE$, so ray AB bisects $\angle A$.

The correct choice is **(2)**.

PART II

36. a. The given difference is:

If possible, simplify the fractions before combining them. Factor out 3 from the numerator of the first fraction. Also, since the denominator of the first fraction is the difference of two squares, factor it into the product of the sum and difference of the same two terms:

Divide out the factor that is common to the numerator and the denominator of the first fraction:

$$\frac{3x-9}{x^2-9} - \frac{1}{x+3}$$

$$\frac{3(x-3)}{(x-3)(x+3)} - \frac{1}{x+3}$$

$$\frac{3\cancel{(x-3)}^{\,1}}{\cancel{(x-3)}(x+3)} - \frac{1}{x+3}$$

$$\frac{3}{x+3} - \frac{1}{x+3}$$

Since the two fractions have the same denominator, combine them by writing the difference of their numerators over their common denominator:

$$\frac{3-1}{x+3}$$

$$\frac{2}{x+3}$$

The difference in simplest form is $\dfrac{2}{x+3}$.

b. The given product is:

Where possible, factor the numerators and denominators. The first numerator is a quadratic trinomial that can be factored into the product of two binomials, and the first denominator has a common factor of 5:

$$\frac{x^2+3x-4}{5x-5} \cdot \frac{10x^2-40x}{x^2-16x}$$

$$\frac{(x-1)(x+4)}{5(x-1)} \cdot \frac{10x^2-40x}{x^2-16x}$$

The numerator of the second fraction has a common factor of $10x$ and the denominator is the difference of two squares, so it can be factored into the product of the sum and difference of the same two terms:

$$\frac{(x-1)(x+4)}{5(x-1)} \cdot \frac{10x(x-4)}{(x+4)(x-4)}$$

Divide out any factor that appears in both a numerator and a denominator:

$$\frac{\overset{1}{\cancel{(x-1)}}\overset{1}{\cancel{(x+4)}}}{\underset{1}{\cancel{5}\cancel{(x-1)}}} \cdot \frac{\overset{2}{\cancel{10}}x\overset{1}{\cancel{(x-4)}}}{\cancel{(x+4)}\cancel{(x-4)}}$$

Multiply the remaining factors in the numerator, and multiply the remaining factors in the denominator:

$$\frac{2x}{1} \text{ or } 2x$$

The product in simplest form is **2x**.

37. a. Before drawing the graph of $y = -x^2 - 2x + 8$ over the interval $-5 \leq x \leq 3$, prepare a table of values for x and y by substituting each integer value of x, from -5 to 3, into the given equation to obtain the corresponding value of y:

x	$-x^2 - 2x + 8$	$= y$	(x,y)
-5	$-(-5)^2 - 2(-5) + 8 = -25 + 10 + 8$	$= -7$	$(-5,-7)$
-4	$-(-4)^2 - 2(-4) + 8 = -16 + 8 + 8$	$= 0$	$(-4,0)$
-3	$-(-3)^2 - 2(-3) + 8 = -9 + 6 + 8$	$= 5$	$(-3,5)$
-2	$-(-2)^2 - 2(-2) + 8 = -4 + 4 + 8$	$= 8$	$(-2,8)$
-1	$-(-1)^2 - 2(-1) + 8 = -1 + 2 + 8$	$= 9$	$(-1,9)$
0	$-0^2 - 2(0) + 8$	$= 8$	$(0,8)$
1	$-1^2 - 2(1) + 8 = -1 - 2 + 8$	$= 5$	$(1,5)$
2	$-2^2 - 2(2) + 8 = -4 - 4 + 8$	$= 0$	$(2,0)$
3	$-3^2 - 2(3) + 8 = -9 - 6 + 8$	$= -7$	$(3,-7)$

Now plot the points that appear in the last column of the table. Connect these points with a smooth curve that has the shape of a parabola whose turning point, $(-1,9)$, is the highest point on the curve. Label this graph with its equation, $y = -x^2 - 2x + 8$, as shown in the accompanying figure.

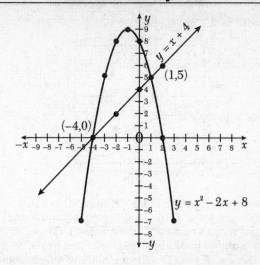

$y = x + 4$

$(1,5)$

$(-4,0)$

$y = x^2 - 2x + 8$

b. To draw the graph of $y = x + 4$, first prepare a table of values for x and y. Choose three convenient values for x, say -2, 0, and 2, and substitute them into the equation $y = x + 4$ to find the corresponding values of y:

x	$x + 4$	$= y$	(x,y)
-2	$-2 + 4$	$= 2$	$(-2,2)$
0	$0 + 4$	$= 4$	$(0,4)$
2	$2 + 4$	$= 6$	$(2,6)$

Now plot the points that appear in the last column of the table. Connect these points with a straight line, and label this line with its equation, $y = x + 4$, as shown in the figure in part **a**.

c. The solution for a system of equations consists of the coordinates of the points, if any, at which the graphs of the equations intersect. Since the graphs drawn in parts **a** and **b** intersect at $(1,5)$ and $(-4,0)$, the coordinates of these points are the solutions for the given system of equations:

$$y = -x^2 - 2x + 8$$
$$y = x + 4$$

The solutions are **(1,5)** and **(-4,0)**.

38. It is given that the vertices of $\triangle ABC$ are $A(-3,-2)$, $B(2,3)$, and $C(5,-4)$
a. See the accompanying figure.

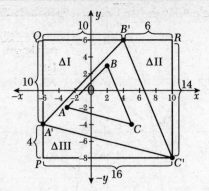

b. The image of point (x,y) under a dilation with a scale factor of 2 is $(2x,2y)$. Therefore, if $\triangle A'B'C'$ is the image of $\triangle ABC$ after a dilation of 2, the coordinates of the vertices of $\triangle A'B'C'$ are $A'(-6,-4)$, $B'(4,6)$, $C'(10,-8)$. The graph of $\triangle A'B'C'$ is shown in the figure in part **a**.

c. To find the area of $\triangle A'B'C'$, circumscribe a rectangle around the triangle as shown in the figure in part **a**. Find the area of $\triangle A'B'C'$ indirectly by subtracting the sum of the areas of right triangles I, II, and III from the area of rectangle $PQRC'$.

- Find the area of rectangle $PQRC'$: $16 \times 14 = 224$.
- Find the sum of the areas of the three right triangles.

$$\text{Area of } \Delta\text{I} = \frac{1}{2}bh = \frac{1}{2}(10)(10) = 50$$

$+$

$$\text{Area of } \Delta\text{II} = \frac{1}{2}bh = \frac{1}{2}(6)(14) = 42$$

$+$

$$\text{Area of } \Delta\text{III} = \frac{1}{2}bh = \frac{1}{2}(16)(4) = 32$$

$$\text{Sum of areas} = 124$$

- Find the area of $\triangle A'B'C'$:

Area of $\triangle A'B'C'$ = Area of rectangle $PQRC'$ – Sum of areas of 3 triangles

$$= \quad 224 \quad - \quad 124$$
$$= \quad 100$$

The area of $\triangle A'B'C'$ is **100** square units.

39.

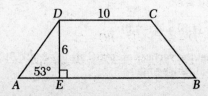

a. In right triangle AED, use the tangent ratio to find AE:

$$\tan \angle A = \frac{\text{side length opposite } \angle A}{\text{side length adjacent to } \angle A}$$

$$= \frac{DE}{AE}$$

$$\tan 53° = \frac{6}{AE}$$

$$1.3270 = \frac{6}{AE}$$

$$1.3270\,AE = 6$$

Use a calculator: $\qquad AE = \dfrac{6}{1.327} \approx 4.52 \approx 4.5$

The length of $\overline{AE}$ correct to the *nearest tenth*, is **4.5**.

b. To find the perimeter of isosceles trapezoid $ABCD$, first determine the lengths of sides $\overline{AD}$, $\overline{BC}$, and $\overline{AB}$.

- In right triangle AED, use the sine ratio to find the length of $\overline{AD}$:

$$\sin \angle A = \frac{\text{side length opposite } \angle A}{\text{hypotenuse}}$$

$$0.7986 = \frac{6}{AD}$$

$$0.7986\,AD = 6$$

$$AD = \frac{6}{0.7986}$$

Use a calculator: $\qquad AD \approx 7.513 \approx 7.5$

- Since $ABCD$ is an isosceles trapezoid, side $\overline{BC}$ has the same length as side $\overline{AD}$:

$$BC = AD = 7.5.$$

- To find the length of base $\overline{AB}$, draw altitude $\overline{CH}$ to $\overline{AB}$. Then $EH = CD = 10$ and $BH = AE = 4.5$. Hence:

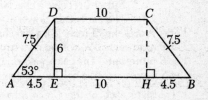

$$AB = AE + EH + BH$$
$$= 4.5 + 10 + 4.5$$
$$= 19$$

- Perimeter of $ABCD = AD + CD + BC + AB$

$$= 7.5 + 10 + 7.5 + 19$$
$$= 44$$

The perimeter of isosceles trapezoid *ABCD*, correct to the *nearest integer*, is **44**.

40. a. The given equation is: $3x^2 + 2x = 7$

Put the quadratic equation into standard form by placing all of the nonzero terms on the same side of the equation: $3x^2 + 2x - 7 = 0$

If a quadratic equation is in the standard form $ax^2 + bx + c = 0$, its roots are given by this formula:

$$x = \frac{-b \pm \sqrt{b^2 - 4ac}}{2a} \quad (a \neq 0)$$

The equation $3x^2 + 2x - 7 = 0$ is in the form $ax^2 + bx + c = 0$ with $a = 3, b = 2,$ and $c = -7$:

$$= \frac{-2 \pm \sqrt{2^2 - 4(3)(-7)}}{2(3)}$$

$$= \frac{-2 \pm \sqrt{4 + 84}}{6}$$

$$= \frac{-2 \pm \sqrt{88}}{6}$$

Using a calculator gives $\sqrt{88} \approx 9.38$:

$$\approx \frac{-2 \pm 9.38}{6}$$

$$x_1 \approx \frac{-2 + 9.38}{6} \quad \text{or} \quad x_2 \approx \frac{-2 - 9.38}{6}$$

Since the question asks for the positive root, discard x_2: $x_1 \approx \frac{7.38}{6} \approx 1.23 \approx 1.2$

The positive solution, correct to the *nearest tenth*, is **1.2**.

b.   Given: If I receive a check for $500, then we will go on a trip.
             If the car breaks down, then we will not go on a trip.
             Either I receive a check for $500 or we will not buy souvenirs.
             The car breaks down.

Let *C* represent: "I receive a $500 check."
Let *T* represent: "We will go on a trip."
Let *B* represent: "The car breaks down."
Let *S* represent: "We will buy souvenirs."

• Translate each of the *Given* into symbolic form:
  "If I receive a check for $500, then we will go on a trip" is the conditional that *C* implies *T*: $C \rightarrow T$
  "If the car breaks down, then we will not go on a trip" is the conditional that *B* implies the negation of *T*: $B \rightarrow \sim T$

"Either I receive a check for $500 or we will not buy souvenirs" is the disjunction of C and the negation of S: $C \lor \sim S$

"The car breaks down" is statement B: B

- Translate the statement to *prove* into symbolic form:

  Prove "We will not buy souvenirs" is the negation of statement S: $\sim S$

- Write a formal proof.

PROOF

Statement	Reason
1. B	1. Given.
2. $B \rightarrow \sim T$	2. Given.
3. $\sim T$	3. Law of Detachment (steps 1 and 2).
4. $C \rightarrow T$	4. Given.
5. $\sim C$	5. Law of *Modus Tollens* (steps 3 and 4).
6. $C \lor \sim S$	6. Given.
7. $\sim S$	7. Law of Disjunctive Inference (steps 5 and 6).

PART III

41. Given: rectangle $ABCD$, $\overline{BNPC}$, $\overline{AEP}$, $\overline{DEN}$, and $\overline{AP} \cong \overline{DN}$.

Prove: a $\triangle ABP \cong \triangle DCN$

      b $\overline{AE} \cong \overline{DE}$

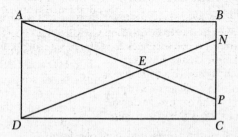

PLAN: **a.** Prove right triangle $ABP \cong$ right triangle DCN by Hyp-Leg $\cong$ Hyp-Leg.

      b. Prove $\overline{AE} \cong \overline{DE}$ by showing that the angles opposite these sides in $\triangle AED$ are congruent:

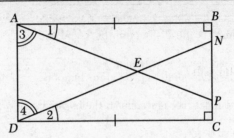

PROOF

Statements	Reasons
a. Prove △ABP ≅ △DCN.	
1. ABCD is a rectangle.	1. Given.
2. ∠A, ∠B, ∠C, and ∠D are right angles.	2. A rectangle contains four right angles.
3. △ABP and △DCN are right triangles.	3. A triangle that contains a right angle is a right triangle.
4. $\overline{AP} \cong \overline{DN}$ (Hyp)	4. Given.
5. $\overline{AB} \cong \overline{CD}$ (Leg)	5. Opposite sides of a rectangle are congruent.
6. △ABP ≅ △DCN.	6. Hyp-Leg $\cong$ Hyp-Leg.
b. Prove $\overline{AE} \cong \overline{DE}$.	
7. m∠1 = m∠2	7. Corresponding angles of congruent triangles are equal in measure.
8. m∠BAD = m∠CDA	8. Right angles are equal in measure.
9. m∠3 = m∠4	9. If equals (m∠1 = m∠2) are subtracted from equals (m∠BAD = m∠CDA), the differences are equal.
10. $\overline{AE} \cong \overline{DE}$	10. If two angles of a triangle have equal measures, the sides opposite these angles are congruent.

42. A quadrilateral is a parallelogram if its diagonals have the same midpoint and, as a result, bisect each other.

- Determine the x- and the y-coordinates of the midpoint of diagonal $\overline{GM}$ by finding the averages of the corresponding coordinates of $G(r,s)$ and $M(t,0)$:

$$\text{Midpoint of } \overline{GM} = \left(\frac{r+t}{2}, \frac{s+0}{2}\right) = \left(\frac{r+t}{2}, \frac{s}{2}\right)$$

- Determine the x- and the y-coordinates of the midpoint of diagonal $\overline{AE}$ by finding the averages of the corresponding coordinates of $A(0,0)$ and $E(t+r,s)$:

$$\text{Midpoint of } \overline{AE} = \left(\frac{0+(t+r)}{2}, \frac{0+s}{2}\right) = \left(\frac{r+t}{2}, \frac{s}{2}\right)$$

- Diagonals $\overline{GM}$ and $\overline{AE}$ of quadrilateral $GAME$ have the same midpoint; hence they bisect each other.

Therefore, quadrilateral $GAME$ is a parallelogram.

Topic	Question Numbers	Number of Points	Your Points	Your Percentage
1. Properties of Number Systems; Def. of Operations	1, 18	2 + 2 = 4		
2. Finite Mathematical Systems	—	—		
3. Linear Function & Graph ($y = mx + b$, slope, eqs. of)	—	—		
4. Quadratic Equation (alg. sol.—factoring, formula)	31, 40a	2 + 4 = 6		
5. Parabola (incl. axis of symmetry, turning point)	32, 37	2 + 10 = 12		
6. Systems of Equations (alg. and graphic solutions)	20	2		
7. Suppls., Compl., Vertical Angles, Angle Measure	—	—		
8. Triangle Properties (eq., isos., sum $\angle$s, 2 sides)	2, 11	2 + 2 = 4		
9. Line ‖ One Side of $\triangle$; Line Joining Midpts. of 2 Sides	—	—		
10. Inequalities in $\triangle$s (ext. $\angle$, ≠ sides, and opp. $\angle$s)	3, 28	2 + 2 = 4		
11. Quadrilateral Properties ($\square$, sq., rhom., rect., trap.)	34, 39b	2 + 6 = 8		
12. Parallel Lines	9, 12	2 + 2 = 4		
13. Alg. Oper.; Verbal Probs.	4, 16, 26, 36	2 + 2 + 2 + 10 = 16		
14. Mean Proportional; Alt. to Hypot. of Right $\triangle$	19	2		
15. Pythag. Th., Special Rt. $\triangle$s (3-4-5, 5-12-13, 30-60-90)	15, 23	2 + 2 = 4		
16. Similar Figures (ratios & proportions)	5, 24	2 + 2 = 4		
17. Areas ($\triangle$, rect., $\square$, rhom., trap.)	10	2		
18. Locus	33	2		
19. Constructions	35	2		
20. Deductive Proofs	29, 41	2 + 10 = 12		
21. Coordinate Geom. (slope, dist., midpt., eq. of circle)	6, 7, 22, 38	2 + 2 + 2 + 10 = 16		
22. Coordinate Geom. "Proofs"	42	10		
23. Logic	17, 21, 27, 40b	2 + 2 + 2 + 6 = 12		
24. Permutations; Arrangements	30	2		
25. Combinations	14	2		
26. Probability	—	—		
27. Trig. of Rt. $\triangle$	25, 39a	2 + 4 = 6		
28. Literal Eqs.	—	—		
29. Transformations	8, 13	2 + 2		

Examination
June 1996
Sequential Math Course II

PART I

Answer 30 questions from this part. Each correct answer will receive 2 credits. No partial credit will be allowed. Write your answers in the spaces provided. Where applicable, answers may be left in terms of π or in radical form. [60]

1 If $a * b$ is defined as $a^2 - 2b$, find the value of $5 * 7$.

1 _____

2 If $\tan A = 1.3400$, find the measure of $\angle A$ to the *nearest degree*.

2 _____

3 What is the identity element in the system defined by the table below?

$\star$	2	4	6	8
2	4	8	2	6
4	8	6	4	2
6	2	4	6	8
8	6	2	8	4

3 _____

4 In the accompanying figure, $\overline{DE} \parallel \overline{BC}$, $AD = 10$, $AB = 24$, and $AC = 36$. Find AE.

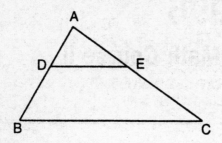

4 _____

5 Evaluate: $_7C_3$

5 _____

6 If one of the roots of the equation $x^2 + kx = 6$ is 2, what is the value of k?

6 _____

7 Solve for the positive value of y: $\dfrac{16}{y} = \dfrac{y}{4}$

7 _____

8 How many different 4-letter arrangements can be formed from the letters in the word "NINE"?

8 _____

9 In $\triangle ABC$, $m\angle B > m\angle C$ and $m\angle C > m\angle A$. Which side of $\triangle ABC$ is the longest?

9 _____

10 In the accompanying diagram of rhombus *ABCD*, diagonal $\overline{AC}$ is drawn. If m∠*CAB* = 35, find m∠*ADC*.

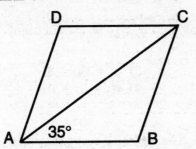

10 _____

11 What is the slope of the line whose equation is $3x + y = 4$?

11 _____

12 The graph of the equation $x^2 + y^2 = 9$ represents the locus of points at a given distance, *d*, from the origin. Find the value of *d*.

12 _____

13 Find the area of the parallelogram whose vertices are (2,1), (7,1), (9,5), and (4,5).

13 _____

14 Express $\dfrac{5x}{6} - \dfrac{x}{3}$ in simplest form.

14 _____

15 The line that passes through points (1,3) and (2,*y*) has a slope of 2. What is the value of *y*?

15 _____

16 What is the length of a side of a square whose diagonal measures $4\sqrt{2}$?

16 _____

Directions (17–35): For *each* question chosen, write in the space provided the *numeral* preceding the word or expression that best completes the statement or answers the question.

17 When factored completely, $x^3 - 9x$ is equivalent to

(1) $x(x - 3)$ (3) $(x + 3)(x - 3)$

(2) $x(x + 3)(x - 3)$ (4) $x(x + 3)$ 17 _____

18 If $(x + 2)^2 + (y - 3)^2 = 25$ is an equation of a circle whose center is $(-2,k)$, then k equals

(1) 1   (3) 3

(2) 2   (4) 4   18 _____

19 In the accompanying diagram of $\triangle ABC$, side $\overline{BC}$ is extended to D, m$\angle B = 2y$, m$\angle BCA = 6y$, and m$\angle ACD = 3y$.

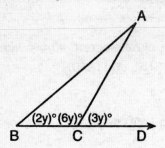

What is m$\angle A$?

(1) 15   (3) 20

(2) 17   (4) 24   19 _____

20 The coordinates of $\triangle ABC$ are $A(0,0)$, $B(6,0)$, and $C(0,4)$. What are the coordinates of the point at which the median from vertex A intersects side $\overline{BC}$?

(1) (1,4)   (3) (3,0)
(2) (2,3)   (4) (3,2)   20 _____

21 Which statement is the equivalent of $\sim(\sim m \wedge n)$?

(1) $m \wedge n$ (3) $m \vee \sim n$
(2) $m \wedge \sim n$ (4) $\sim m \vee \sim n$ 21 _____

22 The translation $(x,y) \rightarrow (x - 2, y + 3)$ maps the point $(7,2)$ onto the point whose coordinates are

(1) (9,5)   (3) (5,–1)
(2) (5,5)   (4) (–14,6)   22 _____

23 In the accompanying diagram, $\triangle FUN$ is a right triangle, $\overline{UR}$ is the altitude to hypotenuse $\overline{FN}$, $UR = 12$, and the lengths of $\overline{FR}$ and $\overline{RN}$ are in the ratio 1:9.

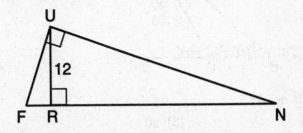

What is the length of $\overline{FR}$?

(1) 1   (3) 36
(2) $1\frac{1}{3}$ (4) 4   23 _____

24 Lines ℓ and m are perpendicular. The slope of ℓ is $\frac{3}{5}$. What is the slope of m?

(1) $-\frac{3}{5}$ (3) $\frac{3}{5}$

(2) $-\frac{5}{3}$ (4) $\frac{5}{3}$

24 _____

25 In the accompanying diagram of $\triangle ABC$, $\overline{AC}$ is extended to D, $\overline{DEF}$, $\overline{BEC}$, $\overline{AFB}$, $m\angle B = 50$, $m\angle BEF = 25$, and $m\angle ACB = 65$.

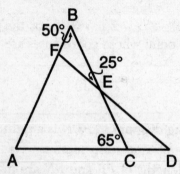

What is $m\angle D$?

(1) 40   (3) 50
(2) 45   (4) 55

25 _____

26 In the accompanying diagram, parallel lines ℓ and m are cut by transversal t.

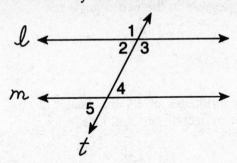

Which statement is true?

(1) m∠1 + m∠2 + m∠5 = 360
(2) m∠1 + m∠2 + m∠3 = 180
(3) m∠1 + m∠2 = m∠2 + m∠3
(4) m∠1 + m∠3 = m∠4 + m∠5   26 _____

27 Which argument below is *not* valid?

(1) Given: $a \rightarrow b$
           a
    Conclusion: b

(2) Given: $a \lor b$
           $\sim b$
    Conclusion: $\sim a$

(3) Given: $a \rightarrow b$
           $\sim b$
    Conclusion: $\sim a$

(4) Given: $a \rightarrow b$
           $b \rightarrow \sim c$
    Conclusion: $a \rightarrow \sim c$ 27 _____

28 The measure of a base angle of an isosceles triangle is 4 times the measure of the vertex angle. The number of degrees in the vertex angle is

(1) 20   (3) 36
(2) 30   (4) 135   28 ____

29 What are the coordinates of R', the image of $R(-4,3)$ after a reflection in the line whose equation is $y = x$?

(1) $(-4,-3)$ (3) $(4,3)$
(2) $(3,-4)$ (4) $(-3,4)$ 29 ____

30 The equation $y = 4$ represents the locus of points that are equidistant from which two points?

(1) $(0,0)$ and $(0,8)$ (3) $(4,0)$ and $(0,4)$
(2) $(0,3)$ and $(0,1)$ (4) $(4,4)$ and $(-4,4)$ 30 ____

31 In equilateral triangle ABC, $\overline{AD}$ is drawn to $\overline{BC}$ such that $BD < DC$. Which inequality is true?

(1) $DC > AC$ (3) $AD > AB$
(2) $BD > AD$ (4) $AC > AD$ 31 ____

32 Which equation represents the axis of symmetry of the graph of the equation $y = 2x^2 + 7x - 5$?

(1) $x = -\frac{5}{4}$ (3) $x = \frac{7}{4}$

(2) $x = \frac{5}{4}$ (4) $x = -\frac{7}{4}$ 32 ____

33 How many congruent triangles are formed by connecting the midpoints of the three sides of a scalene triangle?

(1) 1   (3) 3

(2) 2   (4) 4   33 _____

34 What are the roots of the equation $2x^2 - 7x + 4 = 0$?

(1) $\dfrac{7 \pm \sqrt{17}}{4}$ (3) $4, -\dfrac{1}{2}$

(2) $\dfrac{-7 \pm \sqrt{17}}{4}$ (4) $-4, \dfrac{1}{2}$ 34 _____

35 In the accompanying diagram of quadrilateral $QRST$, $\overline{RS} \cong \overline{ST}$, $\overline{SR} \perp \overline{QR}$, and $\overline{ST} \perp \overline{QT}$.

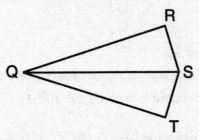

Which method of proof may be used to prove $\triangle QRS \cong \triangle QTS$?

(1) HL   (3) AAS

(2) SAS   (4) ASA   35 _____

PART II

Answer three questions from this part. Clearly indicate the necessary steps, including appropriate formula substitutions, diagrams, graphs, charts, etc. Calculations that may be obtained by mental arithmetic or the calculator do not need to be shown. [30]

36 Answer a, b, and c for all values of x for which these expressions are defined.

a Find the value of $\dfrac{(x+1)^2}{x^2-1}$ if $x = 1.02$. [2]

b Find the positive value of x to the *nearest thousandth*:

$$\frac{1}{x} = \frac{x+1}{1} \quad [5]$$

c Solve for all values of x in simplest radical form:

$$\frac{x+2}{4} = \frac{2}{x-2} \quad [3]$$

37 Triangle ABC has coordinates $A(1,0)$, $B(7,4)$, and $C(5,7)$.

a On graph paper, draw and label $\triangle ABC$. [1]

b Graph and state the coordinates of $\triangle A'B'C'$, the image of $\triangle ABC$ after a reflection in the origin. [3]

c Graph and state the coordinates of $\triangle A''B''C''$, the image of $\triangle A'B'C'$ under the translation $(x,y) \rightarrow (x+1, y+5)$. [3]

d Write an equation of the line containing $\overline{A''B''}$. [3]

38 Solve the following system of equations algebraically or graphically and check:

$$y = x^2 - 6x + 5$$
$$y + 7 = 2x \quad [8,2]$$

39 In the accompanying diagram of rhombus *ABCD*, m∠*CAB* = 25 and *AC* = 18.

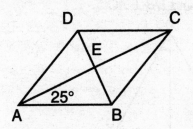

Find, to the *nearest tenth*, the

a perimeter of *ABCD*   [6]

b length of $\overline{BD}$ [4]

40 The vertices of △*NYS* are *N*(−2,−1), *Y*(0,10), and *S*(10,5). The coordinates of point *T* are (4,2).

a Prove that $\overline{YT}$ is a median.   [2]

b Prove that $\overline{YT}$ is an altitude.   [4]

c Find the area of △*NYS*.   [4]

PART III

Answer one question from this part. Clearly indicate the necessary steps, including appropriate formula substitutions, diagrams, graphs, charts, etc. Calculations that may be obtained by mental arithmetic or the calculator do not need to be shown. [10]

41 Given: $\angle 1 \cong \angle 2$ and $\overline{DB} \perp \overline{AC}$.

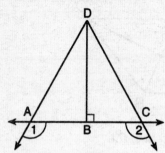

Prove: $\triangle ABD \cong \triangle CBD$ [10]

42 Given: $\sim G \rightarrow F$

$\sim (E \wedge F)$

$\sim E \rightarrow \sim D$

A

$(B \wedge C) \rightarrow D$

$A \rightarrow (B \wedge C)$

Prove: G [10]

Answers
June 1996

Sequential Math Course II

Answer Key

PART I

1. 11	**13.** 20	**25.** (1)
2. 53	**14.** $\frac{x}{2}$	**26.** (3)
3. 6	**15.** 5	**27.** (2)
4. 15	**16.** 4	**28.** (1)
5. 35	**17.** (2)	**29.** (2)
6. 1	**18.** (3)	**30.** (1)
7. 8	**19.** (3)	**31.** (4)
8. 12	**20.** (4)	**32.** (4)
9. $\overline{AC}$	**21.** (3)	**33.** (4)
10. 110	**22.** (2)	**34.** (1)
11. –3	**23.** (4)	**35.** (1)
12. 3	**24.** (2)	

PARTS II AND III See answers explained section.

Answers Explained

PART I

1. If $a * b$ is defined as $a^2 - 2b$, the value of $5 * 7$ is obtained by substituting 5 for a and 7 for b.

The given formula is:

Let $a = 5$ and $b = 7$:

$$a * b = a^2 - 2b$$
$$5 * 7 = 5^2 - 2(7)$$
$$= 25 - 14$$
$$= 11$$

The value of $5 * 7$ is **11**.

2. If $\tan A = 1.3400$, the degree measure of $\angle A$ can be obtained by using a scientific calculator. Some scientific calculators require that you follow these steps:

1. enter 1.34;
2. press the [2nd] or [INV] function key;
3. press the [tan] key since $\tan^{-1}$ is printed directly above it.

The measure of $\angle A$ is approximately 53.267 degrees.
The measure of $\angle A$, correct to the *nearest degree*, is **53**.

3. The identity element of a set is the member of the set that always returns the same element as the one on which it operates. In the given table, look for the row that is identical to the heading at the top and find the column that is identical to the column at the left under the operation symbol, $\star$. Observe that, $6 \star x = x \star 6 = x$ for $x = 2, 4, 6,$ or 8.

The identity element is **6**.

$\star$	2	4	6	8
2	4	8	2	6
4	8	6	4	2
6	2	4	6	8
8	6	2	8	4

4. A line that is parallel to one side of a triangle and intersects the other two sides forms a triangle similar to the original triangle. In the accompanying figure, $\overline{DE} \parallel \overline{BC}$, so $\triangle ADE \sim \triangle ABC$. Since the lengths of corresponding sides of similar triangles are in proportion:

$$\frac{AE}{AC} = \frac{AD}{AB}$$

$$\frac{AE}{36} = \frac{10}{24}$$

Multiplying both sides of the equation by 36 gives $AE = \dfrac{360}{24} = 15$

The length of $\overline{AE}$ is **15**.

5. Evaluate $_7C_3$ by using either a scientific calculator or the formula

$$_nC_r = \frac{n!}{r!(n-r)!}$$

where $n = 7$ and $r = 3$. Thus: $\quad _7C_3 = \frac{7!}{3!(7-3)!}$

$$= \frac{7!}{3!4!}$$

$$= \frac{7 \cdot \overset{1}{\cancel{6}} \cdot 5 \cdot \cancel{4!}}{\cancel{3} \cdot 2 \cdot 1 \cdot \cancel{4!}}$$

$$= 7 \cdot 5$$

$$= 35$$

The value of $_7C_3$ is **35**.

6. Since one of the roots of the equation $x^2 + kx = 6$ is given as 2, the value of k can be obtained by replacing x with 2 and then solving the resulting equation for k. Thus:

$$2^2 + k(2) = 6$$
$$4 + 2k = 6$$
$$2k = 2$$
$$\frac{2k}{2} = \frac{2}{2}$$
$$k = 1$$

The value of k is **1**.

7. The given equation is:

In a proportion, the product of the means equals the product of the extremes (cross-multiply):

$$\frac{16}{y} = \frac{y}{4}$$

$$y \times y = 16 \times 4$$
$$y^2 = 64$$
$$y = \pm\sqrt{64} = \pm 8$$

The positive value of y is **8**.

8. If, in a set of n objects, a of the objects are identical, the number of different ways in which the n objects can be arranged is

$$\frac{n!}{a!}$$

The word "NINE" has four letters, including two identical letter N's. To find the total number of different four-letter arrangements that can be formed from the letters of the word "NINE," let $n = 4$ and $a = 2$:

$$\frac{n!}{a!} = \frac{4!}{2!} = \frac{4 \cdot 3 \cdot \overset{1}{\cancel{2!}}}{\cancel{2!}} = 12$$

There are **12** different four-letter arrangements.

9.

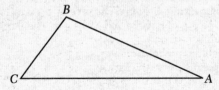

In a triangle, the longest side is opposite the angle with the greatest measure. It is given that, in $\triangle ABC$, $m\angle B > m\angle C$, and $m\angle C > m\angle A$.

Using the transitive property of inequality, we see that $m\angle B > m\angle A$, so $\angle B$ is the greatest angle of the triangle. Then, since side $\overline{AC}$ is opposite $\angle B$, $\overline{AC}$ is the longest side of the triangle.

The longest side of $\triangle ABC$ is $\overline{\textbf{AC}}$.

10. It is given that, in the accompanying diagram, $ABCD$ is a rhombus and $m\angle CAB = 35$. The diagonals of a rhombus bisect the angles of the rhombus, so $m\angle CAD = m\angle CAB = 35$. Hence, $m\angle DAB = 35 + 35 = 70$.

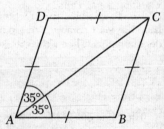

Then, since consecutive angles of a rhombus are supplementary,

$$\begin{aligned} m\angle ADC &= 180 - m\angle DAB \\ &= 180 - \quad 70 \\ &= 110 \end{aligned}$$

The measure of $\angle ADC$ is **110**.

11. If an equation has the form $y = mx + b$, then m is the slope of the line and b is the y-intercept of the line.

To find the slope of the line whose equation is $3x + y = 4$, write the given equation in the form $y = mx + b$:

$$\begin{aligned} 3x + y &= 4 \\ y &= -3x + 4 \end{aligned}$$

Then m, the coefficient of x, is -3.
The slope of the line is **-3**.

12. In general, a circle whose equation has the form $x^2 + y^2 = d^2$ represents the locus of all points d units from the origin. The given equation, $x^2 + y^2 = 9$, has the form $x^2 + y^2 = d^2$ with $d^2 = 9$, so $d = \sqrt{9} = 3$.

The value of d is **3**.

13. The parallelogram whose vertices are (2,1), (7,1), (9,5), and (4,5) is shown in the accompanying diagram. The area of a parallelogram is equal to the product of the length of its base and its height. The length of the base, b, of the parallelogram is $7 - 2$ or 5.

To find the height, h, of the parallelogram, drop a perpendicular to the base from any point on the side that is opposite the base. The height of the parallelogram is $5 - 1$ or 4. Hence:

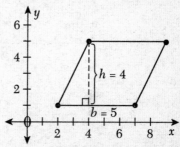

$$\text{Area of the parallelogram} = b \times h$$
$$= 5 \times 4$$
$$= 20$$

The area of the parallelogram is **20**.

14. To combine two fractions, change them into equivalent fractions that have the least common denominator (LCD) of the original fractions as their denominators. Then write the difference of their numerators over the LCD.

The given expression is:
$$\frac{5x}{6} - \frac{x}{3}$$

The LCD of the two fractions is 6 since 6 is the least integer into which 3 and 6 divide evenly. To change the second fraction into an equivalent fraction that has the LCD as its denominator, multiply it by 1 in the form of $\frac{2}{2}$:
$$\frac{5x}{6} - \frac{2}{2}\left(\frac{x}{3}\right)$$

Simplify:
$$\frac{5x}{6} - \frac{2x}{6}$$
$$\frac{5x - 2x}{6}$$

Write the difference of the numerators over the LCD:
$$\frac{3x}{6}$$
$$\frac{x}{2}$$

The result in simplest form is $\dfrac{x}{2}$.

15. The slope, m, of the line that passes through points $A(x_a, y_a)$ and $B(x_b, y_b)$ can be obtained using the formula

$$m = \frac{y_b - y_a}{x_b - x_a}$$

It is given that a line whose slope is 2 passes through points $(1,3)$ and $(2,y)$. To find the value of y, substitute in the slope formula by letting $m = 2$, $y_a = 3$, $x_a = 1$, $x_b = 2$ and $y_b = y$:

$$m = \frac{y_b - y_a}{x_b - x_a}$$

$$2 = \frac{y - 3}{2 - 1}$$

$$2 = \frac{y - 3}{1}$$

$$2 = y - 3$$

$$5 = y$$

The value of y is **5**.

16. Let x represent the length of a side of the square. To find the length of a side of a square whose diagonal measures $4\sqrt{2}$, use the Pythagorean theorem:

$$x^2 + x^2 = \left(4\sqrt{2}\right)^2$$

$$2x^2 = 4\sqrt{2} \times 4\sqrt{2}$$

$$= 16 \times 2$$

$$= 32$$

$$x^2 = \frac{32}{2} = 16$$

$$x = \sqrt{16} = 4$$

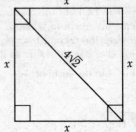

The length of a side of the square is **4**.

17. The given expression is: $\qquad\qquad x^3 - 9x$

Factor out x, the greatest common monomial factor of each term: $\qquad\qquad x(x^2 - 9)$

Since the binomial represents the difference of two squares, it can be factored as the product of the sum and difference of the same two terms: $\qquad\qquad x(x + 3)(x - 3)$

The correct choice is **(2)**.

18. In general, $(x - h)^2 + (y - k)^2 = r^2$ is an equation of a circle whose center is at (h,k) and whose radius length is r. The given equation, $(x + 2)^2 + (y - 3)^2 = 25$, when written in this form is

$$\left(x-(-2)\right)^2 +\left(y-(-3)\right)^2 = 5^2$$

where $h = -2$, $k = 3$, and $r = 5$. Hence, the center of the circle is at $(-2,3)$.

It is given that the center of the circle is $(-2,k)$, so $(-2,k) = (-2,3)$; therefore $k = 3$.

The correct choice is **(3)**.

19.

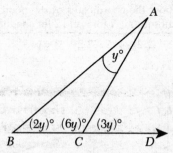

Since the measure of an exterior angle of a triangle is equal to the sum of the two remote (nonadjacent) interior angles:

$$m\angle A + m\angle B = m\angle ACD$$
$$m\angle A + \ 2y \ = \ \ 3y$$
$$m\angle A = 3y - 2y = y$$

Then, since angles ACB and ACD are supplementary:

$$6y + 3y = 180$$
$$9y = 180$$
$$y = \frac{180}{9} = 20$$

Hence, $m\angle A = y = 20$.
The correct choice is **(3)**.

20. The median drawn from vertex A of $\triangle ABC$ to side $\overline{BC}$ intersects $\overline{BC}$ at its midpoint. To find the midpoint $(\bar{x},\bar{y})$ of side $\overline{BC}$, find the averages of corresponding coordinates of $B(6,0)$ and $C(0,4)$. Thus:

$$\bar{x} = \frac{x_B + x_C}{2} \qquad \bar{y} = \frac{y_B + y_C}{2}$$
$$= \frac{6+0}{2} \qquad\qquad = \frac{0+4}{2}$$
$$= 3 \qquad\qquad\qquad = 2$$

The coordinates of the point at which the median from vertex A intersects side $\overline{BC}$ are (3,2).

The correct choice is **(4)**.

21. The given statement is: $\sim(\sim m \wedge n)$

By one of DeMorgan's laws: $\sim(\sim m) \vee \sim n$

Using the Law of Double Negation, replace $\sim(\sim m)$ by m: $m \vee \sim n$

The correct choice is **(3)**.

22. The given translation is defined by the mapping rule, $(x,y) \rightarrow (x-2,y+3)$. Under this translation, the coordinates of the point that (7,2) is mapped onto can be found by substituting 7 for x and 2 for y in the mapping rule. Thus:

$$(7,2) \rightarrow (7-2,2+3) = (5,5)$$

The correct choice is **(2)**.

23.

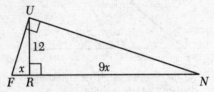

Since it is given that the lengths of $\overline{FR}$ and $\overline{RN}$ are in the ratio $1:9$, let $x = FR$ and $9x = RN$. The altitude drawn to the hypotenuse of a right triangle is the mean proportional between the lengths of the segments into which the hypotenuse is divided. Thus:

$$\frac{FR}{UR} = \frac{UR}{RN}$$

$$\frac{x}{12} = \frac{12}{9x}$$

In a proportion the product of the means equals the product of the extremes (cross-multiply):

$$(x)(9x) = (12)(12)$$

$$9x^2 = 144$$

$$x^2 = \frac{144}{9} = 16$$

$$x = \sqrt{16} = 4$$

Since $FR = x = 4$, the length of $\overline{FR}$ is 4.

The correct choice is **(4)**.

24. If two lines are perpendicular, the product of their slopes is -1. It is given that lines ℓ and m are perpendicular and that the slope of line ℓ is $\frac{3}{5}$.

Then the slope of line m is $-\dfrac{5}{3}$ since

$$\left(\dfrac{3}{5}\right) \times \left(-\dfrac{5}{3}\right) = -1$$

The correct choice is (**2**).

25. Since vertical angles are equal in measure, $m\angle CED = m\angle BEF = 25$. The measure of an exterior angle of a triangle is equal to the sum of the measures of the two remote (nonadjacent) interior angles. Hence:

$$\begin{aligned} m\angle D + m\angle CED &= m\angle ACB \\ m\angle D + \quad 25 \quad &= 65 \\ m\angle D &= 65 - 25 = 40 \end{aligned}$$

The correct choice is (**1**).

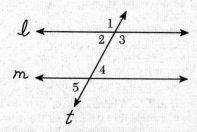

26.

Since angles 1 and 2 are adjacent angles whose exterior sides form a straight line, $m\angle 1 + m\angle 2 = 180$. Examine each statement in turn:

- If choice (1) is true, then $m\angle 5 = 180$, which is false. Hence, choice (1) is not true.
- If choice (2) is true, then $m\angle 3 = 0$, which is false. Hence, choice (2) is not true.
- Since angles 2 and 3 are adjacent angles whose exterior sides form a straight line, $m\angle 2 + m\angle 3 = 180$. Choice (3) is true since the left and right sides of the equation each equal 180.
- Choice (4) is not necessarily true. For example, suppose $m\angle 1 = 100$. Since angles 1 and 3 are vertical angles, $m\angle 3 = 100$. Angles 3 and 4 are supplementary since parallel lines form supplementary interior angles on the same side of the transversal. Hence, $m\angle 4 = 80 = m\angle 5$. Since $m\angle 1 + m\angle 3 = 200$ and $m\angle 4 + m\angle 5 = 160$, choice (4) is not true.

The correct choice is (**3**).

27. The four arguments are:

(1) Given: $a \to b$

a

Conclusion: b

(2) Given: $a \lor b$

$\sim b$

Conclusion: $\sim a$

(3) Given: $a \to b$

$\sim b$

Conclusion: $\sim a$

(4) Given: $a \to b$

$b \to \sim c$

Conclusion: $a \to \sim c$

Examine each argument in turn.

- Choice (1) states the Law of Detachment, so (1) is valid.
- Choice (2) states that, if one of the disjuncts of a disjunction is false, then the other disjunct is also false. However, since the disjunction is given as true, one disjunct (a) must be true when the other disjunct (b) is given as false. Hence, (2) is *not* valid.
- Choice (3) states the Law of *Modus Tollens*, so (3) is valid.
- Choice (4) states the Chain Rule, so (4) is valid.

The correct choice is (**2**).

28. It is given that the measure of a base angle of an isosceles triangle is 4 times the measure of the vertex angle. Let x represent the measure of the vertex angle of the isosceles triangle. Then, since the base angles of an isosceles triangle have equal measures, $4x$ represents the measure of each base angle.

To find x, the measure of the vertex angle, add the measures of the three angles of the triangle and set the sum equal to 180. Thus:

$$x + 4x + 4x = 180$$
$$9x = 180$$
$$x = \frac{180}{9} = 20$$

Hence, the measure of the vertex angle is 20.

The correct choice is (**1**).

29. After a reflection in the line whose equation is $y = x$, the image of point $P(a,b)$ is $P'(b,a)$. Thus, after a reflection in the line $y = x$, the image of $R(-4,3)$ is $R'(3,-4)$.

The correct choice is (**2**).

30. In general, the locus of points equidistant from two fixed points is the line that is the perpendicular bisector of the segment whose endpoints are the two fixed points.

Since it is given that the equation $y = 4$, which is the equation of a *horizontal* line, represents the locus of points that are equidistant from two unknown points, identify the choice that contains two points that determine a *vertical* line that is bisected by $y = 4$.

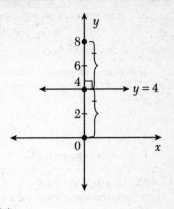

Two points that have the same x-coordinate determine a vertical line. Since only choices (1) and (2) have points with the same x-coordinate, eliminate choices (3) and (4).

The midpoint of the segment whose endpoints, $A(0,0)$ and $B(0,8)$, are given in choice (1), is

$$\left(\frac{0+0}{2}, \frac{0+8}{2}\right) = (0,4)$$

Since the y-coordinate of the midpoint of $\overline{AB}$ is 4, the line $y = 4$ contains the midpoint of $\overline{AB}$, so it is the perpendicular *bisector* of $\overline{AB}$. Hence, the equation $y = 4$ represents the locus of points that are equidistant from $(0,0)$ and $(0,8)$.

The correct choice is (**1**).

31. It is given that in equilateral triangle ABC, $\overline{AD}$ is drawn to $\overline{BC}$ in such a way that $BD < DC$, as shown in the accompanying diagram. Consider each inequality in turn:

- Choice (1): The diagram shows D is between B and C so that $BC > DC$. Since $AC = BC$, then $AC > DC$, so (1) is not true.
- Choice (2): $\angle BAC > \angle 1$ and $\angle B = \angle BAC$, so $\angle B > \angle 1$. In $\triangle ABD$, $AD > BD$ since the longer side lies opposite the larger angle. Hence, (2) is not true.
- Choice (3): $\angle 2 > \angle C$ since an exterior angle of $\triangle ADC$ is greater than either nonadjacent interior angle of the triangle. Since $\angle B = \angle C$, then $\angle 2 > \angle B$. Therefore, in $\triangle ABD$, $AB > AD$. Hence, (3) is not true.
- Choice (4): From the analysis for choice (3), $AB > AD$. Since $AC = AB$, then $AC > AD$. Hence, (4) is true.

The correct choice is (**4**).

32. The graph of an equation that has the form $y = ax^2 + bx + c$ $(a \neq 0)$ is a parabola with a vertical axis of symmetry. An equation for the axis of symmetry of this parabola is $x = -\dfrac{b}{2a}$.

The given equation, $y = 2x^2 + 7x - 5$, is in the form $y = ax^2 + bx + c$, where $a = 2$, $b = 7$, and $c = -5$. Hence, an equation of the axis of symmetry for this parabola is

$$x = -\frac{b}{2a} = -\frac{7}{2(2)} = -\frac{7}{4}$$

The correct choice is **(4)**.

33. In a scalene triangle, no two sides have the same length. Consider a scalene triangle whose side lengths are represented by $2a$, $2b$, and $2c$, as shown in the accompanying diagram.

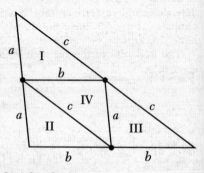

A line joining the midpoints of two sides of a triangle is parallel to the third side and one-half of its length. Hence, when the midpoints of the three sides of the scalene triangle that is shown are conected, four scalene triangles, $\triangle I$, $\triangle II$, $\triangle III$, and $\triangle IV$, are formed. Each of these triangles has side lengths of a, b, and c.

By the Side-Side-Side Theorem of Congruence, $\triangle I \cong \triangle II \cong \triangle III \cong \triangle IV$.
The correct choice is **(4)**.

34. The given equation, $2x^2 - 7x + 4 = 0$, is a quadratic equation. Since some of the four answer choices include irrational roots, solve the equation by using the quadratic formula.

If a quadratic equation is in the form $ax^2 + bx + c = 0$, its roots are given by the quadratic formula:

$$x = \frac{-b \pm \sqrt{b^2 - 4ac}}{2a} \quad (a \neq 0)$$

The given equation is in the form $ax^2 + bx + c = 0$, where $a = 2$, $b = -7$, and $c = 4$:

$$= \frac{-(-7) \pm \sqrt{(-7)^2 - 4(2)(4)}}{2(2)}$$

$$= \frac{7 \pm \sqrt{49 - 32}}{4}$$

$$= \frac{7 \pm \sqrt{17}}{4}$$

The correct choice is **(1)**.

35.

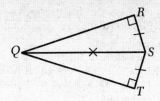

It is given that, in the accompanying diagram, $\overline{RS} \cong \overline{ST}$, $\overline{SR} \perp \overline{QR}$, and $\overline{ST} \perp \overline{QT}$. Since right triangle QRS and right triangle QTS have the same hypotenuse, $\overline{QS}$, and a pair of congruent legs, $\triangle QRS \cong \triangle QTS$ by the *H*ypotenuse-*L*eg (HL) method of proof.

The correct choice is **(1)**.

PART II

36. a. The given expression is:

$$\frac{(x+1)^2}{x^2-1}$$

Rewrite the numerator of the fraction in factored form. Also, since the denominator is the difference of two squares, factor it as the sum and difference of the same two terms:

$$\frac{(x+1)(x+1)}{(x+1)(x-1)}$$

Divide out any factor that appears in both the numerator and the denominator of the fraction since their quotient is 1:

$$\frac{\overset{1}{\cancel{(x+1)}}(x+1)}{\cancel{(x+1)}(x-1)}$$

$$\frac{x+1}{x-1}$$

Since $x = 1.02$:

$$\frac{1.02+1}{1.02-1}$$

Simplify:

$$\frac{2.02}{0.02}$$

$$\frac{202}{2}$$

$$101$$

The value of the given fraction is **101**.

b. The given equation is:

$$\frac{1}{x} = \frac{x+1}{1}$$

In a proportion, the product of the means equals the product of the extremes (cross-multiply):

$$x(x + 1) = 1$$
$$x^2 + x = 1$$

Rearrange the terms of the quadratic equation so that all of the nonzero terms are on the same side:

$$x^2 + x - 1 = 0$$

Use the quadratic formula with $a = 1$, $b = 1$, and $c = -1$:

$$x = \frac{-b \pm \sqrt{b^2 - 4ac}}{2a} \quad (a \neq 0)$$

$$= \frac{-1 \pm \sqrt{1 + 4}}{2}$$

$$= \frac{-1 \pm \sqrt{5}}{2}$$

$$x_1 = \frac{-1 + \sqrt{5}}{2} \text{ or } x_2 = \frac{-1 - \sqrt{5}}{2}$$

Since the question asks for only the positive value of x, discard x_2. Use a calculator to obtain x_1:

$$\frac{-1 + \sqrt{5}}{2} \approx 0.618034$$

The positive value of x, correct to the *nearest thousandth*, is **0.618**.

c. The given equation is:

$$\frac{x+2}{4} = \frac{2}{x-2}$$

In a proportion, the product of the means equals the product of the extremes (cross-multiply):

$$(x + 2)(x - 2) = (4)(2)$$
$$x^2 - 4 = 8$$

Since the quadratic equation does not include a first-degree term, isolate x^2:

$$x^2 = 12$$

Now take the square root of both sides of the equation:

$$x = \pm\sqrt{12}$$

Simplify the radical by factoring the radicand so that one of the two factors is the highest perfect square factor of 12. Rewrite the radical over each factor and simplify:

$$= \pm\sqrt{4}\sqrt{3} = \pm2\sqrt{3}$$

The solutions in simplest radical form are $\pm\mathbf{2\sqrt{3}}$.

37. It is given that $\triangle ABC$ has coordinates $A(1,0)$, $B(7,4)$, and $C(5,7)$.

a. See $\triangle ABC$ on the accompanying diagram.

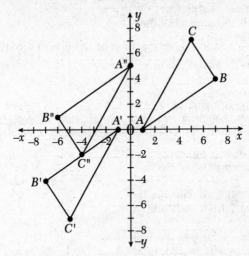

b. In general, the image of $P(x,y)$ after a reflection in the origin is $P'(-x,-y)$. Since $\triangle A'B'C'$ is the image of $\triangle ABC$ after a reflection in the origin:

$$A(1,0) \rightarrow A'(-1,0)$$
$$B(7,4) \rightarrow B'(-7,-4)$$
$$C(5,7) \rightarrow C'(-5,-7)$$

See $\triangle A'B'C'$ on the accompanying diagram.

c. Since $\triangle A''B''C''$ is the image of $\triangle A'B'C'$ under the translation $(x,y) \rightarrow (x+1, y+5)$:

$$A'(-1,0) \rightarrow A''(-1+1, 0+5) = A''(0,5)$$
$$B'(-7,-4) \rightarrow B''(-7+1, -4+5) = B''(-6,1)$$
$$C'(-5,-7) \rightarrow C''(-5+1, -7+5) = C''(-4,-2)$$

See $\triangle A''B''C''$ on the accompanying diagram.

d. In general, $y = mx + b$ represents an equation of a line with slope m and a y-intercept of b. To find an equation of the line that contains $\overline{A''B''}$, find the values of m and b. Then substitute these values into the equation $y = mx + b$.

Since the line containing $\overline{A''B''}$ crosses the y-axis at $A''(0,5)$, the y-intercept is 5, so $b = 5$.

To find the slope m of $\overleftrightarrow{A''B''}$, use the slope formula:

$$m = \frac{y_2 - y_1}{x_2 - x_1}$$

where $(x_1, y_1) = A''(0,5)$ and $(x_2, y_2) = B''(-6,1)$. Thus:

$$m = \frac{y_2 - y_1}{x_2 - x_1} = \frac{1-5}{-6-0} = \frac{-4}{-6} = \frac{2}{3}$$

Since $m = \dfrac{2}{3}$ and $b = 5$, an equation of the line that contains $\overline{A''B''}$ is

$y = \dfrac{2}{3}x + 5$.

38. The given system of equations, $y = x^2 - 6x + 5$ and $y + 7 = 2x$, is a linear-quadratic system that can be solved algebraically or graphically.

Method 1: Algebraic Solution

The given system of equations is:

$$y = x^2 - 6x + 5$$
$$y + 7 = 2x$$

Solve the first-degree equation for y by subtracting 7 from each side of the equation:

$$y = 2x - 7$$

Substitute $2x - 7$ for y in the first equation, thereby obtaining a quadratic equation only in x:

$$2x - 7 = x^2 - 6x + 5$$

Put the quadratic equation in standard form with all terms on one side equal to 0:

$$0 = x^2 - 8x + 12$$

Factor the right side of the equation as the product of two binomials:

$$0 = (x + ?)(x + ?)$$

Find the two missing numbers whose sum is -8 and whose product is $+12$. The two numbers are -2 and -6:

$$0 = (x - 2)(x - 6)$$

If the product of two factors is 0, either factor may equal 0:

$$x - 2 = 0 \quad \text{or} \quad x - 6 = 0$$
$$x = 2 \quad \text{or} \quad x = 6$$

To find the corresponding values of y, substitute each of the solutions for x in the original first-degree equation:

Let $x = 2$	Let $x = 6$
$y + 7 = 2x$	$y + 7 = 2x$
$\quad = 2(2)$	$\quad = 2(6)$
$y = 4 - 7$	$y = 12 - 7$
$\quad = -3$	$\quad = 5$

The solutions are **(2,–3)** and **(6,5)**.

CHECK: Substitute each pair of values of x and y in *both* of the *original* equations to verify that both equations are satisfied.

$$y = x^2 - 6x + 5 \qquad y + 7 = 2x$$

Let $x = 2$ and $y = -3$:

$$-3 \stackrel{?}{=} 2^2 - 6(2) + 5 \qquad -3 + 7 \stackrel{?}{=} 2(2)$$
$$-3 \stackrel{?}{=} 4 - 12 + 5 \qquad\qquad 4 \stackrel{\checkmark}{=} 4$$
$$-3 \stackrel{?}{=} \quad -8 \quad + 5$$
$$-3 \stackrel{\checkmark}{=} -3$$

Let $x = 6$ and $y = 5$:

$$5 \stackrel{?}{=} 6^2 - 6(6) + 5 \qquad 5 + 7 \stackrel{?}{=} 2(6)$$
$$5 \stackrel{?}{=} 36 - 36 + 5 \qquad\qquad 12 \stackrel{\checkmark}{=} 12$$
$$5 \stackrel{?}{=} \quad 0 \quad + 5$$
$$5 \stackrel{\checkmark}{=} 5$$

Method 2: Graphical Solution

- Graph the second-degree equation. The graph of $y = x^2 - 6x + 5$ is a parabola. The x-coordinate of the turning point of the parabola is

$$x = -\frac{b}{2a} = -\frac{-6}{2(1)} = 3$$

Pick three consecutive integer values of x on either side of $x = 3$ and find their y-coordinates. See the accompanying table.

x	$x^2 - 6x + 5$	$= y$
0	$0^2 - 6(0) + 5$	$= 5$
1	$1^2 - 6(1) + 5 = 1 - 6 + 5$	$= 0$
2	$2^2 - 6(2) + 5 = 4 - 12 + 5$	$= -3$
3	$3^2 - 6(3) + 5 = 9 - 18 + 5$	$= -4$
4	$4^2 - 6(4) + 5 = 16 - 24 + 5$	$= -3$
5	$5^2 - 6(5) + 5 = 25 - 30 + 5$	$= 0$
6	$6^2 - 6(6) + 5 = 36 - 36 + 5$	$= 5$

Plot points $(0,5)$, $(1,0)$, $(2,-3)$, $(3,-4)$, $(4,-3)$, $(5,0)$, and $(6,5)$ on a coordinate plane, and connect them with a smooth curve that has the shape of a parabola. See the graph labeled $y = x^2 - 6x + 5$ on the accompanying figure.

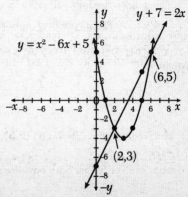

• Graph the first-degree equation using the same set of axes. The graph of $y + 7 = 2x$ is a line. Since $y = 2x - 7$, the line crosses the y-axis at $(0,-7)$. To find a second point on the line, pick any convenient value of x. For example, if $x = 5$, then $y = 2x - 7 = 2(5) - 7 = 3$. Plot $(0,-7)$ and $(5,3)$. Then connect the two points with a straight line. See the graph labeled $y + 7 = 2x$ on the accompanying diagram.

• Find the coordinates of the point(s) at which the graphs intersect.

The solutions are **(2,–3)** and **(6,5)**.

39. It is given that $ABCD$ is a rhombus, m$\angle CAB = 25$, and $AC = 18$.

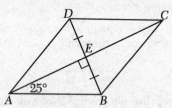

a. The diagonals of a rhombus intersect at right angles and bisect each other. In right triangle AEB, $AE = \frac{1}{2}(AC) = \frac{1}{2}(18) = 9$. To find the length of hypotenuse $\overline{AB}$, use the cosine ratio:

$$\cos \angle CAB = \frac{AE}{AB}$$

$$\cos 25° = \frac{9}{AB}$$

$$AB = \frac{9}{\cos 25°}$$

Use a scientific calculator to obtain $AB \approx 9.93$.
Then, since the four sides of a rhombus all have the same length,

$$\text{Perimeter of rhombus } ABCD \approx 4 \times 9.93 \approx 39.72$$

The perimeter of rhombus $ABCD$, correct to the *nearest tenth*, is **39.7**.

b. To find the length of $\overline{BD}$, first find the length of $\overline{BE}$. In right triangle AEB

$$\tan \angle CAB = \frac{BE}{9}$$

$$\tan 25° = \frac{BE}{9}$$

$$9 \times \tan 25° = BE$$

Use a scientific calculator to obtain $BE \approx 4.197$. Hence, $BD \approx 2 \times 4.197 \approx 8.394$.

The length of $\overline{BD}$, correct to the *nearest tenth*, is **8.4**.

40. It is given that the coordinates of point T are $(4,2)$ and that the vertices of $\triangle NYS$ are $N(-2,-1)$, $Y(0,10)$, and $S(10,5)$.

a. A median of a triangle is a line segment whose endpoints are a vertex of the triangle and the midpoint of the opposite side. To prove that $\overline{YT}$ is a median, show that the midpoint of $\overline{NS}$ is T $(4,2)$.

If point $(\bar{x},\bar{y})$ is the midpoint of $\overline{NS}$, then the coordinates of $(\bar{x},\bar{y})$ are the averages of the corresponding coordinates of the endpoints of $\overline{NS}$. Thus:

$$\bar{x} = \frac{-2+10}{2} = \frac{8}{2} = 4 \quad \text{and} \quad \bar{y} = \frac{-1+5}{2} = \frac{4}{2} = 2$$

Since the midpoint of $\overline{NS}$ is T $(4,2)$, $\overline{YT}$ is a median of $\triangle NYS$.

b. An altitude of a triangle is a line segment drawn from one vertex perpendicular to the opposite side. To prove that $\overline{YT}$ is an altitude, show that $\overline{YT} \perp \overline{NS}$.

Two lines are perpendicular if the product of their slopes is -1. The slope m of a line that contains points (x_1,y_1) and (x_2,y_2) can be determined using the formula

$$m = \frac{y_2 - y_1}{x_2 - x_1}$$

- To find the slope of $\overline{YT}$, use the slope formula with $(x_1,y_1) = Y(0,10)$ and $(x_2,y_2) = T(4,2)$:

$$m = \frac{y_2 - y_1}{x_2 - x_1} = \frac{2-10}{4-0} = \frac{-8}{4} = -2$$

- To find the slope of $\overline{NS}$, use the slope formula with $(x_1,y_1) = N(-2,-1)$ and $(x_2,y_2) = S(10,5)$:

$$m = \frac{y_2 - y_1}{x_2 - x_1} = \frac{5-(-1)}{10-(-2)} = \frac{6}{12} = \frac{1}{2}$$

Since $(-2) \times \left(\dfrac{1}{2}\right) = -1$, $\overline{YT} \perp \overline{NS}$, and therefore $\overline{YT}$ is an altitude of $\triangle NYS$.

c. To find the area of $\triangle NYS$, first find the lengths of altitude $\overline{YT}$ and base $\overline{NS}$. In general, the length of the segment whose endpoints are $A(x_1,y_1)$ and $B(x_2,y_2)$ is given by the formula

$$AB = \sqrt{\left(x_2 - x_1\right)^2 + \left(y_2 - y_1\right)^2}$$

- Find the length of base $\overline{NS}$ by using the distance formula with $(x_1, y_1) =$ $N(-2,-1)$ and $(x_2, y_2) = S(10,5)$:

$$NS = \sqrt{\left(10 - (-2)\right)^2 + \left(5 - (-1)\right)^2}$$
$$= \sqrt{\left(10 + 2\right)^2 + \left(5 + 1\right)^2}$$
$$= \sqrt{144 + 36}$$
$$= \sqrt{180}$$

- Find the length of altitude $\overline{YT}$ by using the distance formula with $(x_1, y_1) =$ $Y(0,10)$ and $(x_2, y_2) = T(4,2)$:

$$YT = \sqrt{\left(4 - 0\right)^2 + \left(2 - 10\right)^2}$$
$$= \sqrt{4^2 + \left(-8\right)^2}$$
$$= \sqrt{16 + 64}$$
$$= \sqrt{80}$$

The area of a triangle is equal to one-half the product of the lengths of a side and of the altitude drawn to that side. Thus:

$$\text{Area of } \triangle NYS = \frac{1}{2}\left(NS \times YT\right)$$
$$= \frac{1}{2} \times \sqrt{180} \times \sqrt{80}$$
$$= \frac{1}{2} \times \sqrt{14,400}$$
$$= \frac{1}{2} \times 120$$
$$= 60$$

The area of $\triangle NYS$ is **60**.

PART III

41. Given: $\angle 1 \cong \angle 2$ and $\overline{DB} \perp \overline{AC}$.

Prove: $\triangle ABD \cong \triangle CBD$

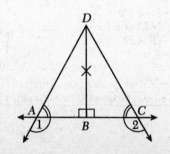

PROOF

Statement	Reason
1. $\overline{DB} \perp \overline{AC}$	1. Given.
2. $\angle DBA$ and $\angle DBC$ are right angles.	2. Perpendicular lines intersect to form right angles.
3. $\angle DBA \cong \angle DBC$ (Angle)	3. All right angles are congruent.
4. $\angle 1 \cong \angle 2$	4. Given.
5. $\angle 3$ is supplementary to $\angle 1$, $\angle 4$ is supplementary to $\angle 2$.	5. If the exterior sides of two adjacent angles form a straight line, the angles are supplementary.
6. $\angle 3 \cong \angle 4$ (Angle)	6. Supplements of congruent angles are congruent.
7. $\overline{DB} \cong \overline{DB}$ (Side)	7. Reflexive property of congruence.
8. $\triangle ABD \cong \triangle CBD$	8. $A.A.S. \cong A.A.S.$

42. $\sim G \rightarrow F$
    $\sim(E \wedge F)$
    $\sim E \rightarrow \sim D$
    A
    $(B \wedge C) \rightarrow D$
    $A \rightarrow (B \wedge C)$

Prove: G

PROOF

Statement	Reason
1. $A \rightarrow (B \wedge C)$, $(B \wedge C) \rightarrow D$	1. Given.
2. $A \rightarrow D$	2. Chain Rule.
3. A	3. Given.
4. D	4. Law of Detachment (2, 3).
5. $\sim E \rightarrow \sim D$	5. Given.
6. $\sim(\sim E)$ or E	6. *Modus Tollens* (4, 5).
7. $\sim(E \wedge F)$	7. Given.
8. $\sim E \vee \sim F$	8. De Morgan's Law.
9. $\sim F$	9. Law of Disjunctive Inference (6, 8)
10. $\sim G \rightarrow F$	10. Given.
11. $\sim(\sim G)$ or G	11. *Modus Tollens* (9, 10).

Topic	Question Numbers	Number of Points	Your Points	Your Percentage
1. Properties of Number Systems; Def. of Operations	1	2		
2. Finite Mathematical Systems	3	2		
3. Linear Function & Graph ($y = mx + b$, slope, eqs. of)	11	2		
4. Quadratic Equation (alg. sol.—factoring, formula)	6, 7, 34, 36b, c	$2 + 2 + 2 + 8 = 14$		
5. Parabola (incl. axis of symmetry, turning point)	32	2		
6. Systems of Equations (alg. and graphic solutions)	38	10		
7. Suppls., Compl., Vertical Angles, Angle Measure	—	—		
8. Triangle Properties (eq., isos., sum ∠s, 2 sides)	19, 25, 28	$2 + 2 + 2 = 6$		
9. Line ‖ One Side of △; Line Joining Midpts. of 2 Sides	4, 33	$2 + 2 = 4$		
10. Inequalities in △s (ext. ∠, ≠ sides, and opp. ∠s)	9, 31	$2 + 2 = 4$		
11. Quadrilateral Properties (▱, sq., rhom., rect., trap.)	10	2		
12. Parallel Lines	26	2		
13. Alg. Oper.; Verbal Probs.	14, 17, 36a	$2 + 2 + 2 = 6$		
14. Mean Proportional; Alt. to Hypot. of Right △	23	2		
15. Pythag. Th., Special Rt. △s (3-4-5, 5-12-13, 30-60-90)	16	2		
16. Similar Figures (ratios & proportions)	—	—		
17. Areas (△, rect., ▱, rhom., trap.)	13, 40c	$2 + 4 = 6$		
18. Locus	12, 30	$2 + 2 = 4$		
19. Constructions	—	—		
20. Deductive Proofs	35, 41, 42	$2 + 10 + 10 = 22$		
21. Coordinate Geom. (slope, dist., midpt., eq. of circle)	15, 18, 20, 24, 37d	$2 + 2 + 2 + 2 + 3 = 11$		
22. Coordinate Geom. "Proofs"	40a, b	6		
23. Logic	21, 27	$2 + 2 = 4$		
24. Permutations; Arrangements	8	2		
25. Combinations	5	2		
26. Probability	—	—		
27. Trig. of Rt. △	2, 39	$2 + 10 = 12$		
28. Literal Eqs.	—	—		
29. Transformations	22, 29, 37 a, b, c	$2 + 2 + 7 = 11$		

Examination January 1997

Sequential Math Course II

PART I

Answer **30** questions from this part. Each correct answer will receive **2** credits. No partial credit will be allowed. Write your answers in the spaces provided. Where applicable, answers may be left in terms of π or in radical form.   [60]

1 Using the accompanying table, solve for x if $x \circ b = a$.

$\circ$	a	b	c
a	a	b	c
b	b	a	c
c	c	c	b

1 _____

2 In the accompanying diagram, △ABC is similar
to △A'B'C', AB = 14.4, BC = 8, CA = 12,
A'B' = x, and B'C' = 4. Find the value of x.

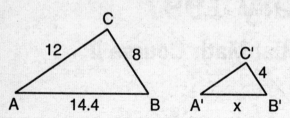

2 _____

3 In the accompanying diagram, parallel lines
$\overleftrightarrow{AB}$ and $\overleftrightarrow{CD}$ are intersected by $\overleftrightarrow{GH}$ at E and
F, respectively. If m∠BEF = 5x − 10 and
m∠CFE = 4x + 20, find x.

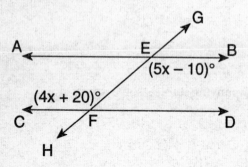

3 _____

4 If tan A = 0.5400, find the measure of ∠A to the
nearest degree.

4 _____

5 Find the length of a side of a square if two
consecutive vertices have coordinates (−2,6) and
(6,6).

5 _____

6 In the accompanying diagram of isosceles triangle *ABC*, *CA* = *CB* and ∠*CBD* is an exterior angle formed by extending $\overline{AB}$ to point *D*. If m∠*CBD* = 130, find m∠*C*.

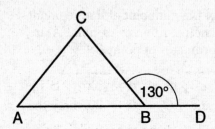

6 _____

7 If $\overleftrightarrow{AB}$ intersects $\overleftrightarrow{CD}$ at *E*, m∠*AEC* = 3*x*, and m∠*AED* = 5*x* − 60, find the value of *x*.

7 _____

8 Point (*x,y*) is the image of (2,4) after a reflection in point (5,6). In which quadrant does (*x,y*) lie?

8 _____

9 In the accompanying diagram, *ABCD* is a parallelogram, $\overline{EC} \perp \overline{DC}$, ∠*B* ≅ *E*, and m∠*A* = 100. Find m∠*CDE*.

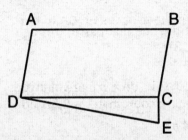

9 _____

10 The lengths of the sides of $\triangle DEF$ are 6, 8, and 10. Find the perimeter of the triangle formed by connecting the midpoints of the sides of $\triangle DEF$.

10 _____

11 The coordinates of the midpoint of line segment $\overline{AB}$ are (1,2). If the coordinates of point A are (1,0), find the coordinates of point B.

11 _____

12 In $\triangle PQR$, $\angle Q \cong \angle R$. If $PQ = 10x - 14$, $PR = 2x + 50$, and $RQ = 4x - 30$, find the value of x.

12 _____

13 What is the image of (–2,4) after a reflection in the x-axis?

13 _____

14 In rectangle $ABCD$, $\overline{AC}$ and $\overline{BD}$ are diagonals. If m$\angle 1 = 55$, find m$\angle ABD$.

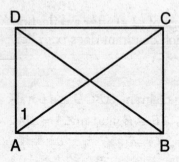

14 _____

15 What is the slope of the line that passes through points (–1,5) and (2,3)?

15 _____

16 The coordinates of the turning point of the graph of the equation $y = x^2 - 2x - 8$ are (1,k). What is the value of k?

16 _____

Directions (17–35): For *each* question chosen, write in the space provided the *numeral* preceding the word or expression that best completes the statement or answers the question.

17 Which equation represents the line that has a slope of $\frac{1}{2}$ and contains the point (0,3)?

(1) $y = \frac{1}{3}x + \frac{1}{2}$ (3) $y = \frac{3}{2}x$

(2) $y = 3x + \frac{1}{2}$ (4) $y = \frac{1}{2}x + 3$ 17 _____

18 If the measures of the angles in a triangle are in the ratio 3:4:5, the measure of an exterior angle of the triangle can *not* be

(1) 165°   (3) 120°
(2) 135°   (4) 105°   18 _____

19 According to De Morgan's laws, which statement is logically equivalent to $\sim(p \wedge q)$?

(1) $\sim p \vee \sim q$ (3) $\sim p \wedge q$
(2) $\sim p \vee q$ (4) $\sim p \wedge \sim q$ 19 _____

20 One angle of a triangle measures 30°. If the measures of the other two angles are in the ratio 3:7, the measure of the largest angle of the triangle is

(1) 15°   (3) 126°
(2) 105°   (4) 147°   20 _____

21 In the accompanying diagram, $ABCD$ is a rectangle, E is a point on $\overline{CD}$, m$\angle DAE = 30$, and m$\angle CBE = 20$.

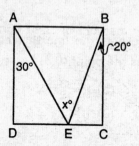

What is m$\angle x$?

(1) 25   (3) 60

(2) 50   (4) 70   21 ____

22 The graph of the equation $y = ax^2 + bx + c$, $a \neq 0$, forms

(1) a circle   (3) a straight line

(2) a parabola   (4) an ellipse   22 ____

23 Which set of numbers can represent the lengths of the sides of a triangle?

(1) {4,4,8}   (3) {3,5,7}

(2) {3,9,14}   (4) {1,2,3}   23 ____

24 Which is an equation of the line that passes through point (3,5) and is parallel to the x-axis?

(1) $x = 3$ (3) $y = 5$

(2) $x = 5$ (4) $y = 3$ 24 ____

25 What are the factors of $y^3 - 4y$?

   (1) $y(y - 2)(y - 2)$ (3) $(y^2 + 1)(y - 4)$

   (2) $y(y + 4)(y - 4)$ (4) $y(y + 2)(y - 2)$ 25 _____

26 In the accompanying diagram of right triangle ABC, $AB = 4$ and $BC = 7$.

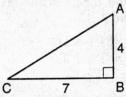

   What is the length of $\overline{AC}$ to the *nearest hundredth*?

   (1) 5.74   (3) 8.06

   (2) 5.75   (4) 8.08   26 _____

27 Which is the converse of the statement "If today is Presidents' Day, then there is no school"?

   (1) If there is school, then today is not Presidents' Day.

   (2) If there is no school, then today is Presidents' Day.

   (3) If today is Presidents' Day, then there is school.

   (4) If today is not Presidents' Day, then there is school.   27 _____

28 How many different eight-letter permutations can be formed from the letters in the word "PARALLEL"?

   (1) $\dfrac{8!}{3!2!}$ (3) 360

   (2) $8!$ (4) $\dfrac{8!}{3!}$ 28 _____

29 Which equation describes the locus of points equidistant from $A(-3,2)$ and $B(-3,8)$?

(1) $x = -3$ (3) $x = 5$
(2) $y = -3$ (4) $y = 5$ 29 _____

30 A translation maps $A(1,2)$ onto $A'(-1,3)$. What are the coordinates of the image of the origin under the same translation?

(1) $(0,0)$ (3) $(-2,1)$
(2) $(2,-1)$ (4) $(-1,2)$ 30 _____

31 The solution set of the equation $x^2 + 5x = 0$ is

(1) $\{0\}$ (3) $\{-5\}$
(2) $\{5\}$ (4) $\{0,-5\}$ 31 _____

32 In the accompanying diagram of parallelogram $MATH$, $m\angle T = 100$ and $\overline{SH}$ bisects $\angle MHT$.

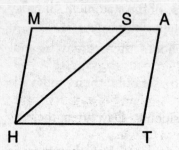

What is $m\angle HSA$?

(1) 80   (3) 120
(2) 100   (4) 140   32 _____

33 What are the roots of the equation
$x^2 + 9x + 12 = 0$?

(1) $\dfrac{-9 \pm \sqrt{33}}{2}$ (3) $\dfrac{-9 \pm \sqrt{129}}{2}$

(2) $\dfrac{9 \pm \sqrt{33}}{2}$ (4) $\dfrac{9 \pm \sqrt{129}}{2}$ 33 _____

34 The vertices of trapezoid *ABCD* are *A*(–3,0),
B(–3,4), *C*(2,4), and *D*(4,0). What is the area of
trapezoid *ABCD*?

(1) 6   (3) 28

(2) 24   (4) 48   34 _____

35 The accompanying diagram shows how
△*A'B'C'* is constructed similar to △*ABC*.

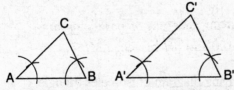

Which statement proves the construction?

(1) If two triangles are congruent, they are
similar.

(2) If two triangles are similar, the angles of one
triangle are congruent to the corresponding
angles of the other triangle.

(3) Two triangles are similar if two angles of one
triangle are congruent to two angles of the
other triangle.

(4) The corresponding sides of two similar triangles are proportional.   35 _____

PART II

Answer three questions from this part. Clearly indicate the necessary steps, including appropriate formula substitutions, diagrams, graphs, charts, etc. Calculations that may be obtained by mental arithmetic or the calculator do not need to be shown. [30]

36 Answer both *a* and *b* for all values of *y* for which these expressions are defined.

  a Express as a single fraction in lowest terms:

$$\frac{y - 4}{2y} + \frac{3y - 5}{5y} \qquad [4]$$

  b Simplify:

$$\frac{y^2 - 7y + 10}{5y - y^2} \div \frac{y^2 - 4}{25y^3} \qquad [6]$$

37 In the accompanying diagram of isosceles triangle KLC, $\overline{LK} \cong \overline{LC}$, m$\angle K = 53$, altitude $\overline{CA}$ is drawn to leg $\overline{LK}$, and $LA = 3$. Find the perimeter of $\triangle KLC$ to the *nearest integer*. [10]

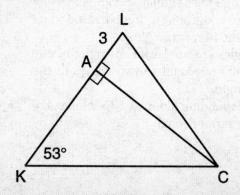

38 *a* On graph paper, draw the graph of the equation $y = -x^2 + 6x - 8$ for all values of x in the interval $0 \le x \le 6$. [6]

 b What is the maximum value of y in the equation $y = -x^2 + 6x - 8$? [2]

 c Write an equation of the line that passes through the turning point and is parallel to the x-axis. [2]

39 At a video rental store, Elyssa has only enough money to rent three videos. She has chosen four comedies, six dramas, and one mystery movie to consider.

 a How many different selections of three videos may she rent from the movies she has chosen? [2]

 b How many selections of three videos will consist of one comedy and two dramas? [3]

 c What is the probability that a selection of three videos will consist of one of each type of video? [3]

 d Elyssa decides to rent one comedy, one drama, and one mystery movie. In how many different orders may she view these videos? [2]

40 In the accompanying diagram of right triangle
ABC, altitude $\overline{BD}$ is drawn to hypotenuse
$\overline{AC}$, $AC = 20$, $AD < DC$, and $BD = 6$.

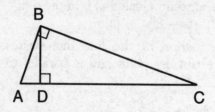

a If $AD = x$, express DC in terms of x. [1]

b Solve for x. [6]

c Find AB in simplest radical form. [3]

PART III

Answer one question from this part. Clearly indicate the necessary steps, including appropriate formula substitutions, diagrams, graphs, charts, etc. Calculations that may be obtained by mental arithmetic or the calculator do not need to be shown.   [10]

41 Given: $\triangle ABC$; $\overline{BD}$ is both the median and the altitude to $\overline{AC}$.

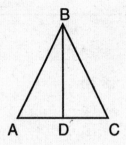

Prove: $\overline{BA} \cong \overline{BC}$ [10]

42 Quadrilateral $ABCD$ has vertices $A(-6,3)$, $B(-3,6)$, $C(9,6)$, and $D(-5,-8)$. Prove that quadrilateral $ABCD$ is

a a trapezoid   [6]

b *not* an isosceles trapezoid   [4]

Answers
January 1997
Sequential Math Course II

Answer Key

PART I

1. b	**13.** (−2,−4)	**25.** (4)
2. 7.2	**14.** 35	**26.** (3)
3. 30	**15.** $-\frac{2}{3}$	**27.** (2)
4. 28	**16.** −9	**28.** (1)
5. 8	**17.** (4)	**29.** (4)
6. 80	**18.** (1)	**30.** (3)
7. 30	**19.** (1)	**31.** (4)
8. I	**20.** (2)	**32.** (4)
9. 10	**21.** (2)	**33.** (1)
10. 12	**22.** (2)	**34.** (2)
11. (1,4)	**23.** (3)	**35.** (3)
12. 8	**24.** (3)	

PARTS II AND III See answers explained section.

Answers Explained

PART I

1. The accompanying table is given. To solve the equation

$$x * b = a$$

we need to locate under the operation symbol $*$, the horizontal row element that intersects vertical column b at element a.

$*$	a	b	c
a	a	b	c
b	b	a	c
c	c	c	b

Since $b * b = a$, the unknown element, x, is b.

$x = \boldsymbol{b}$.

2.

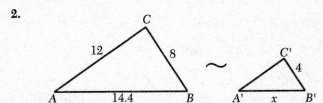

It is given that, in the accompanying diagram, $\triangle ABC$ is similar to $\triangle A'B'C'$. The lengths of corresponding sides of similar triangles are in proportion. Since $BC = 8$ and $B'C' = 4$, the length of each side of $\triangle A'B'C$ is one-half the length of the corresponding side of $\triangle ABC$. Hence:

$$x = \frac{1}{2} AB = \frac{1}{2}(14.4) = 7.2$$

The value of x is **7.2**.

3. It is given that, in the accompanying diagram, lines AB and CD are parallel. Since alternate interior angles formed by parallel lines have equal measures:

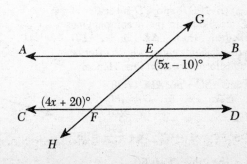

$$m\angle BEF = m\angle CFE$$
$$5x - 10 = 4x + 20$$
$$5x = 4x + 30$$
$$5x - 4x = 30$$
$$x = 30$$

The value of x is **30**.

4. If tan $A = 0.5400$, then the measure of $\angle A$ can be obtained by using a scientific calculator. Some scientific calculators require that you follow these steps:

1. Enter .5400.
2. Press the **[2nd]** or **[INV]** function key.
3. Press the **[tan]** key since $\tan^{-1}$ is printed directly above it.
4. Round off the answer that appears in the display window.

The measure of $\angle A$, correct to the *nearest degree*, is **28**.

5. It is given that the coordinates of two consecutive vertices of a square are $(-2,6)$ and $(6,6)$. Since the y-coordinates of the given vertices are the same, the distance between the vertices, which is the length of a side of the square, is the absolute value of the difference in their x-coordinates:

$$\left|-2 - 6\right| = \left|-8\right| = 8$$

The length of a side of the square is **8**.

6. It is given that, in the accompanying diagram, $\triangle ABC$ is isosceles with $CA = CB$. Since $\angle ABC$ and $\angle DBC$ are supplementary:

$$m\angle ABC = 180 - 130 = 50$$

In an isosceles triangle the angles opposite the congruent sides are congruent. Hence, $m\angle A = m\angle ABC = 50$. Since the sum of the measures of the angles of a triangle is 180:

$$50 + 50 + m\angle C = 180$$
$$m\angle C = 180 - 100 = 80$$

$m\angle C = \mathbf{80}$.

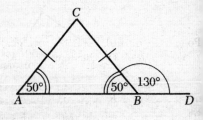

7. If $\overleftrightarrow{AB}$ and $\overleftrightarrow{CD}$ intersect at E, as shown in the accompanying diagram, then $\angle AEC$ and $\angle AED$ are adjacent angles whose exterior sides form a straight line. Hence:

$$m\angle AEC + m\angle AED = 180$$
$$3x + 5x - 60 = 180$$
$$8x = 240$$
$$x = \frac{240}{8} = 30$$

The value of x is **30**.

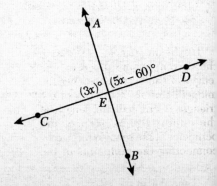

8. It is given that, as shown in the accompanying diagram, point (x,y) is the image of $(2,4)$ after a reflection in point $(5,6)$. To locate (x,y), find x and y such that $(5,6)$ is the midpoint of the segment determined by (x,y) and $(2,4)$.

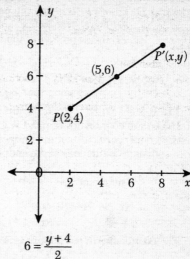

Since the coordinates of the midpoint of a segment are averages of the corresponding coordinates of the endpoints, set 5, the x-coordinate of the midpoint, equal to the average of the x-coordinates of (x,y) and $(2,4)$. Then set 6, the y-coordinate of the midpoint, equal to the average of the y-coordinates of (x,y) and $(2,4)$. Thus:

$$5 = \frac{x+2}{2} \qquad 6 = \frac{y+4}{2}$$
$$10 = x+2 \qquad 12 = y+4$$
$$8 = x \qquad 8 = y$$

Point $(8,8)$, or (x,y), lies in the first quadrant since x and y are both positive. Point (x,y) lies in Quadrant **I**.

9. It is given that, in the accompanying diagram, $ABCD$ is a parallelogram, $\overline{EC} \perp \overline{DC}$, $\angle B \cong \angle E$, and $m\angle A = 100$.

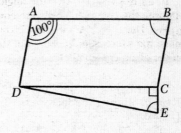

- Consecutive angles of a parallelogram are supplementary, so

  $m\angle B = m\angle E = 180 - 100 = 80$.

- Since $\overline{EC} \perp \overline{DC}$, $m\angle ECD = 90$.

- In $\triangle ECD$, $m\angle CDE + 80 + 90 = 180$, so $m\angle CDE = 180 - 170 = 10$.

$m\angle CDE = \mathbf{10}$.

10. In any triangle, as shown in the accompanying diagram, the length of the segment joining the midpoints of any two sides of the triangle is one-half the length of the opposite side. Hence, the perimeter of the triangle formed by connecting the midpoints of the

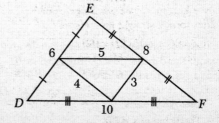

sides of $\triangle DEF$ must be one-half the perimeter of $\triangle DEF$. Since the lengths of the sides of $\triangle DEF$ are given as 6, 8, and 10, the perimeter of $\triangle DEF$ is $6 + 8 + 10$ or 24. Hence, the perimeter of the triangle formed by connecting the midpoints of the sides of $\triangle DEF$ is $\frac{1}{2}(24)$ or 12.

The perimeter is **12**.

11. It is given that the coordinates of the midpoint of line segment $\overline{AB}$ are $(1,2)$, and the coordinates of point A are $(1,0)$. Let the coordinates of point B be (x,y). The coordinates of the midpoint of a segment are the averages of the corresponding coordinates of the endpoints. Hence:

$$^x\text{midpoint} = \frac{1+x}{2} = 1 \qquad\qquad ^y\text{midpoint} = \frac{0+y}{2} = 2$$
$$1 + x = 2 \qquad\qquad\qquad\qquad y = 4$$
$$x = 1$$

The coordinates of point B are **(1,4)**.

12. If two angles of a triangle are congruent, then the lengths of the sides opposite these sides are equal. In $\triangle PQR$, if $\angle Q \cong \angle R$, then $PR = PQ$. Hence:

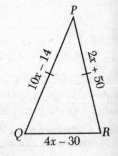

$$2x + 50 = 10x - 14$$
$$14 + 50 = 10x - 2x$$
$$64 = 8x$$
$$\frac{64}{8} = x$$
$$8 = x$$

The value of x is **8**.

13. In general, the image of $P(x,y)$ after a reflection in the x-axis is $P'(x,-y)$. Hence, the image of $(-2,4)$ after a reflection in the x-axis is point $(-2,-4)$.

The image of $(-2,4)$ is **(-2,-4)**.

14. It is given that, in the accompanying diagram, $ABCD$ is a rectangle and $m\angle 1 = 55$. A rectangle contains four right angles, so $m\angle BAC = 90 - 55 = 35$.

Since the diagonals of a rectangle are equal and bisect each other, $AE = BE$ and, as a result, $m\angle ABD = m\angle BAC = 35$.

$$m\angle ABD = \mathbf{35}.$$

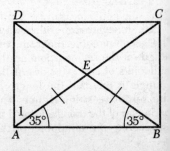

15. The slope m of a line that passes through points $A(x_A, y_A)$ and $B(x_B, y_B)$ is given by the formula

$$m = \frac{y_B - y_A}{x_B - x_A}$$

To find the slope of a line that passes through points $(-1,5)$ and $(2,3)$, let $A(x_A, y_A) = (-1,5)$ and $B(x_B, y_B) = (2,3)$. Then:

$$m = \frac{3-5}{2-(-1)} = \frac{-2}{2+1} = -\frac{2}{3}$$

The slope of the line is $-\dfrac{2}{3}$.

16. It is given that the coordinates of the turning point of the graph of the equation $y = x^2 - 2x - 8$ are $(1,k)$. Since the turning point of a parabola is a point on the graph, the coordinates of point $(1,k)$ must satisfy the given equation. Find the value of k by substituting 1 for x and k for y in the equation of the graph:

$$\begin{aligned} y &= x^2 - 2x - 8 \\ k &= 1^2 - 2(1) - 8 \\ &= 1 - 2 - 8 \\ &= -9 \end{aligned}$$

The value of k is **–9**.

17. An equation of the form $y = mx + b$ represents a line that has a slope of m and a y-intercept of b. It is given that the slope of a line is $\dfrac{1}{2}$, so $m = \dfrac{1}{2}$.

Since the line contains point $(0,3)$, the y-intercept of the line is 3, so $b = 3$.

Hence, an equation of this line is $y = \dfrac{1}{2}x + 3$.

The correct choice is **(4)**.

18. If the measures of the angles of a triangle are in the ratio 3:4:5, then the sum of the measures of these angles can be represented by $3x + 4x + 5x$ or $12x$. Since the sum of the measures of the angles of a triangle is 180, $12x = 180$, so

$$x = \frac{180}{12} = 15$$

The measures of the three angles of the triangle are as follows:

$$\begin{aligned} 3x &= 3(15) = 45 \\ 4x &= 4(15) = 60 \\ 5x &= 5(15) = 75 \end{aligned}$$

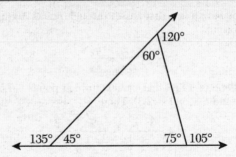

As shown in the accompanying diagram, the measure of an exterior angle of the triangle must be 135 (=180 − 45) or 120 (=180 − 60) or 105 (=180 − 75).

Thus, an exterior angle of the triangle can *not* be 165°.

The correct choice is (**1**).

19. According to one of De Morgan's laws, the negation of a conjunction is logically equivalent to the disjunction of the negation of each of the disjuncts.

The given statement is:　　　　　　　　　　　$\sim(p \wedge q)$

Apply one of De Morgan's laws:　　　　　$\sim(p \wedge q) \leftrightarrow \sim p \vee \sim q$

The correct choice is (**1**).

20. If the measures of two angles of a triangle are in the ratio 3:7, their measures can be represented as $3x$ and $7x$. If the measure of the remaining angle of the triangle is 30, then the sum of $3x$, $7x$, and 30 must be 180:

$$3x + 7x\ 30 = 180$$
$$10x = 150$$
$$x = \frac{150}{10} = 15$$

Since $3x = 3(15) = 45$ and $7x = 7(15) = 105$, the largest angle of the triangle is 105°.

The correct choice is (**2**).

21. It is given that $ABCD$, in the accompanying diagram, is a rectangle. Since a rectangle contains four right angles, m∠BAE = 90 − 30 = 60 and m∠ABE = 90 − 20 = 70.

In △AEB, 60 + x + 70 = 180, so x = 180 − 130 = 50.

The correct choice is (**2**).

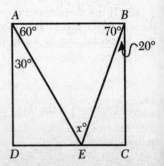

22. The graph of an equation of the form $y = ax^2 + bx + c$, $a \neq 0$, is a parabola.

The correct choice is **(2)**.

23. The length of each side of a triangle must be less than the sum of the lengths of the other two sides. To determine which set of numbers in the four answer choices can represent the lengths of the sides of a triangle, find the set that has the property that each number in the set is less than the sum of the other two numbers.

- Choice (1): Since 8 is *not* less than $4 + 4$, $\{4,4,8\}$ *cannot* represent the lengths of the sides of a triangle.
- Choice (2): Since 14 is *not* less than $3 + 9$, $\{3,9,14\}$ *cannot* represent the lengths of the sides of a triangle.
- Choice (3): Since $3 < 5 + 7$, $5 < 3 + 7$, and $7 < 3 + 5$, $\{3,5,7\}$ can represent the lengths of the sides of a triangle.
- Choice (4): Since 3 is *not* less than $1 + 2$, $\{1,2,3\}$ *cannot* represent the lengths of the sides of a triangle.

The correct choice is **(3)**.

24. A line that is parallel to the x-axis is a horizontal line whose equation has the general form $y = k$, where k is the y-coordinate of each point on the line.

Since it is given that a line parallel to the x-axis passes through point (3,5), as shown in the accompanying diagram, an equation of this line is $y = 5$.

The correct choice is **(3)**.

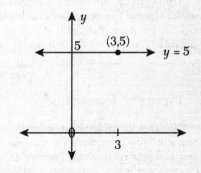

25. The given binomial expression is:

$$y^3 - 4y$$

Factor out y, the greatest common monomial factor of each term:

$$y(y^2 - 4)$$

Since $y^2 - 4$ is the difference of two squares, it can be factored as the sum and difference of the same two terms:

$$y(y + 2)(y - 2)$$

The correct choice is **(4)**.

26. To find the length of a side of a right triangle when the lengths of the other two sides are given, use the Pythagorean theorem. For right triangle ABC, shown in the accompanying diagram:

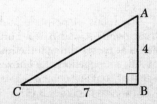

$$(AC)^2 = (AB)^2 + (BC)^2$$
$$= \ 4^2 \ + \ 7^2$$
$$= \ 16 \ + \ 49$$
$$= \ 65$$
$$AC = \ \sqrt{65} \approx 8.06225\ldots$$

Hence, the length of $\overline{AC}$, correct to the *nearest hundredth*, is 8.06.
The correct choice is **(3)**.

27. The converse of a conditional statement of the form "If p, then q" is the conditional statement "If q, then p." Thus, to form the converse of a given statement, interchange the statements that follow the words "If" and "then."

The converse of the statement "If today is Presidents' Day, then there is no school" is the statement "If there is no school, then today is Presidents' Day."
The correct choice is **(2)**.

28. If in a set of n objects a are identical and b are identical, then the number of different ways in which the n objects can be arranged is $\dfrac{n!}{a!\,b!}$.

The word "PARALLEL" contains eight letters, including three identical letters (L) and two other identical letters (A). To find the number of different eight-letter permutations that can be formed from the letters in the word "PARALLEL," let $n = 5$, $a = 3$, and $b = 2$. Thus:

$$\frac{n!}{a!\,b!} = \frac{8!}{3!\,2!}$$

The correct choice is **(1)**.

29. The locus of points equidistant from two given points is the line that is the perpendicular bisector of the segment whose endpoints are the two given points.

As shown in the accompanying diagram, the given points, $A(-3,2)$ and $B(-3,8)$, determine a vertical segment whose midpoint is $\left(-3, \dfrac{2+8}{2}\right)$ $= (-3,5)$.

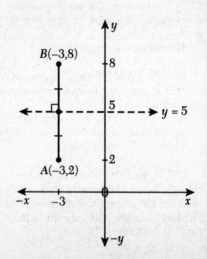

The locus of points equidistant from points A and B is a horizontal line that passes through the midpoint of $\overline{AB}$. An equation of a horizontal line that contains point $(-3,5)$ is $y = 5$.
The correct choice is **(4)**.

30. A translation "slides" each point of a figure fixed amounts in the horizontal and vertical directions.

If under a certain translation $A(1,2)$ is mapped onto $A'(-1,3)$, then this translation slides point A 2 units horizontally to the *left* and 1 unit vertically *up*. Thus, the image of any point (x,y) under the same translation is point $(x - 2, y + 1)$.

To find the coordinates of the image of the origin under the same translation, apply the translation rule $(x,y) \rightarrow (x - 2, y + 1)$, where $x = 0$ and $y = 0$:

$$(0,0) \rightarrow (0 - 2, 0 + 1) = (-2,1)$$

The correct choice is **(3)**.

31. The given equation is: $x^2 + 5x = 0$

Factor out x, the greatest common monomial factor of each term: $x(x + 5) = 0$

If the product of two numbers is 0, then at least one of the numbers is equal to 0: $x = 0$ or $x + 5 = 0$

                                           $x = -5$

Thus, the solution set is $\{0, -5\}$.
The correct choice is **(4)**.

32. It is given that, in the accompanying diagram, *MATH* is a parallelogram, $m\angle T = 100$, and $\overline{SH}$ bisects $\angle MHT$.

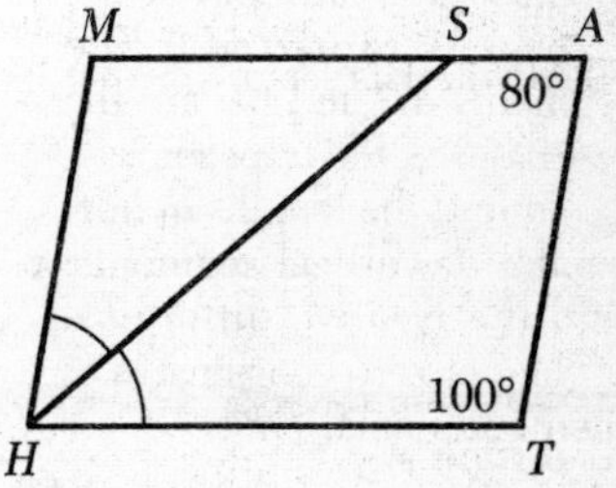

- Since consecutive angles of a parallelogram are supplementary, $m\angle A = 180 - 100 = 80$.
- Opposite angles of a parallelogram have equal measures, so $m\angle MHT = 80$.
- Then $m\angle THS = \frac{1}{2}m\angle MHT = \frac{1}{2}(80) = 40$
- The sum of the measures of the angles of a quadrilateral is 360. In quadrilateral *THSA*:

$$100 + 40 + m\angle HSA + 80 = 360$$
$$m\angle HSA + 220 = 360$$
$$m\angle HSA = 140$$

The correct choice is **(4)**.

33. The given equation, $x^2 + 9x + 12 = 0$, is a quadratic equation. Since each of the four answer choices has irrational roots, solve the quadratic equation by using the quadratic formula.

If a quadratic equation is in the form $ax^2 + bx + c = 0$, its roots are given by the quadratic formula:

$$x = \frac{-b \pm \sqrt{b^2 - 4ac}}{2a} \quad (a \neq 0)$$

The given equation is in the form $ax^2 + bx + c = 0$, where $a = 1$, $b = 9$, and $c = 12$:

$$= \frac{-9 \pm \sqrt{9^2 - 4(1)(12)}}{2(1)}$$

$$= \frac{-9 \pm \sqrt{81 - 48}}{2}$$

$$= \frac{-9 \pm \sqrt{33}}{2}$$

The correct choice is **(1)**.

34. It is given that the vertices of trapezoid $ABCD$ are $A(-3,0)$, $B(-3,4)$, $C(2,4)$, and $D(4,0)$. Sketch the trapezoid, as shown in the accompanying diagram.

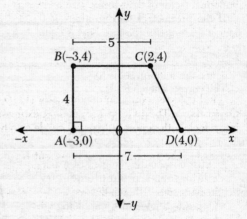

Since $\overline{AB}$ is a vertical segment, it is an altitude of the trapezoid. Horizontal line segments AD and BC are the two bases of the trapezoid.

To find the lengths of horizontal or vertical segments, find the positive difference of the nonzero coordinates of their endpoints. Thus:

$$AB = 4 - 0 = 4$$
$$BC = 2 - (-3) = 2 + 3 = 5$$
$$AD = 4 - (-3) = 7$$

The area of a trapezoid is one-half the product of the altitude and the sum of the lengths of the bases. Hence:

$$\text{Area of } ABCD = \frac{1}{2} AB \, (BC + AD)$$

Since $AB = 4$, $BC = 5$, and $AD = 7$:

$$= \frac{1}{2} \times 4 \times (5 + 7)$$
$$= 2 \times 12$$
$$= 24$$

The correct choice is **(2)**.

35.

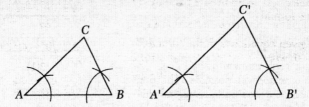

The diagram that is given shows that $\angle A'$ is constructed so that it is congruent to $\angle A$, and $\angle B'$ is constructed so that it is congruent to $\angle B$. Hence, $\triangle ABC$ and $\triangle A'B'C'$ are similar.

The justification is the theorem that states that two triangles are similar if two angles of one triangle are congruent to two angles of the other triangle.

The correct choice is **(3)**.

PART II

36. a. The given sum is:

Find the least common denominator (LCD) of the fractions. The LCD is the smallest expression into which both denominators will divide evenly:

$$\frac{y-4}{2y}+\frac{3y-5}{5y}$$

The LCD for $2y$ and $5y$ is $10y$.

Change the fractions into equivalent fractions having the LCD as their denominators by multiplying the first fraction by 1 in the form of $\frac{5}{5}$ and multiplying the second fraction by 1 in the form of $\frac{2}{2}$:

$$\frac{5}{5}\left(\frac{y-4}{2y}\right)+\frac{2}{2}\left(\frac{3y-5}{5y}\right)$$

$$\frac{5(y-4)}{10y}+\frac{2(3y-5)}{10y}$$

$$\frac{5y-20}{10y}+\frac{6y-10}{10y}$$

Since the fractions now have the same denominator, combine them by writing the sum of their numerators over their common denominator:

$$\frac{(5y-20)+(6y-10)}{10y}$$

Simplify the numerator by combining like terms:

$$\frac{11y-30}{10y}$$

The sum is $\dfrac{11y-30}{10y}$.

b. The given expression is:

$$\frac{y^2 - 7y + 10}{5y - y^2} \div \frac{y^2 - 4}{25y^3}$$

Change the division by a fractional expression to multiplication by inverting the second fraction:

$$\frac{y^2 - 7y + 10}{5y - y^2} \times \frac{25y^3}{y^2 - 4}$$

Factor each numerator and each denominator wherever possible. The first numerator is a quadratic trinomial that can be factored as the product of two binomials using the reverse of FOIL:

$$\frac{(y-5)(y-2)}{5y - y^2} \times \frac{25y^3}{y^2 - 4}$$

Remove a common factor of y from each term of the first denominator. Also, since the second denominator represents the difference of two squares, factor it as the product of the sum and difference of the same two terms:

$$\frac{(y-5)(y-2)}{y(5-y)} \times \frac{25y^3}{(y-2)(y+2)}$$

If the same factor appears in both a numerator and a denominator, divide both of them by that factor so their quotient is 1 (cancel):

$$\frac{(y-5)\overset{1}{\cancel{(y-2)}}}{\cancel{y}(5-y)} \times \frac{25y^{\overset{2}{\cancel{3}}}}{\cancel{(y-2)}(y+2)}$$

$$\frac{\overset{-1}{\cancel{y-5}}}{\cancel{5-y}} \times \frac{25y^2}{y+2}$$

$$\frac{-1}{1} \times \frac{25y^2}{y+2}$$

Multiply together the remaining factors in the numerator, and multiply together the remaining factors in the denominator:

$$\frac{-25y^2}{y+2}$$

The quotient in simplest form is $\dfrac{-25y^2}{y+2}$.

37. It is given, in the accompanying diagram, that $\overline{LK} \cong \overline{LC}$, m$\angle K = 53$, $\overline{CA}$ is an altitude, and $LA = 3$. To find the perimeter of $\triangle KLC$, use right-triangle trigonometry to find the lengths of $\overline{LC}$ and $\overline{KC}$.

- Since $\overline{LK} \cong \overline{LC}$, the angles opposite these sides have the same measure. Hence, m$\angle LCK =$ m$\angle K = 53$. The sum of the

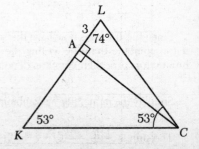

measures of the angles of a triangle is 180 so m$\angle L$ = 180 – (53 + 53) = 74. In right triangle LAC:

$$\cos L = \frac{\text{length of leg adjacent to } \angle L}{\text{hypotenuse}}$$

$$\cos 74° = \frac{LA}{LC}$$

$$0.2756 = \frac{3}{LC}$$

$$LC = \frac{3}{0.2756} \approx 10.89$$

• $LK = LC$ = 10.89, and $AK = LK - LA$ = 10.89 – 3 = 7.89. In right triangle KAC:

$$\cos K = \frac{\text{length of leg adjacent to } \angle K}{\text{hypotenuse}}$$

$$\cos 53° = \frac{AK}{KC}$$

$$0.6018 = \frac{7.89}{KC}$$

$$KC = \frac{7.89}{0.6018} \approx 13.11$$

• The perimeter of $\triangle KLC = LC + LK + KC$ = 10.89 + 10.89 + 13.11 = 34.89.

The perimeter of $\triangle KLC$, correct to the *nearest integer*, is **35**.

38. a. To draw the graph of the equation $y = -x^2 + 6x - 8$ for all values of x in the interval $0 \le x \le 6$, first prepare a table of values for x and y. Then substitute each integer value of x from 0 to 6 into the given equation to obtain the corresponding value of y:

x	$-x^2 + 6x - 8$	y	(x,y)
0	$0 + 0 - 8$	$= -8$	(0,–8)
1	$-(1)^2 + 6(1) - 8 = -1 + 6 - 8$	$= -3$	(1,–3)
2	$-(2)^2 + 6(2) - 8 = -4 + 12 - 8$	$= 0$	(2,0)
3	$-(3)^2 + 6(3) - 8 = -9 + 18 - 8$	$= 1$	(3,1)
4	$-(4)^2 + 6(4) - 8 = -16 + 24 - 8$	$= 0$	(4,0)
5	$-(5)^2 + 6(5) - 8 = -25 + 30 - 8$	$= -3$	(5,–3)
6	$-(6)^2 + 6(6) - 8 = -36 + 36 - 8$	$= -8$	(6,–8)

Now plot the points that appear in the last column of the table. Connect these points with a smooth curve that has the shape of a parabola whose turning point, $(3,1)$, is the highest point on the curve. Label this graph with its equation, $y = -x^2 + 6x - 8$, as shown in the accompanying figure.

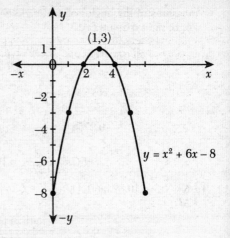

b. The maximum value of y in the equation $y = -x^2 + 6x - 8$ corresponds to the y-coordinate of the turning point in the graph of this equation, which is 1.

The maximum value of y is **1**.

c. In general, $y = k$ is an equation of a horizontal line that passes through the point whose y-coordinate is k. Thus, **$y = 1$** is an equation of the line that passes through the turning point, $(3,1)$, and is parallel to the x-axis.

39. a. Without regard to order, r objects can be selected from a set of n objects in $_nC_r$ ways.

Since it is given that Elyssa has chosen to consider four comedies, six dramas, and one mystery, she is considering a total of $4 + 6 + 1 = 11$ videos. Thus, $_{11}C_3$ represents the number of different selections of three videos Elyssa may rent from the 11 movies she has chosen to consider. Use a scientific calculator to obtain $_{11}C_3 = 165$.

There are **165** different selections of three videos from the movies she is considering.

b. The number of selections of three videos that will consist of one comedy and two dramas is obtained by multiplying the number of different ways in which one comedy can be selected by the number of different ways in which two dramas can be selected.

One comedy can be selected from four comedies in $_4C_1$ ways, and two dramas can be selected from six dramas in $_6C_2$ ways. Use a scientific calculator to evaluate $_4C_1 \times _6C_2$:

$$_4C_1 \times _6C_2 = 4 \times 15 = 60.$$

Thus, **60** different selections of three videos will consist of one comedy and two dramas.

c. The probability that a selection of three videos will consist of one of each type of video is obtained by writing the product of the numbers of ways in which one of each type of video can be selected over the total number of three-video selections determined in part **a.**

One comedy can be selected from four comedies in $_4C_1$ ways, one drama can be selected from six dramas in $_6C_1$ ways, and one mystery can be selected from one mystery in only one way. Hence, the probability that a selection of three videos will consist of one of each type of video is given by the fraction

$$\frac{_4C_1 \times _6C_1 \times 1}{165}$$

Use a scientific calculator to find $_4C_1 = 4$ and $_6C_1 = 6$: $\dfrac{_4C_1 \times _6C_1 \times 1}{165} = \dfrac{4 \times 6 \times 1}{165}$

$$= \frac{24}{165}$$

Thus, the probability that a selection of three videos will consist of one of each type of video is $\dfrac{24}{165}$.

d. If Elyssa rents one comedy, one drama, and one mystery movie, then the number of different orders in which these three videos may be viewed is $3! = 3 \times 2 \times 1 = 6$.

The number of different orders in which she may view these three videos is **6**.

40.

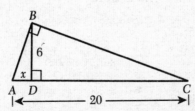

It is given, in the accompanying diagram of right triangle ABC, that $\overline{BD}$ is an altitude to hypotenuse $\overline{AC}$, $AC = 20$, $AD < DC$, and $BD = 6$.

a. If $AD = x$, then $DC = AC - AD = 20 - x$.

b. In a right triangle, the length of the altitude drawn to the hypotenuse is the mean proportional between the lengths of the segments of the hypotenuse. Thus:

$$\frac{AD}{BD} = \frac{BD}{DC}$$

$$\frac{x}{6} = \frac{6}{20 - x}$$

In a proportion, the product of the means equals the product of the extremes (cross-multiply):

Simplify:

$$6(6) = x(20 - x)$$
$$36 = 20x - x^2$$

Rewrite the quadratic equation in standard form so all the nonzero terms are on the same side of the equation and 0 is on the other side:

$$x^2 - 20x + 36 = 0$$

Factor the left-side of the equation as the product of two binomials:

$$(x - 18)(x - 2) = 0$$

If the product of two factors is 0, then either or both factors is 0:

$$x - 18 = 0 \quad \text{or} \quad x - 2 = 0$$
$$x = 18 \quad \text{or} \quad x = 2$$

- If $x = 18$, then $DC = 20 - 18 = 2$. Since it is given that $AD < DC$, reject this solution.
- If $x = 2$, then $DC = 20 - 2 = 18$.

Hence, $x = 2$.

c. To find AB, apply the Pythagorean theorem in right triangle ADB:

$$
\begin{aligned}
(AB)^2 &= (AD)^2 + (BD)^2 \\
&= (2)^2 + (6)^2 \\
&= 4 + 36 \\
&= 40 \\
AB &= \sqrt{40} = \sqrt{4}\,\sqrt{10} = 2\sqrt{10}
\end{aligned}
$$

In simplest radical form, AB is **$2\sqrt{10}$**.

PART III

41. Given: $\triangle ABC$; $\overline{BD}$ is both the median and the altitude to $\overline{AC}$.

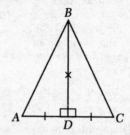

Prove: $\overline{BA} \cong \overline{BC}$

Plan: Prove $\triangle ADB \cong \triangle CDB$ by SAS theorem.

PROOF

Statement	Reason
1. $\overline{BD}$ is a median to $\overline{AC}$.	1. Given.
2. $\overline{AD} \cong \overline{CD}$ (Side)	2. A median divides the side of a triangle to which it is drawn into two congruent segments.
3. $\overline{BD}$ is an altitude to $\overline{AC}$.	3. Given.
4. $\angle ADB$ and $\angle CDB$ are right angles.	4. An altitude intersects the side of a triangle to which it is drawn at right angles.
5. $\angle ADB \cong \angle CDB$ (Angle)	5. All right angles are congruent.
6. $\overline{BD} \cong \overline{BD}$ (Side)	6. Reflexive property of congruence.
7. $\triangle ADB \cong \triangle CDB$	7. $SAS \cong SAS$.
8. $\overline{BA} \cong \overline{BC}$	8. Corresponding sides of congruent triangles are congruent.

42. a. It is given that the coordinates of the vertices of quadrilateral $ABCD$ are $A(-6,3)$, $B(-3,6)$, $C(9,6)$, and $D(-5,-8)$. To prove that quadrilateral $ABCD$ is a trapezoid show that one pair of sides are parallel and the other pair of sides are not parallel.

Two lines are parallel if they have the same slope. The slope m of a line that contains points (x_1,y_1) and (x_2,y_2) can be determined using the formula

$$m = \frac{y_2 - y_1}{x_2 - x_1}$$

- To find the slope of $\overline{AB}$, use the slope formula with $(x_1,y_1) = A(-6,3)$ and $(x_2,y_2) = B(-3,6)$:

$$m = \frac{y_2 - y_1}{x_2 - x_1} = \frac{6-3}{-3-(-6)} = \frac{3}{3} = 1$$

- To find the slope of $\overline{BC}$, use the slope formula with $(x_1,y_1) = B(-3,6)$ and $(x_2,y_2) = C(9,6)$ and:

$$m = \frac{y_2 - y_1}{x_2 - x_1} = \frac{6-6}{9-(-3)} = \frac{0}{12} = 0$$

- To find the slope of $\overline{CD}$, use the slope formula with $(x_1,y_1) = C(9,6)$ and $(x_2,y_2) = D(-5,-8)$:

$$m = \frac{y_2 - y_1}{x_2 - x_1} = \frac{-8-6}{-5-9} = \frac{-14}{-14} = 1$$

- To find the slope of $\overline{AD}$, use the slope formula with $(x_1,y_1) = A(-6,3)$ and $(x_2,y_2) = D(-5,-8)$:

$$m = \frac{y_2 - y_1}{x_2 - x_1} = \frac{-8-3}{-5-(-6)} = \frac{-11}{1} = -11$$

Since the slope of $\overline{AB} = 1$ and the slope of $\overline{CD} = 1$, the slope of $\overline{AB}$ is equal to the slope of $\overline{CD}$ and $\overline{AB}$ is parallel to $\overline{CD}$. Since the slope of $\overline{BC} = 0$ and the slope of $\overline{AD} = -11$, $\overline{BC}$ is *not* parallel to $\overline{AD}$.

Hence quadrilateral $ABCD$ is a trapezoid since it has exactly one pair of parallel sides.

b. To show that $ABCD$ is *not* an isosceles trapezoid, show that its nonparallel sides, $\overline{BC}$ and $\overline{AD}$, do not have the same length. The length of a segment whose endpoints are (x_1,y_1) and (x_2,y_2) is given by the expression $\sqrt{(x_2 - x_1)^2 + (y_2 - y_1)^2}$.

- To find the length of $\overline{BC}$, let $(x_1,y_1) = B(-3,6)$ and $(x_2,y_2) = C(9,6)$:

$$\begin{aligned} BC &= \sqrt{(x_2 - x_1)^2 + (y_2 - y_1)^2} \\ &= \sqrt{(9-(-3))^2 + (6-6)^2} \\ &= \sqrt{144} \end{aligned}$$

- To find the length of $\overline{AD}$, let $(x_1,y_1) = A(-6,3)$ and $(x_2,y_2) = D(-5,-8)$:

$$\begin{aligned} AD &= \sqrt{(x_2 - x_1)^2 + (y_2 - y_1)^2} \\ &= \sqrt{(-5-(-6))^2 + (-8-3)^2} \\ &= \sqrt{1^2 + (-11)^2} \\ &= \sqrt{122} \end{aligned}$$

Since $BC = \sqrt{144}$ and $AD = \sqrt{122}$, sides $\overline{BC}$ and $\overline{AD}$ do *not* have the same length. Hence, quadrilateral $ABCD$ is *not* an isosceles trapezoid.

Topic	Question Numbers	Number of Points	Your Points	Your Percentage
1. Properties of Number Systems; Def. of Operations	—	—		
2. Finite Mathematical Systems	1	2		
3. Linear Function & Graph ($y = mx + b$, slope, eqs. of)	17, 24	2 + 2 = 4		
4. Quadratic Equation (alg. sol.—factoring, formula)	31, 33	2 + 2 = 4		
5. Parabola (incl. axis of symmetry, turning point)	16, 22, 38	2 + 2 + 10 = 14		
6. Systems of Equations (alg. and graphic solutions)	—	—		
7. Suppls., Compl., Vertical Angles, Angle Measure	7	2		
8. Triangle Properties (eq., isos., sum ∠s, 2 sides)	6, 12, 18, 20	2 + 2 + 2 + 2 = 8		
9. Line ‖ One Side of △; Line Joining Midpts. of Two Sides	10	2		
10. Inequalities in △s (ext. ∠, ≠ sides, and opp. ∠s)	23	2		
11. Quadrilateral Properties (▱, sq., rhom., rect., trap.)	9, 14, 21, 32	2 + 2 + 2 + 2 = 8		
12. Parallel Lines	3	2		
13. Alg. Oper.; Verbal Probs.	25, 36	2 + 10 = 12		
14. Mean Proportional; Alt. to Hypot. of Right △	40a, b	7		
15. Pythag. Th., Special Rt. △s (3-4-5, 5-12-13, 30-60-90)	26, 40c	2 + 3 = 5		
16. Similar Figures (ratios & proportions)	2	2		
17. Areas (△, rect., ▱, rhom., trap.)	34	2		
18. Locus	29	2		
19. Constructions	35	2		
20. Deductive Proofs	41	10		
21. Coordinate Geom. (slope, dist., midpt., eq. of circle)	5, 11, 15	2 + 2 + 2 = 6		
22. Coordinate Geom. "Proofs"	42	10		
23. Logic	19, 27	2 + 2 = 4		
24. Permutations; Arrangements	28, 39d	2 + 2 = 4		
25. Combinations	39a, b	5		
26. Probability	39c	3		
27. Trig. of Rt. △	4, 37	2 + 10 = 12		
28. Literal Eqs.	—	—		
29. Transformations	8, 13, 30	2 + 2 + 2 = 6		

Examination
June 1997

Sequential Math Course II

PART I

Answer 30 questions from this part. Each correct answer will receive 2 credits. No partial credit will be allowed. Write your answers in the spaces provided. Where applicable, answers may be left in terms of π or in radical form. [60]

1 Using the table below, compute $(1 \star 5) \star (2 \star 7)$.

$\star$	1	2	5	7
1	2	7	1	5
2	7	5	2	1
5	1	2	5	7
7	5	1	7	2

1 _____

2 In the accompanying diagram, line ℓ is parallel to line k, line $m \perp$ line k, and m$\angle x$ = m$\angle y$. Find m$\angle x$.

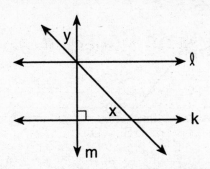

2 _____

3 If ♥ is a binary operation defined as $a ♥ b = \sqrt{a^2 + b^2}$, find the value of 12 ♥ 5.   3 _____

4 In the accompanying diagram of similar triangles ABE and ACD, $\overline{ABC}$, $\overline{AED}$, $AB = 6$, $BC = 3$, and $ED = 4$. Find the length of $\overline{AE}$.

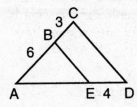

4 _____

5 How many different 5-letter arrangements can be formed from the letters in the word "DANNY"?   5 _____

6 Evaluate: $\dfrac{9!}{3!5!}$ 6 _____

7 In the accompanying diagram of △ABC, AB is extended to E and D, exterior angle CBD measures 130°, and m∠C = 75. Find m∠CAE.

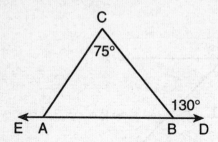

7 _____

8 In right triangle ABC, ∠C is a right angle and m∠B = 60. What is the ratio of m∠A to m∠B?

8 _____

9 In △ABC, m∠A = 3x + 40, m∠B = 8x + 35, and m∠C = 10x. Which is the longest side of the triangle?

9 _____

10 A bookshelf contains seven math textbooks and three science textbooks. If two textbooks are drawn at random without replacement, what is the probability both books are science textbooks?

10 _____

11 Express the product in lowest terms:

$$\frac{x^2 - x - 6}{3x - 9} \cdot \frac{2}{x + 2}$$

11 _____

12 In rhombus ABCD, the measure of ∠A is 30° more than twice the measure of ∠B. Find m∠B.

12 _____

13 The endpoints of the diameter of a circle are (–6,2) and (10,–2). What are the coordinates of the center of the circle?

13 _____

14 Find the area of a triangle whose vertices are (1,2), (8,2), and (1,6).

14 _____

15 Find the distance between points (–1,–1) and (2,–5).

15 _____

16 In the accompanying diagram, the bisectors of ∠A and ∠B in acute triangle ABC meet at D, and m∠ADB = 130. Find m∠C.

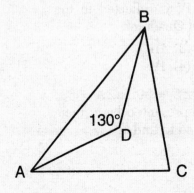

16 _____

17 Point P is on line m. What is the total number of points 3 centimeters from line m and 5 centimeters from point P?

17 _____

18 The diagonals of a rhombus are 8 and 10. Find the measure of a side of the rhombus to the *nearest tenth*.

18 _____

Directions (19–34): For *each* question chosen, write in the space provided the *numeral* preceding the word or expression that best completes the statement or answers the question.

19 In isosceles triangle ABC, $\overline{AB} \cong \overline{BC}$, point D lies on $\overline{AC}$, and $\overline{BD}$ is drawn. Which inequality is true?

 (1) $m\angle A > m\angle ADB$ (3) $BD > AB$
 (2) $m\angle C > m\angle CDB$ (4) $AB > BD$ 19 _____

20 If the statements m, $m \to p$, and $r \to \sim p$ are true, which statement must also be true?

 (1) $\sim r$ (3) $r \wedge \sim p$
 (2) $\sim p$ (4) $\sim p \vee \sim m$ 20 _____

21 If a point in Quadrant IV is reflected in the y-axis, its image will lie in Quadrant

 (1) I   (3) III
 (2) II   (4) IV   21 _____

22 In right triangle ABC, $m\angle C = 90$, $m\angle A = 63$, and $AB = 10$. If BC is represented by a, then which equation can be used to find a?

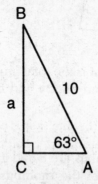

 (1) $\sin 63° = \dfrac{a}{10}$ (3) $\tan 63° = \dfrac{a}{10}$
 (2) $a = 10 \cos 63°$ (4) $a = \tan 27°$ 22 _____

23 If point $R'(6,3)$ is the image of point $R(2,1)$ under a dilation with respect to the origin, what is the constant of the dilation?

(1) 1   (3) 3

(2) 2   (4) 6   23 _____

24 What is an equation of a line that passes through the point $(0,3)$ and is perpendicular to the line whose equation is $y = 2x - 1$?

(1) $y = -2x + 3$ (3) $y = -\frac{1}{2}x + 3$

(2) $y = 2x + 3$ (4) $y = \frac{1}{2}x + 3$ 24 _____

25 What is an equation of the function shown in the accompanying diagram?

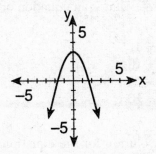

(1) $y = x^2 + 3$ (3) $y = -x^2 - 3$

(2) $y = -x^2 + 3$ (4) $y = (x - 3)^2$ 25 _____

26 What is an equation of the line that is parallel to the y-axis and passes through the point $(2,4)$?

(1) $x = 2$ (3) $x = 4$

(2) $y = 2$ (4) $y = 4$ 26 _____

27 In the accompanying diagram, the altitude to the hypotenuse of right triangle ABC is 8.

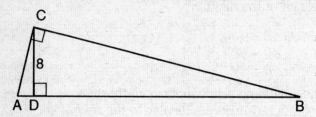

The altitude divides the hypotenuse into segments whose measures may be

(1) 8 and 12   (3) 6 and 10

(2) 3 and 24   (4) 2 and 32   27 ____

28 If the coordinates of the center of a circle are (–3,1) and the radius is 4, what is an equation of the circle?

(1) $(x - 3)^2 + (y + 1)^2 = 4$

(2) $(x + 3)^2 + (y - 1)^2 = 16$

(3) $(x + 3)^2 + (y - 1)^2 = 4$

(4) $(x - 3)^2 + (y + 1)^2 = 16$ 28 ____

29 Which expression is a solution for the equation $2x^2 - x = 7$?

(1) $\dfrac{-1 \pm \sqrt{57}}{2}$ (3) $\dfrac{-1 \pm \sqrt{57}}{4}$

(2) $\dfrac{1 \pm \sqrt{57}}{2}$ (4) $\dfrac{1 \pm \sqrt{57}}{4}$ 29 ____

30 If the complement of $\angle A$ is greater than the supplement of $\angle B$, which statement *must* be true?

(1) $m\angle A + m\angle B = 180$
(2) $m\angle A + m\angle B = 90$
(3) $m\angle A < m\angle B$
(4) $m\angle A > m\angle B$ 30 _____

31 How many different four-person committees can be formed from a group of six boys and four girls?

(1) $\frac{10!}{4!}$ (3) $_6C_2 \cdot {}_4C_2$
(2) $_{10}P_4$ (4) $_{10}C_4$ 31 _____

32 Which equation represents the axis of symmetry of the graph of the equation $y = x^2 - 4x - 12$?

(1) $y = 4$ (3) $y = -2$
(2) $x = 2$ (4) $x = -4$ 32 _____

33 What is $\frac{1}{x} + \frac{1}{1-x}$, $x \neq 1, 0$, expressed as a single fraction?

(1) $\frac{1}{x(1-x)}$ (3) $\frac{2}{-x}$
(2) $\frac{-1}{x(x+1)}$ (4) $\frac{1}{x(x-1)}$ 33 _____

34 In the accompanying diagram, $\overline{RL} \perp \overline{LP}$, $\overline{LR} \perp \overline{RT}$, and M is the midpoint of $\overline{TP}$.

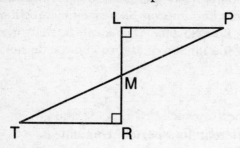

Which method could be used to prove $\triangle TMR \cong \triangle PML$?

(1) SAS ≅ SAS   (3) HL ≅ HL

(2) AAS ≅ AAS   (4) SSS ≅ SSS   34 _____

Directions (35): Leave all construction lines on the answer sheet.

35 *On the answer sheet*, construct an equilateral triangle in which $\overline{AB}$ is one of the sides.

PART II

Answer three questions from this part. Clearly indicate the
necessary steps, including appropriate formula substitutions,
diagrams, graphs, charts, etc. Calculations that may be
obtained by mental arithmetic or the calculator do not need
to be shown. [30]

36 *a* On graph paper, draw the graph of the equation $y = x^2 - 8x + 2$, including all values of x in
the interval $0 \le x \le 8$.   [6]

  b Find the roots of the equation $x^2 - 8x + 2 = 0$
to the *nearest hundredth*. [*Only an algebraic
solution will be accepted*.]   [4]

37 The coordinates of the endpoints of $\overline{AB}$ are
$A(-2,4)$ and $B(4,1)$.

  a On a set of axes, graph $\overline{AB}$.   [1]

  b On the same set of axes, graph and state the
coordinates of

    (1) $\overline{A'B'}$, the image of $\overline{AB}$ after a reflection in
the x-axis   [2]

    (2) $\overline{A''B''}$, the image of $\overline{A'B'}$ after a transla-
tion that shifts (x,y) to $(x + 2,y)$ [2]

  c Using coordinate geometry, determine if
$\overline{A'B'} \cong \overline{A''B''}$. Justify your answer.   [5]

38 Answer both *a* and *b* for all values for which these expressions are defined.

   a Solve for *x*: $-\dfrac{2}{5} + \dfrac{x+4}{x} = 1$ [4]

   b Express the difference in simplest form:

$$\frac{3y}{y^2 - 4} - \frac{2}{y + 2} \qquad [6]$$

39 Solve the following system of equations algebraically and check:

$$\begin{array}{l} y = 2x^2 - 4x - 5 \\ 2x + y + 1 = 0 \end{array} \qquad [8,2]$$

40 In the accompanying diagram of $\triangle ABC$, altitude $AD = 13$, $\overline{AB} \cong \overline{AC}$, and m$\angle BAC = 70$.

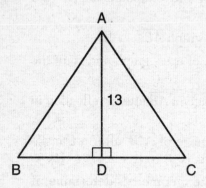

   a Find *BC* to the *nearest tenth*.   [4]

   b Using the answer from part *a*, find, to the *nearest tenth*, the

     (1) area of $\triangle ABC$ [2]

     (2) perimeter of $\triangle ABC$ [4]

PART III

Answer one question from this part. Clearly indicate the necessary steps, including appropriate formula substitutions, diagrams, graphs, charts, etc. Calculations that may be obtained by mental arithmetic or the calculator do not need to be shown. [10]

41 Given: If Sue goes out on Friday night and not on Saturday night, then she does not study.

If Sue does not fail mathematics, then she studies.

Sue does not fail mathematics.

If Sue does not go out on Friday night, then she watches a movie.

Sue does not watch a movie.

Let A represent: "Sue fails mathematics."
Let B represent: "Sue studies."
Let C represent: "Sue watches a movie."
Let D represent: "Sue goes out on Friday night."
Let E represent: "Sue goes out on Saturday night."

Prove: Sue goes out on Saturday night. [10]

42 Given: parallelogram $ABCD$, $\overline{DFC}$, $\overline{AEB}$, $\overline{ED}$ bisects $\angle ADC$, and $\overline{FB}$ bisects $\angle ABC$.

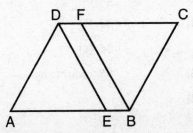

Prove: $\overline{EB} \cong \overline{DF}$ [10]

Answers
June 1997
Sequential Math Course II

Answer Key

PART I

1. 2	**13.** $(2, 0)$	**25.** (2)
2. 45	**14.** 14	**26.** (1)
3. 13	**15.** 5	**27.** (4)
4. 8	**16.** 80	**28.** (2)
5. 60	**17.** 4	**29.** (4)
6. 504	**18.** 6.4	**30.** (3)
7. 125	**19.** (4)	**31.** (4)
8. $\frac{1}{2}$	**20.** (1)	**32.** (2)
9. $\overline{AC}$	**21.** (3)	**33.** (1)
10. $\frac{1}{15}$	**22.** (1)	**34.** (2)
11. $\frac{2}{3}$	**23.** (3)	**35.** construction
12. 50	**24.** (3)	

PARTS II AND III See answers explained section.

Answers Explained

PART I

1. The expression to be evaluated using the accompanying table is

$$(1 \star 5) \star (2 \star 7).$$

$\star$	1	2	5	7
1	2	7	1	5
2	7	5	2	1
5	1	2	5	7
7	5	1	7	2

- Evaluate $(1 \star 5)$ by finding the table element at which the horizontal row labeled 1 intersects the vertical column labeled 5. Since this row and column intersect at element 1, $(1 \star 5) = 1$.

- Evaluate $(2 \star 7)$ by finding the table element at which the horizontal row labeled 2 intersects the vertical column labeled 7. Since this row and column intersect at element 1, $(2 \star 7) = 1$.

Thus, $(1 \star 5) \star (2 \star 7) = 1 \star 1$.

Finally, since the horizontal row labeled 1 intersects the vertical column labeled 1 at element 2, $1 \star 1 = 2$.

The expression $(1 \star 5) \star (2 \star 7) = \mathbf{2}$.

2. It is given that, in the accompanying diagram, line $m \perp$ line k and $m\angle x = m\angle y$. Since vertical angles are equal in measure, $m\angle ABC = m\angle y$. Since the acute angles of right triangle ABC are equal ($m\angle x = m\angle y$) and complementary, the degree measure of each of these acute angles is 45.

The degree measure of $\angle x$ is **45**.

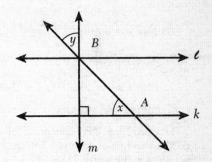

3. It is given that the binary operation $\heartsuit$ is defined as $a \heartsuit b = \sqrt{a^2 + b^2}$. To find the value of $12 \heartsuit 5$, replace a with 12 and b with 5.

The given formula is:

$$a \heartsuit b = \sqrt{a^2 + b^2}$$

Let $a = 12$ and $b = 5$:

$$12 \heartsuit 5 = \sqrt{12^2 + 5^2}$$
$$= \sqrt{144 + 25}$$
$$= \sqrt{169}$$

The value of $12 \heartsuit 5$ is **13**. $= 13$

4.

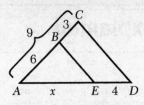

It is given that, in the accompanying diagram, triangles ABE and ACD are similar.

Since the lengths of corresponding sides of similar triangles are in proportion:

$$\frac{AE}{AD} = \frac{AB}{AC}$$

$$\frac{AE}{AE + ED} = \frac{AB}{AB + BC}$$

Let $x = AE$:

$$\frac{x}{x+4} = \frac{6}{6+3}$$

Simplify:

$$\frac{x}{x+4} = \frac{6}{9}$$

$$\frac{x}{x+4} = \frac{2}{3}$$

In a proportion the product of the means is equal to the product of the extremes (cross-multiply):

$$3x = 2(x + 4)$$
$$= 2x + 8$$

Combine like terms:

$$3x - 2x = 8$$
$$x = 8$$

The length of $\overline{AE}$ is **8**.

5. If in a set of n objects a of those objects are identical, then the number of different ways in which the n objects can be arranged is $\dfrac{n!}{a!}$.

The word "DANNY" contains 5 letters, including 2 identical letters (N). To find the number of different 5-letter arrangements that can be formed from the letters in the word "DANNY," let $n = 5$ and $a = 2$. Thus:

$$\frac{n!}{a!} = \frac{5!}{2!}$$

$$= \frac{5 \times 4 \times 3 \times 2!}{2!}$$

$$= 60$$

There are **60** different 5-letter arrangements.

6. The given expression is:

$$\frac{9!}{3!\,5!}$$

Expand the factorials:

$$\frac{9\times 8\times 7\times 6\times 5!}{(3\times 2\times 1)\times 5!}$$

If any factor appears in both the numerator and the denominator, divide both of them by that factor so their quotient is 1 (cancel):

$$\frac{9\times 8\times 7\times \overset{1}{\cancel{6}}\times \overset{1}{\cancel{5!}}}{\cancel{(3\times 2\times 1)}\times \cancel{5!}}$$

Multiply the remaining factors together: 504

The value of the given expression is **504**.

7.

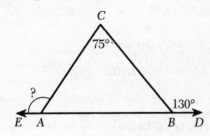

Since it is given that, in the accompanying diagram, m∠CBD = 130, then m∠ABC = 180 − 30 = 50.

The measure of an exterior angle of a triangle is equal to the sum of the measures of the two remote (nonadjacent) interior angles of the triangle. Thus:

$$\begin{aligned}
\text{m}\angle CAE &= \text{m}\angle C + \text{m}\angle ABC\\
&= \quad 75 \quad + \quad 50\\
&= 125
\end{aligned}$$

The degree measure of ∠CAE is **125**.

8. In a right triangle the measures of the two acute angles add up to 90. If, in △ABC, ∠C is a right angle and m∠B = 60, then m∠A = 90 − 60 = 30.

Hence, the ratio of m∠A to m∠B is equal to the ratio of 30 to 60, that is, $\frac{30}{60}$ or, equivalently, $\frac{1}{2}$.

The ratio of m∠A to m∠B is $\dfrac{1}{2}$.

9. The longest side of a triangle is opposite the angle of the triangle with the greatest measure. Find the measures of the three angles of △ABC by first solving for x.

Since the sum of the measures of the angles of a triangle is 180:

$$m\angle A \ + \ m\angle B \ + m\angle C = 180$$
$$(3x + 40) + (8x + 35) + (10x) = 180$$
$$21x + 75 = 180$$
$$21x = 105$$
$$x = \frac{105}{21} = 5$$

Then, as shown in the accompanying diagram:

$$m\angle A = 3x + 40 = 3(5) + 40 = 55$$
$$m\angle B = 8x + 35 = 8(5) + 35 = 75$$
$$m\angle C = 10x = 10(5) = 50$$

Since the angle with the greatest measure is $\angle B$, the side opposite $\angle B$, $\overline{AC}$, is the longest side of $\triangle ABC$.
The longest side of $\triangle ABC$ is $\overline{AC}$.

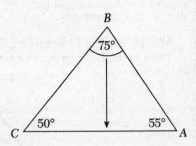

10. It is given that a bookshelf contains 7 math textbooks and 3 science textbooks. If 2 textbooks are drawn at random without replacement, the probability that both books will be science textbooks is the probability that the first book drawn is a science book *multiplied* by the probability that the second book drawn is a science book.

- On the first pick, there is a total of $7 + 3$ or 10 textbooks, so the probability of picking a science textbook is $\frac{3}{10}$.

- Assuming that a science textbook is drawn first, and given that there is no replacement, 2 of the remaining 9 books are science textbooks. Hence, the probability of picking a science textbook on the second draw is $\frac{2}{9}$.

Thus, the probability that both books are science textbooks is $\frac{3}{10} \times \frac{2}{9} = \frac{6}{90}$ or $\frac{1}{15}$.

The probability that both books drawn are science textbooks is $\frac{1}{15}$.

11. The given product is:

$$\frac{x^2 - x - 6}{3x - 9} \cdot \frac{2}{x + 2}$$

Factor where possible. The first numerator is a quadratic trinomial that can be factored as the product of two binomials. In determining the constant terms in the binomial factors, look for two integers whose sum is –1 and whose product is –6:

$$\frac{(x-3)(x+2)}{3x-9} \cdot \frac{2}{x+2}$$

Remove a common factor of 3 from the first denominator:

$$\frac{(x-3)(x+2)}{3(x-3)} \cdot \frac{2}{x+2}$$

If the same factor appears in both a numerator and a denominator, divide both of them by that factor so their quotient is 1 (cancel):

$$\frac{\overset{1}{\cancel{(x-3)}}(x+2)}{3\cancel{(x-3)}} \cdot \frac{2}{\underset{1}{\cancel{x+2}}}$$

Multiply the remaining factors in the numerator and multiply the remaining factors in the denominator:

$$\frac{2}{3}$$

The product in lowest terms is $\frac{2}{3}$.

12. Since it is given that in rhombus $ABCD$ the measure of $\angle A$ is 30 more than twice the measure of $\angle B$, let $x = m\angle B$ and $2x + 30 = m\angle A$. In a rhombus, the consecutive angles are supplementary. Thus:

$$\begin{aligned}
m\angle A + m\angle B &= 180 \\
(2x + 30) + \quad x \;\; &= 180 \\
3x + 30 &= 180 \\
3x &= 150 \\
x &= \frac{150}{3} = 50
\end{aligned}$$

The degree measure of $\angle B$ is **50**.

13. The center of a circle is the midpoint of each diameter of the circle. If the endpoints of the diameter of a circle are $(-6,2)$ and $(10,-2)$, then the coordinates of the center of the circle are the averages of the corresponding coordinates of the endpoints of the diameter.

- The x-coordinate of the center of the circle is the average of –6 and 10:

$$\frac{-6+10}{2} = \frac{4}{2} = 2$$

- The y-coordinate of the center of the circle is the average of 2 and –2:

$$\frac{2+(-2)}{2} = \frac{0}{2} = 0$$

The coordinates of the center of the circle are **(2,0)**.

14. As shown in the accompanying diagram, sketch the graph of the triangle whose vertices are given as $(1,2)$, $(8,2)$, and $(1,6)$. These vertices determine a right triangle in which the length of the base is 8 – 1 or 7, and the height is 6 – 2 or 4. Thus:

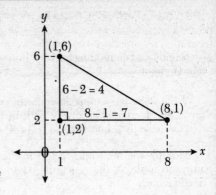

$$\text{Area of triangle } = \frac{1}{2} \times \text{base} \times \text{height}$$

$$= \frac{1}{2} \times \ 7 \ \times \ 4$$

$$= \frac{1}{2} \times 28$$

$$= 14$$

The area of the triangle is **14** square units.

15. To find the distance between points $(-1,-1)$ and $(2,-5)$, use the distance formula.

The formula for the distance d between points (x_a, y_a) and (x_b, y_b) is:

Let $x_a = -1$, $y_a = -1$, $x_b = 2$, and $y_b = -5$:

$$d = \sqrt{(x_b - x_a)^2 + (y_b - y_a)^2}$$

$$= \sqrt{(2 - (-1))^2 + (-5 - (-1))^2}$$

$$= \sqrt{(3)^2 + (-4)^2}$$

$$= \sqrt{9 + 16}$$

$$= \sqrt{25}$$

$$= 5$$

The distance between the given points is **5**.

16. It is given that, in the accompanying diagram, the bisectors of $\angle A$ and $\angle B$ in acute triangle ABC meet at D.

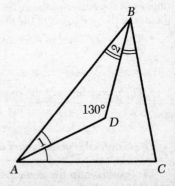

- In $\triangle ADB$, the sum of the measures of angles 1 and 2 is 180 – 130 or 50.
- Since the measure of $\angle 1$ is one-half the measure of $\angle A$ and the measure of $\angle 2$ is one-half the measure of $\angle B$, $m\angle A + m\angle B = 2 \times 50 = 100$.
- In $\triangle ABC$,

$$m\angle C = 180 - (m\angle A + m\angle B)$$
$$= 180 - \qquad 100$$
$$= 80$$

The degree measure of $\angle C$ is **80**.

17. It is given that point P is on line m. To determine the number of points 3 centimeters from line m [condition 1] and 5 centimeters from point P [condition 2], represent the two locus conditions as shown in the accompanying diagram and count the number of points at which the loci intersect.

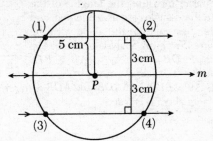

- The locus of points 3 centimeters from line m is a pair of lines each parallel to line m and each 3 centimeters from line m.
- The locus of points 5 centimeters from point P is a circle with center at P and a radius length of 5 centimeters.

Since the radius of the circle is greater than 3, the circle intersects each of the parallel lines at two points. Therefore, the two locus conditions intersect at a total of four points.

The total number of points that satisfy the given conditions is **4**.

18. The diagonals of a rhombus bisect each other and intersect at right angles. If the lengths of the diagonals of a rhombus are 8 and 10, then each side of the rhombus is the hypotenuse of a right triangle with legs that measure $\frac{1}{2} \times 8$ or 4 and $\frac{1}{2} \times 10$ or 5.

To find the measure of a side of the rhombus, use the Pythagorean theorem:

$$x^2 = 4^2 + 5^2$$
$$= 16 + 25$$
$$= 41$$
$$x = \sqrt{41} \approx 6.403$$

Each side of the rhombus measures **6.4**, correct to the *nearest tenth*.

19. It is given that in isosceles triangle ABC, $\overline{AB} \cong \overline{BC}$, point D lies on $\overline{AC}$, and $\overline{BD}$ is drawn. Since $\overline{AB} \cong \overline{BC}$, m$\angle A$ = m$\angle C$.

Determine whether the inequality in each answer choice is true or false.

- Choice (1): Is m$\angle A$ > m$\angle ADB$? Since $\angle ADB$ is an exterior angle of $\triangle DBC$, m$\angle ADB$ > m$\angle C$. Since m$\angle A$ = m$\angle C$, then, according to the substitution principle, m$\angle ADB$ > m$\angle A$. Hence, inequality (1) is false.
- Choice (2): Is m$\angle C$ > m$\angle CDB$? Since $\angle CDB$ is an exterior angle of

$\triangle ADB$, m$\angle CDB >$ m$\angle A$. Since m$\angle A =$ m$\angle C$, then, according to the substitution principle, m$\angle CDB >$ m$\angle C$. Hence, inequality (2) is false.

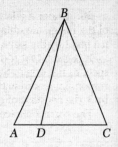

- Choice (3): Is $BD > AB$? If two angles of a triangle are unequal in measure, the lengths of the sides opposite these angles are also unequal, and the longer side lies opposite the angle with the greater measure. From the analysis of choice (1), in $\triangle ADB$, m$\angle ADB >$ m$\angle A$, so $AB > BD$. Hence, inequality (3) is false.

- Choice (4): Is $AB > BD$? In $\triangle ADB$, m$\angle ADB >$ m$\angle A$ implies that $AB > BD$. Hence, inequality (4) is true.

The correct choice is **(4)**.

20. It is given that statements m, $m \rightarrow p$, and $r \rightarrow \sim p$ are true.

- According to the Law of Contrapositive Inference, negating and interchanging the parts of the true conditional $r \rightarrow \sim p$ produces the true conditional $p \rightarrow \sim r$.
- According to the Chain Rule, if $m \rightarrow p$ and $p \rightarrow \sim r$, then $m \rightarrow \sim r$.
- According to the Law of Detachment, if m and $m \rightarrow \sim r$ are true, then $\sim r$ is true.

The correct choice is **(1)**.

21. To reflect a point in the y-axis, "flip" the point across the y-axis by replacing the original x-coordinate with its opposite.

If a point in Quadrant IV, which has a positive x-coordinate, is reflected in the y-axis, the x-coordinate of the image of the point will be negative. The y-coordinate will remain negative, thus placing the image in Quadrant III.

The correct choice is **(3)**.

22. The measures of an acute angle and the hypotenuse of right triangle ABC are given, as shown in the accompanying diagram. Since the length, a, of the leg *opposite* the given angle, $\angle A$, must be determined, use the sine ratio. Thus:

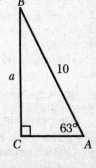

$$\sin A = \frac{\text{leg opposite } \angle A}{\text{hypotenuse}}$$

$$= \frac{BC}{AB}$$

$$\sin 63° = \frac{a}{10}$$

The correct choice is **(1)**.

23. Under a dilation of a point with respect to the origin, the coordinates of the image are obtained by multiplying each of the coordinates of the original point by the same fixed number, called the *constant of dilation*.

It is given that $R'(6,3)$ is the image of point $R(2,1)$ under a dilation with respect to the origin. Since the coordinates of R' can be obtained from the corresponding coordinates of R by multiplying the x- and the y-coordinates of R by 3, the constant of dilation is 3.

The correct choice is **(3)**.

24. A line whose equation has the form $y = mx + b$ has a slope of m and intercepts the y-axis at $(0,b)$. If two lines are perpendicular, then their slopes are negative reciprocals. The slope of the given line, whose equation is $y = 2x - 1$, is 2, the coefficient of x.

Since the desired line is perpendicular to the line $y = 2x - 1$, its slope is $-\dfrac{1}{2}$, the negative reciprocal of 2. Also the desired line passes through point $(0,3)$, so $b = 3$.

Since $m = -\dfrac{1}{2}$ and $b = 3$, an equation of the desired line is $y = -\dfrac{1}{2}x + 3$.

The correct choice is **(3)**.

25. The graph in the accompanying diagram has the shape of a parabola. Since the turning point of the parabola is a maximum point on the graph, the coefficient of the x^2-term must be negative. Also, the axis of symmetry is the y-axis, so the equation will not have a linear term containing x.

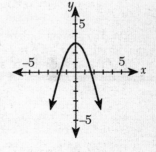

Hence, the general form of an equation of the function shown in the diagram is $y = -x^2 + k$, where k is the y-intercept of the graph. From the graph, $k = 3$, so an equation of this function is $y = -x^2 + 3$.

The correct choice is **(2)**.

26. A line parallel to the y-axis is a vertical line whose equation has the form $x = k$, where k is the x-coordinate of each point on the line. Hence, an equation of the line that is parallel to the y-axis and passes through point $(2,4)$ is $x = 2$.

The correct choice is **(1)**.

27.

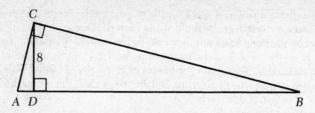

The length of the altitude drawn to the hypotenuse of a right triangle is the mean proportional between the lengths of the two segments of the hypotenuse. In the accompanying diagram, CD is the mean proportional between AD and DB. Thus:

$$\frac{AD}{CD} = \frac{CD}{DB} \quad \text{or} \quad \frac{AD}{8} = \frac{8}{DB}$$

From the proportion, $AD \times DB = 8 \times 8 = 64$. Choose the answer choice in which the product of the given pair of segment measures is 64.

- Choice (1): $8 \times 12 = 96$
- Choice (2): $3 \times 24 = 72$
- Choice (3): $6 \times 10 = 60$
- Choice (4): $2 \times 32 = 64$. Thus, the measures of the segments of the hypotenuse may be 2 and 32.

The correct choice is **(4)**.

28. The general form of an equation of a circle with center at (h,k) and radius length r is $(x - h)^2 + (y - k)^2 = r^2$.

To find an equation of a circle that has a center at $(-3,1)$ and a radius length of 4, let $h = -3$, $k = 1$, and $r = 4$ in the general equation:

$$\left(x - (-3)\right)^2 + \left(y - 1\right)^2 = 4^2$$
$$\left(x + 3\right)^2 + \left(y - 1\right)^2 = 16$$

The correct choice is **(2)**.

29. The given equation, $2x^2 - x = 7$, is a quadratic equation. Since each of the four answer choices has irrational roots, solve the equation by using the quadratic formula.

The given equation is: $2x^2 - x = 7$

Rearrange the terms of the quadratic equation so all of the nonzero terms are on the same side of the equation: $2x^2 - x - 7 = 0$

If a quadratic equation is in the form $ax^2 + bx + c = 0$, its roots are given by the quadratic formula:

$$x = \frac{-b \pm \sqrt{b^2 - 4ac}}{2a} \quad (a \neq 0)$$

Let $a = 2$, $b = -1$, $c = -7$:

$$= \frac{-(-1) \pm \sqrt{(-1)^2 - 4(2)(-7)}}{2(2)}$$

Simplify:

$$= \frac{1 \pm \sqrt{1 + 56}}{4}$$

$$= \frac{1 \pm \sqrt{57}}{4}$$

The correct choice is (4).

30. It is given that the complement of $\angle A$ $(90 - m\angle A)$ is greater than the supplement of $\angle B$ $(180 - m\angle B)$. Hence, $90 - m\angle A > 180 - m\angle B$ or, equivalently, $m\angle B = m\angle A + 90$.

Since $m\angle B$ always exceeds $m\angle A$ by 90, it must be true that $m\angle A < m\angle B$. The correct choice is (3).

31. Without paying attention to order, r people can be selected for a committee from a set of n people $(r \leq n)$ in ${}_nC_r$ ways.

To represent the number of different four-person committees that can be formed from a group of six boys and four girls, let $r = 4$ and $n = 6 + 4 = 10$. Thus, ${}_{10}C_4$ different four-person committees can be formed from a group of six boys and four girls.

The correct choice is (4).

32. The equation $x = -\dfrac{b}{2a}$ is an equation of the axis of symmetry for the parabola whose equation is $y = ax^2 + bx + c$.

To find an equation for the axis of symmetry of the graph of the equation $y = x^2 - 4x - 12$, use the formula $x = -\dfrac{b}{2a}$, where $a = 1$ and $b = -4$. Thus:

$$x = -\frac{b}{2a} = -\frac{(-4)}{2(1)} = \frac{4}{2} = 2$$

The correct choice is (2).

33. The given sum is:

$$\frac{1}{x} + \frac{1}{1-x} \quad (x \neq 1, 0)$$

The least common denominator (LCD) of the fractions is $x(1 - x)$ since this product is the smallest expression into which each of the denominators divides evenly. Change the fractions into equivalent fractions having the LCD as their denominators by multiplying the first fraction by 1 in the form of $\dfrac{1-x}{1-x}$ and multiplying the second fraction by 1 in the form of $\dfrac{x}{x}$:

$$\frac{1-x}{1-x}\cdot\frac{1}{x}+\frac{x}{x}\cdot\frac{1}{1-x}$$

Write the sum of the numerators over the common denominator:

$$\frac{(1-x)1+x}{x(1-x)}$$

Simplify:

$$\frac{1-x+x}{x(1-x)}$$

$$\frac{1}{x(1-x)}$$

The correct choice is (**1**).

34.

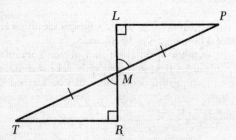

In the accompanying diagram, it is given that:

- $\overline{RL} \perp \overline{LP}$ and $\overline{LR} \perp \overline{RT}$, so right angle $R \cong$ right angle L. (**A**ngle $\cong$ **A**ngle)
- $\angle TMR \cong \angle PML$ since vertical angles are congruent. (**A**ngle $\cong$ **A**ngle)
- M is the midpoint of $\overline{TP}$, so $\overline{TM} \cong \overline{PM}$. (**S**ide $\cong$ **S**ide)

Hence, $\triangle TMR \cong \triangle PML$ by AAS $\cong$ AAS.
The correct choice is (**2**).

35. To construct an equilateral triangle in which $\overline{AB}$ is one of the sides, follow the three steps described below and illustrated in the accompanying diagram.

STEP 1: With the point of the compass on A, set the radius length of the compass equal to AB by placing the pencil point of the compass on point B.

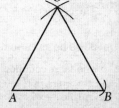

STEP 2: With the point of the compass on A and radius length AB, swing an arc.

STEP 3: With the point of the compass on B and radius length AB, swing an arc. Label as C the point at which the two arcs intersect.

Since $AB = AC = BC$, $\triangle ABC$ is equilateral.

PART II

36. a. To draw the graph of the equation $y = x^2 - 8x + 2$ for all values of x in the interval $0 \le x \le 8$, first prepare a table of values for x and y. Substitute each integer value of x from 0 to 8 into the equation to obtain the corresponding value of y:

x	$x^2 - 8x + 2$	$= y$	(x,y)
0	$0^2 - 8(0) + 2$	$= 2$	$(0,2)$
1	$1^2 - 8(1) + 2 = 3 - 8$	$= -5$	$(1,-5)$
2	$2^2 - 8(2) + 2 = 6 - 16$	$= -10$	$(2,-10)$
3	$3^2 - 8(3) + 2 = 11 - 24$	$= -13$	$(3,-13)$
4	$4^2 - 8(4) + 2 = 18 - 32$	$= -14$	$(4,-14)$
5	$5^2 - 8(5) + 2 = 27 - 40$	$= -13$	$(5,-13)$
6	$6^2 - 8(6) + 2 = 38 - 48$	$= -10$	$(6,-10)$
7	$7^2 - 8(7) + 2 = 51 - 56$	$= -5$	$(7,-5)$
8	$8^2 - 8(8) + 2 = 64 - 64 + 2$	$= 2$	$(8,2)$

Now plot the points that appear in the last column of the table. Connect these points with a smooth curve that has the shape of a parabola whose turning point, $(4,-14)$, is the lowest point on the curve.

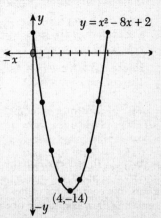

Label this graph with its equation, $y = x^2 - 8x + 2$, as shown in the accompanying figure.

b. The given equation, $x^2 - 8x + 2 = 0$, is a quadratic equation. Since the roots must be determined to the *nearest hundredth*, use the quadratic formula.

The given equation is: $\qquad x^2 - 8x + 2 = 0$

If a quadratic equation is in the form $ax^2 + bx + c = 0$, its roots are given by the quadratic formula:

$$x = \frac{-b \pm \sqrt{b^2 - 4ac}}{2a} \quad (a \neq 0)$$

The given equation is in the form $ax^2 + bx + c = 0$, where $a = 1$, $b = -8$, and $c = 2$:

$$= \frac{-(-8) \pm \sqrt{(-8)^2 - 4(1)(2)}}{2(1)}$$

$$= \frac{8 \pm \sqrt{64 - 8}}{2}$$

$$= \frac{8 \pm \sqrt{56}}{2}$$

Use a calculator to determine $\sqrt{56}$:

$$\approx \frac{8 \pm 7.483}{2}$$

$$x_1 \approx \frac{8 + 7.483}{2} \quad \text{or} \quad x_2 \approx \frac{8 - 7.483}{2}$$

$$\approx \frac{15.483}{2} \qquad\qquad \approx \frac{0.517}{2}$$

$$\approx 7.74 \qquad\qquad\quad \approx 0.26$$

The roots correct to the *nearest hundredth* are **0.26** and **7.74**.

37. It is given that the coordinates of the endpoints of $\overline{AB}$ are $A(-2,4)$ and $B(4,1)$.

a. See the accompanying figure for the graph of $\overline{AB}$.

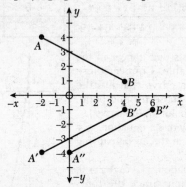

b. (1) To reflect $\overline{AB}$ in the x-axis, reflect the endpoints of $\overline{AB}$ in the x-axis and then connect the image points with a segment. Under a reflection in the x-axis, the coordinates of the images of the endpoints of $\overline{AB}$ are obtained by replacing the y-coordinate of each point with its opposite. Thus:

$$A(-2,4) \rightarrow A'(-2,-4) \quad \text{and} \quad B(4,1) \rightarrow B'(4,-1)$$

The graph of $\overline{A'B'}$ is shown in the figure for part **a**. The coordinates of $\overline{A'B'}$ are $A'(-2,-4)$ and $B'(4,-1)$.

(2) Under a translation that shifts (x,y) to $(x + 2,y)$, the image of:

- $A'(-2,-4)$ is $A''(-2 + 2,-4) = A''(0,-4)$.
- $B'(4,-1)$ is $B''(4 + 2,-1) = B''(6,-1)$.

The graph of $\overline{A''B''}$ is shown in the figure for part **a**. The coordinates of $\overline{A''B''}$ are $A''(0,-4)$ and $B''(6,-1)$.

c. To show $\overline{A'B'} \cong \overline{A''B''}$ using the methods of coordinate geometry, use the distance formula to find the length of each segment. The distance d between points (x_a,y_a) and (x_b,y_b) is given by the expression

$$d = \sqrt{(x_b - x_a)^2 + (y_b - y_a)^2}$$

- To find the length of $\overline{A'B'}$, let $A'(x_a,y_a) = A'(-2,-4)$ and $B'(x_b,y_b) = B'(4,-1)$:

$$
\begin{aligned}
A'B' &= \sqrt{(x_b - x_a)^2 + (y_b - y_a)^2} \\
&= \sqrt{(4 - (-2))^2 + (-1 - (-4))^2} \\
&= \sqrt{(4 + 2)^2 + (-1 + 4)^2} \\
&= \sqrt{(6)^2 + (3)^2} \\
&= \sqrt{36 + 9} \\
&= \sqrt{45}
\end{aligned}
$$

- To find the length of $\overline{A''B''}$, let $A''(x_a,y_a) = A''(0,-4)$ and $B''(x_b,y_b) = B''(6,-1)$:

$$
\begin{aligned}
A''B'' &= \sqrt{(x_b - x_a)^2 + (y_b - y_a)^2} \\
&= \sqrt{(6 - 0)^2 + (-1 - (-4))^2} \\
&= \sqrt{(6)^2 + (-1 + 4)^2} \\
&= \sqrt{(6)^2 + (3)^2} \\
&= \sqrt{36 + 9} \\
&= \sqrt{45}
\end{aligned}
$$

Thus, $A'B' = A''B'' = \sqrt{45}$. Since $\overline{A'B'}$ and $\overline{A''B''}$ have the same length, $\overline{A'B'} \cong \overline{A''B''}$.

38. a. The given equation is:

$$-\frac{2}{5} + \frac{x+4}{x} = 1$$

Add $\frac{2}{5}$ to each side of the equation:

$$+\frac{2}{5} \qquad\qquad = \quad +\frac{2}{5}$$

$$\frac{x+4}{x} = 1 + \frac{2}{5}$$

Replace 1 with $\frac{5}{5}$ and add:

$$\frac{x+4}{x} = \frac{7}{5}$$

In a proportion, the product of the means is equal to the product of the extremes (cross-multiply):

$$7x = 5(x+4)$$
$$= 5x + 20$$
$$7x - 5x = 20$$
$$2x = 20$$
$$x = \frac{20}{2} = 10$$

The value of x is **10**.

b. The given difference is:

$$\frac{3y}{y^2 - 4} - \frac{2}{y+2}$$

To help determine the least common denominator (LCD) of the fractions, factor the denominators where possible. The denominator of the first fraction is the difference of two perfect squares, so it can be factored as the sum and difference of the same two terms:

The LCD is $(y+2)(y-2)$ since this is the smallest expression into which each of the denominators divides evenly. To change the second fraction into an equivalent fraction that has the LCD as its denominator, multiply it by 1 in the form of $\frac{y-2}{y-2}$:

$$\frac{3y}{(y+2)(y-2)} - \frac{2}{y+2}$$

$$\frac{3y}{(y+2)(y-2)} - \left(\frac{y-2}{y-2}\right) \cdot \frac{2}{y+2}$$

Write the difference in the numerators over the LCD:

$$\frac{3y - 2(y-2)}{(y+2)(y-2)}$$

Simplify the numerator:

$$\frac{3y - 2y + 4}{(y+2)(y-2)}$$

$$\frac{y+4}{(y+2)(y-2)}$$

The difference in simplest form is $\dfrac{y+4}{(y+2)(y-2)}$.

39. The given system of equations is:

$$y = 2x^2 - 4x - 5$$
$$2x + y + 1 = 0$$

Eliminate y in the second equation by replacing it with its equal obtained from the first equation:

$$2x + (2x^2 - 4x - 5) + 1 = 0$$

Combine like terms:

$$2x^2 - 2x - 4 = 0$$

Divide each member of the equation by 2:

$$x^2 - x - 2 = 0$$

Solve the resulting quadratic equation by factoring the left side of the equation as the product of two binomials:

$$(x + ?)(x + ?) = 0$$

Find the two missing numbers whose sum is -1 and whose product is -2. The two numbers are $+1$ and -2:

$$(x + 1)(x - 2) = 0$$

If the product of two binomials is 0, then either binomial may equal 0:

$$x + 1 = 0 \quad \text{or} \quad x - 2 = 0$$
$$x = -1 \quad | \quad x = 2$$

To find the corresponding values of y, substitute each of the solutions for x in the original first-degree equation and solve for y:

Let $x = -1$:	Let $x = 2$:
$2x + y + 1 = 0$	$2x + y + 1 = 0$
$2(-1) + y + 1 = 0$	$2(2) + y + 1 = 0$
$-2 + y + 1 = 0$	$4 + y + 1 = 0$
$y = 1$	$y = -5$

The solutions are $(-1, 1)$ and $(2, -5)$.

<u>*CHECK*</u>: Substitute each pair of values for x and y in *both* of the *original* equations to verify that both equations are satisfied at the same time.

	$y = 2x^2 - 4x - 5$	$2x + y + 1 = 0$
Let $x = -1$ and $y = 1$:	$1 = 2(-1)^2 - 4(-1) - 5$	$2(-1) + 1 + 1 = 0$
	$1 = 2(1) + 4 - 5$	$-2 + 2 = 0$
	$1 = 2 - 1$	$0 = 0$
	$1 = 1$	
Let $x = 2$ and $y = -5$:	$-5 = 2(2)^2 - 4(2) - 5$	$2(2) - 5 + 1 = 0$
	$-5 = 2(4) - 8 - 5$	$4 - 5 + 1 = 0$
	$-5 = 8 - 8 - 5$	$-1 + 1 = 0$
	$-5 = -5$	$0 = 0$

40. It is given that, in the accompanying diagram, altitude $AD = 13$, $\overline{AB} \cong \overline{AC}$, and m$\angle BAC = 70$. Since an altitude drawn to the base of an isosceles triangle bisects the vertex angle:

$$\text{m}\angle DAB = \text{m}\angle DAC = \frac{1}{2} \times 70 = 35$$

a. In right triangle ADB:

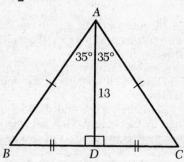

$$\tan\angle DAB = \frac{BD}{AD}$$

$$\tan 35° = \frac{BD}{13}$$

$$0.7002 = \frac{BD}{13}$$

$$0.7002 \times 13 = BD$$

$$9.103 = BD$$

Since the altitude drawn to the base of an isosceles triangle bisects the base:

$$BC = 2 \times BD = 2 \times 9.103 = 18.206$$

Thus, $BC = \textbf{18.2}$, correct to the *nearest tenth*.

b. (1) Area of $\triangle ABC = \frac{1}{2} \times \text{base} \times \text{height}$

$$= \frac{1}{2} \times BC \times AD$$

$$= \frac{1}{2} \times 18.2 \times 13$$

$$= 9.1 \times 13$$

$$= 118.3$$

The area of $\triangle ABC$, correct to the *nearest tenth*, is **118.3** square units.

(2) Use the Pythagorean theorem to find the length of $\overline{AB}$. In right triangle ADB:

$$(AB)^2 = (AD)^2 + (BD)^2$$
$$= (13)^2 + (9.1)^2$$
$$= 169 + 82.81$$
$$= 251.81$$
$$AB = \sqrt{251.81} = 15.87$$

Since $\overline{AB} \cong \overline{AC}$, $AC = AB = 15.87$. The perimeter of the $\triangle ABC$ is the sum of the lengths of its sides. Hence:

$$\text{Perimeter} = AB + AC + BC$$
$$= 15.87 + 15.87 + 18.20$$
$$= 49.94$$

The perimeter of $\triangle ABC$, correct to the *nearest tenth*, is **49.9**.

PART III

41. Given: If Sue goes out on Friday night and not on Satruday night, then she does not study.

If Sue does not fail mathematics, then she studies.

Sue does not fail mathematics.

If Sue does not go out on Friday night, then she watches a movie.

Sue does not watch a movie.

Let A represent: "Sue fails mathematics."
Let B represent: "Sue studies."
Let C represent: "Sue watches a movie."
Let D represent: "Sue goes out on Friday night."
Let E represent: "Sue goes out on Saturday night."

- Write each statement in the Given in symbolic form:

"If Sue goes out on Friday night and not on Saturday night, then she does not study" is the conditional that the conjunction of D and the the negation of E implies the negation of B: $(D \wedge \sim E) \to \sim B$

"If Sue does not fail mathematics, then she studies" is the conditional that the negation of A implies B: $\sim A \to \sim B$

"Sue does not fail mathematics" is the negation of A: $\sim A$

"If Sue does not go out on Friday night, then she watches a movies" is the conditional that the negation of D implies C: $\sim D \to C$

"Sue does not watch a movie" is the negation of C: $\sim C$

- Write the statement in the Prove in symbolic form:
Prove: "Sue goes out on Saturday night" is statement E: E

- Write a formal proof.

PROOF

Statement	Reason
1. $\sim A$	1. Given.
2. $\sim A \to B$	2. Given.
3. B	3. Law of Detachment (steps 1 and 2).
4. $\sim D \to C$	4. Given.
5. $\sim C$	5. Given.
6. $\sim(\sim D)$ or D	6. Modus Tollens (steps 4 and 5).
7. $(D \wedge \sim E) \to \sim B$	7. Given.
8. $\sim(D \wedge \sim E)$	8. Modus Tollens (steps 3 and 7).
9. $\sim D \vee E$	9. De Morgan's Law.
10. E	10. Law of Disjunctive Inference (steps 6 and 9).

42. Given: Parallelogram $ABCD$,
$\overline{ED}$ bisects $\angle ADC$,
$\overline{FB}$ bisects $\angle ABC$.

Prove: $\overline{EB} \cong \overline{DF}$

Plan: Show $\triangle DAE \cong \triangle BCF$
by ASA $\cong$ ASA. then
$AE = CF$ and, by sub-
traction, $EB = DF$.

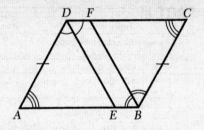

PROOF

Statement	Reason
1. $ABCD$ is a parallelogram.	1. Given.
2. $\angle A \cong \angle C$. (Angle)	2. Opposite angles of a parallelogram are congruent.
3. $\overline{AD} \cong \overline{BC}$. (Side)	3. Opposite sides of a parallelogram are congruent.
4. $m\angle ADC = m\angle ABC$.	4. Opposite angles of a parallelogram have equal measures.
5. $\overline{ED}$ bisects $\angle ADC$ $\overline{FB}$ bisects $\angle ABC$.	5. Given.
6. $m\angle ADE = \frac{1}{2} m\angle ADC$ $m\angle CBF = \frac{1}{2} m\angle ABC$	6. An angle bisector divides an angle into two angles with equal measures.
7. $m\angle ADE = m\angle CBF$	7. Halves of equals are equal.
8. $\angle ADE \cong \angle CBF$ (Angle)	8. If two angles are equal in measure, they are congruent.
9. $\triangle DAE \cong \triangle BCF$.	9. ASA $\cong$ ASA.
10. $AB = CD$.	10. Opposite sides of a parallelogram have equal lengths.
11. $AE = CF$.	11. Corresponding sides of congruent triangles have equal lengths.
12. $EB = DF$.	12. Subtraction property of equality.
13. $\overline{EB} \cong \overline{DF}$.	13. If two segments are equal in length, they are congruent.

Topic	Question Numbers	Number of Points	Your Points	Your Percentage
1. Properties of Number Systems; Def. of Operations	3	2		
2. Finite Mathematical Systems	1	2		
3. Linear Function & Graph ($y = mx + b$, slope, eqs. of)	24, 26	2 + 2 = 4		
4. Quadratic Equation (alg. sol.—factoring, formula)	29, 36b	2 + 4 = 6		
5. Parabola (incl. axis of symmetry, turning point)	25, 32, 36a	2 + 2 + 6 = 10		
6. Systems of Equations (alg. and graphic solutions)	39	10		
7. Suppls., Compl., Vertical Angles, Angle Measure	2, 30	2 + 2 = 4		
8. Triangle Properties (eq., isos., sum ∠s, 2 sides)	8, 9, 16	2 + 2 + 2 = 6		
9. Line ∥ One Side of △; Line Joining Midpts. of 2 Sides	—	—		
10. Inequalities in △s (ext. ∠, ≠ sides, opp. ∠s)	7, 19	2 + 2 = 4		
11. Quadrilateral Properties (▱, sq., rhom., rect., trap.)	12, 18	2 + 2 = 4		
12. Parallel Lines	—	—		
13. Alg. Oper.; Verbal Probs.	11, 33, 38	2 + 2 + 10 = 14		
14. Mean Proportional; Alt. to Hypot. of Right △	27	2		
15. Pythag. Th., Special Rt. △s (3-4-5, 5-12-13, 30-60-90)	—	—		
16. Similar Figures (ratios & proportions)	4	2		
17. Areas (△, rect., ▱, rhom., trap.)	14, 40b	2 + 6 = 8		
18. Locus	17	2		
19. Constructions	35	2		
20. Deductive Proofs	34, 42	2 + 10 = 12		
21. Coordinate Geom. (slope, dist., midpt., eq. of circle)	13, 15, 28, 37	2 + 2 + 2 + 10 = 16		
22. Coordinate Geom. "Proofs"	—	—		
23. Logic	20, 41	2 + 10 = 12		
24. Permutations; Arrangements	5, 6	2 + 2 = 4		
25. Combinations	31	2		
26. Probability	10	2		
27. Trig. of Rt. △	22, 40a	2 + 4 = 6		
28. Literal Eqs.	—	—		
29. Transformations	21, 23	2 + 2 = 4		

Examination
January 1998
Sequential Math Course II

PART I

Answer 30 questions from this part. Each correct answer will receive 2 credits. No partial credit will be allowed. Write your answers in the spaces provided. Where applicable, answers may be left in terms of π or in radical form. [60]

1 If a binary operation is defined as $a \ast b = \dfrac{2a+b}{b}$, evaluate $6 \ast 3$.

1 _____

2 In the accompanying diagram, rectangle $ABCD$ is similar to rectangle $EFGH$, $AD = 3$, $AB = 5$, $EF = 8$, and $FG = x$. find the value of x.

 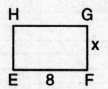

2 _____

3 In the accompanying diagram, $\overleftrightarrow{ALB} \parallel \overleftrightarrow{CJD}$ and $\overleftrightarrow{LJ}$ is a transversal. If $m\angle JLB = 6x - 7$ and $m\angle LJD = 7x + 5$, find the value of x.

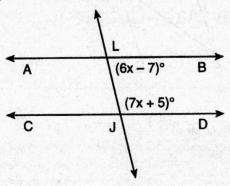

3 _____

4 Factor completely: $2x^2 - 18$ 4 _____

5 In the accompanying diagram, $m\angle ECB = 6x$, $m\angle ECD = 3x - 11$, and $m\angle DCB = 74$. What is the value of x?

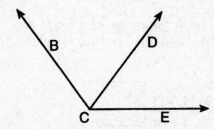

5 _____

6 In $\triangle MEC$, an exterior angle at C measures $115°$, and the measure of $\angle M$ is $60°$. Which is the *shortest* side of $\triangle MEC$?

6 _____

7 In the accompanying diagram of rhombus $ABCD$, m$\angle CAB = 35$. Find m$\angle CDA$.

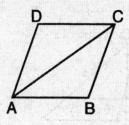

7 _____

8 Find the positive root of $\dfrac{1}{x-1} = \dfrac{x+2}{4}$, $x \neq 1$.

8 _____

9 The length of a side of a square is 5. In simplest radical form, find the length of a diagonal of the square.

9 _____

10 In which quadrant does the image of $(4,-7)$ lie after the translation that shifts (x,y) to $(x - 6, y + 3)$?

10 _____

11 If the endpoints of the diameter of a circle are $A(5,2)$ and $B(-3,4)$, find the coordinates of the center of the circle.

11 _____

12 Solve for x: $\dfrac{2}{x} + \dfrac{4}{3} = \dfrac{14}{3x}$

12 _____

13 In right triangle ABC, m$\angle C = 90$ and altitude $\overline{CD}$ is drawn to hypotenuse $\overline{AB}$. If $AD = 4$ and $DB = 5$, find AC.

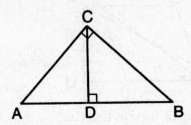

13 _____

14 Find the slope of a line that passes through points $(-6,8)$ and $(2,-4)$.

14 _____

Directions (15–34): For *each* question chosen, write in the space provided the *numeral* preceding the word or expression that best completes the statement or answers the question.

15 If the statements $s \rightarrow t$ and $t \rightarrow u$ are true, then what is a logically valid conclusion?

  (1) $\sim u \rightarrow \sim s$ (3) $u \rightarrow \sim t$
  (2) $\sim u \rightarrow t$ (4) $t \rightarrow \sim u$ 15 _____

16 What is the image of $(-4,-5)$ when reflected in the x-axis?

  (1) $(5,-4)$ (3) $(-4,5)$
  (2) $(-5,-4)$ (4) $(4,-5)$ 16 _____

17 In the accompanying diagram of $\triangle CDE$, m$\angle D =$ 90, m$\angle C = 28$, and $ED = 15$.

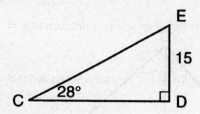

Which equation can be used to find CD?

(1) $\sin 28° = \dfrac{15}{CD}$ (3) $\tan 28° = \dfrac{15}{CD}$

(2) $\sin 28° = \dfrac{CD}{15}$ (4) $\tan 28° = \dfrac{CD}{15}$ 17 ____

18 The expression $\dfrac{12!}{8!\,4!}$ is equivalent to

(1) 1   (3) 2970
(2) 495   (4) 3960   18 ____

19 What is the locus of points at a given distance from a line?

(1) 1 point   (3) 1 circle
(2) 2 points   (4) 2 parallel lines   19 ____

20 Which statement is *false* about the line whose equation is $y = -2x - 5$?

(1) Its slope is -2.
(2) It is parallel to the line whose equation is $y = 2x + 5$.
(3) Its y-intercept is -5.
(4) It is perpendicular to the line whose equation is $y = \frac{1}{2}x - 5$.

20 _____

21 What is the total number of different six-letter permutations that can be formed from the letters in the word "MUUMUU"?

(1) 6   (3) 120
(2) 15   (4) 180

21 _____

22 In the accompanying diagram, $\overline{ACE}$, $\overline{BCD}$, $\overline{AB}$, and $\overline{DE}$, $\angle A \cong \angle E$, and C is the midpoint of $\overline{AE}$.

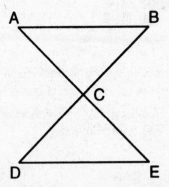

Which theorem justifies $\triangle ABC \cong \triangle EDC$?

(1) $SSS \cong SSS$ (3) $ASA \cong ASA$
(2) $SAS \cong SAS$ (4) $SSA \cong SSA$

22 _____

23 What is the value of $(P \blacksquare S) \blacksquare (L \blacksquare U)$ in the system defined below?

$\blacksquare$	P	L	U	S
P	U	S	P	L
L	S	P	L	U
U	P	L	U	S
S	L	U	S	P

(1) P (3) U

(2) L (4) S

23 _____

24 In right triangle ABC, angle C is the right angle. If the coordinates of A are $(-1,1)$ and the coordinates of B are $(4,-2)$, the coordinates of C may be

(1) $(-1,-2)$ (3) $(1,2)$

(2) $(-1,2)$ (4) $(1,-2)$

24 _____

25 In the accompanying diagram, parallel lines $\overleftrightarrow{AB}$ and $\overleftrightarrow{CD}$ are cut by transversal $\overleftrightarrow{EF}$ at P and Q, respectively.

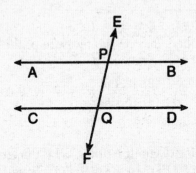

Which statement must always be true?

(1) $m\angle APE = m\angle CQF$
(2) $m\angle APE < m\angle CQF$
(3) $m\angle APE + m\angle CQF = 90$
(4) $m\angle APE + m\angle CQF = 180$ 25 _____

26 What is the distance between points $(6,-9)$ and $(-3,4)$?

(1) $\sqrt{34}$ (3) $\sqrt{178}$
(2) $\sqrt{106}$ (4) $\sqrt{250}$ 26 _____

27 Which equation represents the axis of symmetry of the graph of the equation $y = x^2 - 6x + 5$?

(1) $y = 3$ (3) $x = 3$
(2) $y = -3$ (4) $x = -3$ 27 _____

28 If the statements $\sim(n \wedge \sim c)$ and n are true, then which statement is a logical conclusion?

  (1) c (3) $\sim n \wedge c$

  (2) $\sim c$ (4) $\sim n \vee \sim c$ 28 _____

29 Which set of numbers may be the measure of the sides of a triangle?

  (1) {10,10,20}   (3) {2,4,6}

  (2) {4,6,12}   (4) {8,10,12}   29 _____

30 In the accompanying diagram, altitude $\overline{EH}$ is drawn in trapezoid $DEFG$, $DE = 10$, $EF = 9$, $FG = 8$, and $GD = 15$.

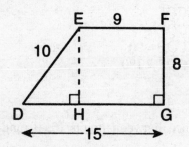

What is m∠D to the *nearest degree*?

  (1) 37   (3) 60

  (2) 53   (4) 80   30 _____

31 Which set is closed under the operation of subtraction?

  (1) odd numbers   (3) integers

  (2) counting numbers (4) prime numbers   31 _____

32 What are the roots of the equation $x^2 - 2x - 1 = 0$?

  (1) $x = -1 \pm \sqrt{2}$ (3) $x = -1 \pm 2\sqrt{2}$

  (2) $x = 1 \pm \sqrt{2}$ (4) $x = 1 \pm 2\sqrt{2}$ 32 ____

33 What are the coordinates of the image of point $(-1,2)$ under a dilation of 3 with respect to the origin?

  (1) $(-6,3)$ (3) $(3,6)$

  (2) $(6,-3)$ (4) $(-3,6)$ 33 ____

34 The number of degrees in the measure of one exterior angle of a regular pentagon is

  (1) 72   (3) 360

  (2) 108   (4) 540   34 ____

35 Construct the perpendicular bisector of $\overline{AB}$, a chord of circle O.

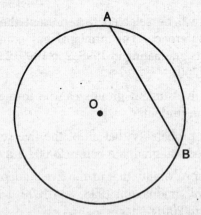

PART II

Answer three questions from this part. Clearly indicate the necessary steps, including appropriate formula substitutions, diagrams, graphs, charts, etc. Calculations that may be obtained by mental arithmetic or the calculator do not need to be shown. [30]

36 *a* On graph paper, draw the graph of the equation $y = x^2 + 2x - 3$ for all values in the interval $-4 \le x \le 2$. [6]

    b On the same set of axes, draw the graph of the equation $(x + 1)^2 + (y + 4)^2 = 16$. [3]

    c Determine the total number of points the graphs drawn in parts *a* and *b* have in common. [1]

37 Solve the following system of equations algebraically and check:

$$y = x^2 + 2x - 4 \quad [8,2]$$
$$y - 5 = 2x$$

38 Five students will be selected to represent their school at a conference. The principal has nominated 4 students graduating in 1998, 2 in 1999, 2 in 2000, and 1 in 2001.

    a How many five-student groups can be formed from the nine students? [2]

    b What is the probability that all of the five students selected will graduate before 2000? [2]

    c What is the probability that of the five students selected 2 will graduate in 1998, 1 in 1999, 1 in 2000, and 1 in 2001? [4]

    d What is the probability that all of the five students selected will graduate after 1999? [2]

39 In the accompanying diagram, *ABCD* is a trapezoid with altitudes $\overline{DW}$ and $\overline{CZ}$ drawn, *CD* = 17.3, *DA* = 8.6, m∠*A* = 68, and m∠*B* = 53. Find, to the *nearest tenth*, the perimeter of *ABCD*. [10]

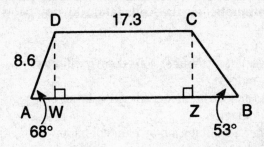

40 *a* In the accompanying diagram of △*CAT*, *W* is a point on $\overline{AC}$ and *G* is a point on $\overline{TC}$ such that $\overline{WG}$ is parallel to $\overline{AT}$, *TG* = *x*, *GC* = *x* − 1, *CW* = *x* + 5, and *WA* = 2*x* + 6. Find the length of $\overline{TG}$. [*Only an algebraic solution will be accepted.*] [6]

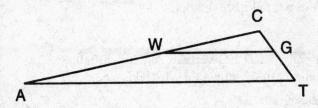

b For all values of *y* for which these expressions are defined, express the product in simplest form.

$$\frac{y^2 - 49}{y^2 - 3y - 28} \cdot \frac{3y + 12}{y^2 + 5y - 14} \quad [4]$$

PART III

Answer one question from this part. Clearly indicate the necessary steps, including appropriate formula substitutions, diagrams, graphs, charts, etc. Calculations that may be obtained by mental arithmetic or the calculator do not need to be shown.   [10]

41 Given: If I get a summer job, then I will earn
                  money.
              If I fail mathematics, then I will not earn
                  money.
              I get a summer job or I am not happy.
              I am happy or I am not successful.
              I am successful.

   Let J represent: "I get a summer job."
   Let E represent: "I will earn money."
   Let F represent: "I fail mathematics."
   Let H represent: "I am happy."
   Let S represent: "I am successful."

   Prove: I did not fail mathematics.   [10]

42 Quadrilateral $ABCD$ has vertices $A(-3,6)$, $B(6,0)$,
   $C(9,-9)$, and $D(0,-3)$. Prove that $ABCD$ is

   a a parallelogram   [8]
   b *not* a rhombus   [2]

Answers
January 1998
Sequential Math Course II

Answer Key

PART I

1. 5	**11.** (1,3)	**21.** (2)	**31.** (3)
2. 4.8	**12.** 2	**22.** (3)	**32.** (2)
3. 14	**13.** 6	**23.** (1)	**33.** (4)
4. $2(x + 3)(x - 3)$	**14.** −1.5	**24.** (1)	**34.** (1)
5. 21	**15.** (1)	**25.** (4)	**35.** construction
6. $\overline{MC}$	**16.** (3)	**26.** (4)	
7. 110	**17.** (3)	**27.** (3)	
8. 2	**18.** (2)	**28.** (1)	
9. $5\sqrt{2}$	**19.** (4)	**29.** (4)	
10. III	**20.** (2)	**30.** (2)	

PARTS II AND III See answers explained section.

Answers Explained

PART I

1. A binary operation works with two numbers of a set at a time. It is given that the binary operation $\circ$ is defined as $a \circ b = \dfrac{2a+b}{b}$. To evaluate $6 \circ 3$, replace a with 6 and b with 3.

The given formula is:

$$a \circ b = \frac{2a+b}{b}$$

Let $a = 6$ and $b = 3$:

$$6 \circ 3 = \frac{2(6)+3}{3}$$

Simplify:

$$= \frac{12+3}{3}$$
$$= \frac{15}{3}$$
$$= 5$$

The value of $6 \circ 3$ is **5**.

2.

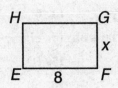

The lengths of corresponding sides of similar polygons are in proportion. Since it is given that, in the accompanying diagram, rectangle $ABCD$ is similar to rectangle $EFGH$, the ratio of the width to the length of each rectangle must be the same. Thus:

$$\frac{\text{width}}{\text{length}} = \frac{AD}{AB} = \frac{GF}{EF}$$

In a proportion, the product of the means is equal to the product of the extremes (cross-multiply):

$$\frac{3}{5} = \frac{x}{8}$$
$$5x = 24$$
$$x = \frac{24}{5}$$
$$= 4.8$$

The value of x is **4.8**.

3. It is given that, in the accompanying diagram, $\overleftrightarrow{ALB} \parallel \overleftrightarrow{CJD}$. If two lines are parallel, interior angles on the same side of the transversal are supplementary, so their degree measures add up to 180. It is also given that $m\angle JLB = 6x - 7$ and $m\angle LJD = 7x + 5$. Thus:

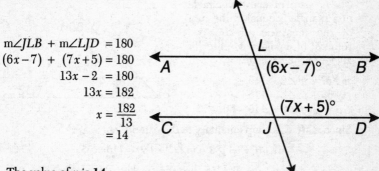

$$m\angle JLB + m\angle LJD = 180$$
$$(6x - 7) + (7x + 5) = 180$$
$$13x - 2 = 180$$
$$13x = 182$$
$$x = \frac{182}{13}$$
$$= 14$$

The value of x is **14**.

4. The given binomial expression is: $2x^2 - 18$

First factor out 2, the greatest common monomial factor of each term of the binomial: $2(x^2 - 9)$

Since $x^2 - 9$ is the difference of two squares, it can be factored as the sum and difference of the same two terms: $2(x + 3)(x - 3)$

Factored completely, the given expression is $2(x + 3)(x - 3)$.

5. It is given that, in the accompanying diagram, $m\angle ECB = 6x$, $m\angle ECD = 3x - 11$, and $m\angle DCB = 74$. Since $\angle ECB$ is comprised of angles ECD and DCB:

$$m\angle ECD + m\angle DCB = m\angle ECB$$
$$(3x - 11) + 74 = 6x$$
$$3x + 63 = 6x$$
$$63 = 3x$$
$$\frac{63}{3} = x$$
$$21 = x$$

The value of x is **21**.

6. The shortest side of a triangle lies opposite the angle of the triangle having the smallest degree measure. It is given that $m\angle M = 60$ and the degree measure of an exterior angle at C is 115, as shown in the accompanying diagram.

To find the shortest side of $\triangle MEC$, first find the degree measures of $\angle E$ and $\angle MCE$.

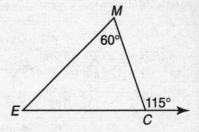

- The measure of an exterior angle of a triangle is equal to the sum of the measures of the two remote (nonadjacent) interior angles of the triangle:

$$m\angle M + m\angle E = 115$$
$$60 + m\angle E = 115$$
$$m\angle E = 115 - 60 = 55$$

- Since $\angle MCE$ is supplementary to the exterior angle at C:

$$m\angle MCE = 180 - m\angle C = 180 - 115 = 65$$

- Angle E, which measures 55, has the smallest degree measure. Therefore, since MC lies opposite $\angle E$, it is the shortest side of $\triangle MEC$.

The *shortest* side of $\triangle MEC$ is $\overline{MC}$.

7. It is given that, in the accompanying diagram, $ABCD$ is a rhombus and $m\angle CAB = 35$. Each diagonal of a rhombus bisects opposite pairs of angles. Hence, $m\angle CAD = m\angle CAB = 35$, so $m\angle DAB$ = 35 + 35 = 70. Since consecutive angles of a rhombus are supplementary, their degree measures add up to 180:

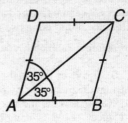

$$m\angle CDA + m\angle DAB = 180$$
$$m\angle CDA + \quad 70 \quad = 180$$
$$m\angle CDA = 180 - 70 = 110$$

Thus, $m\angle CDA = \mathbf{110}$.

8. The given equation is:

In a proportion, the product of the means is equal to the product of the extremes (cross-multiply):

$$\frac{1}{x-1} = \frac{x+2}{4}, \quad x \neq 1$$

$$(x-1)(x+2) = 4$$

Multiply the two binomials together using FOIL:

$$\overset{\text{First}}{\overbrace{x \cdot x}} + \left(\overset{\text{Outer}}{\overbrace{2x}} + \overset{\text{Inner}}{\overbrace{-1x}} \right) + \overset{\text{Last}}{\overbrace{(-1)(2)}} = 4$$

$$x^2 + \quad x \quad - \quad 2 \quad = 4$$

On each side of the quadratic equation subtract 4 so all of the nonzero terms appear on the left side of the equation:

$$x^2 + x - 6 = 0$$

Factor the left side of the equation as the product of two binomials that have the form $(x + ?)(x + ?)$. The missing numbers are the two factors of –6 that add up to +1, the coefficient of x. The correct factors of –6 are –2 and +3:

$$(x - 2)(x + 3) = 0$$

Set each binomial factor equal to 0 and then solve the resulting equations:

$$x - 2 = 0 \quad \text{or} \quad x + 3 = 0$$
$$x = 2 \quad \text{or} \quad x = -3$$

The positive root of the given equation is **2**.

9. The diagonal of a square forms the hypotenuse of a right triangle in which the two legs have the same length.

Let x represent the length of a diagonal of a square in which the length of each side is 5, as given. Apply the Pythagorean theorem:

$$x^2 = 5^2 + 5^2$$
$$= 25 + 25$$
$$= 50$$
$$x = \sqrt{50} = \sqrt{25} \cdot \sqrt{2} = 5\sqrt{2}$$

In simplest radical form, the length of the diagonal of the square is $5\sqrt{2}$.

10. Use the given translation rule, $(x, y) \rightarrow (x - 6, y + 3)$, to obtain the image of $(4, -7)$, which is $(4 - 6, -7 + 3)$ or $(-2, -4)$. This point lies in Quadrant III. After the given translation, the image of $(4, -7)$ lies in Quadrant **III**.

11. The center of a circle is the midpoint of any diameter of that circle. The midpoint $(\bar{x}, \bar{y})$ of the segment whose endpoints are $A(x_A, y_A)$ and $B(x_B, y_B)$ can be determined by using the formulas

$$\bar{x} = \frac{x_A + x_B}{2} \quad \text{and} \quad \bar{y} = \frac{y_A + y_B}{2}$$

To find the coordinates of the center of a circle in which the endpoints of a diameter are $A(5, 2)$ and $B(-3, 4)$, use the midpoint formulas with $A(x_A, y_A) = A(5, 2)$ and $B(x_B, y_B) = B(-3, 4)$:

$$\bar{x} = \frac{x_A + x_B}{2} = \frac{5 + (-3)}{2} \quad \text{and} \quad \bar{y} = \frac{y_A + y_B}{2} = \frac{2 + 4}{2}$$

$$= \frac{2}{2} \qquad\qquad\qquad = \frac{6}{2}$$

$$= 1 \qquad\qquad\qquad\quad = 3$$

Hence, $(\overline{x}, \overline{y}) = (1, 3)$.

The coordinates of the center of the circle are **(1,3)**.

12. The given equation is: $\dfrac{2}{x} + \dfrac{4}{3} = \dfrac{14}{3x}$

Eliminate the fractions by multiplying each term of the given equation by
$3x$, the lowest multiple of all of the
denominators:

$$3x\left(\dfrac{2}{x}\right) + 3x\left(\dfrac{4}{3}\right) = 3x\left(\dfrac{14}{3x}\right)$$

$$3(2) + x(4) = 1(14)$$
$$6 + 4x = 14$$
$$4x = 8$$
$$x = \dfrac{8}{4} = 2$$

The value of x is **2**.

13.

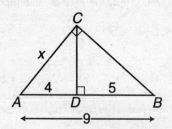

It is given that, in the accompanying diagram, altitude $\overline{CD}$ is drawn to
hypotenuse $\overline{AB}$ of right triangle ABC with $AD = 4$ and $DB = 5$. When an altitude is drawn to the hypotenuse of a right triangle, the length of either leg is
the mean proportional between the length of the segment of the hypotenuse
adjacent to the leg and the length of the entire hypotenuse. Thus:

$$\dfrac{AD}{AC} = \dfrac{AC}{AB}$$
$$\dfrac{4}{x} = \dfrac{x}{4+5}$$
$$\dfrac{4}{x} = \dfrac{x}{9}$$
$$x^2 = 36$$
$$x = \sqrt{36} = 6$$

Hence, $AC = $ **6**.

14. The slope, m, of a nonvertical line that passes through points $A(x_A, y_A)$ and $B(x_B, y_B)$ is given by the formula

$$m = \frac{y_B - y_A}{x_B - x_A}$$

To find the slope of a line that passes through points $(-6,8)$ and $(2,-4)$, use the slope formula with $A(x_A, y_A) = (-6,8)$ and $B(x_B, y_B) = (2,-4)$:

$$m = \frac{-4 - 8}{2 - (-6)} = \frac{-12}{2 + 6} = \frac{-12}{8} = -1.5$$

The slope of the line is **–1.5**.

15. It is given that the conditional statements $s \to t$ and $t \to u$ are true.

- According to the Chain Rule, if the statements $s \to t$ and $t \to u$ are both true, the statement $s \to u$ is also true.
- According to the Law of Contrapositive Inference, negating and interchanging the parts of the true conditional $s \to u$ produces the true conditional $\sim u \to \sim s$.

Hence, $\sim u \to \sim s$ represents a logically valid conclusion.
The correct choice is **(1)**.

16. Under a reflection in the x-axis, the image of (x, y) is $(x, -y)$ since the image lies on the opposite side of the x-axis and the same distance from it. Hence, under a reflection in the x-axis the image of $(-4,-5)$ is $(-4 -(-5))$ or $(-4,5)$, as shown in the accompanying diagram.
The correct choice is **(3)**.

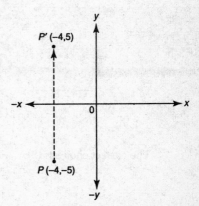

17.

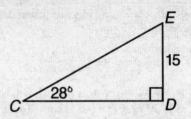

In a right triangle, the tangent of an acute angle is equal to the ratio of the length of the leg opposite that angle to the length of the leg adjacent to the angle. In the accompanying diagram of $\triangle CDE$, m$\angle D = 90$, m$\angle C = 28$, and $ED = 15$. Since 15 is the length of the leg opposite $\angle C$ and CD is the length of the side adjacent to $\angle C$, use the tangent ratio to find CD:

$$\tan C = \frac{ED}{CD}$$
$$\tan 28° = \frac{15}{CD}$$

The correct choice is **(3)**.

18. The given expression is:

$$\frac{12!}{8!\,4!}$$

$$\frac{12 \cdot 11 \cdot 10 \cdot 9 \cdot \cancel{8!}^{\,1}}{\cancel{8!}_{\,1}\, 4!}$$

$$\frac{\cancel{12}\cdot 11 \cdot \cancel{10}^{\,5} \cdot 9}{4 \cdot \cancel{3} \cdot \cancel{2} \cdot 1}$$

$$\frac{11 \cdot 5 \cdot 9}{1}$$

$$495$$

The correct choice is **(2)**.

19. The set of points that are the same distance d from a given line must lie on another line that is parallel to the given line and d units from the line. Since these points may be located on either side of the given line, the locus of points at a given distance from a line consists of *two* parallel lines, as illustrated in the accompanying diagram.

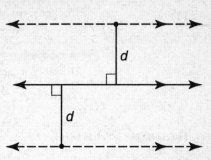

The correct choice is (**4**).

20. If an equation of a line has the form $y = mx + b$, its slope is m and its y-intercept is b.

For the given equation $y = -2x - 5$, $m = -2$ and $b = -5$. Hence, the slope of the given line is -2 and its y-intercept is -5. Consider each choice in turn.

- Choice (1): Since the slope of the given line is -2, choice (1) is true.
- Choice (2): Two lines are parallel if they have the same slope. For the line whose equation is $y = 2x + 5$, $m = 2$ so the slope of this line is 2. Since the lines $y = -2x - 5$ and $y = 2x + 5$ do *not* have the same slope, they are *not* parallel. Hence, choice (2) is *false*.
- Choice (3): Since the y-intercept of the original line is -5, choice (3) is true.
- Choice (4): Two lines are perpendicular if the product of their slopes is -1. Since the slope of the line whose equation is $y = \frac{1}{2}x - 5$ is $\frac{1}{2}$ and $\left(\frac{1}{2}\right) \times (-2) = -1$, the line whose equation is $y = \frac{1}{2}x - 5$ is perpendicular to the line whose equation is $y = -2x - 5$. Hence, choice (4) is true.

Thus, only choice (2) is *false*.
The correct choice is (**2**).

21. The word "MUUMUU" contains six letters, including two identical letters (M) and four other identical letters (U). The number of different permutations of a set of n objects when a objects of the set are identical and b objects of the set are identical is given by the formula $\dfrac{n!}{a!\,b!}$.

To find the total number of different six-letter permutations that can be formed from the letters in the word "MUUMUU," use the formula $\dfrac{n!}{a!\,b!}$, where $n = 6$, $a = 2$, and $b = 4$: $\dfrac{n!}{a!\,b!}$

Since $n = 6$, $a = 2$, and $b = 4$: $\dfrac{6!}{2!\,4!}$

$$\frac{\overset{1}{6 \cdot 5 \cdot \cancel{4!}}}{2! \, \cancel{4!}}$$

$$\frac{\overset{3}{\cancel{6} \cdot 5}}{\cancel{2} \cdot 1}$$

$$3 \cdot 5$$

$$15$$

The correct choice is **(2)**.

22.

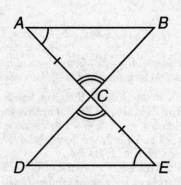

It is given that, in the accompanying diagram, $\angle A \cong \angle E$ and C is the midpoint of $\overline{AE}$. Since a midpoint divides a segment into two congruent segments, $\overline{AC} \cong \overline{EC}$. Vertical angles are congruent, so $\angle ACB \cong \angle ECD$. Thus:

- $\angle A \cong \angle E$ (Angle $\cong$ Angle)
- $\overline{AC} \cong \overline{EC}$ (Side $\cong$ Side)
- $\angle ACB \cong \angle ECD$ (Angle $\cong$ Angle)

Since triangles ABC and EDC agree in two angles and their included side, $\triangle ABC \cong \triangle EDC$ as a result of ASA $\cong$ ASA.
The correct choice is **(3)**.

23. The expression to be evaluated in the system defined by the accompanying table is $(P \blacksquare S) \blacksquare (L \blacksquare U)$.

- Evaluate $(P \blacksquare S)$ by finding the table element at which the horizontal row labeled P intersects the vertical column labeled S. Since this row and column intersect at L, $(P \blacksquare S) = L$.

$\blacksquare$	P	L	U	S
P	U	S	P	L
L	S	P	L	U
U	P	L	U	S
S	L	U	S	P

- Evaluate $(L \blacksquare U)$ by finding the table element at which the horizontal row labeled L intersects the vertical column labeled U. Since this row and column intersect at L, $(L \blacksquare U) = L$.
- Thus, $(P \blacksquare S) \blacksquare (L \blacksquare U) = L \blacksquare L$. Then, since the horizontal row labeled L intersects the vertical column labeled L at P:

$$(P \blacksquare S) \blacksquare (L \blacksquare U) = P$$

The correct choice is **(1)**.

24. It is given that, in right triangle ABC, $\angle C$ is the right angle, the coordinates of A are $(-1,1)$, and the coordinates of B are $(4,-2)$.

Since $\angle C$ is the right angle, $\overline{AB}$ is the hypotenuse. Draw $\overline{AB}$ on the coordinate plane, as shown in the accompanying diagram.

Complete the right triangle by drawing vertical and horizontal segments through points A and B. Although the coordinates of C may be at either $(-1,-2)$ or $(4,1)$, point $(4,1)$ is not included among the answer choices.

The correct choice is **(1)**.

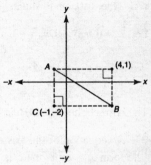

25.

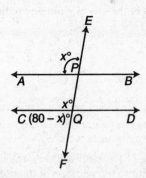

It is given that, in the accompanying diagram, $\overleftrightarrow{AB}$ and $\overleftrightarrow{CD}$ are parallel lines. Since the four answer choices ask that a conclusion be drawn about how the measures of angles APE and CQF compare, let $m\angle APE = x$ and represent $m\angle CQF$ in terms of x.

- Since corresponding angles formed by parallel lines have equal measures, $m\angle CQE = m\angle APE = x$.
- Angles CQE and CQF are supplementary, so $m\angle CQF = 180 - x$.
- Since $m\angle APE = x$ and $m\angle CQF = 180 - x$, $m\angle APE + m\angle CQE = 180$.

The correct choice is **(4)**.

26. In general, distance d between points (x_A, y_A) and (x_B, y_B) is given by the formula

$$d = \sqrt{(x_B - x_A)^2 + (y_B - y_A)^2}$$

To find the distance between the given points, $(6, -9)$ and $(-3, 4)$, use the distance formula with $(x_A, y_A) = (6, -9)$ and $(x_B, y_B) = (-3, 4)$.

Write the distance formula: $\qquad d = \sqrt{(x_B - x_A)^2 + (y_B - y_A)^2}$

Let $x_A = 6, y_A = -9, x_B = -3$, and $y_B = 4$: $\quad = \sqrt{(-3 - 6)^2 + (4 - (-9))^2}$

$$= \sqrt{(-9)^2 + (4 + 9)^2}$$
$$= \sqrt{81 + 169}$$
$$= \sqrt{250}$$

The correct choice is **(4)**.

27. An equation of the axis of symmetry for the parabola whose equation has the form $y = ax^2 + bx + c$ is $x = -\dfrac{b}{2a}$.

To find an equation of the axis of symmetry of the graph of $y = x^2 - 6x + 5$, let $a = 1$ and $b = -6$. Thus:

$$x = -\frac{(-6)}{2(1)} = \frac{6}{2} = 3$$

The correct choice is **(3)**.

28. It is given that $\sim(n \wedge \sim c)$ and n are true statements. To draw a logical conclusion, first remove the parentheses in the statement $\sim(n \wedge \sim c)$ and then decide which of the two disjuncts is true.

- According to one of De Morgan's laws, the negation of a conjunction is logically equivalent to the negation of the disjunction of each part of the conjunction. Thus:

$$\sim(n \wedge \sim c) \leftrightarrow \sim n \vee c$$

- Therefore, $\sim n \vee c$ and n are true statements. If a disjunction is true, then at least one of the disjuncts must also be true. Since $\sim n$ is a false statement, the other disjunct, c, must be a logical conclusion.

The correct choice is **(1)**.

29. The measure of each side of a triangle must be less than the sum of the measures of the other two sides. To determine which set of numbers in the four answer choices can represent the measures of the sides of a triangle, find the set of numbers that has the property that each number in the set is less than the sum of the other two numbers. Consider each choice in turn.

- Choice (1): Since 20 is not less than 10 + 10, {10, 10, 20} *cannot* represent the measures of the three sides of a triangle.
- Choice (2): Since 12 is not less than 4 + 6, {4,6,12} *cannot* represent the measures of the three sides of a triangle.
- Choice (3): Since 6 is not less than 2 + 4, {2,4,6} *cannot* represent the measures of the three sides of a triangle.
- Choice (4): Since 8 < 10 +12, 10 < 8 + 12, and 12 < 8 + 10, {8,10,12} can represent the measures of the three sides of a triangle.

The correct choice is (**4**).

30.

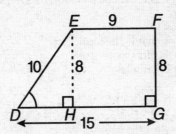

It is given that, in the accompanying diagram, altitude $\overline{EH}$ is drawn in trapezoid $DEFG$, $DE = 10$, $EF = 9$, $FG = 8$, and $GD = 15$.

Since the bases of a trapezoid are parallel, they are everywhere equidistant. Hence, $EH = FG = 8$. In right triangle DHE:

$$\sin D = \frac{\text{length of leg opposite } \angle D}{\text{length of hypotenuse}}$$

$$= \frac{EH}{ED}$$

$$= \frac{8}{10}$$

$$= 0.8$$

Use a scientific calculator to find that the angle whose sine has a value of 0.8 is, correct to the *nearest degree*, 53.

The correct choice is (**2**).

31. A set of numbers is closed under a subtraction if the result of taking the difference between any two numbers of the set is also a member of that set. Consider each choice in turn.

- Choice (1): Since $7 - 5 = 2$ and 2 is not an odd number, the set of odd numbers is *not* closed under subtraction.
- Choice (2): Since $1 - 3 = -2$ and -2 is not a counting number, the set of counting numbers is *not* closed under subtraction.
- Choice (3): Since the difference between any two integers is always another integer, the set of integers is closed under subtraction.
- Choice (4): Since $7 - 3 = 4$ and 4 is not a prime number, the set of prime numbers is *not* closed under subtraction.

The correct choice is **(3)**.

32. The given equation, $x^2 - 2x - 1 = 0$, is a quadratic equation. Since the four answer choices include irrational numbers, solve the equation by using the quadratic formula.

The given equation is:

$$x^2 - 2x - 1 = 0$$

If a quadratic equation is in the form $ax^2 + bx + c = 0 \ (a \neq 0)$, its roots are given by the quadratic formula:

$$x = \frac{-b \pm \sqrt{b^2 - 4ac}}{2a}$$

Let $a = 1$, $b = -2$, and $c = -1$:

$$= \frac{-(-2) \pm \sqrt{(-2)^2 - 4(1)(-1)}}{2(1)}$$

$$= \frac{2 \pm \sqrt{4 + 4}}{2}$$

$$= \frac{2 \pm \sqrt{8}}{2}$$

$$= \frac{2 \pm \sqrt{4} \cdot \sqrt{2}}{2}$$

$$= \frac{2 \pm 2 \cdot \sqrt{2}}{2}$$

$$= \frac{2\left(1 \pm \sqrt{2}\right)}{2}$$

$$= 1 \pm \sqrt{2}$$

The correct choice is **(2)**.

33. A dilation with respect to the origin is a transformation in which each of the coordinates of a point (x, y) is multiplied by the same nonzero quantity, called the *scale factor*.

Hence, under a dilation having a scale factor of 3 with respect to the origin, the coordinates of the image of point (–1,2) are (3(–1),3(2)) or (–3,6).

The correct choice is (**4**).

34. Since a regular polygon is equiangular, each exterior angle has the same degree measure.

An n-sided regular polygon has n exterior angles, provided that one is drawn at each vertex. The sum of the measures of the exterior angles of any polygon is 360, so the measure of an exterior angle of an n-sided regular polygon is $\frac{360}{n}$.

Since a regular pentagon has five sides, the degree measure of each exterior angle of a regular pentagon is $\frac{360}{5}$ or 72.

The correct choice is (**1**).

35.

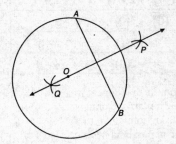

To construct the perpendicular bisector of chord $\overline{AB}$, follow the steps below, which are illustrated in the accompanying diagram.

STEP 1: With the point of the compass at A, set the radius length of the compass equal to more than one-half of the length of $\overline{AB}$.

STEP 2: With center A and the same compass setting, draw a pair of arcs on either side of $\overline{AB}$.

STEP 3: With center B and the same compass setting, draw a second pair of arcs on either side of $\overline{AB}$. Label the points at which the pairs of arcs intersect as P and Q.

STEP 4: Draw $\overline{PQ}$.

The arcs were constructed in such a way that, if points $A,P,B,$ and Q are connected, the figure that results is a rhombus in which $\overline{AB}$ and $\overline{PQ}$ are diagonals. Since the diagonals of a rhombus intersect at right angles and bisect each other, $\overline{PQ}$ is the perpendicular bisector of $\overline{AB}$.

PART II

36. a. To draw the graph of the equation $y = x^2 + 2x - 3$ for all values of x in the interval $-4 \leq x \leq 2$, first prepare a table of values for x and y. Substitute each integer value of x from -4 to 2 into the equation to obtain the corresponding value of y.

x	$x^2 + 2x - 3$	$= y$	(x,y)
-4	$(-4)^2 + 2(-4) - 3 = 16 - 8 - 3$	$= 5$	$(-4,5)$
-3	$(-3)^2 + 2(-3) - 3 = 9 - 6 - 3$	$= 0$	$(-3,0)$
-2	$(-2)^2 + 2(-2) - 3 = 4 - 4 - 3$	$= -3$	$(-2,-3)$
-1	$(-1)^2 + 2(-1) - 3 = 1 - 2 - 3$	$= -4$	$(-1,-4)$
0	$(0)^2 + 2(0) - 3 = 0 - 3$	$= -3$	$(0,-3)$
1	$1^2 + 2(1) - 3 = 1 + 2 - 3$	$= 0$	$(1,0)$
2	$2^2 + 2(2) - 3 = 4 + 4 - 3$	$= 5$	$(2,5)$

Now plot the points that appear in the last column of the table. Connect these points with a smooth curve that has the shape of a parabola whose turning point, $(-1,-4)$, is the lowest point on the curve.

Label this graph with its equation, $y = x^2 + 2x - 3$, as shown in the accompanying figure.

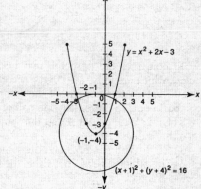

b. The graph of an equation that has the form $(x-h)^2 + (y-k)^2 = r^2$ is a circle whose center is located at (h,k) and whose radius length is r. The given equation, $(x+1)^2 + (y+4)^2 = 16$, has the form $(x-h)^2 + (y-k)^2 = r^2$ with $h = -1$, $k = -4$, and $r = 4$. Hence, the graph of the given equation is a circle with its center at $(-1,-4)$ and a radius length of 4. To draw the graph of $(x+1)^2 + (y+4)^2 = 16$:

- Adjust your compass for a radius length of 4 units by placing the compass point at the origin and measuring an arc that extends 4 units along the x-axis.
- Keeping the radius length of the compass fixed, place the compass point at $(-1,-4)$, the center of the circle, and draw the required circle.

Label the circle with its equation, $(x+1)^2 + (y+4)^2 = 16$, as shown in the accompanying figure.

c. The number of points that the graphs drawn in parts **a** and **b** have in common is **2**.

37. The given system of equations is:
$$y = x^2 + 2x - 4$$
$$y - 5 = 2x$$

Solve the first-degree equation for y by adding 5 on each side of the equation:

$$y = 2x + 5$$

Substitute $2x + 5$ for y in the first equation, thereby obtaining a quadratic equation only in x:

$$2x + 5 = x^2 + 2x - 4$$

Rearrange the terms of the quadratic equation so all of the nonzero terms appear on the same side:

$$0 = x^2 - 9$$

Since the binomial on the right side of the equation represents the difference of two perfect squares, it can be factored as the sum and difference of the same two terms:

$$0 = (x - 3)(x + 3)$$

If the product of two factors is 0, then either factor may equal 0:

$$x - 3 = 0 \text{ or } x + 3 = 0$$
$$x = 3 \text{ or } \quad x = -3$$

To find the corresponding values of y, substitute each of the solutions for x in the original first-degree equation:

$\underline{\text{Let } x = 3}$	$\underline{\text{Let } x = -3}$
$y - 5 = 2x$	$y - 5 = 2x$
$= 2(3)$	$= 2(-3)$
$= 6$	$= -6$
$y = 11$	$y = -1$

<u>CHECK:</u> Substitute each pair of values of x and y in *both* of the *original* equations to verify that both equations are satisfied.

	$\underline{y = x^2 + 2x - 4}$	$\underline{y - 5 = 2x}$
Let $x = 3$ and $y = 11$:	$11 \overset{?}{=} 3^2 + 2(3) - 4$	$11 - 5 \overset{?}{=} 2(3)$
	$11 \overset{?}{=} 9 + 6 - 4$	$6 \overset{\checkmark}{=} 6$
	$11 \overset{\checkmark}{=} 11$	

Let $x = -3$ and $y = -1$

$$-1 \overset{?}{=} (-3)^2 + 2(-3) - 4 \qquad \Big| \qquad -1 - 5 \overset{?}{=} 2(-3)$$

$$-1 \overset{?}{=} 9 - 6 - 4 \qquad\qquad\qquad 6 \overset{\checkmark}{=} 6$$

$$-1 \overset{\checkmark}{=} -1$$

The solutions are **(3,11)** and **(-3,-1)**.

38. It is given that 5 students will be selected from a group of 9 students to represent their school at a conference. The 9 students nominated by the principal include 4 students graduating in 1998, 2 in 1999, 2 in 2000, and 1 in 2001.

a. Without regard to order, r objects can be selected from a group of n objects in $_nC_r$ ways, where $_nC_r$ can be evaluated by using a scientific calculator or the formula

$$_nC_r = \frac{n!}{r!(n-r)!}$$

The number of 5-student groups that can be formed from the 9 students can be represented by $_9C_5$. Use a scientific calculator to determine that $_9C_5 = 126$.

The number of 5-student groups that can be formed from the 9 students is **126**.

b. Since 4 students will graduate in 1998 and 2 students will graduate in 1999, 4 + 2 or 6 students will graduate *before* 2000. The probability that all of the 5 students selected will graduate before 2000 is obtained by writing a fraction whose numerator is the number of ways in which 5 students can be selected from the set of 6 student nominees who will graduate before 2000 and whose denominator is the number of ways in which 5 students can be selected from the original group of 9 students.

- Five students can be selected from the set of 6 students who will graduate before 2000 in $_6C_5 = 6$ ways.
- From part **a**, 5 students can be selected from the original group of 9 students in $_9C_5 = 126$ ways.
- Probability $= \dfrac{_6C_5}{_9C_5} = \dfrac{6}{126}$.

The probability that all of the 5 students selected will graduate before 2000 is $\dfrac{6}{126}$.

c. The question asks for the probability that of the 5 students selected 2 will graduate in 1998, 1 in 1999, 1 in 2000, and 1 in 2001. To find this probability, multiply the number of ways in which students in each graduation category can be selected and then divide the product by 126, the total number of ways in which 5-student groups can be selected from the original 9 students, as determined in part **a**.

- Two students can be selected from the 4 students who will graduate in 1998 in $_4C_2$ ways, 1 student can be selected from the 2 students who will graduate in 1999 in $_2C_1$ ways, 1 student can be selected from the 2 students who will graduate in 2000 in $_2C_1$ ways, and 1 student can be selected from the 1 student who will graduate in 2001 in 1 way. Thus:

$$\text{Probability} = \frac{_4C_2 \cdot {_2C_1} \cdot {_2C_1} \cdot 1}{_9C_5}$$

Use a scientific calculator to find that $_4C_2 = 6$, and $_2C_1 = 2$. Thus:

$$\text{Probability} = \frac{6 \cdot 2 \cdot 2 \cdot 1}{126}$$

$$= \frac{24}{126}$$

The probability that of the 5 students selected 2 will graduate in 1998, 1 in 1999, 1 in 2000, and 1 in 2001 is $\frac{24}{126}$.

d. Since the set of 9 student nominees includes only 3 students who will graduate after 1999, it is impossible that all of the 5 students selected will graduate after 1999.

Since the probability of an impossibility is 0, the probability that all of the 5 students selected will graduate after 1999 is **0**.

39.

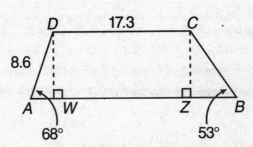

It is given that, in the accompanying diagram, $ABCD$ is a trapezoid with altitudes $\overline{DW}$ and $\overline{CZ}$ drawn, $CD = 17.3$, $DA = 8.6$, m$\angle A = 68$, and m$\angle B = 53$.

The perimeter of trapezoid $ABCD$ is obtained by adding the lengths of its four sides.

- Working in right triangle DWA, find the lengths of $\overline{AW}$ and $\overline{DW}$.

<u>To find *AW*, use the cosine ratio:</u>

$$\cos A = \frac{\text{length of leg adjacent to } \angle A}{\text{length of hypotenuse}}$$

$$\cos 68° = \frac{AW}{8.6}$$

$$0.3746 = \frac{AW}{8.6}$$

$$AW = 0.3476 \times 8.6 = 3.22$$

<u>To find *DW*, use the sine ratio:</u>

$$\sin A = \frac{\text{length of leg opposite } \angle A}{\text{length of hypotenuse}}$$

$$\sin 68° = \frac{DW}{8.6}$$

$$0.9272 = \frac{DW}{8.6}$$

$$DW = 0.9272 \times 8.6 = 7.97$$

- Working in right triangle *CZB*, find the lengths of $\overline{BZ}$ and $\overline{BC}$. Since the bases of a trapezoid are parallel, bases $\overline{CD}$ and $\overline{AB}$ are everywhere the same distance apart. Hence, $CZ = DW = 7.97$.

<u>To find *BZ*, use the tangent ratio:</u>

$$\tan B = \frac{\text{length of leg opposite } \angle B}{\text{length of adjacent to } \angle B}$$

$$\tan 53° = \frac{CZ}{BZ}$$

$$1.3270 = \frac{7.97}{BZ}$$

$$BZ = \frac{7.97}{1.3270} = 6.01$$

<u>To find *BC*, use the sine ratio:</u>

$$\sin B = \frac{\text{length of leg opposite } \angle B}{\text{length of hypotenuse}}$$

$$\sin 53° = \frac{CZ}{BC}$$

$$0.7986 = \frac{7.97}{BC}$$

$$BC = \frac{7.97}{0.7986} = 9.98$$

- Find the length of $\overline{AB}$ by adding the lengths of the segments that comprise it. Since *DWZC* is a rectangle, $WZ = CD = 17.3$. Thus:

$$AB = AW + WZ + BZ = 3.22 + 17.3 + 6.01 = 26.53$$

- Add the lengths of the four sides of trapezoid *ABCD* to find the perimeter.

$$\text{Perimeter of trapezoid } ABCD = AD + CD + BC + AB$$
$$= 8.6 + 17.3 + 9.98 + 26.53$$
$$= 62.41$$

The perimeter of trapezoid *ABCD*, correct to the *nearest tenth*, is **62.4**.

40. a.

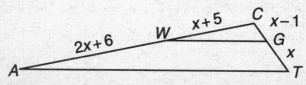

It is given that, in the accompanying diagram of $\triangle CAT$, *W* is a point on $\overline{AC}$ and *G* is a point on $\overline{TC}$ such that $\overline{WG}$ is parallel to $\overline{AT}$. If a line intersecting two sides of a triangle is parallel to the remaining side of a triangle, it

divides the two sides proportion-
ately. Then, since $\overline{WG}$ is parallel to
$\overline{AT}$, the line divides $\overline{CA}$ and $\overline{CT}$
proportionately:

$$\frac{CW}{WA} = \frac{GC}{TG}$$

$$\frac{x+5}{2x+6} = \frac{x-1}{x}$$

In a proportion, the product of
the means equals the product of
the extremes (cross-multiply):

$$(2x+6)(x-1) = x(x+5)$$

Remove the parentheses on the
right side of the equation by multiplying each term inside the parentheses by x:

$$(2x+6)(x-1) = x^2 + 5x$$

Multiply the two binomials
together using FOIL:

$$2x \cdot x + 2x(-1) + 6 \cdot x + 6(-1) = x^2 + 5x$$
$$2x^2 - 2x + 6x - 6 = x^2 + 5x$$
$$2x^2 + 4x - 6 = x^2 + 5x$$

Collect all the nonzero terms
on the left side of the equation,
leaving 0 on the right side:

$$x^2 - x - 6 = 0$$

Factor the left side of the equation as the product of two binomials that have the form $(x + ?)(x + ?)$.
The missing numbers are the two
factors of –6 that add up to –1, the
coefficient of x. The correct factors of –6 are –3 and +2:

$$(x-3)(x+2) = 0$$

Set each binomial factor equal
to 0 and then solve the resulting
equations:

$$x - 3 = 0 \text{ or } x + 2 = 0$$
$$x = 3 \text{ or } x \quad = -2$$

Since x must be positive, reject
the solution $x = -2$. Hence, $x = TG$
= 3.

The length of $\overline{TG}$ is **3**.

b. The given product is:

$$\frac{y^2 - 49}{y^2 - 3y - 28} \cdot \frac{3y+12}{y^2 + 5y - 14}$$

Where possible, factor any
numerator and any denominator.
The first numerator is the difference of two squares, and the first
denominator is a quadratic trino-

mial that can be factored as the product of two binomials:

$$\frac{(y+7)(y-7)}{(y-7)(y+4)} \cdot \frac{3y+12}{y^2+5y-14}$$

The second numerator contains a common factor of 3, and the second denominator is a quadratic trinomial that can be factored as the product of two binomials:

$$\frac{(y+7)(y-7)}{(y-7)(y+4)} \cdot \frac{3(y+4)}{(y+7)(y-2)}$$

If the same factor appears in both a numerator and a denominator, divide both of them by that factor so their quotient is 1 (cancel out common factors):

Multiply together the remaining factors in the numerator, and multiply together the remaining factors in the denominator:

$$\frac{\overset{1}{\cancel{(y+7)}}\,\overset{1}{\cancel{(y-7)}}}{\cancel{(y-7)}\,(y+4)} \cdot \frac{3\,\overset{1}{\cancel{(y+4)}}}{\cancel{(y+7)}\,(y-2)}$$

The product in simplest form is $\frac{3}{y-2}$.

$$\frac{3}{y-2}$$

PART III

41. Given: If I get a summer job, then I will earn money.
   If I fail mathematics, then I will not earn money.
   I get a summer job or I am not happy.
   I am happy or I am not successful.
   I am successful.

Let J represent: "I get a summer job."
Let E represent: "I will earn money."
Let F represent: "I fail mathematics."
Let H represent: "I am happy."
Let S represent: "I am successful."

Prove: I did not fail mathematics.

• Write each statement in the Given in symbolic form:

"If I get a summer job, then I will earn money" is the conditional J implies E:

$$J \to E$$

"If I fail mathematics, then I will not earn money" is the conditional F implies the negation of E:

$$F \to {\sim} E$$

"I get a summer job or I am not happy" is the disjunction of J and the negation of H:

$$J \lor {\sim} H$$

"I am happy or I am not successful" is the disjunction of H and the negation of S:

$H \lor \sim S$

"I am successful" is statement S:

S

- Write the statement in the Prove in symbolic form:
"I did not fail mathematics" is the negation of F:

$\sim F$

- Write the formal proof.

PROOF

Statement	Reason
1. $H \lor \sim S$	1. Given.
2. S	2. Given.
3. H	3. Law of Disjunctive Inference (1,2)
4. $J \lor \sim H$	4. Given.
5. J	5. Law of Disjunctive Inference (3,4)
6. $J \rightarrow E$	6. Given.
7. E	7. Law of Detachment (5,6)
8. $F \rightarrow \sim E$	8. Given.
9. $\sim F$	9. *Modus Tollens* (7,8)

42. It is given that quadrilateral $ABCD$ has vertices $A(-3,6)$, $B(6,0)$, $C(9,-9)$, and $D(0,-3)$.

a. If the diagonals of a quadrilateral bisect each other, then the quadrilateral is a parallelogram. To prove that $ABCD$ is a parallelogram, show that the diagonals have the same midpoint and, as a result, bisect each other.

The midpoint $(\bar{x}, \bar{y})$ of a segment whose endpoints are $A(x_A, y_A)$ and $B(x_B, y_B)$ can be determined by using the formulas

$$\bar{x} = \frac{x_A + x_B}{2} \quad \text{and} \quad \bar{y} = \frac{y_A + y_B}{2}$$

- To find the midpoint of diagonal $\overline{AC}$, use the midpoint formulas with $(x_A, y_A) = A(-3, 6)$ and $(x_C, y_C) = C(9, -9)$:

$$\bar{x} = \frac{x_A + x_C}{2} = \frac{-3+9}{2} = \frac{6}{2} = 3 \quad \text{and} \quad \bar{y} = \frac{y_A + y_C}{2} = \frac{6+(-9)}{2} = -\frac{3}{2}$$

Hence, the midpoint of $\overline{AC}$ is $\left(3, -\frac{3}{2}\right)$.

- To find the midpoint of diagonal $\overline{BD}$, use the midpoint formulas with $(x_B, y_B) = B(6, 0)$, and $(x_D, y_D) = D(0, -3)$:

$$\bar{x} = \frac{x_B + x_D}{2} = \frac{6+0}{2} = 3 \quad \text{and} \quad \bar{y} = \frac{y_B + y_D}{2} = \frac{0+(-3)}{2} = -\frac{3}{2}$$

Hence, the midpoint of $\overline{BD}$ is $\left(3, -\dfrac{3}{2}\right)$.

Since diagonals $\overline{AC}$ and $\overline{BD}$ have the same midpoint, they bisect each other and, as a result, quadrilateral $ABCD$ is a parallelogram.

OTHER METHODS OF SOLUTION: To prove quadrilateral $ABCD$ is a parallelogram, you could do any one of the following:

1. Use the distance formula to show that both pairs of opposite sides have the same length and, as a result, the quadrilateral is a parallelogram.
2. Use the slope formula to show that both pairs of opposite sides have the same slope and, as a result, are parallel, so the quadrilateral is a parallelogram.
3. Use the distance and slope formulas to show that the same pair of sides have the same length and are parallel, so the quadrilateral is a parallelogram.

b. If the adjacent sides of a parallelogram have the same length, the parallelogram is a rhombus. To prove that quadrilateral $ABCD$ is *not* a rhombus, use the distance formula to show that a pair of adjacent sides do *not* have the same length.

In general, distance d between points (x_A, y_A) and (x_B, y_B) is given by the formula

$$d = \sqrt{(x_B - x_A)^2 + (y_B - y_A)^2}$$

- To find the length of side $\overline{AB}$ between the given points, use the distance formula with $(x_A, y_A) = (-3, 6)$ and $(x_B, y_B) = (6, 0)$.

Write the distance formula: $\qquad d = \sqrt{(x_B - x_A)^2 + (y_B - y_A)^2}$

Let $x_A = -3$, $y_A = 6$, $x_B = 6$,
and $y_B = 0$: $\qquad d_{\overline{AB}} = \sqrt{(6 - (-3))^2 + (0 - (-6))^2}$

$$= \sqrt{(6 + 3)^2 + (6)^2}$$
$$= \sqrt{81 + 36}$$
$$= \sqrt{117}$$

Hence, $AB = \sqrt{117}$.

- To find the length of side $\overline{AD}$, use the distance formula with $(x_A, y_A) = (-3, 6)$ and $(x_B, y_B) = (0, -3)$.

Write the distance formula: $\qquad d = \sqrt{(x_B - x_A)^2 + (y_B - y_A)^2}$

Let $x_A = -3, y_A = 6, x_B = 0,$
and $y_B = -3$:

$$d_{\overline{AD}} = \sqrt{(0-(-3))^2 + (-3-6)^2}$$
$$= \sqrt{(3)^2 + (-9)^2}$$
$$= \sqrt{9+81}$$
$$= \sqrt{90}$$

Hence, $AD = \sqrt{90}$.

Since $AD = \sqrt{90}$ and $AB = \sqrt{117}$, adjacent sides of parallelogram $ABCD$ are not equal and, as a result, quadrilateral $ABCD$ is a *not* a rhombus.

ANOTHER METHOD OF SOLUTION: Since the diagonals of a rhombus must be perpendicular to each other, you can prove that parallelogram $ABCD$ is *not* a rhombus by proving that its diagonals are *not* perpendicular to each other. To do this, use the slope formula and show that the product of the slopes of diagonals $\overline{AC}$ and $\overline{BD}$ is not -1 and, as a result, the diagonals are *not* perpendicular to each other.

Topic	Question Numbers	Number of Points	Your Points	Your Percentage
1. Properties of Number Systems; Def. of Operations	1, 31	2 + 2 = 4		
2. Finite Mathematical Systems	23	2		
3. Linear Function & Graph ($y = mx + b$, slope, eqs. of)	20	2		
4. Quadratic Equation (alg. sol.—factoring, formula)	32	2		
5. Parabola (incl. axis of symmetry, turning point)	27, 36a, 36c	2 + 6 + 1 = 9		
6. Systems of Equations (alg. and graphic solutions)	37	10		
7. Suppls., Compl., Vertical Angles, Angle Measure	5, 34	2 + 2 = 4		
8. Triangle Properties (eq., isos., sum ∠s, 2 sides)	29	2		
9. Line ‖ One Side of △; Line Joining Midpts. of 2 Sides	40a	6		
10. Inequalities in △s (ext. ∠, ≠ sides, opp. ∠s)	6	2		
11. Quadrilateral Properties (▱, sq., rhom., rect., trap.)	7, 9	2 + 2 = 4		
12. Parallel Lines	3, 25	2 + 2 = 4		
13. Alg. Oper.; Verbal Probs.	4, 12, 40b	2 + 2 + 4 = 8		
14. Mean Proportional; Alt. to Hypot. of Right △	13	2		
15. Pythag. Th., Special Rt. △s (3-4-5, 5-12-13, 30-60-90)	—	—		
16. Similar Figures (ratios & proportions)	2, 8	2 + 2 = 4		
17. Areas (△, rect., ▱, rhom., trap.)	—	—		
18. Locus	19	2		
19. Constructions	35	2		
20. Deductive Proofs	22, 41	2 + 10 = 12		
21. Coordinate Geom. (slope, dist., midpt., eq. of circle)	11, 14, 24, 26, 36b	2 + 2 + 2 + 2 + 3 = 11		
22. Coordinate Geom. "Proofs"	42	10		
23. Logic	15, 28,	2 + 2 = 4		
24. Permutations; Arrangements	18, 21	2 + 2 = 4		
25. Combinations	38a, 38c, 38d	2 + 4 + 2 = 8		
26. Probability	38b	2		
27. Trig. of Rt. △	17, 30, 39	2 + 2 + 10 = 14		
28. Literal Eqs.	—	—		
29. Transformations	10, 16, 33	2 + 2 + 2 = 6		

Regents Scholarship Dollars

BARRON'S

Receive up to $10,000
for continuing education from Barron's
plus...get a computer for your school!*

FIRST PRIZE winner will receive a $10,000 scholarship for continuing education.

FOUR RUNNERS-UP will each receive a $2,500 scholarship for continuing education.

*First-prize winner will have a desktop computer donated to his/her school.

Please enter me in the Barron's Regents Scholarship Dollars essay contest. *(Must be filled out in entirety and enclosed with essay).*

Name _____

Address _____

City _____

State _____ Zip _____

Phone ( ) _____ Age _____

School Name _____

School Address _____

Advising Teacher/Subject _____